All-American Massacre

EDITED BY ERIC MADFIS
AND ADAM LANKFORD

ALL-AMERICAN MASSACRE

The Tragic Role of American Culture
and Society in Mass Shootings

TEMPLE UNIVERSITY PRESS
Philadelphia • *Rome* • *Tokyo*

TEMPLE UNIVERSITY PRESS
Philadelphia, Pennsylvania 19122
tupress.temple.edu

Library of Congress Cataloging-in-Publication Data

Names: Madfis, Eric, editor. | Lankford, Adam, 1979– editor.
Title: All-American massacre : the tragic role of American culture and
   society in mass shootings / edited by Eric Madfis and Adam Lankford.
Description: Philadelphia : Temple University Press, 2023. | Includes
   bibliographical references and index. | Summary: "In this edited
   collection, topic experts report on the social and cultural roots of
   various motivations and correlates of American mass shootings. The
   examinations of each contributing social problem center the question of
   why mass shootings are such an American phenomenon"— Provided by
   publisher.
Identifiers: LCCN 2022041983 (print) | LCCN 2022041984 (ebook) | ISBN
   9781439923122 (cloth) | ISBN 9781439923139 (paperback) | ISBN
   9781439923146 (pdf)
Subjects: LCSH: Mass shootings—Social aspects—United States. | Social
   problems—United States. | United States—Social conditions.
Classification: LCC HV6536.5 .A533 2023 (print) | LCC HV6536.5 (ebook) |
   DDC 364.152/340973—dc23/eng/20230329
LC record available at https://lccn.loc.gov/2022041983
LC ebook record available at https://lccn.loc.gov/2022041984

Printed in the United States of America

9 8 7 6 5 4 3 2 1

Contents

PART III: MASS SHOOTINGS AND WHITE SUPREMACY IN AMERICA

PART IV: MASS SHOOTINGS AND AMERICAN MASS MEDIA AND SOCIAL MEDIA

PART V: MASS SHOOTINGS AND AMERICAN POLITICS

PART VI: MASS SHOOTINGS AND AMERICAN EDUCATION

PART VII: MASS SHOOTINGS, FIREARMS, AND MENTAL HEALTH IN AMERICA

    Mass Shootings in the United States: Logically Obvious but
    Analytically Evasive / Paul Reeping   285

21 Do Gun Control Laws Prevent Mass Shootings in the
    United States?: A Review of the Evidence / Emma E. Fridel   295

22 Gun Purchasing Patterns in the United States: Trends
    Surrounding Mass Shootings / Lacey N. Wallace   306

23 Mass Shootings and Mental Health in the United States:
    Key Dynamics and Controversies / Jillian Peterson
    and James Densley   319

    Contributors   337

    Index   345

Acknowledgments

Eric Madfis and Adam Lankford would like to acknowledge generous funding support for this project from Stefan Vatheuer, Jamie Nelson, and the Vatheuer Family Foundation, as well as from the Department of Criminology and Criminal Justice at the University of Alabama.

All-American Massacre

PART I

Editors' Introduction

1

Mass Shootings and American Culture and Society

ERIC MADFIS AND ADAM LANKFORD

"What kind of society is this?" These were the last words screamed by a sixty-four-year-old man before he began a shooting rampage at the 1979 Battle of the Flowers parade in San Antonio, Texas. His attack killed two women and wounded more than fifty people, including six police officers (Chester, 1993, p. 67; Guajardo et al., 2019).

The mission of this book is to answer precisely this question: What kind of society is the United States, and what elements of contemporary American life contribute to our having the greatest number and highest share of public mass shootings around the globe? We asked scholars across a range of disciplines to answer this question, including sociologists, criminologists, psychologists, political scientists, media scholars, epidemiologists, historians, and education specialists. They took on this challenge to explore how gender, racism, media, politics, education, gun culture, firearm access, and mental health influence the causes of mass shootings in the United States. With a specific focus on exploring how American culture, institutions, and social structures influence the circumstances, frequency, and severity of mass shootings in the United States, this volume advances emergent theoretical perspectives and forges fresh approaches, new research questions, and innovative data and conclusions. By bringing together pioneering scholars to broaden this discourse, this book helps to clarify the unique nature and salience of mass shootings in American life.

Diagnosing America's Mass Shooting Problem

Sometimes a problem is so obvious that people can see it for themselves without consulting experts. For instance, most Alaskans are probably aware that their state gets more snow than California does. Sophisticated methods are not required to recognize the difference.

America's mass shooting problem is similar. Many people have recognized that something terrible has been happening in the United States and that this particular type of tragedy does not seem to occur in other countries nearly as often. This was obvious long before the mass killings at Sandy Hook, Aurora, Charleston, Orlando, Las Vegas, Parkland, and Uvalde—and even before scholars attempted to quantify it formally.

But it is helpful to understand the data and what they show. In one of the first explorations of this subject, Böckler et al. (2013) found that "more [rampage] school shootings have occurred to date in the United States than in all other countries combined" (p. 10). A year later, Lemieux (2014) compared mass shootings in the United States with those in twenty-four other industrialized countries and found that the United States had more than double the number of attacks in "all other 24 countries combined in the same 30-year period" (p. 81). The next major finding came from Lankford (2016b), who found that although the United States has less than 5 percent of the world's population, it had 31 percent of public mass shooters who attacked from 1966 to 2012. This suggests that America's public mass shooting problem is approximately six times larger than its proportionate share.

Of course, these findings should be understood in context. For instance, countries with the most public mass shootings are not necessarily the most dangerous places to live. Although the United States has the highest rates of violent crime in the developed world (Messner & Rosenfeld, 2012), if cross-national comparisons are made that include other forms of violence—such as single-victim homicides, armed conflict, and civil war—then many countries have deadlier problems than the United States does (Lankford, 2020). A second consideration is that some mass shootings may go undocumented. In general, homicide is one of the most frequently reported types of crime, and mass shootings seem even more likely to be reported, given their severity. However, it is impossible to know the unknown, and it seems less likely that the American mass media would fail to report a mass killing than media in developing countries. Based on their hypotheses about missing data, Duwe et al. (2021) suggest the United States may have experienced four times its global share of mass shootings, rather than six. Documenting missing cases would be the best way to know for sure. A third point to consider is that because public mass shootings are (fortunately) relatively rare, mass shootings rates are only reliable if we examine large population areas. Otherwise, the smallest countries would appear to have misleadingly high rates simply because of a few incidents. As the fact-checking service Snopes warns, outside the United States, "mass shootings are very rare in most countries, so . . . when they do happen, they have an outsized statistical effect" (MacGuill, 2018).

Apples-to-apples comparisons can be made by contrasting America's mass shooting problem with that of large countries or blocks of countries. For instance, Lankford (2016b, 2019) found that in raw numbers, the United States had far more public mass shooters than both China and India, despite those nations exceeding the U.S. population by over one billion. His analysis of other data suggests that America's mass shooting rate appears significantly higher than that of any entire continent outside of North America (Lankford, 2019). In a more recent study with updated data through 2019, Silva (2022) compared mass shootings in the United States with incidents in thirty-six developed countries. His results show that America had approximately three times as many mass shootings as all other developed countries combined (Silva, 2022).

As we attempt to diagnose America's mass shooting problem, one approach is to conduct these types of cross-national comparisons. If you are experiencing pain in one leg, doctors will sometimes look at your other leg to confirm what the healthy one looks like. By observing the difference, it can be easier to recognize the extent of the damage.

But another approach is to focus very closely on the painful area. Where does it hurt most? Are there some parts that show bruising? Does it no longer function as effectively as it should? Is there something malignant within the body—and can it be cured?

This book provides that type of close examination. It uncovers what America's mass shooting problem tells us about the American social body and our country's underlying ailments. The experts gathered in this book trace this prominent symptom back to its insidious causes, both fringe and mainstream. Many of their chapters focus on public mass shootings, which is what most people think of when they hear the phrase *mass shooting*. These are the attacks at schools, workplaces, churches, malls, movie theaters, and other public locations where the perpetrator uses a firearm to kill at least four victims, according to traditional definitions (Peterson & Densley, 2020). But the United States suffers other types of mass shootings as well, including family killings within people's homes and mass shootings associated with other forms of crime, such as gang conflict and drug trafficking. While mass shootings— even using the broadest definitions—represent only a small and extreme portion of all U.S. violence in a given year, they are consistently and hauntingly a troubling American phenomenon.

Mass shootings have become more frequent (Peterson & Densley, 2020) and deadlier (Lankford & Silver, 2020) since the turn of the twenty-first century. Research on mass murder, and public mass shootings in particular, has also increased exponentially during this time (Fox et al., 2021). However, little research specifically investigates why it is that the United States experiences such a large proportion of these devastating events. Numerous books delve into mass murder, mass shootings, and school shootings, and even a few do so in a way that rigorously explores a particular social cause of these crimes (such as Klarevas, 2016). But most prior books have examined mass shootings in the United States with only passing consideration of the American context—as if these incidents could have occurred anywhere on the globe. Very little research has studied why these violent phenomena are so much more common in the United States and examined American culture, institutions, and social structures as interlocking sources of explanation. This is lamentable, as the American causes of mass shootings are multifaceted but vitally necessary to understand in order to prevent future attacks. In this volume, contributors advance a variety of social and cultural explanations for the prevalence and overrepresentation of mass shootings in the United States.

American Culture and Society as Explanatory Factors in Mass Shootings

Below, we present the layout of the book and brief summaries of each chapter, highlighting current research on key themes. The volume is constructed into six separate sections, each of which links American culture, institutions, and/or social structures to mass shootings.

Mass Shootings and American Masculinities

Part II of the book presents perspectives and research on the role of gender (and masculinities in particular) as contributing to these deadly events. A truly striking fact is that approximately 98 percent of public mass shooters in the United States are male and roughly that same percentage identify as heterosexual (Peterson & Densley, 2021). These data support the claim that mass shootings in the United States are an overwhelmingly hetero-masculine endeavor (Madfis, 2014), and the scholars in this book examine the role that gender and sexuality play in American mass shootings in important new ways.

In the first chapter in this section, Tristan Bridges, Tara Leigh Tober, and Melanie Brazzell explore the importance of American masculinity in contributing to mass shootings. They investigate how men who feel their masculinity has been threatened are especially prone to overcompensate in hypermasculine ways. Because of America's unique gun culture, that often involves purchasing firearms in the name of security and personal protection even if what they are really attempting to protect are their own fragile egos. This interaction of insecurity, overcompensation, and guns helps clarify why men commit mass shootings in the United States so much more than men elsewhere.

In the second chapter, Alison J. Marganski looks at the enduring legacy of patriarchy in the United States by studying common features of hegemonic masculinity found among cases of mass murder. Through this analysis, she finds six unique dimensions of hegemonic masculinity (the Provider, the Procreator, the Protector, the Punisher, the Prestige-seeker, and the Pleasure-seeker) that help contribute to these highly gendered, performative crimes.

Next, Jillian J. Turanovic and Kristen J. Neville investigate mass shootings involving harm to romantic partners. They find that shooters tend to be men who experienced jealousy or rejection, who were angry about relationships ending, and who experienced recent stress or crisis. Numerous shootings were preceded by domestic violence, emotional abuse, and stalking; and in several instances, men were ridiculed and emasculated by intimate partners prior to carrying out their attack. These mass shooting incidents are analyzed in the context of American masculinity, wherein aggrieved men use violence in response to "humiliated fury" and in attempts to reconcile affronts to their masculine identity.

Sarah E. Daly provides our next entry: an overview of the involuntary celibate, or "incel," community, referencing violent attacks associated with the group. She offers theoretical explanations and interpretations of the ways online incel communities developed as a result of marginalized masculinities, gender role expectations, and societal norms about relationships, dating, and sex. Her analysis helps explain why sexually frustrated men in America may be especially prone to react in unhealthy and problematic ways.

In the final chapter of the section on gender and masculinity, Daniel Gascón utilizes the theoretical constructs of intersectionality and structural strain to help explain the motivations and behaviors of the 2014 Isla Vista mass killer. Gascón demonstrates how the converging entitlements of race, class, gender, and sexuality weakened the shooter's ability to adapt to personal challenges. As anger and frustration built and perceived failures accumulated, the attacker felt that he had no other way to eliminate his strain than to carry out his violent "Day of Retribution."

Mass Shootings and White Supremacy in America

Part III focuses upon the role that the ongoing legacy of racism and white supremacy in the United States plays in mass shootings. While public mass shooters are not more likely to be white than their share of the population, this form of mass murder remains the only subset of homicide that is committed predominantly by white people (Madfis, 2014). Further, many mass shooters who were technically nonwhite still identified with white identity politics or some version of fascist or racist ideology (such as the Native American shooter in Red Lake, Minnesota, in 2005 or the biracial Isla Vista shooter in 2014). In addition, white supremacist ideology has been directly linked to the motivations of numerous mass shooting perpetrators in recent years, including the 2015 Charleston church shooting, the 2018 Pittsburgh synagogue shooting, and the 2019 El Paso Walmart shooting. The chapters in this section explore how racist ideology, institutionalized and internalized racism, and white supremacist organizations contribute to mass shootings in general and hate-motivated mass shootings in particular.

First, Betsy Friauf and Michael Phillips explore the ways in which numerous mass shootings can be understood as a continuation of a long historical legacy of white supremacist ideology and violence in the United States. They argue that the same distorted racist fears of "white genocide" and "the great replacement" expressed by some mass shooters can be seen among English settlers in colonial Massachusetts, in stories about the Battle of the Alamo, and in decades of rhetoric from the Ku Klux Klan and neo-Nazi organizations. They argue that we must recognize the ways these myths persist and have been increasingly normalized in recent years because they motivate many contemporary mass killers.

In the next chapter in this section, Stanislav Vysotsky examines the ways in which white supremacist online networks discuss mass shootings as an "accelerationist" strategy to encourage further acts of violence, with the ultimate goal of instigating a race war. He finds that the white supremacist movement's online discourse frames the actions of mass shooters as heroic deeds in service of its ideology and goals. If the mass shooters praised in these forums achieve their aims, their attacks will be just the beginning of a long sequence of similarly motivated attacks.

Next, Simon Gottschalk, Daniel Okamura, Jaimee Nix, and Celene Fuller explore the link between participation in white supremacist websites and the mass shootings they inspire. Based on their scholarship and initial findings, they suggest that participation in white supremacist websites poses a more dangerous threat than face-to-face interactions of this type. Because online behavior incites violent emotions and induces derealization, participation in white supremacist websites escalates the risk that some members will commit acts of extreme violence.

In the last chapter in this section, Scott Duxbury examines how media coverage of mass shootings frames white perpetrators differently than typical forms of moral panic focused on racial minorities. Whereas white perpetrators are often depicted as abnormal members of their race who are mentally ill, those same frames are typically denied to offenders of color, whose violence is frequently portrayed as both normal and expected. Double standards in media coverage of mass shootings perpetuate damaging racial stereotypes in American culture.

Mass Shootings and American Mass Media and Social Media

In Part IV, scholars concentrate on mass media and social media and the ways these cultural institutions contribute to the problem of mass shootings in the United States. Increasingly, in America—more than in any other country on the globe—fame is revered as the ultimate marker of success, and becoming a celebrity is the main goal of many Americans. Worse yet, the distinction between fame and infamy is blurring, with some people willing to do almost anything to get their names in the headlines or go viral on social media (Levin et al., 2005). Fame-seeking mass shooters are the deadliest product of these cultural trends. By killing large numbers of victims, they can get more attention than is typically earned by movie stars and professional athletes (Lankford, 2016a, 2018). And, as with other American celebrities, they can inspire fans, followers, and copycats who want to be just like them—but with far more dangerous consequences (Lankford & Madfis, 2018a, 2018b).

In the first chapter of this section, Jason R. Silva starts by examining the perilous relationship between the mass media and fame-seeking mass shooters in the United States. He then demonstrates how some of America's highest-profile mass shooters have been influencing and inspiring copycat attackers in other countries. In other words, the consequences of creating celebrity killers are not restricted to U.S. soil. America's mass shooting problem is being exported to other countries. He also suggests strategies for addressing the problem, including early detection and denying shooters the attention and notoriety they so often seek.

Next, Stephanie Howells, Ryan Broll, and Patrick F. Parnaby explore how, in addition to the attention mass shooters receive from the mass media, these perpetrators can also achieve "micro fame" through social media, online forums, blogs, and fan sites. They argue that while movements such as No Notoriety are important to reduce fame and infamy generated by news media, these efforts should be combined with better regulation of dangerous content on sites like Twitter, Facebook, YouTube, and Instagram. Although important challenges exist, it may be possible to reduce the notoriety that mass shooters receive on social media as well.

In the third chapter of this section, Lindsay Steenberg investigates the way school shootings are depicted in television and film. Her analysis of *We Need to Talk about Kevin*, *Zero Day*, and *Run Hide Fight* reveals how school shootings are filtered through the lens of popular genres, such as art cinema, the found footage mockumentary, and the action film. Her close examination of these films, along with excerpts from *Buffy the Vampire Slayer* and *Bowling for Columbine*, clarifies how the entertainment industry may shape audiences' perceptions of American mass shootings.

Mass Shootings and American Politics

Part V analyzes the state of American politics and the ways public opinion and legislation shape the social context of mass shootings. As mass shootings have become increasingly politicized in recent years—with Democrats, Republicans, lobbyists, and special interest groups often taking strong, adversarial positions—our system of governance has had a profound impact on how Americans understand and react to this threat. The mass shooting literature has much to gain from a direct engagement with politics and contributions from contemporary political science.

In the first chapter covering American politics, Tom Diaz analyzes the battle between gun rights groups and gun control advocates, drawing on decades of professional experience, including his work for the Congressional House Subcommittee on Crime and Criminal Justice. He suggests the NRA (National Rifle Association) and gun rights supporters have consistently won major victories by framing their struggle as part of the culture war and mobilizing grassroots support. Diaz argues that strategies from Chinese scholar Sun Tzu and General Carl von Clausewitz may help gun control advocates navigate this highly contested political terrain and reduce gun violence and mass shootings.

Next, Mark R. Joslyn examines how Democrats and Republicans react when one of their own political leaders is shot in a mass attack. He identifies two natural experiments—the 2011 shooting of Gabrielle Giffords, a House Democrat from Arizona, and the 2017 shooting of Steve Scalise, a House Republican from Louisiana. Then he tests for the effects of these tragic incidents on each party's attitudes about mass shootings. This raises a fascinating question: Do Americans' deeply held views about the causes of mass shootings and the best ways to prevent them *change* when the subject becomes deeply personal instead of merely political?

In the final chapter on politics, Donald P. Haider-Markel, Abigail Vegter, and Patrick J. Gauding analyze national polls from 2000 to 2018 to trace how three overlapping groups—gun owners, Republicans, and conservatives—have increasingly aligned around shared interests. In this case, that leads them to believe that there is nothing the U.S. government or society can do to stop mass shootings. The authors suggest their findings illustrate how gun owners' adherence to rugged individualism as a means to face a dangerous world fits a worldview that is broadly in line with those of Republicans and conservatives. They discuss the implications for the future of the gun debate and public policy in America.

Mass Shootings and American Education

Part VI focuses upon school mass shootings and the American education system. In particular, authors explore how current educational practices and policies in the United States contribute to mass school shootings being more common. For example, strict discipline policies and tight surveillance and security regimes in American schools are ineffective at preventing rampage attacks and may actually increase the likelihood of their occurrence (Madfis, 2020). Further, effective school violence prevention strategies are often underfunded and understaffed, while schools continue to spend millions of dollars on unproven and harmful practices (Kupchik, 2010; Kupchik & Monahan, 2006; Gottfredson et al., 2020).

In the first chapter of this section on education, Brooke Miller Gialopsos, Cheryl Lero Jonson, Melissa M. Moon, and William A. Stadler propose that American schools have created a unique opportunity structure that increases the likelihood of mass shootings. They use Sampson et al.'s (2010) concept of super controllers to explain how the U.S. Department of Education, government regulatory agencies, courts, insurance companies, school boards, school resource officers, and families influence how schools respond to threats and which violence prevention efforts are implemented. They suggest that the composition of super controllers is uniquely American, and by utilizing evidence-based practices, each of these factors should play a role in preventing opportunities for future school shootings.

Then, in the second chapter on education, Aaron Kupchik, Benjamin W. Fisher, F. Chris Curran, and Salvatore D'Angelo seek to better understand common responses to gun violence in schools within American society. They perform an exploratory analysis of how the 2018 tragedy at Marjory Stoneman Douglas High School in Parkland, Florida, was discussed by major news outlets. They find that news media portrayals suggest that views of the Parkland incident and responses to it are heavily influenced by an ethos of individualism and the political quagmire of the gun control debate, both of which have uniquely American features.

Finally, Jessie Klein examines the way that American society and schools are organized around values of individual competition and success that pressure people to "pull themselves up by their bootstraps" and provide limited empathy for anyone who needs help. She discusses the many devastating consequences that arise out of this individualistic culture, including isolation, trauma, bullying, and school shootings. Klein argues that more cooperative and compassionate schools may lead the way to a less violent society with far fewer mass shootings and other pathologies that result from individuals' unhealthy pursuit of various forms of capital.

Mass Shootings, Firearms, and Mental Health in America

The final section, Part VII, will present contemporary research and perspectives on two of the most commonly cited factors related to mass shootings: firearms and mental health. While aspects of the firearms debate remain contentious and complicated, clear relationships exist between America's disproportionate mass shooting problem and its notorious status as the world leader in civilian firearms (Lankford, 2016b; Reeping et al., 2019). Similarly, while it is clear that many mass shooters have had mental health problems (Lankford & Cowan, 2020), the effects of this factor on their behavior are certainly complex. Readers may benefit from careful explorations of what exactly "mental illness" means and how it can be measured, how mental health and the responses to it are shaped by social and cultural forces, and what challenges the American mental health care system must contend with on this sensitive but important issue.

In the first piece in this section, Paul Reeping argues that despite the obvious logic that access to firearms is a cause of mass shootings, it has been hard to "prove" formally. He examines the difficulties researchers must contend with related to firearm access measurement, study design, reverse causation, and the common co-occurrence of other variables, including gun culture and gun laws. Ultimately, he questions whether researchers even need to prove causation analytically to make sound, commonsense recommendations for violence prevention.

Emma E. Fridel explores the evidence on various American gun control laws that have been hypothesized to prevent mass shootings, including bans on assault weapons and large-capacity magazines, concealed carry permits, extreme risk protection orders and "red flag" laws, and possession prohibitions for perpetrators of domestic violence. Do they actually work? Are mass shootings less common in the places where these laws have been passed? As Fridel wisely points out, the best thing for America would be if its gun legislation not only reduces mass shootings but also helps prevent more common forms of gun violence, such as homicide and suicide.

In the next chapter, Lacey N. Wallace examines the patterns of gun purchasing that occur in the aftermath of highly publicized mass shootings. She analyzes the terrible irony: although civilian firearm ownership is associated with higher risks of mass shootings, gun sales often *increase* after a recent attack—which could then make America's problem even worse. Wallace explores how consumers' fears of victimization, perceptions of risk, and concerns about future gun legislation affect supply and demand for firearms in the United States.

Finally, Jillian Peterson and James Densley examine the landscape of mental illness and mental health treatment in the United States. They review the key dynamics and controversies and how this landscape relates to broader discussions about America's unique experience of mass shootings. After discussing the shortcomings of our mental health system and the problematic manner in which society stigmatizes and even criminalizes mental illness, Peterson and Densley then draw data from The Violence Project to clarify the roles of various mental health issues in mass shootings and to make policy recommendations for mass violence prevention.

Ending the Horror of American Mass Shootings

All-American Massacre. This title was intended to reflect that nowhere else in the world has a mass shooting problem quite like America's, and that these massacres may be better understood though the lens of American culture, institutions, and social structures. Shortly after choosing this title, we discovered that this is also the title of an unreleased horror film meant as a spin-off of *The Texas Chainsaw Massacre* franchise. As scholars who frequently think, write, research, and talk publicly about mass shootings, watching the rising number of incidents and deaths in recent years has indeed felt, at times, like being in a horror film. It is both our sincere hope and empirically informed view that more can be done to combat this threat. We are not suggesting that the United States is inherently or inevitably predisposed to having more than our share of mass shooters. There is still reason for hope about reversing these trends. As concerned citizens and scholars, we are passionate about saving our nation from experiencing more of these terrible tragedies. And that is why we need to investigate more thoroughly the sources of America's mass shooting problem—so we know what to do about it. Our country needs far more clarity, shared understanding, and desire to make progress on the issues covered in this volume. Otherwise, it will be a long time before we end this traumatizing cycle of horror and death.

REFERENCES

Böckler, N., Seeger, T., Sitzer, P., & Heitmeyer, W. (2013). School shootings: Conceptual framework and international empirical trends. In N. Böckler, T. Seeger, P. Sitzer & W. Heitmeyer (Eds.), *School shootings: International research, case studies, and concepts for prevention* (pp. 1–24). New York: Springer.

Chester, G. (1993). *Berserk!* New York: St. Martin's.

Duwe, G., Sanders, N., Rocque, M., & Fox, J. A. (2021, November 30). *Estimating the global prevalence of mass public shootings* [Presentation]. https://nij.ojp.gov/media/video/27696

Fox, J. A., Duwe, G., & Rocque, M. (2021). The nature, trends, correlates, and prevention of mass public shootings in America, 1976–2018. Project Summary, National Institute of Justice.

Fox, J. A., Levin, J., & Fridel, E. E. (2018). *Extreme killing: Understanding serial and mass murder.* Thousand Oaks, CA: Sage.

Gottfredson, D., Crosse, S., Tang, Z., Bauer, E., Harmon, M., Hagen, C., & Greene, A. (2020). Effects of school resource officers on school crime and responses to school crime. *Criminology & Public Policy, 19*(3), 905–940.

Guajardo, A., Leal, M., & Floyd, J. (2019, April 26). *Deadly Battle of Flowers parade shooting remembered 40 years later.* KENS 5. https://www.kens5.com/article/entertainment/events/fiesta/deadly-battles-of-flowers-parade-shooting-remembered-40-years-later/273-883c5b74-7cfa-44b1-89dc-d1687fa4526f

Klarevas, L. (2016). *Rampage nation: Securing America from mass shootings.* Amherst, NY: Prometheus.

Kupchik, A. (2010). *Homeroom security: School discipline in an age of fear.* New York: NYU Press.

Kupchik, A., & Monahan, T. (2006). The new American school: Preparation for postindustrial discipline. *British Journal of Sociology of Education, 27*(5), 617–631.

Lankford, A. (2016a). Fame-seeking rampage shooters: Initial findings and empirical predictions. *Aggression and Violent Behavior, 27*(1), 122–129.

Lankford, A. (2016b). Public mass shooters and firearms: A cross-national study of 171 countries. *Violence and Victims, 31*(2), 1–13.

Lankford, A. (2018). Do the media unintentionally make mass killers into celebrities? An assessment of free advertising and earned media value. *Celebrity Studies, 9*(3), 340–354.

Lankford, A. (2019). Confirmation that the United States has six times its global share of public mass shooters, courtesy of Lott and Moody's data. *Econ Journal Watch, 16*(1), 69–83.

Lankford, A. (2020). The importance of analyzing public mass shooters separately from other attackers when estimating the prevalence of their behavior worldwide. *Econ Journal Watch, 17*(1), 40–55.

Lankford, A., & Cowan, R. (2020). Has the role of mental health problems in mass shootings been significantly underestimated? *Journal of Threat Assessment and Management, 7*(3–4), 135–156.

Lankford, A., & Madfis, E. (2018a). Media coverage of mass killers: Content, consequences, and solutions. *American Behavioral Scientist, 62*(2), 151–162.

Lankford, A., & Madfis, E. (2018b). Don't name them, don't show them, but report everything else: A pragmatic proposal for denying mass killers the attention they seek and deterring future offenders. *American Behavioral Scientist, 62*(2), 260–279.

Lankford, A., & Silver, J. (2020). Why have public mass shootings become more deadly? Assessing how perpetrators' motives and methods have changed over time. *Criminology & Public Policy, 19*(1), 37–60.

Lemieux, F. (2014). Effect of gun culture and firearm laws on gun violence and mass shootings in the United States: A multi-level quantitative analysis. *International Journal of Criminal Justice Sciences, 9*(1), 74–93.

Levin, J., Fox, J. A., & Mazaik, J. (2005). Blurring fame and infamy: A content analysis of cover-story trends in *People* magazine. *Internet Journal of Criminology,* 1–17.

MacGuill, D. (2018, March 9). *Does the United States have a lower death rate from mass shootings than European countries?* Snopes Media Group. https://www.snopes.com /fact-check/united-states-lower-death-shootings/

Madfis, E. (2014). Triple entitlement and homicidal anger: An exploration of the inter-sectional identities of American mass murderers. *Men and Masculinities, 17*(1), 67–86.

Madfis, E. (2020). *How to stop school rampage killing: Lessons from averted mass shootings and bombings.* New York, NY: Palgrave Macmillan.

Messner, S., & Rosenfeld, R. (2012). *Crime and the American dream.* Belmont, CA: Wadsworth.

Peterson, J., & Densley, J. (2020). *The Violence Project database of mass shootings in the United States, 1966–2020.* Retrieved November 2, 2022, from https://www.theviolence project.org

Peterson, J., & Densley, J. (2021). *The Violence Project: How to stop a mass shooting epidemic.* New York: Abrams Press.

Reeping, P., Cerda, M., Kalesan, B., Wiebe. D., Galea, S., & Branas, C. (2019). Research state gun laws, gun ownership, and mass shootings in the US: Cross sectional time series. *The BMJ, 364,* I542.

Sampson, R., Eck, J. E., & Dunham, J. (2010). Super controllers and crime prevention: A routine activity explanation of crime prevention success and failure. *Security Journal, 23*(1), 37–51.

Silva, J. R. (2022). Global mass shootings: Comparing the United States against developed and developing countries. *International Journal of Comparative and Applied Criminal Justice.*

PART II

Mass Shootings and American Masculinities

2

Mass Shootings and American Masculinity

TRISTAN BRIDGES, TARA LEIGH TOBER,
AND MELANIE BRAZZELL

Introduction

While there is some disagreement about what kinds of incidents qualify as mass shootings, regardless of how they are defined, two facts are clear from virtually all of the research on the subject: (1) mass shootings are overwhelmingly committed by men; and (2) mass shootings occur in the United States more than any other society in the world (Lankford, 2016; Lemieux, 2014). To understand the relationship between mass shootings and masculinity, attention must be paid to both of these issues. In this chapter, we summarize theory and scholarship that helps to address these important points.

We first explain what scholars who study this kind of violence mean when they refer to "gun culture" in addition to the bodies of scholarship that help us better understand what social scientists mean when they say that guns have gendered meaning. In the United States, guns have strong associations with masculinity and should not be analyzed in gender-neutral ways. And fully appreciating that fact can help us understand rates of gun ownership, use, and violence. This understanding of guns and gun culture is an important component of our two-part explanation of the relationship between American masculinity and mass shootings (see Bridges & Tober, 2016, 2019). We argue that this question is best understood as two questions. One question is why men commit mass shootings at such higher rates. To answer that, we suggest, requires a social psychological explanation. The second question considers why American men commit mass shootings more than men anywhere else in the world. That question requires a separate, and cultural, explanation. Together, these offer a theory of a masculine American gun culture that can explain the unique prevalence of mass shootings in the United States.

On the Gendered Meanings of Guns and "Gun Culture"

"Guns don't kill people; people kill people" is a well-known slogan associated with the National Rifle Association as well as pro-gun activists in the United States. Their argument is that guns are not actually the real problem when it comes to homicides, suicides, and other gun-related crimes. The slogan takes an *instrumental* approach to guns, suggesting that a gun is nothing more than a tool. Organizations that profit off gun use and sales are provided with discursive forms of plausible deniability when gun-related "accidents" happen or guns are used by people for "illegitimate" purposes (e.g., violence). Any harm done with guns, from this perspective, is best understood as "user error."

The problem with the slogan is that it treats guns and gun holders as though they are separable in ways they are not. When humans interact with guns, the interaction is laden with transformative potential that is implicitly (and perhaps intentionally) obscured with the NRA's simple slogan. Indeed, as Wade and Sharpe (2012) note, as early as the 1960s, psychologists became interested in the "law of the instrument." Maslow (1966, p. 15) distilled this law simply in his writing on the topic in this way: "I suppose it is tempting, if the only tool you have is a hammer, to treat everything as if it were a nail." The law of the instrument recognizes the interaction between humans and technology as complex and transformative. Maslow argued that holding a hammer alters the ways hammer holders see the world around them. The act of holding the tool is transformative. When holding a hammer, the world around you takes on a distinct kind of form and shape. No longer simply composed of people and possible things with which to interact, to someone with a hammer, nails and nail-like things come into sharp relief. A hammer is a tool with a specific purpose, and to anyone aware of the meaning and use of the tool, holding it recommends considering those uses. Guns are no different (see Wade & Sharpe, 2012); carrying a gun can alter one's sense of threat, one's willingness to escalate conflict, or the perceived availability of alternative conflict resolution strategies. But guns do not *mean* the same thing everywhere and take on different kinds of meaning for different groups even within a single society. And in many societies, guns are gendered "masculine" (e.g., Levin & Madfis, 2009).

For instance, advocates for fewer gun restrictions in the United States often identify Switzerland and Israel as important comparisons to argue that more guns do not necessarily lead to more gun violence (Klein 2012). Switzerland does indeed have a high rate of guns per capita, coupled with a small number of mass shootings (Rosenbaum, 2012; Lemieux, 2014). Nevertheless, Lankford (2016) finds that Switzerland does fit an overall global trend in a sample of 171 countries where civilian firearm ownership has a positive relationship to the numbers of mass shootings. What troubles any international comparison with the United States is the fact that U.S. gun ownership is a global outlier. The United States not only ranks first in rates of gun ownership around the world, but no other country is even close. In terms of raw numbers, the 2017 Small Arms Survey estimated that there are 393,300,000 civilian-owned guns in the United States, while the next-closest country, India, has 71,000,000 (Karp, 2018). That means there are approximately 120.5 guns per 100 people in the U.S. population (Karp, 2018), more than double the rate of the next highest, Yemen, with 52.8 firearms per 100 people. Canada's rate of gun ownership was only 34.7, but even that was large enough to situate Canada at the higher end of the list. And Canada is a useful comparison. Despite high rates of gun ownership, rates of firearm homicide are dramatically lower in Canada—0.61 per 100,000 people as of 2016. That rate is almost eight times smaller than the United States the same year, though in Canada it qualifies as the highest rate of homicide by firearms since 2005 (David, 2017).

The fact that there is a collection of nations with high rates of gun ownership and radically different rates of gun violence has prompted scholars studying guns and society to conceptualize gun culture. *Gun culture* broadly refers to each country's specific historic and contemporary attitudes, norms, and laws surrounding gun ownership and use. Many scholars studying gun cultures internationally have commented on the uniqueness of the gun culture in the United States (e.g., Carlson, 2015a, 2015b; Stroud, 2016; Yamane, 2017). Simply put, *gun culture* refers to the meanings attributed to guns within specific cultural settings (e.g., Yamane, 2017).

Consider the fact that civilian gun ownership is heavily concentrated in the United States. The Small Arms Survey estimates that while Americans account for 4 percent of the world's population in 2017, American civilians own nearly 46 percent of the world's 857 million civilian guns (Karp, 2018). The United States has become an outlier in this respect: a society with more guns than people. Yet Carlson's (2015a, 2015b) comparison of Canada and the United States suggests that something as complex as gun culture cannot be fully captured by variables like gun ownership. To explain this fact, she considers the dominant kinds of guns owned in these two countries as a partial explanation of this larger point: in Canada, long guns are more commonly owned than handguns; in the United States, the reverse is true. Long guns and handguns have different meanings and uses. Indeed, long guns are more likely to be used for hunting and kept at home, while a primary use of handguns is for self-defense and they are more likely to be carried with owners when they enter public spaces, increasing potential risk of harm to other people. And these differences in firearms are by design—handguns are designed to be smaller so they can more easily be carried in a holster or kept close (in a glove compartment or backpack). Those differences in design entail different meanings, attitudes, and uses. And these distinctions illustrate some of the differences surrounding gun culture, or the meanings guns carry in two different national contexts.

In her qualitative study of gun owners in Michigan, Carlson (2015b) connects this interest in self-defensive weapons to an ideology of male protectionism and breadwinning in the United States. Hofstadter (1970) offers a historical genealogy for this uniquely U.S. gun culture, dating back to the nation's foundational mythology about the protective role of a popular militia and an armed citizenry in the American Revolution. And Kautzer (2021) sees the fruits of this legacy in contemporary white supremacist militias claiming to "defend the Constitution" and the rise of a militarized gun culture he calls "tactical gun culture" in the United States.

In contrast, findings suggest that Canadian gun owners are more likely to treat their weapons as tools, whereas in the United States, they are viewed as forms of entertainment (Carlson, 2015a). Even gun owners in the United States who purchase weapons as tools for hunting tend to buy more extreme firearms: nearly 25 percent of surveyed U.S. hunters who purchased a firearm in July or August 2017 reported buying a sporting rifle or semiautomatic assault weapon (Karp, 2018).

Gun culture goes beyond guns themselves to include the organizational contexts and affective experiences of U.S. gun owners and users. America is "a nation of gun clubs, training classes, shooting events, network meet-ups, and gun collectors and shooters associations" (Yamane, 2017, p. 7). Gun ownership and advocacy in the United States produces so much collective effervescence for those entranced that it is among the issues that sway so-called single-issue voters in elections. The National Rifle Association was for many years one of the most powerful political organizations in the country. The United States is also potentially the only nation in the world to host a dating website specifically for gun owners—ProGunDating.org—which advertises to potential users by encouraging them to "Date a *Real* American." These facts suggest a unique gun culture in the United States, and one that is deeply gendered.

Explaining the Relationship between Mass Shootings and Masculinity in the U.S. Sociologically

Gun-related fatalities are disproportionately committed by men. Men commit more homicides and are more likely to commit suicide with firearms than are women. This gender gap in gun violence grows even larger when we look at mass shootings. Men commit the overwhelming majority of mass shootings, and this general trend is dramatically exaggerated in the United States (Madfis, 2014). This means that mass shootings are a gendered issue: they have to do with the relationship between men, masculinity, and guns. But men in other societies with high rates of gun ownership do not commit mass shootings in the same numbers as American men do. We suggest that explaining this sociologically requires understanding that guns, men, and America are all necessary components of any explanation of mass shootings in the United States. But it is only through understanding the relationships between all three of these elements that we can better understand mass shootings as a gendered phenomenon in the United States.

Thus, we suggest that answering the question of why American men commit the overwhelming majority of mass shootings requires a two-part feminist sociological explanation —a *social psychological explanation* to explain why men turn to this type of violence so much more frequently than women and a *cultural explanation* to clarify what it is about American masculinity that causes the United States to stand out internationally when it comes to this particular type of gun violence (Bridges & Tober 2016, 2019).

A Social Psychological Explanation

In the 1990s, sociologists studying masculinity charted new intellectual ground on the relationship between masculinity and violence, including critically important work by Messerschmidt (2000a, 2000b). In a nuanced life history analysis of U.S. American adolescent boys, Messerschmidt (2000b) is particularly interested in what he refers to as "masculinity challenges," which he defines as "contextual interactions that result in masculine degradation" (2000b, p. 13). Because he understands masculinity (and gender more broadly) as performance (e.g., West & Zimmerman, 1987), he is particularly interested in how masculinity is accomplished in contexts and moments when adolescent boys' claims to masculinity have been challenged. In such moments, Messerschmidt argues, the boys in his study reached for what he terms *masculine resources* to bolster their claims to a threatened gender identity. Pyke (1996) coined the term *compensatory masculinity* to describe these specific displays of masculinity. This offers an interesting social scientific way of attempting to define something as slippery as *masculinity*. Examining what men whose masculinity has been experimentally threatened reach for to over-demonstrate masculinity offers a unique window into what is understood as masculine in the first place. By first identifying extreme or heightened forms of masculinity, it may be easier to then identify the more common or subtle forms. In Messerschmidt's (2000b) language, sometimes *masculine resources* are easiest to see when we examine responses to *masculinity challenges*.

Fast-forward a few decades, and social psychologists have brought Messerschmidt's notion of masculinity challenges into the lab and subjected it to new kinds of scrutiny. Social psychologists have used experiments to study so-called masculinity threat. People come into labs on university campuses, scholars experimentally "threaten" some of their gender identities, and then see whether those whose gender identities have been threatened respond differently and in patterned ways. Men are brought into a lab where they are asked to take a short test measuring their gender identity. Following this, the researchers give a randomly selected group gender-confirming feedback (e.g., "You tested in the 'masculine' range"), and a separate randomly selected group of men receive gender-disconfirming feedback. That latter group has had their masculinities experimentally "threatened."

Masculinity threat is a subset of a larger concept of *social identity threat*, and scholarship on the latter has come up with a few important and testable findings. One of the most important is that when people are invested in a particular identity and that identity is called into question or challenged, responses are socially patterned. A predictable response is to engage in exaggerated behavior that might symbolically authenticate their membership in the questioned identity category (Branscombe et al., 1999). The work that has applied this specifically to masculinity tests what Willer et al. (2013) refer to as the *masculine overcompensation hypothesis*: the notion that men whose gender identities as masculine have been challenged will respond with exaggerated demonstrations of masculinity. The next step in the social psychologists' experiments after offering gender-confirming or -disconfirming feedback is to ask the two groups to complete different kinds of tasks. This allows researchers to study differences between the groups' responses to masculinity threat.

This body of scholarship is still new, but various studies have produced a collection of disturbing results that help us better understand the relationship between masculinity and violence (e.g., Schmitt & Branscombe 2001; Maass et al., 2003; Munsch & Willer, 2012; Willer et al., 2013; Wellman et al., 2021; Ching, 2022). Men whose masculinity has been experimentally threatened reach for hypermasculine behaviors to demonstrate masculinity in exaggerated ways. For instance, Munsch and Willer (2012) had men read scenarios involving sexual coercion or force by men against women and found that men whose masculinity had been threatened were less likely to identify sexual coercion as such and more likely to blame the women victimized in the scenario. Willer et al. (2013) subjected the masculinity overcompensation thesis to a larger number of issues, discovering that men whose masculinity had been threatened were more supportive of violence and war as a solution to problems, more likely to agree with male supremacist statements, more supportive of sexual prejudice toward gay men, more likely to identify as Republican, and even more likely to say that they wanted to purchase a sport utility vehicle. This research helps explain that violence is a masculine resource on which men are more likely to rely when their masculinities have been challenged. Indeed, as Levin and Madfis argue, "in American culture, the masculine role is frequently defined by elements of dominance, violence, and militarism" (2009, p. 1242). Social psychological research on masculinity threat simply offers us new methods of appreciating this relationship.

And some work specifically links threats to gender identity with guns in the United States. For instance, a recent study found that worsening economic conditions for men were associated with increased gun sales, and men who perceived higher levels of masculinity threat were less supportive of gun control measures (Cassino & Besen-Cassino, 2020). Cassino and Besen-Cassino (2020) argue that owning or carrying a gun is a symbolic gendered enactment among American men—it helps men construct and affirm their gendered identities. And other work has shown that in the United States, guns offer a masculine resource that helps to explain men's relationship with guns and the relationship between mass shootings and masculinity in particular (Levin & Madfis, 2009; Madfis, 2014).

And while the most popular rhetoric justifying gun ownership among American men is "protection," Warner et al. (2022) recently discovered that in this discourse, men who are parents and/or partners are no more likely to rely on this justification of gun ownership than men who are not, implying that protective gun ownership and men's relationships with guns in the United States is perhaps less about protecting one's family and more about protecting claims to masculinity and gendered forms of power and authority. And both studies found economic precarity to be meaningfully related to guns among American men—both interest in owning guns and understanding them as emotionally empowering. This work and others suggest that masculinity threats may not only happen interpersonally at what we call an interactional level but that they might also be something we can study at a broader level (see also Carian & Sobotka, 2018). A great deal of scholarship on mass shootings suggests that interpersonal/interactional-level masculinity challenges are important factors precipitating mass murder, particularly for school shooters (Leary et al., 2003; Fox et al., 2005; Madfis, 2014). Less work has explicitly considered the ways masculinity challenges can, at times, occur at structural and cultural levels as well. In the next section, we examine masculinity threats posed at a structural and cultural level in the United States in particular and how they may be factors in the United States' unique masculine gun culture.

Messerschmidt's (2000b) research with young boys is supportive of this notion as well. He found that violence is not simply a masculine resource, but *the* resource boys and young men turn to in a crisis. This understanding of mass shootings as violent gendered behavior helps explain why crimes like mass shootings are so overwhelmingly committed by men—these crimes are enactments of masculinity. This body of social psychological scholarship answers an important question about mass shootings: why they are so overwhelmingly committed by men. But it does not help us answer a separate question: Why *American* men? That question requires a cultural explanation.

A Cultural Explanation

Boys and men in the United States occasionally have their masculinity challenged and sometimes feel their masculinity has been threatened. But boys and men in other nations experience challenges to their gender identities as well. And a fully sociological explanation of the relationship between masculinity and mass shootings has to account for why *American* boys and men commit these crimes more than boys and men anywhere else. To answer this question requires a *cultural* explanation—one that attends to the unique role that American culture plays in influencing boys and young men in the United States to turn to this type of violence at such higher rates than boys and men elsewhere. Addressing this requires shifting our attention away from the individual characteristics of the shooters themselves to focus on the sociocultural contexts in which violent masculinities are produced and valorized (e.g., Carlson, 2015a; Tonso, 2009). These include structural masculinity threats via both economic instability and political changes wrought by movements for equity and justice like the civil rights and feminist movements.

Yamane (2017) summarizes what it means to study U.S. *gun culture* sociologically in a smart analysis that traces the history of the use and meanings associated with firearms in the United States. Yamane helps to outline what an analysis of gun *culture* might look like. One way of getting at this, according to Yamane (2017), is to examine the shifting meanings associated with firearms throughout American history. Yamane shows that colonial-era Americans thought of guns as tools, necessary for life on the frontier. But this changed over time as sport hunting and shooting came into fashion as pastimes and lifestyle pursuits as well as things like gun collecting among American men. Indeed, among the unique elements of gun ownership in the United States is the fact that the average gun owner in the United States owns far more firearms than the average gun owner in other comparable societies around the world—gun-owning households in the United States own an average of about eight guns (Ingraham, 2018). The Pew Research Center found that among gun owners in the United States, only about one-third own only a single firearm. Another third own between two and four guns, and a full third of American gun owners own five or more guns (Parker et al., 2017).

And while Yamane argues that these recreational meanings associated with guns and gun culture are still present in the United States, the meanings associated with guns have shifted in the most recent era toward notions of armed self-defense—something Yamane refers to as "Gun Culture 2.0." And surveys of American gun owners support this shift as well. In 2017, only 8 percent of gun owners claimed to own a gun for work, 13 percent claimed to be collectors, 30 percent for sport shooting, 38 percent for hunting, but a full 67 percent claimed the major reason for owning a gun was "for protection" (Parker et al., 2017).[1] Indeed, what sociologists now refer to as *protective gun ownership* is on the rise, and important research documents the gendered ways men in particular lean on this logic (e.g., Stroud, 2012, 2016; Carlson, 2015a, 2015b). Indeed, both Carlson (2015a) and Stroud (2016) also comment on the racialized nature of this discourse, nothing that white men in particular lean on this logic of gun ownership and armed protection—a detail supported by the fact that white men in the United States are much more likely to own guns than white women or men of color (Parker et al., 2017). Kautzer (2021) describes the militarization of U.S. gun culture particularly by white supremacist militias claiming to defend the Constitution, the border, and other symbols of U.S. nationalism.

What attracts white men in particular to this U.S. gun culture? One structural masculinity threat may offer a clue: downward economic mobility (Madfis, 2014). In Carlson's (2015a, 2015b) research on gender and American gun ownership, she found many men she interviewed spoke about a very specific kind of "nostalgic longing for a particular version of America" (2015b, p. 390). Some invoked it by name, referring to it as "Mayberry," referencing the fictional U.S. town from the 1960s American family sitcom *The Andy Griffith Show*, depicting a family's life in a small white community of suburban single-family homes, safety, and security. Carlson argues that Mayberry represents a symbolic image of some of what is perceived as lost among the gun-owning American men she studied. In an age of economic decline, the men in Carlson's study are living through the evaporation of the manufacturing economy that may have afforded previous generations of men an ability to accomplish masculinity through economic provision for their families. And the men in Carlson's study use guns to mourn this social, cultural, and economic transition—a cultural process she refers to as *mourning Mayberry*. No longer as able to accomplish masculinity through the provider role, gun-owning American men increasingly lean on *protection* as a way of accomplishing masculinity—white men in particular (see also Stroud, 2012, 2016). The entitlement that accompanies privilege ironically renders more privileged men more vulnerable; as Madfis explains, "it is the very entitlements of his race and gender which make any subsequent life-course struggles and failures all the more unexpected, and thus all the more painful and humiliating" (2014, p. 80).

Another structural masculinity threat that may account for Gun Culture 2.0, as Yamane (2017) refers to it, is its emergence alongside early victories by the civil rights movement and shifts in our understandings of inequality and privilege in America. Indeed, Madfis (2014) comments on the ways boys and young men who have committed school shootings disproportionately belong to privileged groups in society: young, white, class and education privileged, and heterosexual. Gun Culture 2.0 emerged right around the same time that the intersecting privileges associated with these identity categories started to become more visible than perhaps ever before. As Connell (1995a) wrote in mid-1990s, these shifts have produced "a major loss of legitimacy for patriarchy," and she went on to argue that "different groups of men are now navigating that loss in very different ways" (1995, p. 202). So, too, did Tonso (2009) argue that many young men in the United States experience a sense of shame and humiliation that stems, in part, from their perceived loss of privilege—an occurrence acutely felt in small social networks.

Mass shootings can thus be understood as responses to these structural and cultural masculinity threats. Mencken and Froese (2017) found that men, and particularly white men, who had recently experienced an economic setback or even feared experiencing one were more likely to see owning a gun as emotionally and morally empowering. As Mencken and Froese write, "White men in economic distress find comfort in guns as a means to reestablish a sense of individual power and moral certitude in the face of changing times" (2017, p. 22). Mass shootings become an opportunity for revenge or even a final moment of infamy.

Gun culture in the United States is something that has shifted over time, and understanding that fact is important in making sense of mass shootings. For instance, while different scholars have defined mass shootings in different ways, another fact supported by a good deal of the work on mass shootings and mass shooting–related incidents in the United States is that these incidents have increased in frequency and severity (Lankford & Silver, 2019) over time. There are different reasons that this might be the case, and certainly some have to do with the availability of guns in the United States and the relative lack of restrictions for obtaining a firearm in comparison to other nations with high rates of guns per capita. But a cultural explanation for why American men commit mass shootings more than anywhere else in the world needs to acknowledge that rates of gun ownership/access to guns is a necessary but insufficient explanation for rates of mass shootings in the United States. It is not simply guns or simply masculinity. Explaining the relationship between American men, masculinity, and mass shootings requires an understanding and appreciation of U.S. gun culture.

Conclusion

Mass shootings are so common in the United States that we classify them by type. We have school shootings, workplace shootings, church shootings, mall shootings, and more. The media often frames the most frightening of these incidents as *random* mass shootings, in which figuring out why the shooter selected a particular place and group of victims is challenging to understand. Mass shootings do not only occur in the United States. But the scale and scope of this social problem are unique to the United States. And rates of gun ownership and access to and availability of firearms are important components of this problem as well. But when we shift our focus out from the gun itself to the people wielding the gun and then out again to the gun culture within which mass shootings occur, gender and nation becomes impossible to ignore.

Mass shootings are typically enactments of masculinity. But before this can be true, guns and masculinity have to be connected with each other, as does masculinity and violence. Men otherwise unable to access a gendered sense of status in their social hierarchies only turn to guns and violence as masculine resources in societies in which violence is culturally understood as so-called proof of masculinity.

And men only enact masculinity in these ways in cultural contexts in which these enactments are legitimized and granted cultural status and authority. The gun culture in the United States is uniquely toxic in this respect. Real change will require *cultural* change as well, and this is more challenging. As Connell writes, "When pictures of men with guns are rare, and pictures of men with [strollers] are common, we will really be getting somewhere" (1995b).

NOTE

1. Figures add to more than 100 percent here, as respondents were able to claim multiple reasons for their gun ownership in response to questions asking gun owners to report whether protection, hunting, sport shootings, gun collecting, or their occupation was a "major reason for owning a gun."

REFERENCES

Branscombe, N. R., Ellemers, N., Spears, R., & Doosje, B. (1999). The context and content of social identity threat. In N. Ellemers, R. Spears, & B. Doosje (Eds.), *Social identity: context, commitment, content* (pp. 35–58). Wiley.

Bridges, T., & Tober, T. L. (2016). Mass shootings and masculinity. In M. Stombler & A. Jungels (Eds.), *Focus on social problems: A contemporary reader* (pp. 507–512). Oxford University Press.

Bridges, T., & Tober, T. L. (2019). Mass shootings, masculinity, and gun violence as feminist issues. In V. Taylor, N. Whittier, & L. Rupp (Eds.), *Feminist Frontiers* (10th ed.) (pp. 498–505). Rowman and Littlefield.

Carian, E. K., & Sobotka, T. C. (2018). Playing the Trump card: Masculinity threat and the US 2016 Presidential Election. *Socius, 4*, 1–6.

Carlson, J. (2015a). *Citizen-protectors: The everyday politics of guns in an age of decline.* Oxford University Press.

Carlson, J. (2015b). Mourning Mayberry: Guns, masculinity, and socioeconomic decline. *Gender & Society, 29*(3), 386–409.

Cassino, D., & Besen-Cassino, Y. (2020). Sometimes (but not this time), a gun is just a gun: Masculinity threat and guns in the United States, 1999–2018. *Sociological Forum, 35*(1), 5–23.

Ching, B. H. (2022). The effect of masculinity threat on transprejudice: Influence of different aspects of masculinity contingent self-worth. *Psychology & Sexuality, 13*(3), 550–564. https://doi.org/10.1080/19419899.2021.1883724

Connell, R. (1995a). *Masculinities.* University of California Press.

Connell, R. (1995b). The politics of changing men. *Australian Humanities Review, 4.* http://australianhumanitiesreview.org/1996/12/01/politics-of-changing-men/

Cotter, A. (2014). *Firearms and violent crime in Canada, 2012* (Component of Statistics Canada catalogue no. 85-002-X). Canadian Centre for Justice statistics, Canadian Minister of Industry. http://www.statcan.gc.ca/pub/85-002-x/2014001/article/11925-eng.htm#a1

David, J-D. (2017, November 22). *Homicide in Canada, 2016* (Statistics Canada Catalogue no. 85-002-X). Canadian Centre for Justice Statistics, Canadian Minister of Industry. https://www150.statcan.gc.ca/n1/en/pub/85-002-x/2017001/article/54879-eng.pdf?st=dVsy-9bX

Fox, J. A., Levin, J., & Quinet, K. (2005). *The will to kill: Making sense of senseless murder* (2nd ed.). Allyn & Bacon.

Hofstadter, R. (1970). America as a gun culture. *American Heritage, 21*(6). https://www.americanheritage.com/america-gun-culture.

Ingraham, C. (2018, June 19). There are more guns than people in the United States, according to a new study of global firearm ownership. *The Washington Post.* https://www.washingtonpost.com/news/wonk/wp/2018/06/19/there-are-more-guns-than-people-in-the-united-states-according-to-a-new-study-of-global-firearm-ownership/

Karp, A. (2018). *Estimating global civilian-held firearms numbers.* Briefing Paper for the 2017 Small Arms Survey. Australian Department of Foreign Affairs and Trade. https://www.smallarmssurvey.org/sites/default/files/resources/SAS-BP-Civilian-Firearms-Numbers.pdf

Kautzer, C. (2021, December 17). America as a tactical gun culture. *Boston Review.* https://bostonreview.net/articles/america-as-a-tactical-gun-culture/.

Klein, E. (2012, December 14). Mythbusting: Israel and Switzerland are not gun-toting utopias. *The Washington Post.* http://www.washingtonpost.com/blogs/wonkblog/wp/2012/12/14/mythbusting-israel-and-switzerland-are-not-gun-toting-utopias/

Krouse, W. J. (2012, November 14). *Gun control legislation.* Congressional Research Report for Congress, Federation of American Scientists. http://fas.org/sgp/crs/misc/RL32842.pdf

Lankford, A. (2016). Public mass shooters and firearms: A cross-national study of 171 countries. *Violence and Victims, 31*(2), 187–199.

Lankford, A., & Silver, J. (2019). Why have public mass shootings become more deadly?: Assessing how perpetrators' motives and methods have changed over time. *Criminology & Public Policy, 19*(1), 37–60.

Leary, M., Kowalski, R., Smith, L., & Phillips, S. (2003). Teasing, rejection, and violence: Case studies of the school shootings. *Aggressive Behavior, 29,* 202–214.

Lemieux, F. (2014). Effect of gun culture and firearm laws on gun violence and mass shootings in the United States: A multi-level quantitative analysis. *International Journal of Criminal Justice Sciences, 9*(1), 74–93.

Levin, J., & Madfis, E. (2009). Mass murder at school and cumulative strain: A sequential model. *American Behavioral Scientist, 52*(9), 1227–1245.

Maass, A., Cadinu, M., Guarnieri, G., & Grasselli, A. (2003). Sexual harassment under social identity threat: The computer harassment paradigm. *Journal of Personality and Social Psychology, 85,* 853–870.

Madfis, E. (2014). Triple entitlement and homicidal anger: An exploration of the intersectional identities of American mass murderers. *Men and Masculinities, 17*(1), 67–86.

Maslow, A. (1966). *The psychology of science: A reconnaissance.* Harper & Row.

Mencken, F. C., & Froese, P. (2017). Gun culture in action. *Social Problems, 66*(1), 3–27.

Messerschmidt, J. W. (2000a). Becoming "real men": Adolescent masculinity challenges and sexual violence. *Men and Masculinities, 2*(3), 286–307.

Messerschmidt, J. W. (2000b). *Nine lives: Adolescent masculinities, the body, and violence.* Westview Press.

Munsch, C., & Willer, R. (2012). The role of gender identity threat in perceptions of date rape and sexual coercion. *Violence against Women, 18,* 1125–1146.

Parker, K., Menasce Horowitz, J., Igielnik, R., Oliphant, J. B., & Brown, A. (2017). *America's complex relationship with guns.* Pew Research Center. https://www.pewresearch.org /social-trends/2017/06/22/americas-complex-relationship-with-guns/?utm_content =bufferf2d4e&utm_medium=social&utm_source=twitter.com&utm_campaign=buffer

Pyke, K. D. (1996). Class-based masculinities: The interdependence of gender, class, and interpersonal power. *Gender & Society, 10*(5), 527–549.

Rosenbaum, J. (2012). Gun utopias? Firearm access and ownership in Israel and Switzerland. *Journal of Public Health Policy, 33*(1), 46–58.

Schmitt, M. T., & Branscombe, N. R. (2001). The good, the bad, and the manly: Threats to one's prototypicality and evaluations of fellow in-group members. *Journal of Experimental Social Psychology, 37,* 510–517.

Stroud, A. (2012). Good guys with guns: Hegemonic masculinity and concealed handguns. *Gender & Society, 26*(2), 216–238.

Stroud, A. (2016). *Good guys with guns: The appeal and consequences of conceal carry.* University of North Carolina Press.

Tonso, K. (2009). Violent masculinities as tropes for school shooters: The Montreal massacre, the Columbine attack, and rethinking schools. *American Behavioral Scientist, 52*(9), 1266–1285.

United States Bureau of Alcohol, Tobacco, Firearms, and Explosives. (2017). *Firearms commerce in the United States: Annual statistical update 2017.* U.S. Department of Justice. https://www.atf.gov/resource-center/docs/undefined/firearms-commerce-united-states -annual-statistical-update-2017/download

Wade, L., & Sharpe, G. (2012). The transformative potential of technology. *The Sociological Images.* Retrieved October 1, 2021, from https://thesocietypages.org/socimages /2012/12/20/the-transformative-potential-of-technology-the-bushmaster-223/

Warner, T., Tober, T. L., Bridges, T., & Warner, D. F. (2022). To provide or protect? Masculinity, economic insecurity, and protective gun ownership in the United States. *Sociological Perspectives, 65*(1), 97–118.

Wellman, J. D., Beam, A. J., Wilkins, C. L., Newell, E. E., & Mendez, C. A. (2021). Masculinity threat increases bias and negative emotions toward feminine gay men. *Psychology of Men & Masculinities, 22*(4), 787–799.

West, C., & Zimmerman, D. (1987). Doing gender. *Gender & Society, 1*(2), 125–151.

Willer, R., Rogalin, C. L., Conlon, B., & Wojnowicz, M. T. (2013). "Overdoing gender: A test of the masculine overcompensation thesis." *American Journal of Sociology, 118*(4), 980–1022.

Yamane, D. (2017). The sociology of U.S. gun culture. *Sociology Compass, 11*, 1–10.

3

The Patriarchal Patterns
of Male Mass Killers in America

A Typology

Alison J. Marganski

Mass shooters/murderers are products of our social world. Although they are commonly portrayed as individuals with serious mental health issues and their crimes have been dubbed "random" acts of violence, research reveals a more complicated picture: they are more often than not male actors who engage in premeditated and calculated acts (Silver et al., 2018). Their behavior reflects deep-seated, cultural beliefs that have been learned and taken to the extreme to remedy a sense of disempowerment through the one solution taught and touted as the most appropriate (and manliest) response: violence (Kimmel, 2013; Madfis, 2014; Marganski, 2019). As such, the study of mass shootings/murders warrants investigation into the sociocultural contexts of these crimes. By investigating macro-level structures that shape offenders in the places they thrive (e.g., the United States), we can make sense of what has incorrectly been dubbed "senseless" violence.

Patriarchy: An Overview

Patriarchy, a male-oriented and male-dominated sociopolitical system, structures gender norms, expectations, relations, and behaviors (Connell, 1995). In this system, narrow and distinct concepts are held up as ideals. In Western cultures, masculine standards (e.g., toughness, self-sufficiency, sexual prowess) are socialized into boys at an early age and shape what it means to "be a man." The most dominant form, hegemonic masculinity (Connell, 1987,

1995; Connell & Messerschmidt, 2005) "structures and legitimates hierarchal gender relations between men and women, between masculinity and femininity, and among masculinities" (Messerschmidt, 2019, p. 10). In other words, it creates unequal gender relations and rationalizes inequalities that superordinate men/hegemonic masculinity and subordinate women/femininity, nondominant masculinities, and others (Connell, 1987). This informs institutions and operations that reinforce and maintain the system—and patriarchy does not act alone, but rather in conjunction with other systems of domination such as white supremacy, heteronormativity, and capitalism.[1]

The enactment of hegemonic masculinity, then, is an act of male supremacy that must be understood in context. As West and Zimmerman (1987), Butler (1990), and others note, gender is performative and relational; it comes into play as people act in institutional and social settings that are interpreted by others who make meaning of it. Although not without internal contradictions (Pleck, 1995), gender norms have been baked into social institutions in ways that reinforce, reproduce, and sustain inequalities, making it appear "normal" for men to be powerful and in control (Connell & Messerschmidt, 2005). Compounded with other characteristics (e.g., race, class), this influences the way individuals view, treat, and respond to one another. Historically, well-off heterosexual white men have been valued above all others (Connell, 1995), born with rights people of color, women, and LGBTQA+ individuals had to fight for and treated more favorably in "justice" proceedings (Alexander, 2012; Weissman, 2021). Consequently, they accumulated vast power and resources, which has allowed them to dominate, control, and keep existing structures in place.

Patriarchy Packs a Punch!

Patriarchy, a great *un*equalizer, informs practices that influence individual cognitions (binary gender scripts), beliefs (gendered attitudes like sexism/misogyny), and behavior (violence against women), which impact gender relations, institutions, and structures. Individuals who adhere to rigid gender ideologies that have been learned through socialization sources are at risk for committing violence when they experience threats or challenges to their social identity (Kimmel, 2013). Conformity to hegemonic masculine norms increases men's distress and aggressive tendencies yet decreases their willingness to seek help in times of need (Good & Wood, 1995). While some cope with shortcomings or a sense of emasculation in prosocial ways, others may develop maladaptive strategies such as internalizing strain and masking depression or suicidal ideation (Seidler et al., 2016) or externalizing strain and channeling rage toward people they blame for their distress (Broidy & Agnew, 1997).

Gender role strain can lead to negative emotions such as anger, depression, or fear, which may, in turn, influence revenge seeking and violence (Agnew, 1992). Men who more strongly support traditional gender roles and arrangements, and who believe their masculine identity is under attack, are at risk for hypermasculine displays of power that emphasize toughness, aggression, homophobia, transphobia, and/or the devaluation of women (Willer et al., 2013). Such exaggerated gender performances are designed to prove one's worth or secure status (Dahl et al., 2015; Willer et al., 2013). Relatedly, men who report experiencing acceptance and status threats have greater attraction to guns and more aggressive responses to perceived conflict (Scaptura & Boyd, 2022). Economically and racially advantaged men are especially likely to fit this description, which signifies the need for intersectional perspectives (e.g., Madfis, 2014) and better understandings of what Levin and Madfis (2009) call cumulative strain.

Social Context Is Key

Violence is a means by which some men establish dominance over others, physically and symbolically (Katz, 2011). Men learn this through popular culture, various institutions, and sociopolitical systems. For example, powerful and pervasive industries like media entertainment (e.g., films, music, radio shows, advertising) build hegemonic ideals normalizing men's violence and how it is achieved (Katz, 2011) while subordinating/subjugating women, girls, and others (APA, 2007). Further, guns are promoted as masculine tools (Levin & Madfis, 2009) with rewarding qualities (Katz, 2011), often across racialized lines (Carlson, 2015), which is reflective in ownership: there are more guns than citizens in America, and these are disproportionately owned by white men (Schaeffer, 2021)—not coincidentally, those who feel most victimized by social progress (Kimmel, 2013).

Individuals, groups, and institutions reinforce patriarchal ideals, which contribute to many manifestations of violence ranging from everyday sexism (Bates, 2012) to intimate partner and sexual violence (Munsch & Willer, 2012) to terrorism and extremism (Rottweiler et al., 2021). Virulently misogynistic messages and banter, on- and offline, are frequently trivialized or met with inaction, yet they have catalyzed mass killings (Center on Extremism, 2018). Violent individuals are not acting alone, but rather with support of peers (see DeKeseredy & Schwartz, 2013) and institutions that tolerate and sometimes encourage offending. Individuals in toxic online communities, for instance, have vocalized support for killers' acts, cited manifestos, and blamed others for personal failings while bonding over shared grievances and visions of power (Myketiak, 2016), which has influenced the thoughts and actions of some men in crisis.

The Importance of Intersectionality

Mass murder, like gendered violence, relates to ideologies centering on sub-ordinating others and superordinating oneself. There is evidence of hostile, discriminatory attitudes in these crimes including sexism, racism, homopho-bia, xenophobia, and more. Violence against women and girls is one of the most common features of mass murder, and many offenders also exhibit prob-lematic attitudes toward others based on race, religion, and other social iden-tity markers (Marganski, 2019). This presents complex transgressions war-ranting investigation into the masculinity-violence nexus as observed in a white, heteronormative, capitalist patriarchy. While many concepts can be applied, intersectionality (Crenshaw, 1989, 1991) is particularly pertinent, as it affords a complex understanding of how social identity markers collide to influence efforts at domination or oppression.

For most of America's history, cisgender, heterosexual, wealthy, white men have been the beneficiaries of patriarchal arrangements. They have enjoyed the vast majority of power, influence, and money—and benefited from the best of what the United States has offered. This has been so entrenched in the American experience that many white men have come to believe they are en-titled to supremacy, as if it were their birthright. Meanwhile, women and girls, persons of color, and others have suffered tremendous inequalities. In recent decades, America has made important progress with people of all races, gen-ders, and sexual orientation increasingly gaining social, financial, and po-litical power, yet true equality has certainly not been achieved. These advance-ments, nevertheless, pose a "threat" in the eyes of entitled men. If unable to secure status via conventional routes, violence can offer an appealing solu-tion. Carlson (2015), for example, demonstrates how some men who have failed to be successful professionally embrace guns to achieve power socially. In the neoliberal era, these deadly weapons have been packaged as an answer to men's empowerment. America possesses more firepower than the next twenty-five countries combined (Karp, 2018), with white, heterosexual, conservative males overwhelmingly being owners (Carlson, 2015).

In line with multiracial feminism, it is essential to consider social identity (individual and collective) and interrelated systems of domination/oppres-sion (Crenshaw, 1989, 1991; Hill Collins & Bilge, 2016). To this end, some re-search highlights how mass shooters can be understood through social iden-tity. Kimmel and Mahler (2003) found that male school shooters who were targets of homophobic bullying, violence, and social marginalization in schools responded with retaliatory violence to these masculinity threats (Kimmel & Mahler, 2003). Additionally, Madfis (2014) found that white, middle-class, heterosexual males engaged in a disproportionate number of mass murders, largely due to the fusion between the "triple entitlement" of white heterosexual masculinity and class frustration stemming from their precarious position in a postindustrial economy. Also, Lankford (2016) underscored how structural advantage and aggrieved entitlement experienced by whites may explain their offending while social disadvantage and inequalities more accurately captures offending for members of other racial backgrounds. Intersectional approaches, therefore, are valuable for theoretical and analytic musing, as they situate persons and events in critical social contexts.

Still, there is a paucity of research on mass shootings/murders examining offender dynamics involving victims and survivors (for notable exceptions, see Klein, 2005; Marganski, 2019; Yardley & Richards, 2021). American women and children are overrepresented in mass murder fatalities (Everytown for Gun Safety, 2017; USA Today, 2018) and, like American men, face a greater risk of firearm death in general than individuals in other high-income countries (Grinshteyn & Hemenway, 2019). Mass murderers are disproportionately male offenders with histories of gender violence (Marganski, 2019), and their motivations commonly center on gaining power through controlling others or putting them "in their place." In some cases, these men and boys believed they were owed sex from women and girls, and in others, they decided it was okay to abuse them. We live in a nation where men have killed women for being too sexual (spa killings) *and* not sexual enough (incel-related killings) and where men killed women when women ended or threatened to leave abusive relationships *and* when they stayed. We also live in a nation where men have killed when humiliated and their reputations were at stake (e.g., job loss, crumbling marriage) *and* when they wanted to humiliate others. They acted as if their right to kill superseded others' right to live.

From an intersectional standpoint, it is not simply sexism, racism, et cetera, that factors into oppression, but also, for example, *racist sexism*. In the Georgia spa shootings involving the murder of Asian American women, the male offender employed techniques of neutralization to minimize responsibility for the attack by telling police that *he* was the victim of a sex addiction and, reportedly, that he wanted to eliminate all Asians and the temptation of massage parlors (Agathangelou & Killian, 2021). After the attack, the sheriff's office spokesman officials reported to the public that the offender was "having a really bad day." Patriarchal, heteronormative racism shapes how this male offender viewed these women—and how he, too, was viewed by the male officers, media, and public. Further, there is a long history of hypersexualizing Asian women, not only by men and media, but also in governmental policies (Shimizu, 2007). Another case in California points to beliefs reflective of male entitlement to women's bodies based on self-perceived race and class superiority: "How could an inferior, ugly black boy be able to get a white girl and not me? I am beautiful, and I am half white myself. I am descended from British aristocracy. *He* is descended from slaves. I deserve it more" (Melzer, 2018, p. 136). Beyond blatant discrimination, covert bias has been observed among offenders who killed in the name of "good-guy" politics (e.g., benevolent sexism), as seen in the South Carolina church slayings: "You rape *our* women and you're taking over *our* country" (Wade, 2015). Such violence signals aggrieved entitlement based on social hierarchies that views oneself as superior and others as inferior.

Analyzing Mass Murders through Patriarchy

Mass murder typologies help make sense of and differentiate offender motivations (Fox & Levin, 1998; Holmes & Holmes, 1994). To date, however, scholars have degendered a gendered problem and overlooked patriarchal cultural frames. If mass murders are predominantly perpetrated by male offenders who adhere to rigid gender ideologies, perceive threats to their social standing from others, believe in violence as an appropriate solution to remedy emasculation, and have histories of violence against others, then mass murder typologies must reflect patriarchal ideals that underlie murderous behavior. Without a gender-conscious analysis of (racist, capitalist, heteronormative) patriarchy, research is missing the big picture.

Male offenders exemplify archetypes of patriarchal gender role expectations that center on *power and control*, yet also reflect various dimensions of hegemonic masculinity. In the following section, I explore what I term **Patriarchy's Six Patterns of Male Mass Killers—the Provider, Procreator, Protector, Punisher, Prestige-seeker, and Pleasure-seeker**—which all represent unique facets of hegemonic masculinity that have aided and abetted mass shootings:

> **"The Provider" reflects the ideal of self-sufficiency**. It centers on the breadwinner philosophy, the man whose wages support him/family ("bringing home the bacon" or "putting a roof over heads"). These economically motivated offenders turn to violence when they fail to achieve success (e.g., unemployed), can no longer provide (e.g., fired), or experience financial conflict. Examples include persons unable to secure positions in the conventional workforce; those facing job loss, bankruptcy, or other hardships; and those shorted in drug sales or whose wage positions are threatened.

> **"The Procreator" relates to sexual conquest/success** (or the lack thereof and an inability to secure/maintain romantic relationships). These male offenders commodify, objectify, and feel entitled to others' bodies and may have histories of violence against women and/or girls they desire, have been intimate with, or supposedly love(d). Such offend-

ers include those obsessed with sex, whether too much or not enough, and those who abuse, dehumanize, or otherwise see women and girls as property.

"The Protector" connects with safety/defense. He prioritizes protecting people he believes to be at risk from harm. This offender views it as his duty to act and convinces himself that his behaviors are for a greater good. This may involve killing one's family to prevent them from perceived evil (mercy killings), "the enemy" to save/defend one's ingroup (hate crimes), or others who posed a threat.

"The Punisher" illustrates toughness. This is grounded in the warrior mentality and notions of strength/dominance (alpha male), adherence to authoritative codes ("push me and I'll push back"), and admiration for or involvement in military/war. These offenders view themselves as soldiers, rule enforcers, or freedom fighters on the front line of justice. They police and punish others and seek retaliation for perceived wrongs.

"The Prestige-seeker" is linked to leadership and loyalties. This reflects a fixation with fame, excellence, and a sense of superiority, and it may be tied to ingroup validation. These offenders, who occasionally co-offend with others like them, attack for popularity, peer acceptance, et cetera, to increase status, position, or rank, or to gain peer approval.

"The Pleasure-seeker" corresponds with risk-taking. It consists of offenders who exhibit hedonistic, impulsive, or antisocial behaviors and those who are fascinated by murder or kill for a thrill.

If patriarchal culture matters, then one or more of the six typologies should be evidenced among many male mass shooters. To examine whether they apply, all known cases of *male-perpetrated mass murders* involving firearms in 2019 were analyzed using open-source information (n = 27).[2] The findings are in Table 3.1.

Discussion

The data presented suggest that patriarchal culture deeply matters. The descriptions, albeit brief, show male offenders upholding hegemonic masculine ideals turned toxic when interacting with gendered strain in a culture that has championed violence as a manly (and heroic) solution. These offenders

	TABLE 3.1 TYPES OF PATRIARCHY AMONG MALE-PERPETRATED MASS MURDERS INVOLVING FIREARMS IN 2019	
Location	Type	Description
El Paso, TX	Punisher, Provider, Protector	Male killed twenty-three in a Walmart; posted a manifesto to 8chan filled with hate, blamed immigrants for taking jobs from "native-born Americans"; lamented college debt and dwindling jobs; peers described him as a bullied loner who "liked to take charge" (Elmahrek et al., 2019).
Virginia Beach, VA	Provider, Punisher, Pleasure-seeker	Male killed twelve in workplace; military background; allegedly held a grievance against his wife who divorced him, outranked him, and took disciplinary action against him (Jamison, 2021); history of street harassment, catcalling, and intimidating neighbors (Fruen & Ardehali, 2019); legally purchased firearms and used them to respond to a perceived hostile work environment.
Dayton, OH	Punisher, Pleasure-seeker, Procreator	Male killed nine at a bar; authorities searched his home, found writings expressing interest in killing people/mass shootings; in a "pornogrind" band with dark, violent, misogynistic content; previously developed a hit list of boys he wanted to kill and girls he wanted to rape; referred to women as "sluts" and simulated shooting peers (Murphy et al., 2019).
Odessa, TX	Punisher, Protector, Pleasure-seeker	Male killed seven in a shooting spree; fired at officers, motorists, and residents during traffic stop; history of violence against mother, neighbor, and animals (Alfonso & Wagner, 2019); preparing for war against government.
San Diego, CA	Procreator, Punisher	Male killed estranged wife, four children, and himself at a residence the day after wife obtained restraining order; weeks before, he sent her a photo of a handgun displayed in front of beer cans and a bottle of alcohol, stating, "It's sure happening"; repeatedly called, texted, and stalked her despite pleas to stop harassment (City News Service, 2019).
Jersey City, NJ	Protector, Procreator, Provider, Punisher	Team offenders killed four at JC Kosher Supermarket; anti-Semitic and anti–law enforcement beliefs; male offender had a history of violence; arrested years earlier after hurting and threatening to kill girlfriend; choked her, punched a hole in a door, squeezed her face, stating, "I'm going to kill you. I feel like killing you. You made me lose everything, you can leave this world. Call the police, because I'm going to kill you"; told police argument started over having a child and being unable to afford it (Scofield, 2019).
Aurora, IL	Procreator, Punisher, Provider, Pleasure-seeker	Male killed several individuals in workplace; made recurring threatening statements to coworkers about killing them if fired; six prior arrests for domestic violence–related charges, violating a restraining order, and felony aggravated assault conviction (Sakuma, 2019).

TABLE 3.1 TYPES OF PATRIARCHY AMONG MALE-PERPETRATED MASS MURDERS INVOLVING FIREARMS IN 2019 (*continued*)

Location	Type	Description
Sebring, FL	Pleasure-seeker, Punisher	Male killed five women at a bank; former correction officer; served in the army (Rogers & Moore, 2019); was said to have hated people, shared dreams about killing others, and made threats; ex-girlfriend reported his fascination with murder, but no one viewed him as threat (Spencer, 2019).
Elkmont, AL	Punisher, Pleasure-seeker	Teenage male killed family at home; discovered mom was stepmother; history of alarming behavior, including burning animals alive and breaking into school (Remkus, 2019).
St. Louis, MO	Prestige-seekers, Pleasure-seekers	Male co-offenders killed five in drug-related killing; at least one had prior convictions for domestic assault and set girlfriend's car on fire (Bell, 2019).
Clinton, MS	Procreator, Punisher	Male killed wife, her family, and family friends at home; police responded to domestic disturbance call; twelve-hour standoff; man shot at them before being killed; police previously visited for domestic disputes (Kennedy, 2019).
Chippewa Falls, WI	Procreator, Punisher, Provider, Pleasure-seeker	Male killed mother, brother, and nephew at townhouse, then shot woman and her parents at another residence; killed self; sent harassing sexual images to unrelated female victim; police believed offender planned deadly home invasion and abduction of woman to mimic a crime; described as loner and drifter; frequently unemployed; mental health issues; previously, threatened family with a shotgun (Sederstrom, 2019).
Gonzalez, LA	Procreator, Provider, Punisher, Pleasure-seeker	Male killed girlfriend, her brother, and father at residence, then parents at another location after being kicked out of their trailer home; history of physical partner violence and verbal aggression against teachers; drug addiction; previously joined military, but left early; married for eleven days, separated, divorced; court records revealed he "choked, punched, and slapped" partner over three-year relationship (Stole et al., 2019); his mother asked judge to impose a protective order against him, but judge declined, stating wife did not "prove" accusations.
White Swan, WA	Pleasure-seeker, Prestige-seeker	Male offenders (including brothers) killed five in impoverished area of Indian reservation and fled in stolen vehicle; charged with carjacking, kidnapping, and weapons offenses; police said drug related (Berton & Carter, 2019).
Santa Maria, CA	Procreator, Provider, Punisher	Male shot neighbors then drove home, killed family, set home on fire, and killed himself after feud with police; was getting evicted from mobile park community; known for domestic abuse (Neighbors, 2019).

(*continued on next page*)

Location	Type	Description
Livingston, TX	Punisher, Procreator, Pleasure-seeker	Male killed wife after relationship ended, along with his fifteen-month-old daughter, grandparents-in-law, and himself at dwelling; professional boxer; posted Facebook messages stating, "It's time to pay up for all the bad Decisions you made"; arrest history included felony aggravated assault with deadly weapon; charge dropped as part of prosecutor agreement (Cleary, 2019).
Abington, MA	Provider, Procreator	Male killed wife and three children at home; struggling children's book author; posted Facebook status stating he was "unemployed and going crazy" (Voorhees, 2019).
San Jose, CA	Procreator, Provider, Pleasure-seeker	Male killed four family members and himself at home; wife sponsored her family coming to America, but he was barred from doing so because prior robbery conviction (Kukura, 2019); neighbors reported domestic problems.
Chicago, IL	Provider, Punisher, Pleasure-seeker	Male killed neighbors in apartment complex; evidence of economic stress (bankruptcy, foreclosure, eviction); police found letters expressing grievances, belief others were against him; previously assaulted one victim after voted out of position as president of condo association (Charles, 2019).
Rockmart, GA	Pleasure-seeker, Punisher	Male killed aunt, cousin, and friends in two double homicide incidents; targeted victims; stole a truck; paroled for robbery and burglary charges (Fernandes, 2019).
Palm Springs, CA	Pleasure-seeker, Procreator, Protector, Provider	Male killed three friends in car, one on street; drug sale, robbery; intoxicated; police found excessive ammunition; told friend would kill unless he found woman for sex (City News, 2022); posted "wannabe gangster" lyrics on social media; past DUI charge; unemployed one year (Hong et al., 2019).
Beaumont, TX	Provider, Punisher, Pleasure-seeker	Male killed four roommates at trap house; ongoing altercation; police called to site for drugs, theft, and violence (Geiger, 2019).
West Chester, OH	Procreator, Provider	Male killed wife, her parents, and aunt in apartment; staged as burglary gone bad; incapacitated wife with chili powder, postmortem examination revealed she died of asphyxiation; family member said, "We knew there were disputes in the family and we expected fist fights or a divorce but we never expected the whole family to be killed" (Londberg et al., 2019); another reported "about greed . . . wanted his father-in-law's property" (Winter, 2021).
Canoga Park, CA	Procreator, Punisher, Pleasure-seeker	Male killed ex-partner at gas station, then shot his father, brother, mother (survived) at home, and man at bus station; stalked ex after relationships ended; did not want to work; known by police for history of violence toward family and drug problems (Perez, 2019).

TABLE 3.1   TYPES OF PATRIARCHY AMONG MALE-PERPETRATED MASS MURDERS INVOLVING FIREARMS IN 2019 (*continued*)

Location	Type	Description
Kansas City, KS	Pleasure-seeker, Punisher	Male killed several individuals at bar; past violent confrontations, including spitting in face of deputy and civilian when asked to leave, throwing cups at bartender, etc.; gang-affiliated; history of aggravated assault, robbery, burglary, battery, and threatening others (Schmidt & Holt, 2019).
Philadelphia, PA	Punisher	Male killed mother, stepfather, and half-brothers at home; previously diagnosed with schizophrenia, but stopped medication, began substance abuse; night before attack, mother took him to crisis intervention for help, but hospital sent him back for lack of suicidal ideation and because he declined treatment; purchased a firearm next day, killed family, wrote messages on wall with blood (Rushing, 2020).
Fresno, CA	Prestige-seeker, Punisher	Four males attacked group of gang members watching football in a backyard; retaliation for murder earlier that day (Levin, 2020).

perpetrated numerous harms—at home, in the workplace, at commercial/retail establishments, and on the streets—against family/intimate partners, acquaintances, strangers, and nonhuman beings. Examples include the following: misogyny and other forms of discrimination; physical/sexual/psychological violence; and various antisocial behaviors. In all cases, at least one of six types applied, with most cases exhibiting two or three. The most common types among this sample were Punisher (appearing twenty-one times) and Pleasure-seeker (eighteen times), followed by Procreator (fourteen times), Provider (thirteen times), Protector (four times), and Prestige-seeker (three times). Offenders were frequently observed as failing to achieve masculine measures of success—relational, economic, and/or social—which contributed to gender strain and a sense of victimhood derived from the belief that they should be on top because that is the message they received in our patriarchal society.

Whether we examine the family annihilator, disgruntled employee, mass school shooter, or other classifications, a patriarchal lens enriches our understanding of American mass murders by drawing attention to gender and associated social identities, relationships, and processes. The same values that shape mass murder are those that shape other male-perpetrated crimes, including violence against women, children, and other men, while also being values most revered in our culture. In this way, deviance and conformity overlap (Messner & Rosenfeld, 2013). The connection between harmful forms of male socialization and violence necessitates solutions that specifically address

problematic normative pressures men and boys experience while promoting
healthy masculinity scripts for responding to strain and "doing gender" (APA,
2018). We need to change what makes men and boys so susceptible to gender
role strain and strain-induced violence, which involves restructuring norms,
institutions, and society. If we are to end mass murder, social, economic, political, and cultural transformations are needed that are inclusive of and work
to support all, especially the most vulnerable/victimized, in life rather than
only in death.

NOTES

1. Each of these systems warrants its own investigation; this chapter spotlights patriarchy.
2. Four cases were excluded due to unknown offenders.

REFERENCES

Agathangelou, A. M., & Killian, K. (2021). Violence against Asians: When is racial hate
a crime? *Journal of Feminist Scholarship, 18*(18), 154–161.

Agnew, R. (1992). Foundation for a general strain theory of crime and delinquency. *Criminology, 30*(1), 47–88.

Alexander, M. (2012). *The new Jim Crow: Mass incarceration in the age of colorblindness.*
New York: The New Press.

Alfonso, F., & Wagner, M. (2019). *7 killed in West Texas shooting.* CNN. https://www.cnn
.com/us/live-news/west-texas-shooting-odessa-midland/index.html

American Psychological Association (APA). (2007). *Report of the APA task force on the
sexualization of girls.* https://www.apa.org/pi/women/programs/girls/report

American Psychological Association (APA). (2018). *APA guidelines for psychological practice with boys and men.* https://www.apa.org/about/policy/boys-men-practice-guide
lines.pdf

Bates, L. (2016). *Everyday sexism: The project that inspired a worldwide movement.* New
York: Thomas Dunne Books.

Bell, K. (2019). Two men charged in slayings of five men at north St. Louis County apart-
ment. *St. Louis Post-Dispatch.* https://www.stltoday.com/news/local/crime-and-courts
/two-men-charged-in-slayings-of-five-men-at-north-st-louis-county-apartment/arti
cle_edc8905e-8b47-5454-bc5a-5df531f318ae.html

Berton, H., & Carter, M. (2019). Rising tensions and community members' worries. *The
Seattle Times.* https://www.seattletimes.com/seattle-news/law-justice/relatives-won
der-whether-drugs-revenge-figured-in-yakama-reservation-killings/

Broidy, L., & Agnew, R. (1997). Gender and crime: A general strain theory perspective.
Journal of Research in Crime and Delinquency, 34(3), 275–306.

Butler, J. (1990). *Gender trouble: Feminism and the subversion of identity.* New York: Routledge.

Carlson, J. (2015). Mourning Mayberry: Guns, masculinity, and socioeconomic decline.
Gender & Society, 29 (3), 386–409. https://doi.org/10.1177/0891243214554799

Center on Extremism (2018). *When women are the enemy: The intersection of misogyny
and white supremacy.* Anti-Defamation League. https://www.adl.org/resources/reports
/when-women-are-the-enemy-the-intersection-of-misogyny-and-white-supremacy

Charles, S. (2019). "No mercy," declared note on accused shooter's door: prosecutors. *Chicago Sun Times*. https://chicago.suntimes.com/crime/2019/10/14/20913488/krysztof-marek-murder-charges-dunning-apartment-shooting

City News Service. (2019). San Diego shooting: Docs show harassment prior to murder-suicide. *Patch*. https://patch.com/california/san-diego/docs-detail-harassment-prior-paradise-hills-murder-suicide

City News Service (2022). *Testimony for quadruple-murder suspect continues Thursday*. NBC. https://nbcpalmsprings.com/2022/01/03/testimony-for-quadruple-murder-suspect-continues-thursday/

Cleary, T. (2019). *Randy Horn*. Heavy. https://heavy.com/news/2019/02/randy-horn/

Connell, R. W. (1987). *Gender and power*. Sydney: Allen and Unwin.

Connell, R. W. (1995). *Masculinities*. Cambridge: Polity.

Connell, R. W., & Messerschmidt, J. W. (2005). Hegemonic masculinity: Rethinking the concept. *Gender & Society, 19*(6), 829–859. https://doi.org/10.1177/0891243205278639

Crenshaw, K. (1989). Demarginalizing the intersection of race and sex: A black feminist critique of antidiscrimination doctrine, feminist theory and antiracist politics. *University of Chicago Legal Forum, 1989*, Article 8.

Crenshaw, K. (1991). Mapping the margins: Intersectionality, identity politics, and violence against women of color. *Stanford Law Review, 43*, 1241.

Dahl J., Vescio T., & Weaver K. (2015). How threats to masculinity sequentially cause public discomfort, anger, and ideological dominance over women. *Social Psychology, 46*(4), 242–254.

DeKeseredy, W. S., & Schwartz, M. D. (Eds.). (2013). *Male peer support and violence against women: The history and verification of a theory*. Boston: Northeastern University Press.

Elmahrek, A., Etehad, M., & Ormseth, M. (2019). Suspect in El Paso massacre "didn't hold anything back" in police interrogation. *Los Angeles Times*. https://www.latimes.com/world-nation/story/2019-08-03/what-we-know-about-patrick-crusius-el-paso-rampage

Everytown for Gun Safety. (2017). *Women and children in the crosshairs*. https://www.everytown.org/press/women-and-children-in-the-crosshairs-new-analysis-of-mass-shootings-in-america-reveals-54-percent-involved-domestic-violence-and-25-percent-of-fatalities-were-children/

Fernandes, T. (2019). Lone survivor of Georgia mass shooting says he tried to save mother during rampage. *Boston News*. https://www.boston25news.com/news/trending-now/lone-survivor-of-georgia-mass-shooting-says-he-tried-to-save-mother-during-rampage/915472817/

Fox, J. A., & Levin, J. (1998). Multiple homicide: Patterns of serial and mass murder. *Crime and Justice, 23*, 407–455.

Fruen, L., & Ardehali, R. (2019). Pictured: Virginia Beach gunman. *DailyMail.com*. https://www.dailymail.co.uk/news/article-7094943/PICTURED-Virginia-Beach-gunman-40-indiscriminately-shot-dead-12-colleagues.html

Geiger, D. (2019). Texas man accused of gunning down 4 of his roommates in "trap house." *Oxygen*. https://www.oxygen.com/crime-time/lively-stratton-allegedly-shoots-kills-4-beaumont-roomates

Good, G. E., & Wood, P. K. (1995). Male gender role conflict, depression, and help seeking. *Journal of Counseling & Development, 74*(1), 70–75.

Grinshteyn, E., & Hemenway, D. (2019). Violent death rates in the US compared to those of the other high-income countries, 2015. *Preventive Medicine, 123*, 20–26.

Hill Collins, P., & Bilge, S. (2016). *Intersectionality*. Malden, MA: Polity Press.

Holmes, R. M., & Holmes, S. T. (1994). *Murder in America*. Thousand Oaks, CA: Sage.

Hong, J., Damien, C., Atagi, C., DiPierro, A., & Newell, S. (2019). Suspect in Palm Springs quadruple homicide arrested. *Desert Sun*. https://www.desertsun.com/story/news/crime_courts/2019/02/07/palm-springs-mass-homicide-victims-all-linked-friendship-school-work/2802064002/

Jamison, P. (2021). "No evidence": Motive of Virginia Beach mass shooter remains a mystery, report finds. *Washington Post*. https://www.washingtonpost.com/dc-md-va/2021/03/24/virginia-beach-shooter-dewayne-craddock-motive/

Karp, A. (2018). *Estimating global civilian-held firearms numbers*. Small Arms Survey. www.smallarmssurvey.org/fileadmin/docs/T-Briefing-Papers/SAS-BP-Civilian-Firearms-Numbers.pdf

Katz, J. (2006). *Macho paradox: Why some men hurt women and how all men can help*. Naperville, IL: Sourcebooks.

Katz, J. (2011). Advertising and the construction of violent White masculinity. In G. Dines and J. M. Humez (Eds.). *Gender, race, and class in media* (pp. 261–269). Thousand Oaks, CA: Sage.

Kennedy, D. (2019). *Investigators searching for motive in Clinton standoff that left five dead, including suspected shooter*. WLBT. https://www.wlbt.com/2019/02/19/investigators-searching-motive-clinton-standoff-that-left-five-dead-including-suspected-shooter/

Kimmel, M. (2013). *Angry White men: American masculinity at the end of an era*. New York: Nation Books.

Kimmel, M., & Mahler, M. (2003). Adolescent masculinity, homophobia, and violence: Random school shootings, 1982–2001. *American Behavioral Scientist, 46*(10), 1439–1458.

Klein, J. 2006. An invisible problem: Everyday violence against girls in schools. *Theoretical Criminology, 10*(2), 147–77.

Kukura, J. (2019). Quadruple murder-suicide in San Jose apparently motivated by visa dispute. *SFST*. https://sfist.com/2019/06/26/quadruple-murder-suicide-in-san-jose-apparently-motivated-by-visa-dispute/

Lankford, A. (2016). Race and mass murder in the United States: A social and behavioral analysis. *Current Sociology, 64*(3), 470–490.

Levin, J., & Madfis, E. (2009). Mass murder at school and cumulative strain: A sequential model. *American Behavioral Scientist, 52*(9), 1227–1245.

Levin, S. (2020). Fresno mass shooting: police arrest six suspects in deadly November attack. *The Guardian*. https://www.theguardian.com/us-news/2020/jan/02/fresno-mass-shooting-police-arrest-six-suspects-in-deadly-november-attack

Londberg, M., Knight, C., & Chopra, S. (2019). "Heinous crime": West Chester police arrest husband of victim in quadruple homicide. *Cincinnati.com*. https://www.cincinnati.com/story/news/crime/crime-and-courts/2019/07/02/west-chester-police-make-arrest-april-shooting-killed-four-members-sikh-family/1139687001/

Madfis, E. (2014). Triple entitlement and homicidal anger: An exploration of the intersectional identities of American mass murderers. *Men and Masculinities, 17*(1), 67–86.

Marganski, A. J. (2019). Making a murderer: The importance of gender and violence against women in mass murder events. *Sociology Compass, 13*(9), e12730.

Melzer, S. (2018). *Manhood impossible: Men's struggles to control and transform their bodies and work*. New Brunswick, NJ: Rutgers University Press.

Messerschmidt, J. W. (2019). The salience of "hegemonic masculinity." *Men and Masculinities, 22*(1), 85–91.

Messner, S. F., & Rosenfeld, R. (2013). *Crime and the American dream.* Belmont, CA: Cengage.

Munsch, C. L., & Willer, R. (2012). The role of gender identity threat in perceptions of date rape and sexual coercion. *Violence Against Women, 18*(10), 1125–1146.

Murphy, P., Toropin, K., Griffin, D., Bronstein, S., & Levenson, E. (2019). *Dayton shooter had an obsession with violence and mass shootings, police say.* CNN. https://www.cnn .com/2019/08/05/us/connor-betts-dayton-shooting-profile/index.html

Myketiak, C. (2016). Fragile masculinity: Social inequalities in the narrative frame and discursive construction of a mass shooter's autobiography/manifesto. *Contemporary Social Science, 11*(4). https://doi.org/10.1080/21582041.2016.1213414

Neighbors say Santa Maria mobile park killer had history of domestic violence. (2019). *News Channel 3.* https://keyt.com/news/2019/06/25/neighbors-say-santa-maria-mo bile-park-killer-had-history-of-domestic-violence/

Parrott, D. J., & Zeichner, A. (2003). Effects of hypermasculinity on physical aggression against women. *Psychology of Men & Masculinity, 4*(1), 70–78. https://doi.org/10.1037 /1524-9220.4.1.70

Perez, C. (2019). California man kills 4, including dad and brother, during 12-hour shooting spree. *NY Post.* https://nypost.com/2019/07/25/california-man-kills-4-including -dad-and-brother-during-12-hour-shooting-spree/

Pleck, J. H. (1995). The gender role strain paradigm: An update. In R. F. Levant & W. S. Pollack (Eds.), *A new psychology of men* (pp. 11–32). New York: Basic Books.

Remkus, A. (2019). *Teen accused of killing 5 had burned animals, discovered family secret, relative says.* Al.com. https://www.al.com/news/2019/09/teen-accused-of-killing-5-had -burned-animals-discovered-family-secret-relative-says.html

Rogers, E., & Moore, M. H. (2019). Sebring police: SunTrust shooting suspect Zephen Xaver murdered 5 women with 9 mm. *Florida Today.* https://www.floridatoday.com /story/news/2019/01/24/sebring-shooting-zephen-xaver/2665883002/

Rottweiler, B., Clemmow, C., & Gill, P. (2021). *Misogyny, violent extremism and interpersonal violence: Examining the mediating and contingent effects of revenge motivation, hypermasculinity, collective narcissism and group threats.* The European Research Council.

Rushing, E. (2020). Man charged with killing his four family members in West Philly deemed incompetent to stand trial. *The Philadelphia Inquirer.* https://www.inquirer .com/crime/west-philly-murder-maurice-louis-mental-health-mercy-catholic-hospital -20200107.html

Sakuma, A. (2019). *The Aurora shooter had a history of domestic violence and assault. He never should have had a gun.* Vox. https://www.vox.com/2019/2/16/18227655/aurora -shooter-gun-domestic-violence

Scaptura, M. N., & Boyle, K. M. (2022). Protecting manhood: Race, class, and masculinity in men's attraction to guns and aggression. *Men and Masculinities, 25*(3), 355–376. https://doi.org/10.1177/1097184X211023545

Schaeffer, K. (2021). *Key facts about Americans and guns.* Pew Charitable Trust. https:// www.pewresearch.org/fact-tank/2021/05/11/key-facts-about-americans-and-guns/

Schmidt, H., & Holt, J. (2019). *Court records detail criminal history for both suspects in KCK mass shooting at Tequila KC.* Fox News. https://fox4kc.com/news/court-records -detail-criminal-history-for-both-suspects-in-kck-mass-shooting-at-tequila-kc/

Scofield, D. (2019). *"I'm going to kill you": New Jersey shooter previously arrested in Kent for threatening girlfriend.* News 5. https://www.news5cleveland.com/news/local-news

/oh-portage/im-going-to-kill-you-new-jersey-shooter-previously-arrested-in-kent-for
-threatening-girlfriend

Sederstrom, J. (2019). Wisconsin man's alleged shooting rampage may have been inspired
by Jayme Closs case, cops say. *Oxygen.* https://www.oxygen.com/crime-time/wiscon
sin-ritchie-german-jr-gunned-down-four-people-possible-copycat-jayme-closs

Seidler, Z. E., Dawes, A. J., Rice, S. M., Oliffe, J. L., & Dhillon, H. M. (2016). The role of
masculinity in men's help-seeking for depression: a systematic review. *Clinical Psychology Review, 49,* 106–118.

Shimizu, C. P. (2007). *The hypersexuality of race.* Chicago: Duke University Press.

Silver, J., Simons, A., & Craun, S. (2018). *A study of the pre-attack behaviors of active
shooters in the United States between 2000 and 2013.* Washington, D.C.: United States
Department of Justice, Federal Bureau of Investigation.

Spencer, T. (2019). Ex-girlfriend of Sebring bank shooting suspect says he was fascinated
with violence. *Orlando Sentinel.* https://www.orlandosentinel.com/news/breaking
-news/os-ap-ex-girlfriend-of-sebring-bank-shooting-suspect-says-he-was-fascinated
-with-violence-20190124-story.html

Stole, B., Toohey, G., & Kennedy, E. (2019). Dakota Theriot's troubled past. *The Advocate.*
https://www.theadvocate.com/baton_rouge/news/article_65be7950-234f-11e9-a10f
-074e59124a31.html

USA Today (2018). Behind the bloodshed: The untold story of America's mass killings.
www.gannett-cdn.com/GDContent/mass-killings/index.html#title

Vito, C., Admire, A., & Hughes, E. (2018). Masculinity, aggrieved entitlement, and violence: Considering the Isla Vista mass shooting. *Norma, 13*(2), 86–102.

Voorhees, C. (2019). After Abington father's murder-suicide, experts examine why. *South
Coast Today.* https://www.southcoasttoday.com/news/20191013/after-abington-fathers
-murder-suicide-experts-examine-why

Wade, L. (2015). How "benevolent sexism" drove Dylann Roof's racist massacre. *Washington Post.* https://www.washingtonpost.com/posteverything/wp/2015/06/21/how
-benevolent-sexism-drove-dylann-roofs-racist-massacre/

Weissman, D. (2021). Gender violence, the carceral state, and the politics of solidarity.
UC Davis Law Review, 55, 803–873.

West, C., & Zimmerman, D. H. (1987). Doing gender. *Gender & Society, 1*(2), 125–151.

Willer, R., Rogalin, C. L., Conlon, B., & Wojnowicz, M. T. (2013). Overdoing gender: A
test of the masculine overcompensation thesis. *American Journal of Sociology, 118*(4),
980–1022.

Winter, D. (2021). *Man accused of murdering family attends motions hearing.* Dayton247.
https://dayton247now.com/news/local/man-accused-of-murdering-family-attends
-motions-hearing-gurpreet-singh-killing-homicide-crime-aggravated-murder-sha
linder-kaur-death-penalty-plea-trial-hamilton-cincinnati-ohio

Yardley, E., & Richards, L. (2021). The elephant in the room: Towards an integrated,
feminist analysis of mass murder. *Violence against Women.* https://journals.sagepub
.com/doi/10.1177/10778012221101917

4

Mass Shootings Involving Intimate Partners in the United States

Prevalence and Patterns

Jillian J. Turanovic and Kristen J. Neville

Introduction

Deadly mass shootings have emerged as one of the most prominent social problems in contemporary America. And though these incidents account for far less than 1 percent of all homicides in the United States (Fridel, 2021; Krouse & Richardson, 2015), a large majority of adults (79 percent) experience stress over mass shootings, and a third say that the fear of these attacks stops them from going to certain places and events (American Psychological Association, 2019). There are multiple ways in which a mass shooting can be defined (Duwe, 2020; Fox & Levin, 2015), yet the term is typically used to describe deadly attacks in public spaces—specifically, incidents in which four or more victims are fatally shot in a public location within a twenty-four-hour period in the absence of other criminal activity, such as robberies, drug deals, and gang conflict (Peterson & Densley, 2019; Schildkraut & Elsass, 2016; Siegel et al., 2020). These include mass shootings such as those carried out in Orlando, Parkland, Las Vegas, and El Paso—premeditated, high-profile attacks that target innocent victims in places like nightclubs, schools, concerts, and stores (Duwe et al., 2021; Lankford, 2016).

When mass shootings are defined more broadly, however—to recognize *any* event in which four or more individuals are fatally shot—more than half have been found to involve the killing of an intimate partner or family victim, and the bulk occur in private, rather than public, spaces (Everytown for Gun Safety, 2021; Fridel, 2021). Indeed, research shows that between 30 percent and 40 percent of intimate partner homicides involve more than one victim—

typically ranging from between two to seven people killed per incident—including family members, children, friends, and other household members (Kafka et al., 2021; Kivisto, 2015; Liem & Reichelmann, 2013; Smith et al., 2014; Zeoli, 2018). Yet despite their prevalence, multiple-victim intimate partner homicides have received comparatively less attention in the mass shootings literature (Geller et al., 2021). Information is thus lacking on the trends and features of mass shootings that target intimate partners, as well as on the motives and circumstances surrounding such attacks.

Intimate partner homicide is often preceded by, and viewed as an extension of, intimate partner violence (Campbell et al., 2003; Zeoli et al., 2021). Various perspectives have been put forth to explain why intimate partner violence occurs (Lawson, 2012), but at the heart of these are feminist explanations that consider partner abuse as an expression of male hegemony that "cannot be adequately understood unless gender and power are taken into account" (Yllo, 1993, p. 47; see also Dobash & Dobash, 1979). Such perspectives are also rooted in assumptions of gender asymmetry that consider men as more likely to use violence in relationships as a means of asserting dominance and control (Stark, 2007). To be sure, women are at highest risk of both lethal and nonlethal violence when they want to leave, are trying to leave, or have left an intimate relationship (DeKeseredy & Schwartz, 2009). Threats to masculinity and grievances with intimate partners can also be motivating factors for acts of serious violence—either against intimate partners or other individuals (Silva et al., 2021).

The willingness to engage in violence is central to American masculinity because so-called real men are socialized to believe they must show others they are strong, powerful, and unafraid (Messerschmidt, 2000). In American society, the more violently men behave, the more "manly" they are viewed (Madfis, 2014; Neroni, 2000). Carrying out acts of violence in response to rejection, jealously, and humiliation may serve as a self-correction to a crisis of masculinity (Allison & Klein, 2021; Bengtsson, 2016; Scaptura & Boyle, 2020) or to enact retributive justice for transgressions by an intimate partner (Felson, 1997; Hayes et al., 2018). Violence is also salient among men who feel entitled to certain privileges, such as ownership, control, and power over women. When these expected privileges are blocked, or men's position of authority or dominance is threatened, anger and violence are likely to occur. As such, some men use violence against intimate partners as a means of aggrieved entitlement, in which they attempt to avenge their precarious sense of masculinity (Kalish & Kimmel, 2010; Kimmel, 2013).

According to the Centers for Disease Control and Prevention (CDC), an intimate partner can include a current or former spouse, boyfriend or girlfriend, dating partner, or sexual partner (CDC, 2021). In this chapter, we focus exclusively on deadly mass shootings in which an individual shoots and kills an intimate partner and at least three other people. Using unique data compiled on deadly mass shootings in the United States between 1976 and 2019, we provide a descriptive overview of incidents to identify trends and basic characteristics and then provide a qualitative case review to showcase underlying themes. After presenting the data and findings, we conclude with a discussion of gender and American masculinity and directions for future research.

Methods

A dataset was compiled on all deadly mass shootings in the United States from 1976 through 2019 in which the offender shot and killed an intimate partner (N = 208). Similar to existing definitions of mass murder (Duwe, 2020; Fox et al., 2019; Krouse & Richardson, 2015), a deadly mass shooting was defined as the fatal shooting of four or more individuals (excluding the shooter) within twenty-four hours. Mass shootings of all types were included—not only public incidents—but attacks had to involve an intimate partner being shot and killed to qualify.

Although researchers have relied on various other data sources to study mass shootings and intimate partner homicides, these are not without their limitations. For example, the FBI Supplemental Homicide Report (SHR) data suffer from a high degree of missingness, reporting errors, and the listing of multiple records for incidents with large victim counts (Duwe, 2020). Crowdsourced databases are also limited in that they often focus exclusively on public mass shootings, use inconsistent definitions and inclusion criteria, and are of questionable validity (Fridel, 2021; Neville, 2021).

To overcome these issues, the mass shooting data were compiled as follows. First, a master list of homicides with four or more victims was generated using data from the SHR, the FBI Active Shooter Incident reports, the United States Secret Service reports on mass attacks in public spaces, the Florida Supplemental Homicide Reports, the Associated Press/USA Today/Northeastern University Mass Killing Database, Everytown for Gun Safety, Mother Jones, the Stanford Mass Shootings in America database, the New York City Police Department report on active shooters, the Violence Project Mass Shooter Database, and the Gun Violence Archive. Extensive systematic media searches were also conducted to locate mass shootings not included in existing databases. Second, media reports, police reports, and court documents (if applicable) were used to validate each incident. To date, this represents one of the most comprehensive and accurate databases available on deadly mass shootings of intimate partners during the study period. For more information on how the data were compiled, validated, and coded, see Turanovic et al. (2022).

Findings

Trends and Features

Figure 4.1 presents the number of mass shootings per year from 1976 to 2019 in which the offender shot and killed an intimate partner. As can be seen, there is no stark increase or decrease in these incidents over time, though in the past two decades, they tend to occur on a slightly more frequent and consistent basis. The year 2011 had the highest number of incidents (fourteen incidents). Notably, these patterns do not appear to be the same as for public mass shootings in general, which have been increasing in the United States in recent years (Peterson & Densley, 2019). Across forty-four years, 949 victims were killed by gunfire in the shootings where intimate partners were murdered. The average number of victims shot and killed per incident was 4.6, ranging from four to thirteen. The deadliest shooting occurred in Wilkes-Barre, Pennsylvania, in 1982, where a man shot and killed thirteen people at two homes—seven children, his three live-in girlfriends, an ex-girlfriend, his ex-girlfriend's mother, and a bystander in the street.

Table 4.1 presents descriptive statistics on the 208 mass shootings where an intimate partner was killed. As can be seen, all but one incident (99.5 percent) involved at least one female victim, and over three-quarters (76.4 percent) involved at least one child victim. The vast majority (90.9 percent) occurred in private residences, and nearly all were carried out by men (96.2 percent) and lone shooters (97.6 percent). Perpetrators were most often between the ages of thirty to forty-nine (68.7 percent) and were white (56.3 percent). In

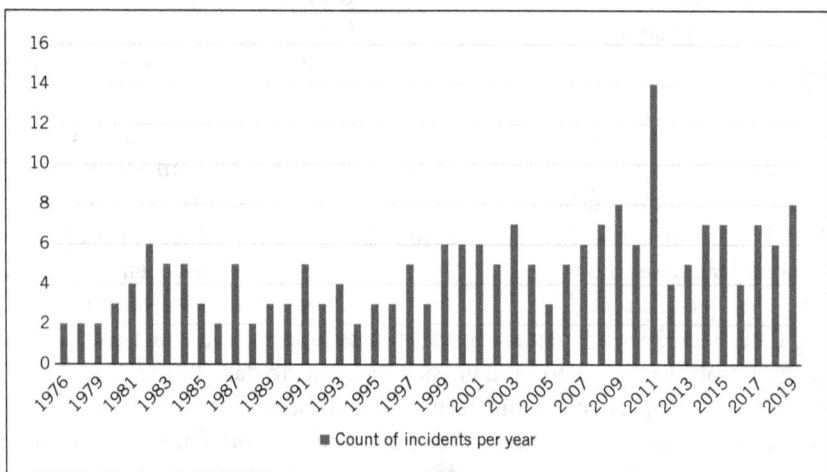

Figure 4.1 Number of Mass Shootings involving an Intimate Partner, 1976–2019.

TABLE 4.1 DESCRIPTIVE STATISTICS OF MASS SHOOTINGS INVOLVING INTIMATE PARTNERS (N = 208)	
Incident Characteristic	Mean (SD) or %
Number of victims	4.6 (1.1)
Females	2.6 (1.1)
Males	1.9 (1.1)
Children	1.9 (1.5)
Female victim(s)	99.5%
Male victim(s)	91.4%
Child victim(s)	76.4%
Primary location	
Private residence	90.9%
Street or sidewalk	2.4%
Office building	1.9%
Other public location	5.9%
Felony related	2.9%
Lone shooter	97.6%
Male shooter(s)	96.2%
Female shooter(s)	3.9%
Age of shooter(s)	
18–24	10.1%
25–29	13.0%
30–39	39.4%
40–49	29.3%
50–59	8.2%
60 and over	1.9%
Race of shooter(s)	
White	56.3%
Black	25.5%
Latinx	10.6%
Asian	3.4%
Other	4.3%
Shooter committed suicide	57.7%
Shooter underwent recent stress or crisis	88.9%
Lost job	11.5%
Financial strain	20.7%
Breakup, separation, or divorce	51.4%
Interpersonal conflict	43.3%
Other acute stress	34.6%
Shooter history of violence	51.4%
Domestic violence	37.0%
Shooter mental health problems	38.0%

more than half of all incidents, shooters committed suicide after the attack, either on- or off-scene (57.7 percent). Although most incidents also involved at least one male victim (91.4 percent), there were differences in the number of victims killed per incident who were male versus female. Overall, the average number of female victims killed per incident was higher, and 51.9 percent of all incidents involved three or more female victims. Figure 4.2 provides more information on these differences. As seen, there were several incidents involving no male victims (compared with only one incident involving no female victims), and a greater portion of incidents with upward of three female victims.

Additionally, as Table 4.1 shows, for most of the intimate partner–related mass shootings (88.9 percent), the offender underwent recent stress or crisis. These stressors, which were not mutually exclusive, were tied to job loss (11.5 percent); financial strain (20.7 percent); a breakup, separation, or divorce (51.4 percent); recent interpersonal conflict (43.3 percent); or some other form of acute stress (34.6 percent). These "other" stressors included, for example, being under intense pressure at a new job, undergoing a custody battle, being arrested, suffering health problems, or experiencing the death of a family member or friend. Given that the majority of shooters were white males, it is possible that the privileges of white masculinity make these losses or stressors more unexpected and shameful and culminate in feelings of failure that precede violence (Madfis, 2014).

In just over half of cases (51.4 percent), the shooter had a documented history of violence. Of those with a history of violence, the majority (71.3 percent) had engaged in violence against intimate partners. In over a third of cases (38.0 percent), the shooter was noted to have suffered prior mental health problems (as diagnosed by a medical professional or as evidenced by prescription medications, hospitalizations, mental health treatment, suicide plans, and suicide attempts).

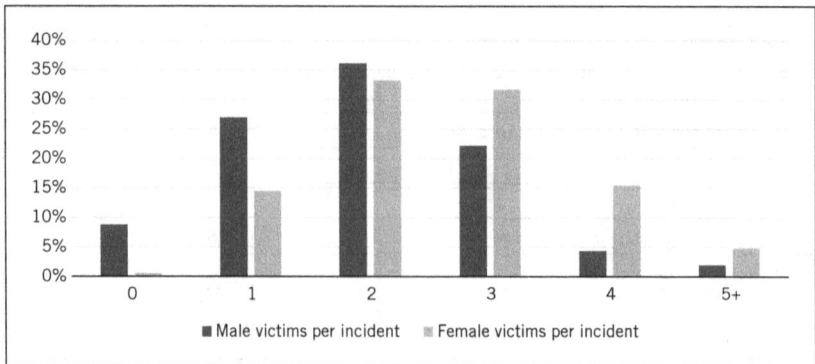

Figure 4.2 Number of Male and Female Victims Killed per Incident.

Based on these descriptive statistics, it seems that mass shootings involving the death of an intimate partner are typically carried out by men in crisis, many of whom who are white and have violent histories, including violence against intimate partners. These shootings typically happen in the home, women and children are victims in most attacks, and perpetrators often commit suicide afterward. While these pieces of data are informative, they do not speak to the deeper motives behind the shootings, the dynamics between shooters and intimate partners, or threats to masculinity. Accordingly, an in-depth review of incidents is required.

Digging Deeper

To showcase deeper themes, a qualitative review of the 208 intimate partner–involved incidents was undertaken using extensive information gathered from official records (court documents, police reports) and reports from the media (triangulated and verified through multiple sources, see Turanovic et al., 2022).[1] This review revealed more complex issues that facilitated mass shootings, namely, involving men's struggles to maintain power and control over their intimate partners, which were closely linked to crises of masculinity.

The term *humiliated fury* has been used to describe violence perpetrated by men when they feel shamed, powerless, and lacking the control to which they believe they are entitled (Hill, 2020, p. 112). Because of American masculine socialization, many men feel entitled to their partner's deference and subordination. When this is withheld, men's sense of shame and humiliation can serve as a powerful precursor to violence. As Hill (2020, p. 116) states, when abusive and controlling men are "confronted with feelings of shame, they take the path of least resistance. Instead of acknowledging their own sense of powerlessness and sitting with their discomfort, they blame others and . . . use violence to achieve a phony—and often short-lived—feeling of power and pride."

Prior to committing mass shootings, several perpetrators became increasingly paranoid or jealous about losing their partners to another man, and they expressed rage over talk of separation or divorce. Several incidents were preceded by the shooters stalking, harassing, or abusing their partners, and these behaviors were often reported to police. As attempts to regain control over women failed, and women continually distanced themselves from abusive relationships, men resorted to lethal violence. The following shooting that took place in Norwalk, Iowa, is one illustration of how a man was sent into turmoil after his wife left him:

In June 1993, a man entered his former family home, shot and killed his estranged wife, Jolene, one of his children, and two children belonging to Jolene's boyfriend. The man also killed two more of his children who lived in the home—one by suffocation and one by strangulation. The year before, Jolene had filed for a dissolution of marriage. Since then, the man had been resisting his wife's efforts to obtain a divorce and had threatened his family's safety. He told one of Jolene's sisters that if he could not have the family no one else could. Prior to the shootings, the man had been arrested and put on probation for domestic abuse and stalking, and was ordered to stay away from the home. Despite the restraining order, relatives and neighbors testified to the man's relentless efforts to follow Jolene and the children. Numerous times a day, the man would drive by or sit outside Jolene's home and observe her activities. He was described as "obsessed" and distraught over the fact Jolene had a male friend and was dating. Three months before the shooting, Jolene's brother overheard the man tell her, "[y]ou are bringing this all on yourself. If you don't quit, I will kill you and the others." The marriage dissolution trial was for scheduled one month after the shootings. The man attempted suicide by gun on scene yet survived.

Another incident in Ardmore, Pennsylvania, was preceded by police contact, stalking, jealousy, and possessive behavior:

In January 2002, after arguing about divorce, a man shot and killed his wife, Sandra, his stepdaughter, and Sandra's parents, before committing suicide. The man had a tumultuous relationship with Sandra. He stalked her, followed her to work, on outings with her girlfriends, and to a local college where she was taking undergraduate night classes. According to a family friend, the man wanted "constantly to have her under his thumb." The man was clinically depressed, jealous, and possessive of his wife, but no clear evidence that he had previously been physically abusive. Five days before the shooting, a family friend called the police to express concern about the man's mental stability, but Sandra would not agree to file a complaint. Two days before the shootings, the man had disrupted a church service by loudly accusing a family friend of having a relationship with Sandra. He was cited for harassment and disorderly conduct. Less than seven hours before the shooting, the man called the police and calmly said that he planned to contest the charges. Police said that he gave no hint he was homicidal or suicidal.

In this case, the shooter's sense of aggrieved entitlement (Kalish & Kimmel, 2010) brought on by his wife's desire for independence and a divorce likely contributed to the mass shooting.

Although threats to masculinity can be inferred in many cases, there were several incidents where it was clear that shooters were ridiculed and emasculated prior to the attack. Feelings of humiliation were central to narratives that explained shooter's motives, where violence was carried out to reinstate "manliness" or to enact retribution. For example, in a mass shooting that took place near Deer Lodge, Montana, the shooter—a controlling man with a history of domestic violence—was upset by his wife "mocking" him:

> In June 2015, a man shot and killed his wife and three of their children in their home, before committing suicide. Prior to shooting himself, the man called an acquaintance to tell him that he shot his family and that "his wife had been mocking and riding him all day." The man was known to be very controlling of his wife. He had cut off contact with most family and friends in the years before the shooting and was living with his wife and children "off the grid" in remote isolation. The man had a history of violence, including physical abuse in a previous marriage.

In other incidents, men's fury stemmed from the inferiority and embarrassment they felt when their partners left them for someone else. Take, for example, the following mass shooting in Willow River, Minnesota:

> In April 1976, a man shot and killed his wife, Ruth, Ruth's lover James, and three of their children. In January 1976, the man learned that Ruth was having an affair with James, their neighbor. The man separated from Ruth and agreed to her request for a divorce, but he did not want her to move in with James until the divorce was finalized. However, in the weeks leading up the shootings, the man felt that Ruth "couldn't get enough" of James, and that she was "going to move in with him regardless of what or who she would hurt." The man had also learned recently that one of Ruth's sons had caught his mother in bed with James in their marital home. The day before the shootings, Ruth ridiculed her husband's ability as a lover, demanded all his farm machinery as part of the division of property, and threatened to deprive him of the opportunity to see their 5-year-old son, the only child of their marriage. The following day, the man returned to his farm to get some belongings. On arrival, he saw that a truck and trailer were being loaded by Ruth, her two sons by a previous marriage, James, and his three sons. The man brandished two loaded pistols with the intention of "scaring the hell out of" Ruth and James. However, as conflicts escalated, he ended up shooting and killing Ruth, James, and three of the children, including his 5-year-old son. Short-

ly after the shootings, the man attempted suicide by taking an over-
dose of alcohol and sleeping pills, yet he survived.

Here, on top of the shame felt by his wife leaving him, aggravating factors
included the ridicule of his lovemaking skills and the loss of his property,
each of which was an affront to his masculinity.

A more poignant case of emasculation can be seen in the following mass
shooting that took place in Channelview, Texas, where a man was humiliated by his ex-wife in front of several people:

> In November 1997, a man shot and killed his ex-wife, Gloria, and three
> men. That night, the man went to Gloria's apartment after indications
> of reconciliation. He hoped she would be alone but, instead, she was
> having a party with her roommate and three other men. It was ap-
> parent that all had been drinking excessively. The man agreed to stay
> and drink with the group even though he was uncomfortable with
> the situation. The man reported that he felt humiliated when, at some
> point during the party, conversations turned sexual, and Gloria flashed
> her breasts to the group. She then went into her bedroom with two
> male partygoers. A short time later, she reappeared with one of the
> men, whose pants were unzipped. She announced that she had given
> him oral sex, and that she was going to have sex with the other par-
> tygoer who was still in the bedroom. The man (shooter) was angry
> and attempted to leave, but someone at the party took away his keys
> and taunted him. Upset, the man grabbed his hunting rifle from his
> truck and went back into the home where he continued to be mocked
> and harassed. Gloria's roommate threw a beer at him, and he fired
> his gun. The man continued to shoot and kill four people at the party,
> including Gloria and the man she was in bed with at the time. The
> roommate survived the shooting.

The combination of failed reconciliation, the flaunting of sexual encounters
with other men, and harassment by several partygoers culminated in an intense crisis of masculinity for the perpetrator.

Discussion

Although not exhaustive, the few examples above highlight underlying themes
of masculinity in mass shootings of intimate partners. These attacks are almost always carried out by men, and nearly all target female victims. In several cases, attacks were carried out in attempts to reassert power and control
over partners and failing relationships. Yet many mass shootings were also

retributive and occurred after instances of emasculation, rejection, and ridicule. According to Leverenz (1986, p. 451), "American manhood has less to do with ensuring male dominance . . . than with minimizing maximum loss. . . . The real fear is not of women but of being ashamed or humiliated in front of other men, or being dominated by stronger men." This quote still rings true decades later, which speaks to the pervasiveness of toxic masculinity in American society.

In our review of incidents, we discussed crises of masculinity in terms of aggrieved entitlement and humiliated fury, but there is much more to explore—particularly with how a precarious sense of masculinity coincides with the use and possession of firearms in the United States (Bridges et al., 2022, this volume). In America, the culture of coercive control and male hegemony that perpetuates violence against women is also one that glorifies male gun ownership (Stroud, 2012). Guns are a necessary component of these events and have long been conceived as symbols of masculinity (Connell, 1995). As Stange and Oyster (2000, p. 22) stated, "In [men's hands], the gun has served a symbolic function that exceeds any practical utility. It has become the symbol par excellence of masculinity: of power, force, aggressiveness, decisiveness, deadly accuracy, cold rationality." Given that a nontrivial portion of intimate partner–related mass shootings were preceded by domestic violence, and over half of shooters had problems with violence in the past, efforts to restrict access to firearms for individuals with violent histories may help to prevent such attacks in the future (Gold, 2020; Lynch et al., 2022; Zeoli & Paruk, 2020). Of course, most cases of intimate partner violence never escalate to homicide. As such, the connection between access to guns, mass shootings, and partner abuse is one that should be explored further.

Further, because the findings presented were purely descriptive, there is far more to explore regarding the extent to which American masculine ideals facilitate mass shootings involving intimate partners. Mainstream discourse on mass violence tends to focus most heavily on mental illness, violent media consumption, and the availability of firearms (Lankford & Cowan, 2020; Skeem & Mulvey, 2020), yet deeper analyses of the patriarchal norms and attitudes that contribute to mass shootings are less common (Scaptura & Boyle, 2020). There were also themes in the literature on American masculinity that we did not focus heavily on in our qualitative case review—such as losses of occupational prestige and financial success. Such stressors are thought to be of significance for men who kill, especially in American society where the demands of the workplace and monetary successes are valued above other noneconomic goals (Messner & Rosenfeld, 2013). The continued downward mobility among American middle and lower classes, coupled with less racial and gender privilege for entitled white males, may be of consequence for these mass shootings involving intimate partners (Madfis, 2014).

There are likely multiple problematic situations, stressors, and opportunities for violence that have cumulative effects on people's lives—factors that, in combination with masculine cultural norms, shape the impacts that short-term "precipitants" (such as job loss or romantic rejection) have on decisions to carry out a mass shooting (Levin & Madfis, 2009). Nearly all perpetrators of intimate partner–related mass shootings were documented to be under recent stress, yet it is exceedingly difficult to determine *why* only some individuals respond to crises or humiliation with extreme violence (Fox et al., 2019). An intersectional approach that incorporates gender, race, and class, such as the one advanced by Madfis (2014) and Gascón (2022, this volume), will be necessary to better understand these phenomena. As research in this area progresses, we emphasize the need to look beyond monolithic explanations, and to be mindful of masculine ideals, to yield more promising directions for policy and practice.

ACKNOWLEDGMENTS

We are thankful the students at Florida State University and Travis Pratt who helped to build the database used for this study. We extend special thanks to Antonia La Tosa, Michaela Wilson, Georgia Watson, Troy Allen, Victoria Hall, Angelina Cole, and Kara Dudley. This project was supported by Award No. 2018-75-CX-0024, awarded by the National Institute of Justice, Office of Justice Programs, U.S. Department of Justice. The opinions, findings, and conclusions or recommendations expressed in this chapter are those of the authors and do not necessarily reflect those of the Department of Justice.

NOTE

1. Details on the specific media reports and official documents from which the qualitative case summaries were constructed are available upon request from the authors. Over 100 documents were reviewed per case. More information also be found in Turanovic et al. (2022).

REFERENCES

Allison, K., & Klein, B. R. (2021). Pursuing hegemonic masculinity through violence: An examination of anti-homeless bias homicides. *Journal of Interpersonal Violence, 36*(13–14), 6859–6882.

American Psychological Association. (2019). One-third of US adults say fear of mass shootings prevents them from going to certain places or events. https://www.apa.org/news/press/releases/2019/08/fear-mass-shooting

Bengtsson, T. T. (2016). Performing hypermasculinity: Experiences with confined young offenders. *Men and Masculinities, 19*(4), 410–428.

Bridges, T., Tober, T. L., & Brazzell, M. (2022). Mass shootings and American masculinity. In E. Madfis & A. Lankford (Eds.), *All American massacre: The tragic role of American culture and society in mass shootings.* Temple University Press.

Campbell, J. C., Webster, D., Koziol-McLain, J., Block, C., Campbell, D., Curry, M. A., Gary, F., Glass, N., McFarlane, J., Sachs, C., Sharps, P., Ulrich, Y., Wilt, S. A., Manganello,

J., Xu, X., Schollenberger, J., Frye, V., & Laughon, K. (2003). Risk factors for femicide in abusive relationships: Results from a multisite case control study. *American Journal of Public Health, 93*(7), 1089–1097.

Centers for Disease Control and Prevention (CDC). (2021). Intimate partner violence. https://www.cdc.gov/violenceprevention/intimatepartnerviolence/

Connell, R. W. (1995). *Masculinities.* Cambridge: Polity.

DeKeseredy, W. S., & Schwartz, M. D. (2009). *Dangerous exits: Escaping abusive relationships in rural America.* New Brunswick, NJ: Rutgers University Press.

Dobash, R. P., & Dobash, R. E. (1979). *Violence against wives: A case against the patriarchy.* New York: Free Press.

Duwe, G. (2020). Patterns and prevalence of lethal mass violence. *Criminology & Public Policy, 19*(1), 17–35.

Duwe, G., Sanders, N. E., Rocque, M., & Fox, J. A. (2021). Forecasting the severity of mass public shootings in the United States. *Journal of Quantitative Criminology,* 1–39.

Everytown for Gun Safety. (2021). *Mass shootings in the United States: 2009–2021.* https://everytownresearch.org/maps/mass-shootings-in-america-2009-2019/

Felson, R. B. (1997). Anger, aggression, and violence in love triangles. *Violence and Victims, 12*(4), 345–362.

Fox, J. A., & Levin, J. (2015). Mass confusion surrounding mass murder. *The Criminologist, 40,* 8–11.

Fox, J. A., Levin, J., & Fridel, E. E. (2019). *Extreme killing: Understanding serial and mass murder* (4th ed.). Thousand Oaks, CA: Sage.

Fridel, E. (2021). A multivariate comparison of family, felony, and public mass murders in the United States. *Journal of Interpersonal Violence, 36*(3–4), 1092–1118.

Gascón, D. (2022). Structural strain, intersectionality, and mass murder: A case study of the Isla Vista shooting. In E. Madfis & A. Lankford (Eds.), *All American massacre: The tragic role of American culture and society in mass shootings.* Temple University Press.

Geller, L. B., Booty, M., & Crifasi, C. K. (2021). The role of domestic violence in fatal mass shootings in the United States, 2014–2019. *Injury Epidemiology, 8*(1), 1–8.

Gold, L. H. (2020). Domestic violence, firearms, and mass shootings. *Journal of the American Academy of Psychiatry and the Law, 48*(1), 35–42.

Hayes, B. E., Mills, C. E., Freilich, J. D., & Chermak, S. M. (2018). Are honor killings unique? A comparison of honor killings, domestic violence homicides, and hate homicides by far-right extremists. *Homicide Studies, 22*(1), 70–93.

Hill, J. (2020). *See what you made me do: Power, control and domestic abuse.* London: Hurst & Company.

Kafka, J. M., Moracco, K. E., Young, B. R., Taheri, C., Graham, L. M., Macy, R. J., & Proescholdbell, S. K. (2021). Fatalities related to intimate partner violence: Towards a comprehensive perspective. *Injury Prevention, 27*(2), 137–144.

Kalish, R., & Kimmel, M. (2010). Suicide by mass murder: Masculinity, aggrieved entitlement, and rampage school shootings. *Health Sociology Review, 19*(4), 451–464.

Kimmel, M. (2013). *Angry white men: American masculinity at the end of an era.* New York: Nation Books.

Kivisto, A. J. (2015). Male perpetrators of intimate partner homicide: A review and proposed typology. *Journal of the American Academy of Psychiatry and the Law, 43*(3), 300–312.

Krouse, W. J., & Richardson, D. J. (2015). *Mass murder with firearms: Incidents and victims, 1999–2013.* Washington: Congressional Research Service.

Lankford, A. (2016). Public mass shooters and firearms: A cross-national study of 171 countries. *Violence and Victims, 31,* 187–199.

Lankford, A., & Cowan, R. G. (2020). Has the role of mental health problems in mass shootings been significantly underestimated? *Journal of Threat Assessment and Management, 7*(3–4), 135–156.

Lawson, J. (2012). Sociological theories of intimate partner violence. *Journal of Human Behavior in the Social Environment, 22,* 572–590.

Leverenz, D. (1986). Manhood, humiliation, and public life: Some stories. *Southwest Review, 71*(4), 442–462.

Levin, J., & Madfis, E. (2009). Mass murder at school and cumulative strain: A sequential model. *American Behavioral Scientist, 52*(9), 1227–1245.

Liem, M., & Reichelmann (2013). Patterns of multiple family homicide. *Homicide Studies, 18*(1), 44–58.

Lynch, K. R., Boots, D. P., Jackson, D. B., & Renzetti, C. M. (2022). Firearm-related abuse and protective order requests among intimate partner violence victims. *Journal of Interpersonal Violence, 37*(15–16), NP12973–NP12997.

Madfis, E. (2014). Triple entitlement and homicidal anger: An exploration of the intersectional identities of American mass murderers. *Men and Masculinities, 17*(1), 67–86.

Messerschmidt, J. W. (2000). Becoming "real men": Adolescent masculinity challenges and sexual violence. *Men and Masculinities, 2*(3), 286–307.

Messner, S. F., & Rosenfeld, R. (2013). *Crime and the American dream* (5th ed.). Boston: Cengage.

Neroni, H. (2000). The men of Columbine: Violence and masculinity in American culture and film. *Journal for the Psychoanalysis of Culture and Society, 5,* 256–263.

Neville, K. J. (2021). *An introduction to comprehensive data on deadly mass shootings in America from 1976 to 2019* [Master's thesis, Florida State University].

Peterson, J., & Densley, J. (2019). *The Violence Project database of mass shootings in the United States, 1966–2019.* The Violence Project. https://www.theviolenceproject.org/wp-content/uploads/2019/11/TVP-Mass-Shooter-Database-Report-Final-compressed.pdf

Scaptura, M. N., & Boyle, K. M. (2020). Masculinity threat, "incel" traits, and violent fantasies among heterosexual men in the United States. *Feminist Criminology, 15*(3), 278–298.

Schildkraut, J., & Elsass, H. J. (2016). *Mass shootings: Media, myths, and realities.* Westport, CT: Praeger.

Siegel, M., Goder-Reiser, M., Duwe, G., Rocque, M., Fox, J. A., & Fridel, E. E. (2020). The relation between state gun laws and the incidence and severity of mass public shootings in the United States, 1976–2018. *Law and Human Behavior, 44*(5), 347.

Silva, J. R., Capellan, J. A., Schmuhl, M. A., & Mills, C. E. (2021). Gender-based mass shootings: an examination of attacks motivated by grievances against women. *Violence Against Women, 27*(12–13), 2163–2186.

Skeem, J., & Mulvey, E. (2020). What role does serious mental illness play in mass shootings, and how should we address it? *Criminology & Public Policy, 19*(1), 85–108.

Smith, S. G., Fowler, K. A., & Niolon, P. H. (2014). Intimate partner homicide and corollary victims in 16 states: National Violent Death Reporting System, 2003–2009. *American Journal of Public Health, 104*(3), 461–466.

Stange, M. Z., & Oyster, C. K. (2000). *Gun women: Firearms and feminism in contemporary America.* New York: New York University Press.

Stark, E. (2007). *Coercive control: The entrapment of women in personal life.* New York: Oxford University Press.

Stroud, A. (2012). Good guys with guns: Hegemonic masculinity and concealed handguns. *Gender & Society, 26*(2), 216–238.

Turanovic, J. J., Pratt, T. C., Neville, K. N., & La Tosa, A. (2022). *A comprehensive assessment of deadly mass shootings, 1980–2018.* Final report prepared for the National Institute of Justice. https://www.ojp.gov/pdffiles1/nij/grants/305090.pdf

Yllo, K. A. (1993). Through a feminist lens: Gender, power, and violence. In R. J. Gelles & D. R. Loseke (Eds.), *Current controversies on family violence* (pp. 47–62). Thousand Oaks, CA: Sage.

Zeoli, A. M. (2018). *Multiple victim homicides, mass murders, and homicide suicides as domestic violence events.* Battered Women's Justice Project. https://www.preventdvgun violence.org/multiple-killings-zeoli.pdf

Zeoli, A. M., Kwiatkowski, C. C., Wallin, M. A., & Brown, K. (2021). Criminal histories of intimate partner homicide offenders. *Homicide Studies.* Advance online publication.

Zeoli, A. M., & Paruk, J. (2020). Potential to prevent mass shootings through domestic violence firearm restrictions. *Criminology & Public Policy, 19*(1), 129–145.

5

Involuntary Celibates, Masculinities, and Violence in American Culture

SARAH E. DALY

Involuntary celibate men, or "incels," have gained increasing attention in recent years. Men associated with inceldom have committed or planned violent attacks including but not limited to the 2014 Isla Vista shooting, the Toronto van attack, multiple stabbing incidents in Canada, and most recently, the mass shooting in the English city of Plymouth in August 2021. However, incels are collectively blamed for these and other events while being portrayed by law enforcement and media as a nefarious group of homicidal, angry men who aim to exact revenge on a society of sexually active people. This depiction is often easily confirmed by screenshots from incel forums that utilize misogynistic, violent, and racist speech or glorify mass shooters. Moreover, a quick Google News search for *incels* results in sensational headlines associating them with violence, hatred, and extremism. As some scholars have noted, relative to the size of the online communities, the number of incels who engage in violence is small (Cottee, 2020), and, as such, it becomes increasingly necessary to understand more nuanced aspects of inceldom. Such examinations should include an understanding of individual experiences, differences between violent and nonviolent members, and cultural influences that have made room for the growth of the online group.

While many agencies and organizations have attempted to use a domestic terrorism and/or radicalization approach to understanding and preventing incel-related violence, researchers and practitioners have often overlooked or ignored the societal and cultural factors that may have contributed to the rise of incel forums and groups. Rather than simply considering the people and the online community as inevitably dangerous, this chapter examines the sociological factors that have created space for incels as an online community not only to grow but also to flourish. Many criminological theories can provide a cultural understanding and a macro-level explanation of the ways in which American society has banished incels to the margins and cultivated a culture rooted in aggrievement, sadness, and often-hateful rhetoric. While the chapter does not condone the actions, speech, or ideas that may be common among incel forums, it attempts to unpack and examine incel grievances and societal expectations that may influence incel experiences and behaviors. While they may be deserving of the criticism of their generally misogynistic, racist, and homophobic rhetoric, a comprehensive analysis of the macro- and micro-level factors that influence participation and engagement in the online groups can offer much needed insights for prevention and intervention. As a result, this chapter aims to offer recommendations for future research and policy.

Incels: A Brief Overview

Incel is a portmanteau for *involuntary celibate*, meaning a person who desires sex but is unable to attain it. Although the term and the idea has appeared in literature for centuries, the research on incels has evolved from "love-shyness" (Gilmartin, 1987) to a life-course perspective of involuntary celibacy (Donnelly et al., 2001) to modern research on incels (see Cottee, 2021; Daly & Reed, 2021; Ging, 2019; Glace et al., 2020). Having transformed from an inclusive, online space in the 1990s to a hostile and seemingly toxic set of forums, the modern iteration of incels were not the only group to use the internet to connect and share ideas. Incels, for the most part, fall under the broader umbrella of the "manosphere," which Nagle (2017) argues is a direct backlash to the proliferation of feminism.

While a more thorough history on the evolution of involuntary celibacy is beyond the scope of this chapter (for a more comprehensive explanation, see Daly & Reed, 2021; Ging, 2019), incels are now understood (both in research and mainstream media) to be an online community of men, spread out over a variety of online platforms, who share similar views lamenting their situation (inceldom). Many discussions on their forums condemn women for not having sex with them, resent people who are successfully having sex, and blame society more broadly for creating these circumstances that make their lives nearly unbearable. They have been often associated with violence (specifically lone-wolf attacks), misogyny, racism, and hatred (Hoffman & Ware, 2020; Scaptura & Boyle, 2020; Texas Department of Public Safety, 2020). Often overlooked, however, are the abnormally high (relative to the general population) rates of suicidal ideations and completed suicides (Daly & Laskovtsov, 2021) in these communities and that only a small number of incels have enacted violence relative to the number of online users.

American Culture and Hegemonic Masculinity

In addition to expectations of femininity for women (Hartley, 2018; Stein, 2015; Trekels & Eggermont, 2018; Wiederman & Hurst, 1998), there still exist notable and pervasive expectations for men to demonstrate masculinity both in appearance and in action. "Manly men" are expected to protect themselves and others, serve as breadwinners, demonstrate bravery, and be physically fit.

As Shachter and Seinfeld (1994) note, "The American culture of violence is reflected in the history, attitudes, belief systems, and coping styles of the population in dealing with conflicts, frustration, and the quest for wealth and power" (p. 347). The manifestation of this is the unfortunate notion that violence, strength, and respect are clear cornerstones of American masculinity. Inherent in this idea of masculinity is also that boys learn that they should have sexual desire for girls (Schrock & Schwalbe, 2009).

In relationships and interactions with girls and women, men "do gender" through masculine acts that are not only sexual but also through behaviors that protect and lead women, whereas women are expected to reciprocate in feminine ways. As West and Zimmerman (1987) write, "The man 'does' masculinity by, for example, taking the woman's arm to guide her across a street, and she 'does' being feminine by consenting to be guided and not initiating such behavior with a man" (p. 135). As a result, we consider the ways that masculinity is inherently tied to notions of femininity and relationships with women and other men. Measures of male role norms not only seek to examine individual elements of masculinity (e.g., toughness or status) but also the clear distinction of anti-femininity (Gallagher & Parrott, 2011).

Connell (2005, 1987) and Messerschmidt (2018) have made significant contributions to gender research. As Connell and Messerschmidt note together in 2005, "Masculinity is not a fixed entity embedded in the body of personality traits of individuals. Masculinities are configurations of practice that are accomplished in social action, and, therefore, can differ according to the gender relations in a particular social setting" (p. 836). Those who cannot achieve this expectation are relegated to nondominant masculinities, including subordinated and marginalized masculinities. In addition to experiencing negative outcomes due to their failure to meet gendered expectations, they may seek other ways to achieve hegemonic masculinity.

Incels: Subordinated and Marginalized Masculinities

Though some incels may be marginalized due to their class, race, or physical appearance, most would also be considered subordinated, as their experiences (or lack thereof) are in opposition to hegemonic ideals. As Carpenter (2002) explains, "Consistent with the sexual double standard, women tended to approach virginity as a gift, whereas men tended to see it as a stigma" (p. 353). For incels, then, their lack of romantic success (through sex and relationships) is viewed as a significant affront to their masculinity. As one incel I interviewed explained, "For me, being a virgin is very embarrassing. People think you must be gay if you never had sex yet" (Steven, twenty-one, personal communication). This echoes the findings from Menzie (2020), who argues that "incels desire a prescribed status and power that they believe is earned through having an objectively desirable romantic partner to display their masculinity and attractiveness to other men" (p. 14).

In analyzing data from my interviews of incels, my colleague Shon Reed and I (2021) found that incels failed to meet standards of manhood and viewed themselves at the bottom of the masculine hierarchy. Specifically, their lack of sexual experiences and interactions only further stigmatized and reinforced their subordination. This sexual failure and lack of masculinity can also lead to male gender role stress (see, for example, Swartout et al., 2014), which often arises when men fail to meet the demands of the gender role: in this case, not having sex or relationships with women.

Strain and Anomie

Incels feel as though they have failed romantically and sexually, and they place blame on themselves for being unattractive, odd, or shy and on others for being shallow, hypersexual, or dismissive of undesirable men. As evidenced by discussions on the forums, there is judgment not simply of *Stacys* (attractive women) but also of *Chads* (attractive men) for engaging in the relationships that incels cannot have. Such burden and failure (relative to Stacys, Chads, and even so-called normies) create strains, events, conditions, or circumstances that are unpleasant for incels. The three types of strain outlined by Agnew (2006)—removal of positive stimuli, presentation of negative stimuli, and, perhaps most relevant to incels, the inability to achieve goals—are both experienced and anticipated (as many believe that their situation of inceldom will continue). As Agnew (2006) argues, these can lead to negative emotions and criminal coping when they are seen as high in magnitude and unjust.

However, incels do not just experience negative emotions due to a lack of romantic relationships and sex. Generally speaking, their perception of failure is a result of the internalization of American cultural goals related to masculinity. Incels know what masculine sexual success is and, as a result, can recognize their own failure at achieving ideal or hegemonic masculinity. Their sexual failure is a direct result of the proscribed cultural goals that have outlined how men are expected to perform gender. However, as they become more embedded in incel culture, they may move from Merton's (1938) notion of innovation to achieve their goals to retreatism, disregarding the expected goals (for which they do not have the physical or social means) and embedding themselves in online incel communities. This disconnect between the accepted goals and the means to achieve them can also lead to a state of sexual anomie.

Sexual Anomie

Durkheim ([1897] 1951) argues that individual happiness is contingent upon needs being proportioned to means. Focusing on broader societal expectations and contributions, his premise states that suicide is the result of an imbalance between social integration and moral resolution. Of particular note is his discussion of anomic suicide. While this is typically applied to economic regulation and wealth (e.g., financial means and individual expectations), this notion can be (and has been) applied to ideas about sexual success. Given widely accepted cultural expectations of masculinity in the United States, incels, then, fall into an anomic state, as they internalize the goals yet lack the means to achieve those goals. Durkheim ([1897] 1951), in a sense, captures the often-shared sentiment of incels long before their online communities arose, writing, "To pursue a goal which is by definition unattainable is to condemn oneself to a state of perpetual unhappiness" (p. 248). While some may argue that incels could achieve romantic and interpersonal success if they engaged in self-improvement techniques (or even simply stopped aligning themselves with other incels), they may often view themselves as being inherently unable or unlikely to do so given their physical appearance, personality, or mental health setbacks.

Changing societal norms have also affected the nature of interpersonal relationships, particularly in heterosexual relationships between men and women. According to Tiryakian (1981), the shift in expectations and opportunities for women that allowed them to work, learn, and earn (and in, turn, resulted in a decreasing reliance on men and their income) affected the nature of intimate relationships and marriage. Given societal advancements toward equity and opportunity, women can now be more selective in their relationship choices, as they can be independent and put off (or reject) marriage and child-bearing expectations.[1] These efforts and successes in past decades have undoubtedly improved educational, professional, and personal outcomes for women, and such social progress is necessary and important for the advancement of societies. Representative of the time, however, Tiryakian (1981) notes of men, "Such a new situation—that is, in effect, the breakdown of spatial, social, and psychological segregation of women—could only from a traditionalist perspective be called 'sexual anomie'" (p. 1044). At the time, and even today, some men (including incels and nonincels alike) refused to accept and adjust to these changing standards and related interpersonal effects, feeling as though they had lost something (e.g., opportunities, rights, access, resources) to which they once were entitled.

Labeling Theory

The media portrayal of incels in response to recent violent attacks can shape the ways in which the public perceives the online community. The demonization and vilification of the broader incel community in American culture, law enforcement, and media coverage have been pervasive, specifically in response to acts of violence committed by individual incels. A quick search of news articles on incels provides results that include terms like *extremists*,[2] *terror threat*,[3] and *nihilist cult*.[4] In 2020, the Texas Department of Public Safety described incels as an "emerging domestic terrorism organization" (p. 3). While it is clear that some topics of discussion in incel forums (specifically those that glorify mass violence) are, in fact, extreme, nihilistic, or misogynistic and warrant concern, such hyperbolic depictions of the group (and the subsequent application of this to presume that all incels are terrorists) can lead to more concerning societal outcomes. As an example, given more widespread concern about incels, the term *incel* has also now become a part of online American rhetoric and mockery—which some would argue is the basis of social media behavior—often used as a slur against a man who holds misogynist beliefs or appears to be a virgin, in addition to widely shared memes that shame or ridicule incels.

To be sure, the violence and horror of incel-related attacks were devastating and tragic, and the rhetoric and discourse on incel forums lends itself to the natural assignment of labels like *misogynistic* or *racist*. The nature of the representation of all incels and its effects, however, cannot be ignored, as this ongoing generalization can, in theory, have profound effects on the ways that incels internalize the labels and the stigma associated with being an incel. While there may be some element of truth to the label, which ultimately refers to the language and discourse on forums (without further context of individual users' perspectives or experiences), criminological theory again allows for a clear understanding of the ways in which others see incels and how, in turn, incels may see themselves.

Lemert (1951, 1967) argues that there is a process by which negative or stigmatizing labels can lead to negative outcomes, ranging in milestones such as prelabeling, primary deviance, social penalties, a crisis reached in tolerance quotient, and ultimately, an acceptance of deviant social status. Participation in forums and conversations could be seen as deviant, although it is not explicitly criminal. Such engagement aligns them with the broader incel community, which ultimately results in social penalties, as incels are often portrayed as homicidal, angry virgins. This representation (or the label) encourages further primary deviation or enhanced embeddedness in the community, and it can lead the individual to the next stage, further deviation with hostilities and resentment. This can look like increased use of violent, misogynistic, or hateful rhetoric in conversations and the reinforcement of common ideas often shared on the forums.

As this cycle of increased deviation or embeddedness and further penalties continues, incels may find themselves internalizing the labels assigned to them in public spheres (which reinforces preexisting notions about themselves) and finding increased need for the support provided in incel groups. This immersion and group identity, particularly in the face of a crisis in the tolerance quotient, may ultimately lead to increased potential for self-harm or retaliation in the form of secondary deviance.

While this theoretical process certainly requires testing and evaluation, there is an obvious need to consider the ways in which American society both covers and labels people who commit crimes as well as those who share similar experiences, ideologies, and feelings. If the demonization and vilification of incels in American culture (through law enforcement and media reporting) can, in any way, radicalize otherwise nonviolent (albeit perhaps disturbed, downtrodden, or hateful) incels, those who share this information must evaluate the consequences of their actions. This aspect of American culture, particularly in concert with the content found on many of the forums, may contribute to future violence and harm.

Other Aspects of American Culture

While these notions of masculinity and media representation may also affect incels across Western culture, there are additional macro-level aspects of American culture that can contribute to the ways that incels respond to their romantic troubles. Access to mental health treatment (and its associated stigma) and the use of mass violence as a tool for retribution and notoriety can and should be examined as contributory factors that may shape individual decisions to enact violence and affect the broader understanding of the incel community.

Mental Health Treatment

According to a March 2020 survey from a popular incel forum, 67.5 percent of respondents shared that they have experienced long-lasting depression, and

74.1 percent report that they "experience anxiety, stress or emotional distress 'in a constant manner'" (N = 665) (ADL, 2020, para. 24). Although the survey does not explicitly ask if the respondents have been formally diagnosed or if they have sought out treatment, the high rates of these self-reported feelings and symptoms are of concern, especially in the context of gendered responses to mental health treatment. As Emslie and colleagues (2006) explain, "Masculinity requires men to be tough and self-reliant, whereas the experience of depression often leaves people feeling weak and vulnerable" (p. 2247).

Even more, while incels may feel more comfortable discussing their experiences with depression, anxiety, autism, and other mental health concerns on incel websites, they may still experience skepticism, doubt, or hesitation about the benefits of mental health treatment. Many incels who proscribe to the BlackPill—the belief that physical appearance matters most in attracting romantic and sexual partners, thus leaving most unattractive men doomed to failure (Glace et al., 2021)—believe that mental health treatment will not address or remedy the underlying cause of their problems.

In the same way, it seems that men, incels and nonincels alike, may experience attitudinal and structural barriers to seeking treatment. One study found that men who did not want to seek mental health treatment were more likely to hide their suffering and doubt that a therapist could address their issues properly (Seidler et al., 2020). Another incel, Simon, explained, "Mental health in America is absolute garbage. For example, I went into a hospital [for a psych eval]. I went in for 10 hours and was released with an autism and anxiety diagnosis (which is not news to me). That being said, the shrink prescribed me TED talks and podcasts and not much else" (Simon, personal communication, 2019).

To add an additional layer of difficulty to the mental health issues that many incels may face, there also exists the issue of access to mental health resources. As quality health-care coverage in the United States is often linked to steady, lucrative employment, many incels who are not educated, employed, or trained (NEET) may lack the opportunity and resources necessary to get high-quality treatment for their mental health, even if they want to seek treatment and therapy. Simon pointed out that therapists are too expensive for his budget (and reiterated that he believes that mental health treatment in America is "trash"). Even if people in the United States seeking treatment do have coverage, even with Medicaid, they may still have trouble accessing therapists. The National Alliance on Mental Illness (NAMI) found that "a third of respondents reported difficulty finding *any* mental health prescriber who would accept their insurance, either in- or out-of-network" (NAMI, 2017, para. 7).

While the debate between correlation and causation of incels' mental health problems is beyond the scope of this chapter, there is a clear need for consideration of the ways that American resources are limited, particularly as they relate to men who may not have the social or economic capital to utilize them.

Mass Violence as Retribution and Fame

Finally, we cannot ignore the American culture of violence and the ways in which mass violence have become woven into the fabric of society. For individual incels who have indeed committed acts of violence, there have been notable attempts to gain recognition, fame, and notoriety, especially as they have spent much of their lives feeling unnoticed, rejected, and ignored by their peers and their love interests. As Newman and colleagues (2004) explain of school shooters, "If fame and glory are the goal, school shooters know that celebrity status will be granted only if they can outdo the last rampage" (p. 250).

Because the coverage of these attacks splashes the shooters' names and faces across televisions, newspapers, and smart phones, their acts of violence become tragic parts of history, and they become names that the public remembers. As such, these shooters tend to be younger and kill and injure more victims (Lankford, 2016). Even more, the cycle continues, and as Lankford and Madfis (2018) note, "Because many attackers explicitly admit that they want fame and directly reach out to media organization to get it, it has become essentially indisputable that as a society, we have been helping them achieve their goals" (p. 3).

The long history of American mass violence combined with media coverage and the "reward" for their actions make violence a seemingly attractive option to reclaim their masculinity and exact their revenge not only on their targets but on the society that created these conditions. Although it should be obvious that the vast majority of incels will not commit acts of mass violence, we cannot overlook the notion that many of these men who visit these online forums have experienced similar occurrences of victimization, isolation, and marginalization.

In sum, incels are living in a society that demands masculinity of men, punishes and ostracizes them if they cannot achieve it, makes it difficult to find help when they need it, labels them a terrorist when they seek out support from a controversial group, but then rewards them with infamy when they commit mass violence. In this sense, it becomes necessary to consider the social and cultural factors that contribute to incel violence and suicide.

Recommendations Moving Forward

Currently, there seems to exist a spectrum of opinions about the potential danger that incels pose. While some view them as emerging domestic terror threats (Texas Department of Public Safety, 2020; Hoffman & Ware, 2020), others explicitly acknowledge that only a small percentage of incels are likely to engage in violence (Scaptura & Boyle, 2019). Regardless, it seems there is a clear and pressing need to address their problems either from a broader mass violence prevention perspective or from an individual suicide prevention and treatment approach. Even treatment opportunities that aim to address incel concerns and grievances may do well to enhance positive coping in the face of strain and anomie. Given the macro-level research and ongoing work on individual incel experiences, recommendations moving forward should focus on more inclusive masculinities and counterhegemonic practices (Messerschmidt, 2018), opportunities for men to seek help and support, and closer examination of media coverage and general treatment of incels.

There are, in fact, some positive elements of masculinity, but research has made it abundantly clear than hegemonic masculinity harms women and LGBTQ+ individuals while also marginalizing and subordinating many men. By encouraging men and boys to gain self-confidence through a variety of positive ways and reimagining what "doing gender" looks like, the future may be more liberating for those who struggle to achieve more dominant masculinities. In addition, if men are socially permitted to seek help and admit when they are struggling (through positive outlets outside of toxic online forums), they may be more comfortable sharing their incel status and seeking treatment.

As such, in addition to the obvious recommendation of making treatment easier to access across the United States, practitioners (e.g., psychologists, psychiatrists, therapists, school counselors) need training and education to address issues related to inceldom and familiarize themselves with the rhetoric and ideas that are commonly shared among incels. The American Psychological Association (APA) recommends that "psychologists strive to reduce the high rates of problems boys and men face and act out in their lives such as aggression, violence, substance abuse, and suicide" (APA, Boys and Men Guidelines Group, 2018, p. 15), and the therapeutic community (and society, more generally) has an obligation to destigmatize vulnerability, mental health struggles, and treatment.

Related to coverage and responses to incels, journalists, law enforcement professionals, and legislators must consider effects of labeling. For incels who may not have otherwise considered violence, the negative stigma of their situation may radicalize them through the labeling process and serve as a type of recruiting for those who may be seeking outlets for their grievances and did not previously know about incels. Future reporting on incels should focus on the fact that while a single attacker may have proclaimed to be an incel, the vast majority of incels will still likely not go on to commit violence. This can avoid the ongoing associations made between incels and violence and hopefully lead to shift in perceptions about incels such that they may be able to freely discuss their grievances offline and find the support that they need.

Finally, those who consider themselves progressive in their understanding of and advocacy for gender equity should reevaluate the ways in which they use the term *incel*. As the term has evolved, social media users and others using it to describe both incels and nonincels only reinforces the worst notions of hegemonic masculinity. Moreover, mocking them, sharing their posts, and, in the most extreme retaliation, advocating for their suicide may only serve to confirm their beliefs that society hates them. For those who are considering violence or posting about it, feeding the trolls and responding to shit-posts may fuel their desire to post and share more hateful interactions, thus continuing the cycle of society hating incels and incels blaming society for their suffering.

NOTES

1. Although circumstances have changed as a result of pushes toward equality for women, incel discussions often focus on *hypergamy*, the practice of women "marrying up" in terms of social, educational, financial success (Esteve et al., 2012), creating a contradictory argument that women are shallow and aim to improve their status through relationships with men while also criticizing a society in which women do not need men to achieve success.

2. See C. Tye, "Inside the Warped World of Incel Extremists," *The Conversation*, August 16, 2021, https://theconversation.com/inside-the-warped-world-of-incel-extremists-166142.

3. See D. Casciani and D. De Simone, "Incels: A New Terror Threat to the UK?" *BBC News*, August 13, 2021, https://www.bbc.com/news/uk-58207064.

4. See D. Barrett, "Threat Posed by 'Nihilist Cult' of 'Incels' Was Raised Six Months Ago: Home Office-Backed Report Warned Anti-Extremism Laws Had Not Kept Pace with Woman-Hating Movement Which Influence Plymouth Gunman," *Daily Mail UK*, August 13, 2021, https://www.dailymail.co.uk/news/article-9891119/The-rising-threat-incels-Plymouth-gunman-expressed-solidarity-misogynistic-movement.html.

REFERENCES

Agnew, R. (2006). *Pressured into crime: An overview of general strain theory.* Roxbury Publishing.

American Psychological Association (APA), Boys and Men Guidelines Group. (2018). *APA guidelines for psychological practices with boys and men.* http://www.apa.org/about/policy/psychological-practice-boys-men-guidelines.pdf

Anti-Defamation League (ADL). (2020, September 10). *Online poll results provide new insights into incel community.* https://www.adl.org/blog/online-poll-results-provide-new-insights-into-incel-community

Carpenter, L. M. (2002). Gender and the meaning and experience of virginity loss in the contemporary United States. *Gender & Society, 16*(3), 345–365.

Connell, R. W. (1987). *Gender and power: Society, the person and sexual politics.* Stanford University Press.

Connell, R. W. (2005). *Masculinities* (2nd ed.). University of California Press.

Connell, R. W., & Messerschmidt, J. W. (2005). Hegemonic masculinity: Rethinking the concept. *Gender & Society, 19*(6), 829–859. https://doi.org/10.1177/0891243205278639

Cottee, S. (2020). Incel (e)motives: Resentment, shame and revenge. *Studies in Conflict & Terrorism, 44*(2), 93–114. https://doi.org/10.1080/1057610X.2020.1822589

Daly, S. E., & Laskovtsov, A. (2021). "Goodbye, my friendcels": An analysis of incel suicide posts. *Journal of Qualitative Criminology and Criminal Justice.* https://doi.org/10.21428/88de04a1.b7b8b295

Daly, S. E., & Reed, S. (2021). "I think society hates us": A qualitative thematic analysis of interviews with incels. *Sex Roles.* https://doi.org/10.1007/s11199-021-01250-5

Donnelly, D., Burgess, E., Anderson, S., Davis, R., & Dillard, J. (2001). Involuntary celibacy: A life course analysis. *Journal of Sex Research, 38*(2), 159–169. https://doi.org/10.1080/00224490109552083

Durkheim, E. ([1897] 1951). *Suicide: A study in sociology.* Free Press.

Emslie, C., Ridge, D., Ziebland, S., & Hunt, K. (2006). Men's accounts of depression: Reconstructing or resisting hegemonic masculinity? *Social Science & Medicine, 62,* 2246–2257. https://doi.org/10.1016/j.socscimed.2005.10.017

Esteve, A., Garcia-Roman, J., & Permanyer, I. (2012). The gender-gap reversal in education and its effect on union formation: The end of hypergamy? *Population and Development Review, 38*(3), 535–546. http://www.jstor.org/stable/41857404

Gallagher, K. E., & Parrott, D. J. (2011). What accounts for men's hostile attitudes toward women? The influence of hegemonic male role norms and masculine gender role stress. *Violence Against Women, 17*(5), 568–583. https://doi.org/10.1177/1077801211407296

Gilmartin, B. G. (1987). Peer group antecedents of severe love-shyness in males. *Journal of Personality, 55*(3), 467–489. https://doi.org/10.1111/j.1467-6494.1987.tb00447.x

Ging, D. (2019). Alphas, betas, and incels: Theorizing the masculinities of the Manosphere. *Men and Masculinities, 22*(4), 638–657. https://doi.org/10.1177/1097184X17706401

Glace, A. M., Dover, T. L., & Zatkin, J. G. (2021). Taking the Black Pill: An empirical analysis of the "incel." *Psychology of Men & Masculinities, 22*(2), 288–297. https://psycnet.apa.org/doi/10.1037/men0000328

Hartley, G. (2018). *Fed up: Emotional labor, women, and the way forward.* Harper One.

Hoffman, B., & Ware, J. (2020). Incels: America's newest domestic terrorism threat. *Lawfare.* https://www.lawfareblog.com/incels-americas-newest-domestic-terrorism-threat

Lankford, A. (2016). Fame-seeking rampage shootings: Initial findings and empirical predictions. *Aggression and Violent Behavior, 27,* 122–129. http://dx.doi.org/10.1016/j.avb.2016.02.002

Lankford, A., & Madfis, E. (2018). Don't name them, don't show them, but report everything else: A pragmatic proposal for denying mass killers the attention they seek and deterring future offenders. *American Behavioral Scientist, 62*(2), 260–279. https://doi.org/10.1177/0002764217730854

Lemert, E. M. (1951). *Social pathology: A systematic approach to the theory of sociopathic behavior.* McGraw-Hill.

Lemert, E. M. (1967). *Human deviance, social problems, and social control.* Prentice Hall.

Menzie, L. (2020). Stacys, Beckys, and Chads: The construction of femininity and hegemonic masculinity within incel rhetoric. *Psychology & Sexuality.* Advance online publication. https://doi.org/10.1080/19419899.2020.1806915

Merton, R. K. (1938). Social structure and anomie. *American Sociological Review, 3*(5), 672–682. https://doi.org/10.2307/2084686

Messerschmidt, J. W. (2018). *Hegemonic masculinity: Formulation, reformulation, and amplification.* Rowman & Littlefield.

Nagle, A. (2017). *Kill all normies: Online culture wars from 4Chan and Tumblr to Trump and the alt-right.* Zero Books.

National Alliance on Mental Illness (NAMI). (2017). *The doctor is out: Continuing disparities in access to mental and physical health care.* https://www.nami.org/Support-Education/Publications-Reports/Public-Policy-Reports/The-Doctor-is-Out

Newman, K., Fox, C., Harding, D. J., Mehta, J., & Roth, W. (2004). *Rampage: The social roots of school shootings.* Basic Books.

Scaptura, M. N., & Boyle, K. M. (2019). Masculinity threat, "incel" traits, and violent fantasies among heterosexual men in the United States. *Feminist Criminology, 15*(3), 277–298. https://doi.org/10.1177/1557085119896415

Schrock, D., & Schwalbe, M. (2009). Men, masculinity, and manhood acts. *Annual Review of Sociology, 35,* 277–295. https://doi.org/10.1146/annurev-soc-070308-115933

Seidler, Z. E., Rice, S. M., Kealy, D., Oliffe, J. L., & Ogrodniczuk, J. S. (2020). What gets in the way? Men's perspectives of barriers to mental health services. *International Journal of Social Psychiatry, 66*(2), 105–110. https://doi.org/10.1177/0020764019886336

Shachter, B., & Seinfeld, J. (1994). Personal violence and the culture of violence. *Social Work, 39*(4), 347–350. https://www.jstor.org/stable/23717044

Stein, J. (2015, June 29). Nip. Tuck. Or Else: Why you'll be getting cosmetic procedures even if you don't really want to. *Time.* https://time.com/3926042/nip-tuck-or-else/

Swartout, K. M., Parrot, D. J., Cohn, A. M., Hagman, B. T., & Gallagher, K. E. (2014). Development of the Abbreviated Masculine Gender Role Stress Scale. *Psychological Assessment, 27*(2), 489–500. https://dx.doi.org/10.1037/a0038443

Texas Department of Public Safety. (2020). *Texas domestic terrorism threat assessment.* https://www.dps.texas.gov/sites/default/files/documents/director_staff/media_and_communications/2020/txterrorthreatassessment.pdf

Tiryakian, E. A. (1981). Sexual anomie, social structure, societal change. *Social Forces, 59*(4), 1025–1053.

Trekels, J., & Eggermont, S. (2018). "I can/should look like a media figure": The association between direct and indirect media exposure and teens' sexualizing appearance behaviors. *Journal of Sex Research, 55*(3), 320–333. https://doi.org/10.1080/00224499.2017.1387754

West, C., & Zimmerman, D. H. (1987). Doing gender. *Gender & Society, 1*(2), 125–151. https://doi.org/10.1177/0891243287001002002

Wiederman, M. W., & Hurst, S. R. (1998). Body size, physical attractiveness, and body image among young adult women: Relationships to sexual experience and sexual esteem. *Journal of Sex Research, 35*(3), 272–281. https://www.jstor.org/stable/3813247

6

Structural Strain, Intersectionality, and Mass Murder

A Case Study of the Isla Vista Shooting

Daniel Gascón

On May 23, 2014, in the small town of Isla Vista adjacent to the campus of the University of California, Santa Barbara (UCSB), an attacker—a twenty-two-year-old biracial heterosexual male and unemployed college student—stabbed three young men, went on a shooting spree at several public areas in quick succession, and used his BMW to run over several pedestrians between stops. After two separate gun battles with county sheriff's officers, a bullet struck the attacker's hip. With the vehicle still in motion, the attacker shot himself in the head and crashed the BMW into a row of parked cars. He was dead at the scene. The attack resulted in six dead and fourteen wounded (Brown, 2015).

Structured action, or the ways that societal expectations shape our actions and the ways we interact with others in a variety of different contexts, is an increasingly popular framework among scholars examining the social structural determinants of violent behavior (Messerschmidt, 2013). Related studies have linked violence involvement with structural elements through social class (such as unemployment, receiving welfare, and residence in a poor neighborhood (Brownfield, 1986)), family and school ties (Wright & Fitzpatrick, 2006), racial identity and differential lived experiences (McNulty & Bellair, 2003), and the social confinement of women in heterosexual relationships (Michalski, 2004).

This chapter demonstrates how mass murder is another type of a structured action. I will adopt the case study method in examining the 2014 attack on IV. My primary source of data is the attacker's one-hundred-forty-one-page manifesto, entitled "My Twisted World," supplemented with police reports. This chapter builds on Madfis's (2014) study that combines structural strain theory, which seeks to explain how societal expectations of men shape their decisions about using violence in situations where their manhood is challenged, and intersectionality theory, which seeks to understand how broader social structures, such as race, class, and gender, manifest in the identities and experiences of individuals. Using intersectional theory will reveal how some shooters feel challenged in their relationships and by their perceived positions within larger structural arrangements. I will show that the converging entitlements of white heterosexual masculinity weakened the IV shooter's ability to adapt to personal challenges. Anger, resentment, and a sense of injustice built as episodes of perceived failure accumulated, until the attacker felt that he had no other way to eliminate his strain than to carry out his "Day of Retribution."

Structural Strain and Intersectionality

Recent studies of structural strain focus on men's patterned responses to masculinity challenges. Messerschmidt's (2013) structured action theory explains how social structures inform social action through the enactment of a dynamic set of corresponding discourses. One key set of discourses for Messerschmidt deals with dominant expectations of manhood, or what he calls *hegemonic masculinity*. These discourses shape men's thoughts and identities and others' perceptions of men, as well as the social interactions between them. When men behave in accordance with hegemonic masculine expectations, they reify dominant discourses and take a particular subject position within society. Messerschmidt explains how discourses coordinate men's activities as they perform, or "do," gender in situationally dependent ways.

Each time a man performs a sanctioned behavior and puts structured knowledge into practice, he engages gendered structures. These discourses can be "anxiety-producing," according to Messerschmidt. When young men attempt and fail to perform competent masculine behaviors, they become frustrated and are more likely to use violence to reassert their masculinity. Messerschmidt (2018) gives the examples of two of his research respondents, Lenny and Perry, who engaged in assaultive violence after having their masculinity challenged through experiences with victimization. Whereas Lenny's assault was an attempt to fight back against schoolyard bullies, Perry's was an attempt to defend himself against a physically abusive stepfather. In both instances, however, assaultive violence served to eliminate the frustration they felt over direct challenges to their manhood.

Building on previous studies, Madfis (2014) seeks to explain how structural strain can engage multiple discourses at once. He argues that, more than any other group, white middle-class heterosexual men perpetrate mass shootings because they fail to receive the classed, gendered, and racialized privileges that they expect. Intersectional analysis enables researchers to understand how structures simultaneously pattern human actions. The goal is to outline how a person's position within established social hierarchies dictates their experience with subordination or superordination. Identifying with dominant social categories leads many white middle-class heterosexual men to expect the privileges that correspond to each category, or what Madfis calls *triple entitlement*. When these men's strains accumulate, Madfis explains, their innovative masculine responses involve extreme violence that serves to eliminate the perceived sources of their strain. Whether mass shooters are motivated by their hatred for women, people of color and immigrants, their classmates, or former employers, they adapt to accumulated strain by targeting people in public who resemble the objects of their hatred.

Gendered and Sexual Strain: Subordinated Masculinity

The IV shooter exuded what Messerschmidt (2013) calls *subordinated masculinity*, which includes those young men who some describe as "shy . . . nonathletic, 'geekish,' or weird" (Kimmel & Mahler, 2003, p. 1445). The attacker suffered from a crippling shyness that prevented him from building and maintaining peer and romantic relationships. He described himself as a "shy, quiet kid" who classmates called "weird." The shooter barely spoke, and when he did, it was in a low voice. His mother was forced to set up playdates because he was too shy to build his own friendships and needed lots of reassurance before engaging with his peers (Brown, 2015). Throughout his manifesto, the attacker writes of attempting to change his physical appearance and become fitter and stronger, but that over time, insecurities about his body compounded. The shooter's ability to "do" competent masculinity and sexuality was circumscribed by these frustrations.

By the time the attacker was a young adult, he became frustrated when confronted with sexual competitors. In the following excerpt, written not long before the attack about a memory six years prior, the shooter encountered a childhood acquaintance, Leo, at a local restaurant. The shooter met Leo when they were twelve. He hated Leo ever since. Here, the shooter explains how Leo, though younger, performed a dominant form of masculinity:

> I kept thinking about Leo ********, and how he kissed that girl Nicole at the Sagebrush Cantina when he was only twelve. Twelve! He was able to have an intimate experience with a girl when he was only twelve; and there I was at eighteen, still a kissless virgin. My envy of Leo became an obsession. I kept asking my sister for information about him,

but she refused to tell me anything. I frightfully wondered if he had lost his virginity already, and he most likely had. He was a popular kid, and girls desired him. Leo was happily living his heavenly life with the knowledge that he's worth something to the world, while I had to wallow in my misery and loneliness.

The shooter's perception of Leo as a competent sexual male was an intense source of strain. He saw himself and Leo as being locked in a relationship circumscribed by social expectations of masculine performance. The shooter recognized that kissing women is a competent masculine behavioral style. When Leo kissed a girl in public, this move confirmed his manhood. By contrast, the IV shooter seldom felt that women confirmed his masculinity through sexual interest and so felt as though he had failed to live up to dominant expectations. Compared with Leo, the shooter believed that women perceived him as less sexually desirable.

Throughout his life, the attacker felt that he was less physically capable than his male peers. The shooter wrote that he was short for his age, often the shortest in class. One episode in which the shooter was denied access to a carnival ride at six years old because he was too short to meet the height requirement made him hypersensitive about his small frame. This experience, he thought, presaged the corporeal difficulties he would have later in his life. Even girls were taller than him in middle school. And next to his male high school classmates, the shooter thought he looked and sounded like a ten-year-old.

Though the attacker was overcome with sexual urges, his inability to realize these desires became a huge source of frustration. The attacker thought of himself as having a very high sex drive but also felt that going into puberty "was the start of hell." When school let out, he would rush home to masturbate to mental images and fantasies of the blonde girls in his class. However, his sexuality was confined to fantasy because when the shooter did encounter sexually explicit material, the kind that excited his male peers, he reacted with shock, confusion, and disgust. Joining a group of boys huddled around a pornographic magazine while on a school camping trip, being exposed to pornographic images in a chat room, and catching another gamer in an internet café watching pornography were "traumatizing" events. The shooter felt incapable of performing sexually competent masculine behavior.

The shooter externalized blame for his sexual incompetence. Into his young adult years, the shooter became convinced that women were harming him through their refusal to confirm his masculinity: "It was society's fault for rejecting me. It was women's fault for refusing to have sex with me," he wrote. This feeling of sexualized anger is an example of what Messerschmidt (2018) refers to as a *body betrayal*. The shooter lived in a man's body, so he should benefit from men's privileges, including sexual possession of women's bodies. A year before the attack, the shooter fumed at the thought that his masculine desires had been denied: "Those girls deserved to be dumped in boiling water for the crime of not giving me the attention and adoration I so rightfully deserve!"

Racial Strain: Unconfirmed Whiteness

Madfis (2014) explains that racial strain can motivate mass violence when white men do not experience the racial privileges they expect. Given their access to some of these privileges throughout their lives, racial privilege occludes many white men from developing suitable coping mechanisms and renders them psychologically vulnerable to strain when their privileges fail to materialize. In the shooter's case, these entitlements extended to men who were half-white as well. Straining events for white men in this situation include relationship losses or, in the attacker's case, unrealized relationships. They feel their racial privilege is threatened in a rapidly changing and increasingly diverse society and that, as a result, their chances of success are significantly diminished because opportunities formerly available to them are now going to nonwhites (Madfis, 2014). Their sense of loss and awareness of unrealized expectations leads them to externalize their blame (upon others, often people of color), eventually leading to violent attacks (Duque et al., 2019).

Although there were early signs in the manifesto, racial strain manifested most noticeably as the shooter entered college. By this point, the shooter drank alcohol to deaden his shyness and insecurities that gradually turned into "drunken night walks" in which he would go out alone hoping to make friends and meet women. But these attempts were often fruitless because even when he did manage to join a group of partiers, he could not engage with them because he would either be overcome by his insecurities or his drunkenness. And as his resentment built over time, the attacker's behavior became increasingly problematic. In the following excerpt written ten months before the attack, he took a drunken night walk, stumbled into a party, encountered a mixed-race couple, and assaulted the man:

> I came across this Asian guy who was talking to a white girl. The sight of that filled me with rage. I always felt as if white girls thought less of me because I was half-Asian, but then I see this white girl at the party talking to a full-blooded Asian. I never had that kind of attention from a white girl! And white girls are the only girls I'm attracted to, especially the blondes. How could an ugly Asian attract the attention of a white girl, while a beautiful Eurasian like myself never had any attention from them? I thought with rage.

I glared at them for a bit, and then decided I had been insulted enough. I angrily walked toward them and bumped the Asian guy aside, trying to act cocky and arrogant to both the boy and the girl. My drunken state got the better of me, and I almost fell over to the floor after a few minutes of this. They said something along the lines that I was very drunk and that I needed to get some water, so I angrily left them and went out to the front yard, where the main partying happened. Rage fumed inside me as I realized that I just walked away from that confrontation, so I rushed back into the house and spitefully insulted the Asian before walking outside again.

The attacker's anger in this moment was induced by a sense of racial strain. The shooter perceived the blonde woman's choice of the "ugly" "full-blooded Asian" over him as a denial of his whiteness. Messerschmidt (2013) might term this a body betrayal of his whiteness. The shooter had a complex racial identity; he at once embraced his half-white side and felt embarrassed by his half-Asian side. As a kid, being half-Asian made him feel inferior, and he felt that others treated him differently than the white kids in his classes. While his mother was Malaysian and he presented as Asian, the shooter felt proud that he came from a wealthy British family on his father's side. He saw himself as a "beautiful Eurasian."

Identifying with his father's whiteness was a dominant structure that may have shaped his desires for women. As he indicates in the excerpt above, the shooter saw blonde women as the most desirable. Over time, his inability to realize relationships with blonde girls became a chronic source of frustration: "To have a beautiful blonde girl by my side, to feel her hand clasping my own as we walk everywhere together, to feel her love! That is what I want in life."

The shooter externalized the blame for his failed racial performances. At some points, just hearing that his peers were sexually active or seeing young couples together in public, especially mixed-race couples, sent the attacker into a rage. The manifesto reveals the attacker's extreme dislike of his "ugly" and "repulsive" Asian roommates, the "ugly, pig-faced," and "obnoxious Mexican kid" who boasted of bedding blonde women, and his middle school classmate Lucky, the "ugly black filth," who lost his virginity to a blonde girl. The attacker became particularly jealous in one episode when he encountered a mixed-race couple in a Santa Barbara restaurant. A "dark-skinned Mexican" kid was sitting with a "hot blonde white girl" at a nearby table. Seeing the couple together instantly stirred feelings of inferiority in the attacker, and his father's presence only amplified his sense of racial strain:

I was ashamed to be in such an inferior position in front my father. When I saw the two of them kissing, I could barely contain my rage.

I stood up in anger, and I was about to walk up to them and pour my glass of soda all over their heads. I probably would have, if father wasn't there. I was seething with envious rage, and my father was there to watch it all. It was so humiliating. I wasn't the son I wanted to present to my father. I should be the one with the hot blonde girl, making my father proud. Instead, my father had to watch me suffer in a pathetic position.

This restaurant encounter was a failed racial performance for the attacker, a challenge to his white masculinity, and a sign of his increasing agitation. The attacker felt humiliated, particularly in front of his father, that he was not the sexually competent son with a charmed girlfriend that he thought his father wanted him to be. Other public encounters did result in verbal insults and eventually escalated to physical attacks, including splashing young couples with hot coffee or water-gunning them with orange juice. These attacks would temporarily alleviate his strain. After one incident, he wrote, "I was panicking as I got into my car and drove off, shaking with rage-fueled excitement. I drove all the way to the Vons at the Fairview Plaza and spent three hours in my car trying to contain my tumultuous emotions." But once the initial buzz of excitement wore off, the shooter would retreat to his room feeling even more isolated and alone.

Class Strain: Economic Immobility

Madfis (2014) explains that many mass shooters are either working or lower middle class and downwardly mobile with respect to their careers and job prospects, so they resort to extreme violence as a form of class-based vengeance. The IV attacker was much like previous mass shooters in being strained over the mismatch between their status expectations and inability to achieve them. But unlike many previous shooters, the IV shooter came from a prominent family. His status frustrations came from his economic immobility, or the failure to leverage his family's status to build a career or personal wealth. Extending Merton's classic take on economic strain, Messner and Rosenfeld (2012) argue that not only do working-class people experience strain from having their opportunities for advancement blocked by outside forces but so, too, do some wealthier people whose desire for excessive wealth is so powerful that they resort to crime to attain it.

While his parents gave the shooter a privileged upbringing, the shooter felt it was not enough compared with his wealthier peers. The shooter was fiercely jealous of them. This strain was further compounded by his numerous failed attempts to claim wealth. After one of the shooter's childhood friends cut ties with him over his increasingly disturbing views, as I will discuss later, the shooter sank into a deep depression. Feeling as though he had no prospects for a social life, the shooter convinced himself that becoming wealthy and successful was among the few remaining options he had, and "that was a form of happy, peaceful revenge, and it became my only hope." Further, he wrote the following:

> There had to be a way for me to become wealthy. I continued to see it was the only way I would ever have a beautiful girlfriend and lose my virginity. My ultimate dream was to experience the pleasures of love and sex with girls once I become rich enough to be worthy of them, and then I would settle down with a beautiful girlfriend and have beautiful children with her, whom I would raise up to live a much better life than the one I've had to suffer through. That would be the most satisfying vengeance against all those young people who thought they were better than me. If I could show them that I lived such a life, my purpose on this world would be complete. To see the look on all of their faces once I've risen above them. . . . I couldn't imagine anything sweeter.

The shooter wrote proudly of his family's prominence. He told stories of the time he spent in "beautiful and opulent" locales in fully stocked hotel rooms across the globe, how he was raised with immigrant nannies, and how he ate at expensive restaurants. He loved that his parents were Hollywood insiders who received regular invitations to red-carpet movie premiers and private concerts with top talents. Attending these events validated the shooter's classed expectations.

Off the red carpet and on his own, the attacker failed to claim the wealth and status he wanted. The shooter had a very problematic schooling record. In middle school, the attacker requested to go from a public school to a private all-boys school so that he could avoid contact with girls. This inconsistent educational record continued into high school due to bullying. Unable to resolve these conflicts, the shooter's parents moved him to a continuation school. But upon entering the school, he was displeased with its "low-class" appearance and felt he was superior to his classmates. These negative feelings motivated the attacker to work hard and graduate high school early. The shooter's college career was even more inconsistent, however. He went to three colleges from his late teens into his early twenties. As in middle school, this reluctance to stay in one school for more than a semester was due to the shooter's inability to contain negative emotions at the sight of "hot blondes" on campus.

Once the attacker dropped out of school, his mother forced him to look for work. But the attacker felt that none of the jobs "suited" him. He briefly worked with a family friend who owned a construction business. But the attacker did not believe in starting from the bottom and felt that his parents' status entitled him to a position higher up the ranks. To him, the work was "lowly and laborious," though he did enjoy the limited social interaction. He also took a custodial job for a day but was immediately displeased with the nature of the work, again, because he thought it was beneath him.

The attacker became convinced that his last option to attract women was to win the lottery. Now in his early twenties, the shooter recognized that he had no marketable skills. He felt that he would never date a "beautiful blonde girlfriend" unless he became instantly rich. The attacker began using his savings to buy lottery tickets. He would drive to liquor stores up and down the 101 corridor between the San Fernando Valley and Santa Barbara for lottery tickets. But despite spending nearly $2,000, he lost frequently and was utterly crushed. In one last desperate attempt, he drove to Arizona to buy fifty tickets at once. When he lost, the shooter wrote that he felt "cold and dead," then he "threw a wild tantrum" and over the next several nights had numerous drunken "crying fits."

Strain Elimination: Violence as "Doing" Masculinity

Madfis (2014) explains that extreme violence is a masculine reaction to the perceived injustice and shame that white heterosexual male mass shooters experience. Their attacks serve to embody manhood and take the place of their previous failed masculine performances. Violence helped attackers achieve dominant hegemonic masculine power. In his discussion of assaultive violence as a perceived solution to masculinity challenges, Messerschmidt (2018) explains that such actions were structured in relation to the shooter's place in localized perceptions of masculinity. To the attacker, being masculine meant responding to the perceived harm of being "refused" and "denied" a social and sexual life by his peers as a provocation, and over time his violent thoughts crystallized.

By his early twenties, both the shooter's real and fantasy lives were taking a "darker turn," as he describes. After two years in Santa Barbara, he had not made real friends or dated. By then, the shooter's violent fantasies became increasingly vivid. He was convinced that committing murder-suicide was the only way to eliminate his accumulated strains. He wrote:

> There is nowhere in the world I can go anymore. There is no more life to live. The Day of Retribution is all I have. It is the final solution to all of the injustices of this twisted world. By doing this, I will set right all of the wrongs I've had to face in my sorry excuse of a life.
>
> Every single time I've seen a guy walk around with his beautiful girlfriend, I've always wanted to kill them both in the most painful

way possible. They deserve it. They must be punished. The males deserve to be punished for living a better and more pleasurable life than me, and the females deserve to be punished for giving that pleasurable life to those males instead of me. On the Day of Retribution, I will finally be able to punish them ALL.

Prior to reaching this point in his thinking, though, shortly after graduating high school, the shooter was becoming increasingly seduced by the sense of empowerment he felt when ruminating over violent revenge. He said, for instance, "My anger made me stronger inside." Even if others could deny him a sex life, he felt that he could in turn prevent others from having sex lives: "I began to have fantasies of becoming very powerful and stopping everyone from having sex. I wanted to take their sex away from them, just like they took it away from me." He pictured running couples over in his dad's Mercedes SUV or entering their homes while they had sex so he could knife them both to death. After the attack, police also found violent hand-drawn images in the shooter's bedroom (Brown, 2015).

The shooter had been slowly amassing weapons for a year prior to the attack. Police found several weapons in his possession: three handguns, two large hunting knives, a machete, and a sledgehammer. The attacker explained that he purchased these weapons during times of increased strain, like after dropping out of school and losing big in the lottery. When his mother bought him the BMW a month before the attack, he was content that she had given him another weapon. Initially, these objects gave the shooter a sense of empowerment and alleviation, but eventually these would devolve into feelings of dread. Months prior to the attack, for instance, the shooter visited a firing range. While practicing on the paper targets down the lane, he became physically ill at the thought that his violent fantasies were becoming a reality.

The shooter planned to carry out his attack in three distinct phases. He designed to kill his roommates first. Then he would move on to the second phase, the "War on Women," where he planned to target Alpha Phi, the "hottest" sorority at UCSB. In the final phase, the attacker planned to target random people in the community. Though he chose dates for the attack, the shooter postponed several times because he was sick, his father came back home early from a business trip abroad, or he wanted to give life another chance.

In the days before his attack, the perpetrator took to the internet to validate his violent inclinations. Peterson and Densley (2020) explain that a common pathway for mass shooters in the social media age is to validate their fantasies through contact with and encouragement from likeminded online communities and look for "scripts," or examples of plans of attack that prospective shooters can mimic. According to police, the IV attacker's browser history included searches for misogynistic forums and chat rooms, torture techniques, and episodes of mass violence, most notably the 2009 attack at LA Fitness in Collier Township, Pennsylvania, where a white male who had complained about his own sexual frustration shot and killed three and injured nine female victims before shooting himself at the scene (Pittsburgh Post-Gazette, 2009a).

Discussion

Kimmel (2017) and others have pointed out that mass shootings are regularly linked with various forms of violence against women (VAW). A recent study showed that shooters motivated by their hatred for women are much more likely to have histories of domestic violence than other mass shooters and suggested that given the increased national attention to feminism through the #MeToo movement and Women's March, for instance, women may be under increased threat of mass violence in public spaces, particularly from men who identify with misogynistic ideologies (Silva et al., 2021). Both the IV and LA Fitness attackers have become symbols of the now-prominent "involuntary celibacy," or "incel," movement, which is composed of men across the globe who feel entitled to and denied the privileges over women's bodies. This collective emotional register speaks to a widespread experience of masculinity challenges (Kimmel, 2017).

Madfis (2014) argues that structural strain enables researchers to see how dominant discourses shape how mass shooters perceive the opportunities and challenges in their lives but also how they respond to these strains over time. Examining the IV shooter's manifesto reveals how his actions were structured in part by anxiety-producing discourses. Beyond the LA Fitness shooter, who kept an online blog wherein he made misogynistic remarks and justified the sexual slavery of white women (Anonymous, 2009b), the Violence Project's mass shooter database indicates that since 1966, there have been at least fifteen mass shooters whose misogynistic feelings toward women were primary motivators in their attacks. Future studies should systematically analyze these cases to glean a deeper understanding of the factors that contributed to the attacks in each case.

The intersectionality perspective offers mass shooting researchers an insight into how internal strains related to race, class, and gender can engage with multiple discourses. My findings raise questions about the development of mass shooters. Do their strains accumulate over time until they reach a breaking point, as is the case with some school shooters (see Levin & Madfis, 2009)? Do their strains have compounding effects on the thoughts and actions of mass shooters, similar to the way that Crenshaw (1989) describes black women's experiences with "compound discrimination"? My study reveals that racial and classed strains manifested alongside gendered strains in the development of the IV shooter. My findings extend Madfis's (2014) understanding of the potential risks when someone feels entitled to whiteness. White racial identification exerted an intense pressure on the IV shooter and led him to feel entitled to racial privilege, even though he was half-Asian, a comparatively subordinated category in his mind. His half-white identity became the dominant lens through which his sense of entitlement to relationships with blonde women took shape and highlighted the means through which he sought but failed to realize these relationships. The attacker's class-based strains were also important motivators in the attack, although these developed much later in the manifesto than other strains. Madfis (2014) argued that these types of strains are often a response to job loss or blocked opportunities, but the IV attacker's problems in improving his social status seems to have stemmed from his sense of entitlement in somewhat different ways. Although the IV shooter had access to wealthy social circles, he could not leverage these ties to claim wealth and status for himself. He felt entitled to high-status jobs given his family's prominence and was unwilling to work to achieve his financial goals.

In line with Madfis's (2014) framework, the IV attacker's manifesto details the "innovative" process that he underwent to fantasize, validate, and plan his attack, but there remain questions about the buildup to the attack. What is unclear from this analysis is exactly when and how he decided finally to carry out the attacks, as there are several Day of Retribution dates discussed in the manifesto. His decision finally to go through with the attack was somewhat sudden compared with the extensive treatment he gave other decisions in the text. A developmental analysis using the cumulative strain framework (see Levin & Madfis, 2009) is needed to better understand this process. My future work will examine the precise "trigger moment" that propelled the attacker from the "darker turn" in his mood to the point of carrying out his attack.

Madfis (2014) concludes that the continually diminishing class status of whites compared with other racial groups could potentially fuel future cases of mass violence. Taken together with the fact that incidents of mass violence targeting both women (Nicholson & DeVoe, 2020) and people of color (Hill, 2020) are occurring at an increasing rate, it is urgent that scholars advance a more thorough understanding of the relationship between structural pressure and extreme violence.

REFERENCES

Anonymous. (2009a). Four dead in fitness center shooting Among the dead, gunman had note in gym bag. *Pittsburgh Post-Gazette*. https://www.post-gazette.com/local/south/2009/08/05/Four-dead-in-fitness-center-shooting/stories/200908050169

Anonymous. (2009b). *George Sodini's blog: Full text by alleged gym shooter.* ABC News. https://abcnews.go.com/US/story?id=8258001&page=1

Brown, B. (2015). *Isla Vista mass murder, May 23, 2014* [Investigative summary]. Santa Barbara County Sheriff's Office.

Brownfield, D. (1986). Social class and violent behavior. *Criminology, 24*(3), 421–438.

Crenshaw, K. (1989). Demarginalizing the intersection of race and sex: A black feminist critique of antidiscrimination doctrine, feminist theory and antiracist politics. *University of Chicago Legal Forum, 1989,* Article 8.

Duque, R. B., LeBlanc, E. J., & Rivera, R. (2019). Predicting active shooter events: Are regional homogeneity, intolerance, dull lives, and more guns enough deterrence? *Crime & Delinquency, 65*(9), 1218–1261.

Hill, C. (2020). The one Trump record he doesn't want you to talk about: An unprecedented number of mass shootings. *The Independent.* https://www.independent.co.uk/news/world/americas/us-election-2020/trump-mass-shootings-usa-2020-election-biden-guns-nra-b1424716.html

Kimmel, M. (2017). *Angry white men: American masculinity at the end of an era.* Hachette UK.

Kimmel, M. S., & Mahler, M. (2003). Adolescent masculinity, homophobia, and violence: Random school shootings, 1982–2001. *American Behavioral Scientist, 46*(10), 1439–1458.

Levin, J., & Madfis, E. (2009). Mass murder at school and cumulative strain: A sequential model. *American Behavioral Scientist, 52*(9), 1227–1245.

Madfis, E. (2014). Triple entitlement and homicidal anger: An exploration of the intersectional identities of American mass murderers. *Men and Masculinities, 17*(1), 67–86.

McNulty, T. L., & Bellair, P. E. (2003). Explaining racial and ethnic differences in serious adolescent violent behavior. *Criminology, 41*(3), 709–747.

Messerschmidt, J. W. (2013). *Crime as structured action: Doing masculinities, race, class, sexuality, and crime.* Rowman & Littlefield.

Messerschmidt, J. W. (2018). *Masculinities and crime: A quarter century of theory and research.* Rowman & Littlefield.

Messner, S., & Rosenfeld, R. (2012). *Crime and the American dream.* Wadsworth.

Michalski, J. H. (2004). Making sociological sense out of trends in intimate Partnera violence: The social structure of violence against women. *Violence Against Women, 10*(6), 652–675.

Nicholson, J., & DeVoe, E. (2020). *Violence against women and public mass shootings.* BU Office of Research. https://www.bu.edu/ihsip/2020/10/19/violence-against-women-and-public-mass-shootings/

Peterson, J., & Densley, J. (2020). *Mass shooting prevention: An evidence based framework.* Annual Meeting of the Violence Project, Minneapolis, MN.

Silva, J. R., Capellan, J. A., Schmuhl, M. A., & Mills, C. E. (2021). Gender-based mass shootings: An examination of attacks motivated by grievances against women. *Violence Against Women, 27*(12–13). https://doi.org/10.1177/1077801220981154

Wright, D. R., & Fitzpatrick, K. M. (2006). Social capital and adolescent violent behavior: Correlates of fighting and weapon use among secondary school students. *Social Forces, 84*(3), 1435–1453.

PART III

Mass Shootings and White Supremacy in America

7

White Supremacy, Frontier Myths, the "Great Replacement" Theory, and the Making of American Mass Killers

BETSY FRIAUF AND MICHAEL PHILLIPS

Early on the morning of August 3, 2019, a young man left his home in Allen, Texas, an affluent and rapidly growing and diversifying suburb twenty-five miles north of Dallas. He packed an AK-47-style assault weapon. A twenty-one-year-old community college student, he drove about eleven hours across more than 560 miles of the state's vast landscape. He sought a battlefield for a solo racial war. He parked near a Walmart in the border city of El Paso, where almost 81.5 percent of the population is Latinx, and posted online a twenty-three-thousand-word "manifesto" announcing he would soon launch "an attack in response to the Hispanic invasion of Texas." In his apologia for impending mayhem, he portrayed himself as a victim. "They [Mexican immigrants and Mexican Americans] are the instigators, not me," he said. "I am simply defending my country from cultural and ethnic replacement brought on by an invasion." Nineteen minutes after his private declaration of war (titled "The Inconvenient Truth") appeared online, police began to receive 911 calls from the store. The killer relentlessly hunted brown-skinned targets, eventually murdering twenty-three men, women, and children, ranging in age from fifteen to ninety, and wounding dozens (Abutaleb, 2019; Allyn et al., 2019; Arengo et al., 2019; Bogel-Burroughs, 2019; Branham, 2019; Chason et al., 2019; Crusius, 2019; "El Paso," 2020; Moore & Berman, 2019; Phillips & Friauf, 2019; Quick Facts, 2021; Ryan, 2019).

Politicians and the media sought answers. Texas Lt. Gov. Dan Patrick, on the *Fox and Friends* newscast, quickly ticked off a litany of American "culture war" culprits conservatives often blame for mass shootings. "We've always had guns, always had evil, but I see a video game industry that teaches young people to kill," Patrick said. He also blamed a lack of school prayer, declining patriotism, and disrespect for law enforcement (Tenbarge, 2019; Bella, 2019).

Some media outlets offered far more empathy for the El Paso killer than provided Muslims engaged in terrorism, blaming personal or family pathologies (Mingus & Zopf, 2010). The *Wall Street Journal* described the shooter as a "little lost, with few friends," while the *Daily Mail* reported that the murderer's father struggled with alcohol and drug abuse (Ailsworth et al. 2019; Perry & Boswell, 2019). Law enforcement suggested the killer had been "radicalized online," as he spent up to eight hours a day in sinister corners of the internet, such as 8chan. However, "friends and former teachers and classmates say he might have been hardened, too, by the tensions in his changing community in real life," including the fact that the white population in his Collin County community had in recent years dropped from 80 percent to about half (Chason et al., 2019).

Each explanation for the El Paso catastrophe zeroed in on present-day causes such as the influence of racist content on the so-called "dark web." The shooter's rampage, however, has much deeper roots in American history, its genesis long predating the internet or the present-day alt-right. American origin myths have long glorified white supremacist violence as essential to the rise of the American nation as well as its preservation.

His manifesto referenced a conspiracy theory widely shared among the modern far right: that global elites (usually identified as Jews) are conspiring to commit "white genocide" by overwhelming white-majority nations with dark-skinned immigrants who then corrupt the culture and biologically degrade the population through miscegenation. The media treated this white dread of racial erasure as a recent, internet-driven phenomenon, when in fact the El Paso killer drew up a paranoid narrative of much older vintage in American culture, dating back to the Puritan invasion of present-day Massachusetts. The great replacement theory is just the latest iteration of an old narrative depicting American society as ever in danger of collapse due to racial contamination. According to this mythology, these threats necessitate periodic rituals of purity-restoring bloodletting to forestall a racial apocalypse (Crusius, 2019; Slotkin, 1973, pp. 12–13).

The fear that whites might be exterminated by racialized others gripped the first English settlers in colonial Massachusetts. In the early 1600s, English invaders, who already had acquired immunity to a variety of deadly contagions alien to much of North America, brought smallpox and other diseases that quickly destroyed much of the region's indigenous population. With their invisible biogenic weapons, the newcomers acquired a significant population advantage over Native Americans around Cape Cod. Nevertheless, Puritans dreaded massacres by Native Americans from the more distant frontier and used this anxiety to justify genocide of Indians as a defensive maneuver. Seventeenth-century Puritans like William Bradford warned that in North America, the English would be "in continual danger of the savage people, who are cruel, barbarous, and most treacherous . . . not being content only to take away life, [they] delight to torment men in the most bloody manner" (Slotkin, 1973, p. 38). Such language not only represented projection, but provided a license to kill in ensuing centuries (Gibson, 1980; Slotkin, 1973).

As they stole Native American lands and murdered inhabitants regardless of age or infirmity, Europeans and their American descendants accused Indians of scalping still-living victims, desecrating enemies' corpses, and murdering unarmed women and children, acts whites themselves had committed, in what the historian Richard Slotkin calls the myth of savage war. "In its most typical formulations, the myth of 'savage war' blames Native Americans as instigators of a war of extermination," Slotkin wrote. "The accusation . . . made the Indians scapegoats for the morally troubling side of American expansion . . . [and] became a basic ideological convention of a culture that was itself increasingly devoted to the extermination of the Indians and the kidnapping and enslavement of black Africans" (Slotkin, 1998, pp. 12–13). After the United States achieved independence, the myth of savage war persisted. In the white supremacist mind, the outnumbered and out-armed became the threatening, the invaders transformed into the besieged, the conquered turned into the aggressors. Whites widely shared the idea that "savage" and "civilized" races could not live peacefully side by side.

The savage war myth in the El Paso shooter's home state of Texas centered on the Battle of the Alamo in 1836, serving to underscore the supposed peril posed by "aliens." Anglo public memory of the Alamo represents a perfect model for the power inversions dominating the great replacement mindset. Mexicans in the tale are presented as invaders in their own land. Anglo enslavers are portrayed as freedom fighters. An Anglo defeat metamorphoses into a victory because of the higher number of Mexican casualties at the Alamo, evidence suggesting Mexican inferiority. The Mexicans, not Anglos, slaughter prisoners of war, at the Alamo and later at Goliad, the myths insist, thus overlooking Texan war crimes in the Battle of San Jacinto and elsewhere (Brear, 1995, pp. 28, 35–37; Acuña, 1988, pp. 10–11, 28).

The savage war myth of Mexican depravity during the Texas Revolution, 1835–1836, has been foundational to an ongoing racial war in which Anglos, from Gen. Sam Houston's soldiers to the El Paso shooter, have justified any act of violence. Alamo tales instigated Anglos to shoot, club, and stab surrendered Mexican troops in the decisive Battle of San Jacinto that ended the Texas Revolution on April 21, 1836, and to scalp and torture Mexican civilians in the Mexican-American War of 1846–1848. Unitarian minister The-

odore Parker deeply opposed that war but wrote that whites were born to con-
quer and to eliminate all parts of the human family that stood in their way.
"The history of the Anglo-Saxon, for the last hundred years has been one of
continuous aggression, invasion, and extermination," he wrote (Slotkin, 1998,
p. 46). This notion of necessary racial violence continued through sporadic
acts of racial terrorism in Texas, including the murder of "hundreds, possibly
thousands" of Mexicans and Mexican Americans at the hands of vigilantes,
ranchers, and Texas Rangers in the Lone Star State between 1915 and 1920
(Chamberlain, 1956, pp. 87–88; Simon, 1917, pp. 109–110; Johnson, 2003, pp.
1–2, 109, 113, 115, 176).

The exterminationist discourse seen as the province of the racist fringe
today flowed from the pens and mouths of the powerful as, between 1890 and
1910, 11.3 million Poles, Hungarians, Russians, Italians, Greeks, Eastern European Jews, and others immigrated to America (Okrent, 2019, p. 142). These
immigrants did not conform to contemporary definitions of whiteness and
thus were portrayed as a danger to the "white" population. In the words of
one New York worker in the 1890s, "The Russian Jews and the other Jews will
completely control the finances and the Government of this country or they
will all be dead" (Higham, 1955, p. 93; Jacobson, 1998; Roediger, 1991, 1994).

In response to immigration, American eugenicists engaged in lower-in-
tensity, nonlethal schemes of violence in the form of sexual sterilization of
the so-called unfit. Legislatures enacted mandatory sterilization laws in all but
sixteen states; at least 63,480 Americans were placed under the knife in the
twentieth century (Largent, 2011, p. 77). Disproportionately, surgeons subjected African American and Native American women to sterilization (Ordover, 2003, pp. 130–131). Prominent Americans like Theodore Roosevelt embraced eugenics. He disdained the new Italian arrivals as "the most fecund
and the least desirable population of Europe" and despaired the increasing
numbers of "Jew bankers." Unless the birthrate of middle- and upper-class
Americans of "old stock" (Northern and Western European heritage) caught
up with Eastern and Southern European immigrants, the United States would
commit "race suicide." Roosevelt summoned the language of the battlefield
to describe the reproductive race between old-stock Americans and immigrants as the "warfare of the cradle" (Kevles, 1985, p. 74; Dorsey & Harlow,
2003; Okrent, 2019, pp. 82–84, 142).

Eugenics popularizers like the journalist Lothrop Stoddard believed that
the growing numbers of "Under-Men" might eventually make it necessary
for "Nordics" (Northern Europeans) to wage a war of elimination against
racial inferiors as a matter of survival. Stoddard found a mass audience with
his 1920 jeremiad, *The Rising Tide of Color against White World Supremacy*, in
which he warned that the rapid reproduction of people of color around the
world would overwhelm the world's white population. "Let the brown world

once make up its mind that the white man *must* go, and he *will* go, for his position will have become simply impossible," Stoddard warned (1921, p. 83). In a 1922 polemic, *The Revolt against Civilization: The Menace of the Under Man*, Stoddard feared he saw America's future in the 1918 Bolshevik revolution in Russia, a supposed overthrow of enfeebled but still relatively superior white elites by Asiatic primitives. Stoddard urged the racially superior in America to be prepared for a remorseless race war (1922, pp. 23, 29, 62–94, 111–113, 175, 233). "No misguided sentimentality should shield those who plot the disruption of civilization and the degradation of the race," Stoddard wrote. "These irreconcilables should be carefully watched . . . and where anything like revolution is attempted—hunted down and extirpated" (1922, pp. 232–233).

As science historian Elazar Barkan contends, the horrors of race science during the Nazi Holocaust from 1939 to 1945 delegitimized eugenics, even though forced sterilization continued in America through the late twentieth century (Barkan, 1992; Lombardo, 2011). Explicit exterminationist discourse retreated to the margins, but it slowly crept back into the mainstream after the Vietnam War. The legislative triumphs of the civil rights movement, and the North Vietnamese victory over the vaunted technological advantages and vast wealth of the United States, presaged to many whites an end to their racial hegemony. Ku Klux Klan newspapers described whites as victims of "discrimination in the awarding of employment, promotions, scholarships, and college entrances" that favored immigrants and minorities (LeSage, 2002, p. 157). These resentments boiled in the racist underground, beginning in the 1970s, but gradually seeped back into the political mainstream, reaching an apotheosis in the Trump presidency. (Belew, 2018, pp. 3, 5, 7, 9, 97–99, 158, 163–164; Ferber & Kimmel, 2000, pp. 193–194).

Many on the racist religious right believe that the Bible prophesied a race war at the end-times. Adherents of Christian Identity, a sect dating to nineteenth-century Great Britain, identify the white race as the authentic Twelve Tribes of Israel. According to believers, these tribes were promised world dominion by God. The Identity movement recast the Battle of Armageddon, a final struggle between good and evil alluded to in the Christian New Testament's book of Revelation, as a final face-off between racially pure whites and the dark masses created by Satan. However, adherents believe that white survival is not inevitable. Instead, believers insist that they themselves must pave a bloody path to Jesus's Second Coming. "The faithful would be tasked with ridding the world of the unfaithful, the world's non-white and Jewish population, before the return of Christ," historian Kathleen Belew wrote (Belew, 2018, p. 6). This belief would later influence members of a 1980s white terrorist group, the Order, and later American mass killers (Belew, 2018; Barkun, 1994, pp. 111, 119, 226–229).

In 1975, a secular prophecy that called for whites to launch a first strike in an inevitable race war flowed from the pen of William L. Pierce, who at one point taught physics at Oregon State University. He formed a neo-Nazi organization, the National Alliance, and published a novel, *The Turner Diaries*, in serial form in the NA publication *Attack!* from 1975 to 1978. Set in the early 1990s, *The Turner Diaries*, written by Pierce under the pseudonym Andrew MacDonald, takes the form of a fictional journal kept by an engineer, Earl Turner. Turner becomes a leader of an underground terrorist army, the Organization, after the implementation of a ban on all private gun ownership. After guns are seized from most Americans, rapes of white women skyrocket. This, Pierce writes, is part of the Jewish plot to destroy white America, along with opening American borders to nonwhite immigrants. To save the white race, Turner blows up the FBI national headquarters in Washington, D.C., with a truck bomb. Turner sees his eventual murder of thousands as cutting out a lethal cancer (Barkun, 1994, pp. 115, 225–228; Turner, 1978, pp. 1–2, 38, 42). Without mass violence, Turner says, "our whole race will die" (Pierce, 2019, p. 42).

White nationalists take over Vandenberg Air Force Base in Southern California and seize its nuclear missiles, while ethnically cleansing 8.5 million nonwhites. The Organization conducts mass hangings of fifty-five thousand to sixty thousand so-called "race traitors" during the "Day of the Rope." As the white revolution reaches its crescendo, the Organization sets off small nuclear weapons in multiple American cities. A nuclear missile is launched from Vandenberg to destroy the Israeli capital of Tel Aviv. Earl Turner finally defeats "the system" by flying a crop duster armed with a small nuclear weapon into the Pentagon. As a final act, through the use of nuclear, chemical, and biological weapons, the Organization renders sixteen million square miles of Asia uninhabitable and its population "effectively sterilized" (Turner, 2019, pp. 47–48, 61, 140, 147, 152, 155, 161–163, 170, 189, 197–198, 202–205, 209).

The Turner Diaries features all the main themes that appear later in the great replacement theory: that the white race is on the verge of extinction because of "race-mixing" brought about by nefarious Jews who seek white destruction. *The Turner Diaries* "has become one of the most influential texts among white nationalists and right-wing extremists," the *New York Times* reported in 2021. It was removed from the amazon.com website after the siege of the U.S. Capitol by Trump supporters on January 6, 2021, but before then, it "had received hundreds of five-star reviews from readers extolling its message." The *Times* added, "It has inspired dozens of acts of violence, and has been held up as a blueprint for how to enact a violent insurrection." From 1983 to 1984, the Order, a white supremacist terrorist group that took its name from the secret circle Earl Turner joins, robbed a pornography shop, banks, and armored cars, heisting more than $8 million they later distributed to several white supremacist groups with the intent of funding a white revolution. Along the way, they assassinated a Jewish radio talk show host, Alan Berg. A leader of the Order authored the "White Genocide Manifesto" while in prison, articulating the notion of pending extinction for whites and the need for racial war. He later coined what came to be known to the far right as the "14 Words." That slogan, "We must secure the existence of our people and a future for white children," has animated warriors against the supposed Great Replacement, like the El Paso shooter, since the 1980s (Alter, 2021; Barkun, 1994, pp. 228, 231; Belew, 2018, p. 164; "Once Again," 2000; Berger, 2016a).

The obsessive fear of white racial extinction by no means represents a unique American pathology, nor did William Pierce have the great replacement genre to himself. A French writer antagonistic to Muslim immigrants in his nation, Renaud Camus, most fully described an alleged conspiracy to destroy the white race in his 2011 book *Le Grand Remplacement* (Charlton, 2019; Camus, 2011). But Pierce exercised an outsized influence over the American racist far right. Before his terrorist act, the bomber of the Alfred P. Murrah Federal Building in Oklahoma City sold copies of *The Turner Diaries* at gun shows. He modeled his attack on the novel's bombing of the FBI headquarters, and investigators found pages from *The Turner Diaries* in his truck (Zeskind, 2009, pp. 29–32, 93, 399–402, 456; Belew, 2018, p. 110). A murderer and white supremacist said, "We're starting *The Turner Diaries* early," as he drove a truck dragging James Byrd Jr. to his death in Jasper, Texas, in 1998 (Berger, 2016b). Pierce's influence could also be felt in a 1999 shooting spree that killed and wounded African Americans, Jews, and Asian immigrants over a bloody weekend in Illinois and Indiana on the weekend of July 4, 1999 (Slater & Beckham, 1999); the murder of seven at a Sikh temple in Oak Creek, Wisconsin, on August 5, 2012 (Helm, 2012; "Profile," 2012); and the fatal shooting of three at the Jewish Community Center of Greater Kansas City and the Village Shalom retirement home in Overland Park, Kansas, on April 13, 2014 (Keating & Assael, 2021).

The 2015 Charleston shooter did not reference *The Turner Diaries* when he posted his explanation for his butchering of nine churchgoers at the Emanuel African Methodist Episcopal Church, but the fears of white genocide expressed by Pierce and sloganized in the neo-Nazi "14 Words" shape almost every paragraph in the rambling political testament he posted online. The Charleston shooter posted photos of himself holding the flag of the defunct white supremacist Rhodesian regime and a Confederate banner. He raged at wildly inflated black-on-white crime statistics. He expressed his desire for a white homeland in the Pacific Northwest and warned of the impending disappearance of white people unless they waged a war of self-defense, their survival possible only if violent action were taken soon enough. "It is far from being too late for America or Europe," the murderer wrote in a manifesto before his mass shooing. "I believe that even if we made up only 30 percent of the population[,] we could take it back completely. But by no means should we wait any longer to take drastic action" (Robertson & Schwartz, 2012; "Full Text," 2015; Adamczyk, 2020; Gilsinan, 2015).

The last four centuries of American history suggest that violent words precede violent action, particularly when they receive elite sanction. The modern mainstream conservative movement now echoes key buzz phrases of the great replacement theory. Donald Trump won the presidency in 2016 warning that the United States was being swamped with illegal immigrants, famously declaring, "When Mexico sends its people . . . they're sending people that have lots of problems. . . . They're bringing drugs. They're bringing crime. They're rapists." Former Iowa U.S. House Rep. Steve King sounded like Lothrop Stoddard as he tweeted on March 12, 2017, "We can't restore our civilization with somebody else's babies" (Lee, 2015; Bump, 2017).

Mass shootings inspired by racist doomsday warnings rapidly accelerated during the Trump presidency (2017–2021). Trump's white nationalist rhetoric and Pierce's and Camus's warnings of white racial extinction echoed around the globe. Camus deeply influenced an Australian who slaughtered fifty-one Muslims and wounded forty at two different mosques in Christchurch, New Zealand, on March 15, 2019 (Charlton, 2019; Camus, 2011; "Christchurch Shooting," 2020; Tarrant, 2019), as well as the El Paso killer. The great replacement theory seemed in part to have sparked the violence of the man who butchered eleven at the Tree of Life Synagogue in a Pittsburgh suburb in 2018; a mass shooting that killed one and wounded three at a Poway, California, synagogue on April 27, 2019; and the gunning down of three and wounding of seventeen others at the Gilroy Garlic Festival on July 28, 2019, just one week before the El Paso slaughter. All the killers had immersed themselves in a worldview that reversed the realities of American racism and depicted whites as the victims of lethal oppression (Ghansah, 2017; Lord, 2018; Sridhar, 2019; Feis & Brown, 2019).

Meanwhile, as Trump-supporting seditionists invaded the Capitol on January 6, 2021, far-right internet chat rooms such as 4chan and Stormfront noted similarities between the real events unfolding before their eyes and *The Turner Diaries*, including the erection of a scaffold and a noose outside the Capitol that reminded many viewers of Pierce's "Day of the Rope." Someone on the neo-fascist-friendly Telegram app posted, "The turner diaries mentioned this. Keep reading." After the Capitol assault, right-wing media amped up white supremacist rhetoric. *Fox News* host Tucker Carlson channeled the El Paso shooter's claims that Democrats were creating a one-party dictatorship on the strength of ballots from immigrants with fake IDs. Carlson embraced the great replacement theory on air in April 2021. "I know that the left . . . become literally hysterical if you use the term 'replacement,' if you suggest that the Democratic Party is trying to replace the current electorate . . . with new people, more obedient voters from the Third World," Carlson said. "But they become hysterical because that's what happening, actually" (Chait, 2021).

Iterations of the great replacement theory have resulted in a body count since the times of the Pilgrims. The fear of white genocide, in different forms, is older than the United States. Like other forms of eschatological dread, the racial apocalypse is ever on the horizon in American culture. Replacement panic will continue to lurk, mutate, and resurface in a society grounded in ruthless economic competition, ever-changing demographics, persistent white and male insecurity, a hyperactive apocalyptic imagination, and acceptance of gun violence as an intrinsic part of the American way of life.

REFERENCES

Abutaleb, Y. (2019, August 4). What's inside the hate-filled manifesto linked to the alleged El Paso shooter. *Washington Post.* https://www.washingtonpost.com/politics/2019/08/04/whats-inside-hate-filled-manifesto-linked-el-paso-shooter/

Acuña, R. (1988). *Occupied America: A history of Chicanos.* HarperCollins Publishers.

Adamczyk, C. (2020). *Gods vs. Titans: Ideological indicators of Identitarian Violence* [Master's thesis]. Naval Postgraduate School.

Ailsworth, E., Wells, G., & Lovett, I. (2019, August 8). Lost in life, El Paso suspect found a dark world online. *Wall Street Journal.* https://www.wsj.com/articles/lost-in-life-el-paso-suspect-found-a-dark-world-online-11565308783

Allyn, B., Matias, D., Gonzalez, R., & Chappell, B. (2019, August 6). *Stories of El Paso shooting victims show acts of self-sacrifice amid massacre.* NPR.com. https://www.npr.org/2019/08/06/748527564/stories-of-el-paso-shooting-victims-show-acts-of-self-sacrifice-amid-massacre

Alter, A. (2021, January 12). How 'The Turner Diaries' incites white supremacists. *New York Times.* https://www.nytimes.com/2021/01/12/books/turner-diaries-white-supremacists.html

Arengo, T., Bogel-Burroughs, N., & Benner, K. (2019, August 3). Minutes before El Paso killing, hate-filled manifesto appears online. *New York Times.* https://www.nytimes.com/2019/08/03/us/patrick-crusius-el-paso-shooter-manifesto.html

Barkan, E. (1992). *The retreat of scientific racism: Changing concepts of race in Britain and the United States between the World Wars.* Cambridge University Press.

Barkun, M. (1994). *Religion and the racist right: The origins of the Christian Identity movement.* University of North Carolina Press.

Belew, K. (2018). *Bringing the war home: The white power movement and paramilitary America.* Harvard University Press.

Bella, T. (2019, August 5). Politicians suggest video games are to blame for the El Paso shooting. It's an old claim not backed by research. *Washington Post.* https://www.washingtonpost.com/nation/2019/08/05/kevin-mccarthy-dan-patrick-video-games-el-paso-shooting/

Berger, J. M. (2016a, September 16). Alt history: How a self-published, racist novel changed white nationalism and inspired decades of violence. *The Atlantic.* https://www.theatlantic.com/politics/archive/2016/09/how-the-turner-diaries-changed-white-nationalism/500039/

Berger, J. M. (2016b). *The Turner legacy: The storied origins and enduring impact of white nationalism's deadly Bible*. International Centre for Counter-Terrorism. https://icct.nl /publication/the-turner-legacy-the-storied-origins-and-enduring-impact-of-white-na tionalisms-deadly-bible/

Bogel-Burroughs, N. (2019, August 9). "I'm the shooter": El Paso suspect confessed to targeting Mexicans, police say. *New York Times*. https://www.nytimes.com/2019/08 /09/us/el-paso-suspect-confession.html

Branham, D. (2019, August 5). El Paso massacre suspect drove 10 hours from Allen before killing 22 in crowded Walmart, chief says. *Dallas Morning News*. https://www .dallasnews.com/news/texas/2019/08/06/el-paso-massacre-suspect-drove-10-hours -from-allen-before-killing-22-in-crowded-walmart-chief-says/

Brear, H. (1995). *Inherit the Alamo: Myth and ritual at an American shrine*. University of Texas Press.

Bump, P. (2017, March 12). Rep. Steve King warns that "our civilization" can't be restored with "somebody else's babies." *Washington Post*. https://www.washingtonpost.com /news/politics/wp/2017/03/12/rep-steve-king-warns-that-our-civilization-cant-be-re stored-with-somebody-elses-babies/

Camus, R. (2011). *Le grande remplacement*. David Reinharc.

Chait, J. (2021, April 9). Tucker Carlson endorses white supremacist theory by name. *New York*. https://nymag.com/intelligencer/2021/04/tucker-carlson-great-replacement-white -supremacist-immigration-fox-news-racism.html

Chamberlain, S. (1956). *My confessions*. Harper & Row.

Charlton, L. (2019, August 6). What is the great replacement? *New York Times*. https:// www.nytimes.com/2019/08/06/us/politics/grand-replacement-explainer.html

Chason, R., Nevans, A., Gowan, A., & Fuchs, H. (2019, August 9). As his environment changed, suspect in El Paso shooting learned to hate. *Washington Post*. https://www .washingtonpost.com/national/as-his-environment-changed-suspect-in-el-paso -shooting-learned-to-hate/2019/08/09/8ebabf2c-817b-40a3-a79e-e56fbac94cd5_story .html

Christchurch shooting: Gunman Tarrant wanted to kill "as many as possible." (2020, August 24). BBC.com. https://www.bbc.com/news/world-asia-53861456

Crusius, P. (2019). *The inconvenient truth*. Bridgetown Initiative. https://bridge.george town.edu/research/the-manifesto-of-the-el-paso-terrorist/

Dorsey, L., & Harlow, R. (2003). "We want Americans pure and simple": Theodore Roosevelt and the myth of Americanism. *Rhetoric and Public Affairs*, 6(1), 55–78.

El Paso Walmart shooting victim dies, raising death toll to 23. (2020, April 26). NBCNews. com. https://www.nbcnews.com/news/us-news/el-paso-walmart-shooting-victim-dies -death-toll-now-23-n1193016

Feis, A., & L. Brown. (2019, July 29). Gilroy shooter Santino William Legan posted racist rants on social media. *New York Post*. https://nypost.com/2019/07/29/gilroy-shooter -santino-william-legan-posted-racist-rants-on-social-media/

Ferber, A., & Kimmel, M. (2000). Reading right: The Western tradition in white supremacist discourse. *Sociological Focus*, 33(2).

Full text of Charleston suspect Dylann Roof's apparent manifesto. (2015, June 20). Talking Points Memo. https://talkingpointsmemo.com/muckraker/dylann-roof-manifesto -full-text

Ghansah, R. (2017, August 21). A most American terrorist: The making of Dylann Roof. *GQ.com*. https://www.gq.com/story/dylann-roof-making-of-an-american-terrorist

Gibson, A. (1980). *The American Indian: Prehistory to the present*. D. C. Heath & Company.

Gilsinan, K. (2015, June 24). Why is Dylann Roof so worried about Europe? *The Atlantic*. https://www.theatlantic.com/international/archive/2015/06/dylann-roof-world-white-supremacist/396557/

Helm, J. (2012, August 7). Wade Michael Page was steeped in neo-Nazi "hate music" movement. *Washington Post*. https://www.washingtonpost.com/lifestyle/style/wade-michael-page-was-steeped-in-neo-nazi-hate-music-movement/2012/08/07/b879451e-dfe8-11e1-a19c-fcfa365396c8_story.html

Higham, J. (1955). *Strangers in the land: Patterns of American nativism, 1860–1925*. Rutgers University Press.

Jacobson, M. (1998). *Whiteness of a different color: European immigrants and the alchemy of race*. Harvard University Press.

Johnson, B. (2003). *Revolution in Texas: How a forgotten rebellion and its bloody suppression turned Mexicans into Americans*. Yale University Press.

Keating, P., & Assael, S. (2021, June 11). The herald of the far right. *GQ.com*. https://www.gq.com/story/the-herald-of-the-far-right

Kevles, D. (1985). *In the name of eugenics: Genetics and the uses of human heredity*. Harvard University Press.

Largent, M. (2011). *Breeding contempt: The history of coerced sterilization in the United States*. Rutgers University Press.

Lee, M. (2015, July 8). Donald Trump's false comments connecting immigrants and crime. *Washington Post*. https://www.washingtonpost.com/news/fact-checker/wp/2015/07/08/donald-trumps-false-comments-connecting-mexican-immigrants-and-crime/

LeSage, J., Ferber, A., Storrs, D., & Wong, D. (2002). *Making a difference: University students of color speak out*. Rowman & Littlefield.

Lombardo, P. (Ed.). (2011). *A Century of eugenics in America: From the Indiana experiment to the human genome era*. Indiana University Press.

Lord, R. (2018, November 10). How Robert Bowers went from conservative to white nationalist. *Pittsburgh Post-Gazette*. https://www.post-gazette.com/news/crime-courts/2018/11/10/Robert-Bowers-extremism-Tree-of-Life-massacre-shooting-pittsburgh-Gab-Warroom/stories/201811080165

Mingus, W., & Zopf, B. (2010). White means never having to say you're sorry: The racial project in explaining mass shootings. *Social Thought & Research, 31*, 57–77.

Moore R., & Berman, M. (2019, August 9). El Paso suspect said he was targeting "Mexicans," told police he was shooter. *Washington Post*. https://www.washingtonpost.com/national/el-paso-suspect-said-he-was-targeting-mexicans-told-officers-he-was-the-shooter-police-say/2019/08/09/ab235e18-bac9-11e9-b3b4-2bb69e8c4e39_story.html

Okrent, D. (2019). *The guarded gate: Bigotry, eugenics, and the law that kept two generations of Jews, Italians, and other European Americans out of America*. Scribner.

Once again, the Turner Diaries inspires bloodshed. (2000, September 15). Splcenter.org. https://www.splcenter.org/fighting-hate/intelligence-report/2000/once-again-turner-diaries-inspires-bloodshed

Ordover, N. (2003). *American eugenics: Race, queer anatomy, and the science of nationalism*. University of Minnesota Press.

Perry, R., & Boswell, J. (2019, August 4). El Paso Walmart mass shooter Patrick Crusius' father admits to nearly 40 years of drug addiction which tore apart his family and claims he has spoken directly to Jesus. *Daily Mail*. https://www.dailymail.co.uk/news/article-7319821/El-Paso-Walmart-shooter-Patrick-Crusius-father-penned-book-life-drug-addiction.html

Phillips, M., & Friauf, B. (2019, August 12). The world that made the El Paso shooter. *Jacobin*. https://jacobin.com/2019/08/patrick-crusius-texas-el-paso-massacre-shooting-gun-laws

Pierce, W. ([1978] 2019). *The Turner diaries*. Cosmotheist Books.

Profile: Wisconsin Sikh temple shooter Wade Michael Page. (August 7, 2012). BBC.com. https://www.bbc.com/news/world-us-canada-19167324

Quick Facts: El Paso, Texas. (2021). Census.gov. https://www.census.gov/quickfacts/elpasocountytexas

Robertson, C., & Schwartz, J. (2012, March 22). Shooting focuses attention on a program that seeks to avoid guns. *New York Times*. https://www.nytimes.com/2012/03/23/us/trayvon-martin-death-spotlights-neighborhood-watch-groups.html

Roediger, D. (1991). *The wages of whiteness: Race and the making of the American working class*. Verso.

Roediger, D. (1994). *Towards the abolition of whiteness: Essays on race, politics and working class history*. Verso.

Ryan, N. (2019, August 8). El Paso Walmart manager relives mass shooting terror at his store. KVIA.

Simon, J. (1917). *The papers of Ulysses S. Grant* (vol. 1). Princeton University Press.

Slater, E., & Beckham, J. (1999, July 6). Shooter cultivated his racist views in college. *Los Angeles Times*. https://www.latimes.com/archives/la-xpm-1999-jul-06-mn-53387-story.html

Slotkin, R. (1973). *Regeneration through violence: The mythology of the American, 1600–1860*. University of Oklahoma Press.

Slotkin, R. (1998). *Gunfighter nation: The myth of the frontier in twentieth century America*. University of Oklahoma Press.

Sridhar, P. (2019, September 19). *Suspected Poway synagogue shooter unleashed anti-Semitic diatribe in 911 call*. KPBS. https://www.kpbs.org/news/2019/09/19/preliminary-hearing-set-for-poway-synagogue

Stoddard, L. (1921). *The rising tide of color against white world supremacy*. Charles Scribner's Sons.

Stoddard, L. (1922). *The revolt against civilization: The menace of the under man*. Charles Scribner's Sons.

Tarrant, B. (2019, March 15). *The great replacement*. https://img-prod.ilfoglio.it/userUpload/The_Great_Replacementconvertito.pdf

Tenbarge, K. (2019, August 4). In a "Fox and Friends" segment Texas' lieutenant governor suggested violent video games and a lack of prayer in schools could be factors in El Paso mass shooting. *Business Insider*. https://www.businessinsider.in/in-a-fox-friends-segment-texas-lieutenant-governor-suggested-violent-video-games-and-a-lack-of-prayer-in-schools-could-be-factors-in-the-el-paso-mass-shooting/articleshow/70528025.cms

Zeskind, L. (2009). *Blood and politics: The history of the white nationalist movement from the margins to the mainstream*. Farrar, Straus and Giroux.

8

The Accelerationists

White Supremacist Movement Culture and the
Strategy of Mass Shootings in the United States

STANISLAV VYSOTSKY

"**M**any people think that the fight for America is already lost. They couldn't be more wrong. This is just the beginning of the fight for America and Europe. I am honored to head the fight to reclaim my country from destruction." These are the final words of the four-page manifesto written by the 2019 El Paso Walmart mass shooter in which he sought to justify his attack that killed twenty-three people and injured twenty-three others. This incident, which primarily targeted Latinx customers, was the deadliest ideologically inspired far-right mass shooting in the United States and served as the culmination of a series of such attacks between late 2018 and 2019. This period is unique because of the increase in frequency of mass shootings perpetrated by individuals who explicitly cite white supremacist ideology and conspiracy theory as the inspiration and justification for their acts of violence, which marks a distinct shift in the place of such attacks in supremacist movement culture and tactical repertoire.

Far-right mass shooters are on a "mission" to eliminate people whom their ideology deems to be "inferior" or a threat and to inspire others to follow their example (J. Levin & McDevitt, 2002). It is specifically this desire to eliminate people and provide spectacular inspiration that in part drives these acts of violence (Bates, 2012). It is precisely this mission dynamic that drives the higher rates of death and injury at the hands of ideologically motivated mass shooters (Capellan, 2015; Capellan et al., 2019; J. Levin & McDevitt, 2002). While individual incidents of supremacist mass shootings are rare, research indicates that they are on the rise (Capellan, 2015; Capellan et al., 2019; Spaaij, 2010).

As a movement tactic, the mass shooting reflects an accelerationist philosophy that encourages acts of violence to instigate a race war (Beauchamp, 2019; Gartenstein-Ross et al., 2020; Walther & McCoy, 2021). White supremacist accelerationism has its origins in the neoreaction ideas of philosopher Nick Land, as well as the neo-Nazi writings of James Mason's collected works *Siege* and William Pierce's *The Turner Diaries*. Its advocates argue that acts of mass violence committed by supremacists will serve to increase the tensions in society, destabilize political order, and further ideological polarization that will inevitably lead to a race war that whites will win (Beauchamp, 2019; Gartenstein-Ross et al., 2020; Walther & McCoy, 2021). The proponents of accelerationism engage in spectacular, and often violent, actions that are designed to speed up this racial conflict by not only inspiring movement members but also provoking a repressive state response that they believe will be viewed by many in the society as illegitimate and overbearing. The justifications written by mass shooting perpetrators in their manifestos indicate that accelerationism is a key component of contemporary supremacist mass violence.

Much of the scholarly understanding of far-right mass shooters focuses on the specific characteristics of the individuals involved, with particular attention to their gender, age, psychological state, and relationship to other people. As with many other mass shooters, far-right ideologically oriented perpetrators are overwhelmingly male; however, they are generally older than nonideologically oriented mass shooters (Capellan, 2015; Gruenewald et al., 2013). Roughly half of the perpetrators suffered from confirmed or suggested mental health problems (Capellan, 2015; Gruenewald et al., 2013; Langman, 2020). Bubolz and Simi (2019, p. 11) explain this dynamic:

> Of course, not all people who join White supremacist groups or other antidemocratic movements suffer from mental health problems, but rather, there may be a type of synergy that exists between unstable individuals and movements that valorize violence as a preferred mode of expression. . . . These individuals may not be screened during recruitment (Horgan, 2005) and, in fact, may be a preferred type of member because of ideological likeness and unrestrained violent tendencies.

So, while mental illness may not be a distinct causal factor of supremacist mass shootings, it is part of a complex combination of personal and ideological motivations that are exploited by a broader movement for its own ends. It is precisely this movement dynamic that is most evident among far-right ideologically motivated mass shooters. Rather than being isolated loners acting on personal frustration, supremacist-inspired perpetrators are frequently connected in some way to a broader social movement that valorizes violence and calls for the elimination of whole categories of people as a central tenet of its ideology. They frequently have contact with movement propaganda through internet activity and may interact with other movement members either in person or online. Supremacist mass shooters frequently engage with far-right websites and social media to participate in discussions, acquire information, and obtain materials. The online supremacist world creates a dynamic where would-be mass shooters are simultaneously lone actors and active participants in the movement (Gill et al., 2014; Gottschalk, 2020; Hamm & Spaaij, 2017; Holt et al., 2019). Furthermore, internet activity provides justifications and neutralizations for violent activity in the real world by framing them as intrinsic to the movement and its ideology (Gottschalk, 2020; Vysotsky & McCarthy, 2017).

Online supremacist sites serve as "transmovement" free spaces that link movement members, provide a forum for discussion of ideology and tactics, allow for coordination of events, and serve as a means of financially sustaining the movement (Cohen-Almagor, 2018; Daniels, 2009; Futrell & Simi, 2004; B. Levin, 2002; Miller-Idriss, 2020; Simi & Futrell, 2010). White supremacist internet sites provide a forum for racial identity construction through systematic othering of people deemed inferior by the movement, the construction of white victimhood, and the assertion of the importance of racial activism (Miller-Idriss, 2020; Simi & Futrell, 2010; Tischauser & Musgrave, 2020; Wong et al., 2015). Far-right internet activity also generates a distinct culture marked by the deployment of images, memes, and intramovement "humor" that denigrates historically marginalized people as well as ideological opponents and celebrates violence (Bogerts & Fielitz, 2018; Dafaure, 2020; DeCook, 2018; Miller-Idriss, 2020; Simi & Futrell, 2010). While publicly accessible forums such as Stormfront, one of the oldest and largest white supremacist forums, attempt to engage in impression and stigma management of the white supremacist movement by moderating content and toning down the worst expressions of bigotry and violence (Daniels, 2009; Simi & Futrell, 2009, 2010), the relatively recent advent of the dark web, anonymous forums, and social media sites provides a plethora of opportunities for the most violent and bigoted expressions of movement adherents (Dafaure, 2020). This online environment serves as a key point of transmission of white supremacist movement culture and ideology.

This chapter looks beyond the individual level of white supremacist ideologically oriented mass shooters' beliefs and behaviors to situate their actions in the broader cultural context of the social movement with which they are affiliated. In doing so, it bridges the field of social movement studies with criminology (Shank, 1999). This chapter also provides a cultural criminological analysis of the way in which the act of mass shooting is interpreted and deployed by the far right by constructing meaning and symbolic representation (Ferrell et al., 2015). The mass shooting serves as a crucial cultural signifier for the white supremacist movement. The discourse and visual culture of the far right serve as a manifestation of the leaderless resistance model of action venerated by the movement and as a means of enacting an ideology that seeks to maintain structural and systemic hierarchy through violence.

White Supremacist Discourse and Mass Shootings

The ways in which mass shootings are discussed by white supremacists in online forums demonstrate their perception of such actions within the movement. They often celebrate the actions of shooters and encourage others to act. In the context of other forms of dehumanizing discourse in online forums, the comments regarding mass shootings reinforce existing supremacist movement frames and serve to encourage future incidents of violence.

Mass shootings and other terrorist acts by white supremacists are extremely popular topics of discussion on forums like 4chan and 8kun as well as social media and chat platforms like Gab and Telegram. Traffic on these sites and platforms increases significantly in the immediate aftermath of supremacist violence (Wells & Lovett, 2019; Malevich & Robertson, 2020). Discussion of shootings ranges from comments on the death toll—praise when it is high and derision when it is low—to the soundness of the tactics employed by the shooter (Wells & Lovett, 2019). In appraising the El Paso Walmart attack, a commenter on 8chan stated, "The new guy deserves some praise, he reached almost a third of the high score" (Wells & Lovett, 2019, para. 44). The shooters themselves contribute to the discourse through both their active participation in online spaces and their active announcements of their intent and their actions; frequently referencing past supremacist mass shootings as direct inspiration or models for their activity (Cai et al., 2019; Cai & Landon, 2019; Wells & Lovett, 2019). The 2018 Pittsburgh synagogue shooter notoriously announced his attack on the Tree of Life Synagogue by posting, "I can't sit by and watch my people get slaughtered. Screw your optics, I'm going in," on Gab, the Twitter alternative social media site whose libertarian ethos provides a platform for supremacist users and content. Prior to his 2019 anti-Semitic attack on the Chabad of Poway, California, the perpetrator uploaded a manifesto to 8chan in which he praised the site for his radicalization and inspiration to action (Wells & Lovett, 2019). His post also contained a playlist of songs that would be streamed as he engaged in his rampage and a link to a Facebook live stream that he planned to use for the attack (Collins & Blankstein, 2019; Wells & Lovett, 2019). The pattern of activity on these forums and uploads of manifestos indicates an active engagement with the wider white supremacist community that participates on these sites and platforms. White supremacist mass shooters are therefore not merely consuming but actively engaging with the discourse that inspires their actions.

In white supremacist online spaces, the conspiracy theories of "the great replacement" and "white genocide" (as detailed by Friauf & Phillips, 2022, this volume) are taken seriously with out-of-context immigration statistics and news stories about crimes committed by immigrants and people of color being shared frequently. References to migrants from Latin America to the United States as well as Africa and the Middle East being inherently criminal and predatory are common, with terms like *rapefugee*, a portmanteau of *rapist* and *refugee*, being a favorite among users (Dafaure, 2020). These patterns of crime and immigration are explained as the product of a nefarious Jewish plot in both short quips and lengthy diatribes. In this context, the mass shooter is often discussed as a heroic figure willing to take a stand against "invaders" and the Jewish masterminds of the "invasion" (Burley, 2017; Dafaure, 2020; DeCook, 2018; Tischauser & Musgrave, 2020).

Unencumbered by serious content moderation or the need to filter or censor themselves, white supremacists on online forums and platforms express explicitly dehumanizing and violent sentiments. While much of the public-oriented supremacist discourse online seeks to engage in stigma management to provide wider appeal, movement-oriented discussions reflect the violence of its ideology. The conspiracies and celebrations of violence discussed above serve as a means of reinforcing movement beliefs, expressing bigoted attitudes, and providing a series of neutralizations for action (Klein, 2017; Simi & Futrell, 2010; Vysotsky & McCarthy, 2017). The discourse by white supremacists creates a culture where mass murder is not only condoned but encouraged. This cultural aspect is evident in the visual representations posted to forums and platforms in the form of memes and images of violence.

Memes and Mass Shootings

A key feature—and innovation—of the contemporary white supremacist movement is its deployment of visual representations online that reflect their ideology in the form of memes and images. Similar to the discourse discussed above, these visual expressions contribute to a culture that applauds mass shootings by deploying dehumanization, defining enemies, and celebrating ideologically motivated violence, including mass shootings and their perpetrators.

Much like the language used on supremacist-oriented forums and platforms, the visual culture of the movement seeks to denigrate and dehumanize people of color, Jewish people, Muslims, and LGBTQ+ people. Stereotypical images of historically marginalized people abound in supremacist online spaces, frequently taken out of context and presented as affirmation of the poster's and intended audience's prejudices. Similarly, memes trade on these types of images and add text either denigrating the subject of the image or reinforcing conspiracy theories. Memes that depict the criminal person of color or immigrant as well as bloodthirsty or violent Muslims reinforce racist and Islamophobic sentiments (Dafaure, 2020; Miller-Idriss, 2020).

Anti-Semitic conspiracy theories are similarly transmitted in memes that portray Jewish people as nefarious puppet masters behind any number of evils, with George Soros and Jacob Rothschild serving as particularly popular images of stereotypical Jewish power (Dafaure, 2020). Such depictions construct already vulnerable groups of people as an enemy consistent with the frames discussed above.

The stereotypical and dehumanizing depictions in images and memes are offensive on their own, but they exist in a visual culture that glorifies violence and encourages it among supremacist movement adherents. The white supremacist movement has a long history of depicting white men as heroic warriors in racial conflict that predates the modern internet (Daniels, 1997; Dobratz & Shanks-Meile, 1997; Ferber, 1999); however, these images have been amplified in recent decades (Bogerts & Fielitz, 2018; Dafaure, 2020; DeCook, 2018; Miller-Idriss, 2020; Simi & Futrell, 2010). Contemporary supremacist memes range from subtle violent references such as images of Knights Templar and the words *Deus Vult* (Latin for "God's Will" and a supposed battle cry of Crusaders) (Dafaure, 2020) to Holocaust imagery and accompanying text that either minimizes or celebrates it. Posting images of guns, ammunition, and body armor is a common practice on social media by far-right posters (DeCook, 2018). Guns and bullets are frequently adorned with supremacist slogans and coded language indicating the intended victims of these weapons.

If it is typical to celebrate violence in supremacist memes, then the mass shooting and its perpetrator are the ultimate depiction. Supremacist mass shooters are not just lionized in words as described above; they are canonized through images and memes that celebrate their deeds. The mass shooter who murdered nine worshippers at the historically Black Emanuel African Methodist Episcopal Church in Charleston, South Carolina, in 2015 is particularly noteworthy for his celebrity status in the online supremacist world. Memes that featuring his image and quotations from his brief manifesto, "The Last Rhodesian," depict him as a saint or religious icon, or encourage others to adopt his analysis or even actions are common in far-right online spaces. His distinct bowl haircut has been adopted by many of the right and is itself an image referencing racist mass murder. Groups of users and group chats on Gab, Discord, Telegram, and elsewhere use names like "Bowl Gang," "Bowl Patrol," and "Bowlwaffen" to signify their affinity for his ideas and actions. A short-lived podcast, the Bowlcast, explicitly discussed engaging in acts of mass violence and openly praised the Charleston and Pittsburgh mass shooters (Anti-Defamation League, 2019).

The memeification of the white supremacist mass shooting reached its apex with the mass shooter who killed fifty-one people at the Al Noor Mosque and Linwood Islamic Centre in Christchurch, New Zealand, on March 15, 2019. From the beginning, the attack was designed as a meme and readymade to reproduce on 4chan and 8chan. The Christchurch attacker's major innovation in supremacist mass shootings was the use of a Facebook live stream. The attack was broadcast live on Facebook, complete with musical soundtrack, and announced in a post on 8chan (Bart, 2020; Evans, 2019). Although only ten people watched the live stream of the attack, tens of thousands of copies of the video were shared on Facebook, Twitter, and YouTube in the days after the attack (Koh, 2019). While the major social media platforms were able to develop algorithms and processes for banning this video, it is still available to download on unregulated torrent sites and other video streaming sites with less content moderation. The artifacts of the shooting, specifically the perpetrator's weapons and manifesto, reflect many of the memes that circulate on 4chan and 8chan /pol/ forums, as well as supremacist social media. References to "Remove Kebab," a racist and Islamophobic song that celebrates genocidal violence against Muslims, were written on his rifle, featured in the musical soundtrack that accompanied his video live stream, and mentioned in his manifesto. Additionally, the manifesto includes a series of in-jokes and comments meant to be understood by supremacist fellow travelers online such as the reference to Candace Owens and the Navy SEAL copypasta (Bart, 2020; Evans, 2019). The ideological content of his manifesto similarly references the great replacement theory and eco-fascist conspiracy theories in its title and discussion of the Christchurch shooter's motivation (Obaidi et al., 2021; Weill, 2019), which are common far-right memes, as discussed above. The attack as meme comes full circle with the way in which anonymous posters on 4chan and 8chan constructed memes based on the shooter's actions. His "success" in the eyes of his ideological compatriots is evidenced by the reverence with which he is treated on supremacist forums and social media. Discussion of this attack generated an /ourguy/ thread in which posters argued about his ideological affinity with their white supremacy on 4chan, with one post calling him "the first mass meme shooter" (Bart, 2020, p. 38). Like the Charleston shooter before him, the Christchurch shooter was quickly elevated to "Saint" status, with memes rapidly appearing that portray him as a religious icon (Bart, 2020). By constructing his attack as a meme and its aftermath resulting in a flurry of memes among the far right, the Christchurch mass shooter successfully constructed a model to be reproduced by others.

The visual culture of the supremacist movement online reinforces the practice of ideologically motivated mass shootings. The memes and images circulated on far-right forums and social media serve to dehumanize groups of people who are ideologically constructed as inferior or dangerous and to be eliminated. These stereotypical images serve as a kind of target selection for supremacist violence by combining visual representation with ideological messaging. The visual culture of the far right further glorifies violence through active depictions of violence either through coded references or direct representation. Images of racist, anti-Semitic, and Islamophobic violence are common, as are images of individual poster's weapons. Combined with supremacist slogans, these images serve as threats and statements of violent intent. Finally, white supremacist memes and images celebrate and reproduce mass shootings and their perpetrators. Combined, these practices serve to venerate the mass shooting and shooter as heroic deeds performed by heroic men that is reflective of the core of movement ideology and strategy.

Mass Shooting as Ideology and Strategy

As the modern incarnation of fascist ideology, the beliefs of the contemporary far right are grounded in the violent suppression and ultimately elimination of people whom they deem as inferior. This eliminationist violence is, however, not simply a utilitarian progression from a desired goal, but a reflection of a core belief regarding the superiority of the violent individual. Supremacist ideology, rooted in fascism, views the person who uses violence to achieve domination over others as morally and spiritually superior and the embodiment of its ideals. Individual acts of violence then become a key component of far-right strategy as part of a "leaderless resistance" model that encourages lone-actor and small-cell terrorism in order to enact ideology, achieve movement goals, and inspire others (Belew, 2018; Dobratz & Waldner, 2012; Kaplan, 1997; Michael, 2012) and an accelerationist philosophy that encourages acts of violence to instigate a race war (Beauchamp, 2019; Gartenstein-Ross et al., 2020; Walther & McCoy, 2021). In this ideological and strategic context, the mass shooting becomes a crucial element of the supremacist tactical repertoire.

Supremacist movements share a fundamental commitment to violence that is consistent with fascist ideology. Classical fascism is predicated in centering violence as a defining characteristic of both social movements and the state. Whereas many movements view some form of violent action as acceptable as part of their tactical repertoire, for fascist movements, violence serves as not just a means but an end in and of itself. For adherents of fascist ideology, the ideal world is one where violence is venerated as the ultimate display of power and domination. War is venerated as the fulfillment of the historical mission of the state as well as the physical and spiritual superiority of the individual. Fascist movements envision all of life as a state of war and engage in violence as a means of achieving power and maintaining it when they gain control of the state (Berlet, 1992; Burley, 2017; Eco, 1995; Griffin, 1993; Paxton, 2004). In the movement phase of violence, fascists engage in street violence and violent crime as a means of intimidating their political opposition as well as demoralizing and controlling people whom they view as fundamentally inferior (Paxton, 2004). This phase is therefore marked by small-scale acts of interpersonal violence, "mission" bias crimes, and acts of lone-actor and small-cell terrorism (Belew, 2018; Burley, 2017; J. Levin & McDevitt, 2002; Paxton, 2004). The ideologically motivated far-right mass shooting, therefore, reflects many of the ideological aspects of violence embedded in fascist ideology.

In their public statements and manifestos, white supremacist mass shooters describe themselves as men of action who are willing to engage in violence to achieve their ideological goals. Whether it is the Pittsburgh shooter's final tweet discussed earlier in this chapter or the Poway shooter's claim that "there is at least one European man alive who is willing to take a stand against the injustice that the Jew has inflicted upon him," supremacist mass shooters consistently express the fascist belief that people willing to engage in violent action to achieve their goals are acting in accordance to the ideals of their ideology and movement. By targeting racial and religious minorities, white supremacist mass shooters engage in a type of "direct action" consistent with their belief systems in eliminating hated groups of people that they perceive as threats. The mass shooting operates as a distinct manifestation of white supremacist strategy.

Like many contemporary social movements, the white supremacist movement is a broad and diffuse conglomeration of individuals and organizations without central leadership of coordination. While classical fascism was organized around a strong central leader sustained by a cult of personality, contemporary far-right movements adhere to a leaderless resistance strategy that relies heavily on individual and small-cell action, instead of large, centralized organizations, to carry out acts of violence to inspire others to action and to achieve small-scale attacks on their ideological enemies. The links between actors who commit acts of supremacist violence are primarily ideological rather than organizational, with many sharing a common idea that inspires their actions (Belew, 2018; Berlet & Vysotsky, 2006; Burley, 2017; Dobratz & Waldner, 2012; Kaplan, 1997; Michael, 2012). Because of the decentralized nature of these types of actions, they frequently appear to be individualized acts of criminal violence; however, the perpetrators are linked by a core set of ideas and, increasingly, online networks of interaction (Bates, 2012; Gill et al., 2017; Gottschalk, 2020; Hamm & Spaaij, 2017). As a movement tactic, the mass shooting aligns well with the leaderless resistance strategy.

The leaderless resistance strategy is reinforced by a rise in the popularity of accelerationist philosophy within the far right. The supremacist perpetrators of mass shootings in the 2018–2019 surge either had ties to, explicitly referenced, or took inspiration from accelerationist beliefs. They frequently saw their actions as part of a greater strategy to hasten what they believe to be an inevitable race war (Beauchamp, 2019; Gartenstein-Ross et al., 2020; Walther & McCoy, 2021). The Pittsburgh mass shooter was active in online discussion forums that promoted accelerationism; and while he did not articulate this in a manifesto like other mass shooters, his final social media post is a nod to the philosophy with its explicit call to action. The perpetrator of the Christchurch mass shooting makes explicit reference to accelerationist principles in his manifesto, including a discussion of how his acts of mass murder will increase tensions between gun control advocates and gun rights supporters that will result in a civil war in the United States. In a section of his manifesto labeled "Destabilization and Accelerationism: tactics for victory," the Christchurch shooter states the following:

> True change and the change we need to enact only arises in the great crucible of crisis. A gradual change is never going to achieve victory. . . . Therefore we must destabilize and discomfort society where ever [sic] possible. . . . Destabilize, then take control. If we want to radically and fundamentally change society, then we need to radicalize society as much as possible. (B.T., 2019)

Inspired by these statements and actions, the mass shooters in Poway and El Paso pay tribute not only to their predecessors but also included accelerationist language in their manifestos (Beauchamp, 2019; Parker, 2020). The Poway shooter makes this explicit, stating, "I used a gun for the same reason that [the Christchurch shooter] used a gun. In case you haven't noticed we are running out of time. If this revolution doesn't happen soon, we won't have the numbers to win it. The goal is for the US government to start confiscating guns. People will defend their right to own a firearm—civil war has just started" (J.E., 2019). Similarly, the El Paso shooter begins his manifesto by declaring, "I support the Christchurch shooter and his manifesto," and his concluding section states, "INACTION IS A CHOICE. I can no longer bear the shame of inaction knowing that our founding fathers have endowed me with the rights needed to save our country from the brink destruction. . . . America can only be destroyed from the inside-out" (P.C., 2019). In this context, the actions of supremacist mass shooters are designed as much to provoke repression and conflict as inspire action among movement compatriots.

White supremacist mass shooters show many of the hallmarks of the leaderless resistance strategy and accelerationist philosophy. While there are no direct ties between them, all of the recent white supremacist mass shooters clearly adhered to a similar ideology. In keeping with the leaderless resistance strategy, all of the perpetrators indicated that their individual acts of violence are designed both to act directly against their ideologically defined enemies and serve as inspiration for fellow movement members to engage in acts of violence. Indeed, as individual acts, they are linked to each other through clear expressions of inspiration by past mass shooters and their actions through direct references to "Saints" like the Norway, Charleston, and Christchurch mass shooters. As indicated above, the reverence with which their actions are discussed further indicates the way in which a decentralized movement encourages acts of individual violence in service of its ideological goals. White supremacist accelerationist philosophy further encourages major acts of violence such as mass shootings to exacerbate contradictions and conflicts as well as increase tensions within society. These individual acts are therefore linked by their adherence to the leaderless resistance strategy and accelerationist philosophy.

Conclusion

The ideologically motivated mass shooting is a key component of the tactical repertoire of the white supremacist movement. Although mass shooting events by supremacist movement adherents are relatively rare, they are distinctly embedded in movement culture and reflect its ideology as well as strategy. Movement discourse frames the actions of mass shooters as heroic deeds in service of its ideology and goals. The visual culture of the supremacist movement not only encourages individual acts of violence but uniquely lauds mass shooters with titles such as /ourguy/ and Saint. The actions of mass shooters also reinforce movement culture by contributing to the discourse and meme culture popular on online forums and social media. As acts of mass violence against people whom the movement identifies as enemies and undesirables, shootings serve to reflect movement ideology. Mass shooters frequently indicate that they are acting in the service of conspiracy theories that are central to white supremacist ideology. Additionally, both the perpetrators of mass shootings and movement members contextualize these acts as part of an ideological imperative to engage in war and violence to demonstrate strength and domination. Finally, the mass shooting reflects the white supremacist strategy of leaderless resistance where actions taken by individuals and small cells are designed not only to express ideological goals but also inspire other adherents to action. While shooters act as individuals, they are embedded in movement networks (online and off), and their acts clearly serve as inspiration for other adherents. Taken as a whole, the mass shooting holds a key place in the tactical repertoire of the supremacist movement as reflected in its culture, ideology, and strategy.

REFERENCES

Anti-Defamation League. (2019, February 6). *Hardcore white supremacists elevate Dylann Roof to cult hero status.* https://www.adl.org/blog/hardcore-white-supremacists-elevate -dylann-roof-to-cult-hero-status

Bart, T. (2020). *Lone wolves, copycats and the chans: How anonymous, far-right online communities and their vernacular practices radicalize lone wolf terrorists* [Master's thesis]. University of Amsterdam.

Bates, R. (2012). Dancing with wolves: Today's lone wolf terrorists. *Journal of Public and Professional Sociology, 4*(1). https://digitalcommons.kennesaw.edu/jpps/vol4/iss1/1

Beauchamp, Z. (2019, November 11). *The extremist philosophy that's more violent than the alt-right and growing in popularity.* Vox. https://www.vox.com/the-highlight/2019/11/11/20882005/accelerationism-white-supremacy-christchurch

Belew, K. (2018). *Bring the war home: The white power movement and paramilitary America.* Harvard University Press.

Berlet, C. (1992, September 28). *Fascism!* Political Research Associates. https://www.politicalresearch.org/1992/09/28/fascism

Berlet, C., & Vysotsky, S. (2006). Overview of US white supremacist groups. *Journal of Political and Military Sociology, 34*(1), 11.

Bogerts, L., & Fielitz, M. (2018). "Do you want meme war?" Understanding the visual memes of the German far right. In M. Fielitz & N. Thurston (Eds.), *Post-digital cultures of the far right online actions and offline consequences in Europe and the US* (pp. 137–153). Transcript-Verlag.

B.T. (2019). The great replacement: Towards a new society [Manifesto from the 2019 Christchurch shooter].

Bubolz, B. F., & Simi, P. (2019). The problem of overgeneralization: The case of mental health problems and U.S. violent white supremacists. *American Behavioral Scientist,* 1–17. https://doi.org/10.1177/0002764219831746

Burley, S. (2017). *Fascism today: What it is and how to end it.* AK Press.

Cai, W., Griggs, T., Kao, J., Love, J., & Ward, J. (2019, August 4). White extremist ideology drives many deadly shootings. *New York Times.* https://www.nytimes.com/interactive/2019/08/04/us/white-extremist-active-shooter.html

Cai, W., & Landon, S. (2019, April 3). Attacks by white extremists are growing. So are their connections. *New York Times.* https://www.nytimes.com/interactive/2019/04/03/world/white-extremist-terrorism-christchurch.html, https://www.nytimes.com/interactive/2019/04/03/world/white-extremist-terrorism-christchurch.html

Capellan, J. A. (2015). Lone wolf terrorist or deranged shooter? A study of ideological active shooter events in the United States, 1970–2014. *Studies in Conflict & Terrorism, 38*(6), 395–413. https://doi.org/10.1080/1057610X.2015.1008341

Capellan, J. A., Johnson, J., Porter, J. R., & Martin, C. (2019). Disaggregating mass public shootings: A comparative analysis of disgruntled employee, school, ideologically motivated, and rampage Shooters. *Journal of Forensic Sciences, 64*(3), 814–823. https://doi.org/10.1111/1556-4029.13985

Cohen-Almagor, R. (2018). Taking North American white supremacist groups seriously: The scope and challenge of hate speech on the internet. *International Journal for Crime, Justice & Social Democracy, 7*(2), 38–57. https://doi.org/10.5204/ijcjsd.v7i2.517

Collins, B., & Blankstein, A. (2019, April 28). *Anti-Semitic open letter posted under name of synagogue shooting suspect.* NBC News. https://www.nbcnews.com/news/us-news/anti-semitic-open-letter-posted-online-under-name-chabad-synagogue-n999211

Dafaure, M. (2020). The "Great Meme War": The alt-right and its multifarious enemies. *Angles, New Perspectives on the Anglophone World, 10,* Article 10. https://doi.org/10.4000/angles.369

Daniels, J. (1997). *White lies: Race, class, gender, and sexuality in white supremacist discourse.* Routledge.

Daniels, J. (2009). *Cyber racism: White supremacy online and the new attack on civil rights.* Rowman & Littlefield.

DeCook, J. R. (2018). Memes and symbolic violence: #proudboys and the use of memes for propaganda and the construction of collective identity. *Learning, Media and Technology, 43*(4), 485–504. https://doi.org/10.1080/17439884.2018.1544149

Dobratz, B. A., & Shanks-Meile, S. L. (1997). *White power, white pride!: The white separatist movement in the United States.* Prentice Hall.

Dobratz, B. A., & Waldner, L. (2012). Repertoires of contention: White separatist views on the use of violence and leaderless resistance. *Mobilization: An International Quarterly, 17*(1), 49–66. https://doi.org/10.17813/maiq.17.1.3282448743272632

Eco, U. (1995, June 22). Ur-Fascism. *New York Review of Books.* https://www.nybooks.com/articles/1995/06/22/ur-fascism/

Evans, R. (2019, March 15). *Shitposting, inspirational terrorism, and the Christchurch mosque massacre.* Bellingcat. https://www.bellingcat.com/news/rest-of-world/2019/03/15/shitposting-inspirational-terrorism-and-the-christchurch-mosque-massacre/

Ferber, A. L. (1999). *White man falling: Race, gender, and white supremacy.* Rowman & Littlefield.

Ferrell, J., Hayward, K. J., & Young, J. (2015). *Cultural criminology: An invitation.* Sage Publications.

Friauf, B., & Phillips, M. (2022). White supremacy, frontier myths, the "great replacement" theory, and the making of American mass killers. In E. Madfis & A. Lankford (Eds), *All American massacre: The tragic role of American culture and society in mass shootings.* Temple University Press.

Futrell, R., & Simi, P. (2004). Free spaces, collective identity, and the persistence of U.S. white power activism. *Social Problems, 51*(1), 16–42.

Gartenstein-Ross, D., Hodgson, S., & Clarke, C. P. (2020, April 20). *The growing threat posed by accelerationism and accelerationist groups worldwide.* Foreign Policy Research Institute. https://www.fpri.org/article/2020/04/the-growing-threat-posed-by-accelerationism-and-accelerationist-groups-worldwide/

Gill, P., Corner, E., Conway, M., Thornton, A., Bloom, M., & Horgan, J. (2017). Terrorist use of the internet by the numbers. *Criminology & Public Policy, 16*(1), 99–117. https://doi.org/10.1111/1745-9133.12249

Gill, P., Horgan, J., & Deckert, P. (2014). Bombing alone: Tracing the motivations and antecedent behaviors of lone-actor terrorists. *Journal of Forensic Sciences, 59*(2), 425–435. https://doi.org/10.1111/1556-4029.12312

Gottschalk, S. (2020). Accelerators, amplifiers, and conductors: A model of tertiary deviance in online white supremacist networks. *Deviant Behavior, 41*(7), 841–855. https://doi.org/10.1080/01639625.2020.1734746

Griffin, R. (1993). *The nature of fascism.* Routledge.

Gruenewald, J., Chermak, S., & Freilich, J. D. (2013). Far-right lone wolf homicides in the United States. *Studies in Conflict & Terrorism, 36*(12), 1005–1024. https://doi.org/10.1080/1057610X.2013.842123

Hamm, M. S., & Spaaij, R. (2017). *The age of lone wolf terrorism.* Columbia University Press, eBook Collection (EBSCOhost). https://proxy.ufv.ca:2443/login?url=https://search.ebscohost.com/login.aspx?direct=true&db=nlebk&AN=1628732&site=eds-live

Holt, T. J., Freilich, J. D., Chermak, S. M., Mills, C., & Silva, J. (2019). Loners, colleagues, or peers? Assessing the social organization of radicalization. *American Journal of Criminal Justice, 44*(1), 83–105. https://doi.org/10.1007/s12103-018-9439-5

J.E. (2019). An open letter [Manifesto from the 2019 Poway shooter].

Kaplan, J. (1997). Leaderless resistance. *Terrorism & Political Violence, 9*(3), 80. https:// doi.org/10.1080/09546559708427417

Klein, A. (2017). *Fanaticism, racism, and rage online: Corrupting the digital sphere.* Palgrave MacMillan.

Koh, Y. (2019, March 17). Why video of New Zealand massacre can't be stamped out. *Wall Street Journal.* https://www.wsj.com/articles/why-video-of-new-zealand-massacre-cant -be-stamped-out-11552863615

Langman, P. (2020). Desperate identities: A bio-psycho-social analysis of perpetrators of mass violence. *Criminology & Public Policy, 19*(1), 61–84. https://doi.org/10.1111/1745 -9133.12468

Levin, B. (2002). Cyberhate: A legal and historical analysis of extremists' use of computer networks in America. *American Behavioral Scientist, 45*(6), 958–988. https://doi.org/10 .1177/0002764202045006004

Levin, J., & McDevitt, J. (2002). *Hate crimes revisited: America's war against those who are different.* Westview.

Malevich, S., & Robertson, T. (2020). *Violence begetting violence: An examination of extremist content on deep web social networks.* First Monday. https://doi.org/10.5210/fm .v25i3.10421

Michael, G. (2012). *Lone wolf terror and the rise of leaderless resistance.* Vanderbilt University Press.

Miller-Idriss, C. (2020). *Hate in the homeland: The new global far right.* Princeton University Press.

Obaidi, M., Kunst, J., Ozer, S., & Kimel, S. Y. (2021). The "great replacement" conspiracy: How the perceived ousting of whites can evoke violent extremism and Islamophobia. *Group Processes & Intergroup Relations*, 13684302211028292. https://doi.org/10.1177 /13684302211028293

Parker, J. (2020, February 4). *Accelerationism in America: Threat perceptions.* GNET. https:// gnet-research.org/2020/02/04/accelerationism-in-america-threat-perceptions/

Paxton, R. O. (2004). *The anatomy of fascism.* Alfred A. Knopf.

P.C. (2019). The inconvenient truth [Manifesto from the 2019 El Paso Shooter].

Shank, G. (1999). Looking back: Radical criminology and social movements. *Social Justice, 26*(2), 114–134.

Simi, P., & Futrell, R. (2009). Negotiating white power activist stigma. *Social Problems, 56*(1), 89–110.

Simi, P., & Futrell, R. (2010). *American swastika: Inside the white power movement's hidden spaces of hate.* Rowman & Littlefield.

Spaaij, R. (2010). The enigma of lone wolf terrorism: An assessment. *Studies in Conflict & Terrorism, 33*(9), 854–870. https://doi.org/10.1080/1057610X.2010.501426

Tischauser, J., & Musgrave, K. (2020). Far-right media as imitated counterpublicity: A discourse Analysis on racial meaning and identity on Vdare.com. *Howard Journal of Communications, 31*(3), 282–296. https://doi.org/10.1080/10646175.2019.1702124

Vysotsky, S., & McCarthy, A. L. (2017). Normalizing cyberracism: A neutralization theory analysis. *Journal of Crime and Justice, 40*(4), 446–461. https://doi.org/10.1080/0735648X .2015.1133314

Walther, S., & McCoy, A. (2021). US extremism on Telegram: Fueling disinformation, conspiracy theories, and accelerationism. *Perspectives on Terrorism, 15*(2), 100–124.

Weill, K. (2019, August 5). *From El Paso to Christchurch, a racist lie is fueling terrorist attacks.* Daily Beast. https://www.thedailybeast.com/el-paso-shooting-racist-lie-great -replacement-fuels-terrorist-attacks

Wells, G., & Lovett, I. (2019, September 4). "So what's his kill count?": The toxic online world where mass shooters thrive. *Wall Street Journal*. https://www.wsj.com/articles/inside-the-toxic-online-world-where-mass-shooters-thrive-11567608631

Wong, M. A., Frank, R., & Allsup, R. (2015). The supremacy of online white supremacists—an analysis of online discussions by white supremacists. *Information & Communications Technology Law, 24*(1), 41–73. https://doi.org/10.1080/13600834.2015.1011845

9

Violent Revenge, Derealization, and Deadly Violence

White Supremacist Websites and Mass Shootings

Simon Gottschalk, Daniel Okamura,
Jaimee Nix, and Celene Fuller

Introduction: White Supremacist Websites and Mass Shootings

In a 2018 interview, KKK leader David Duke remarked that "the internet will begin a chain reaction of racial enlightenment that will shake the world by the speed of its intellectual conquest" (Daniels, 2018). Unfortunately, he was correct. As the mass shootings at the Poway Chabad synagogue (2019), the New Zealand Christchurch mosques (2019), the El Paso Walmart (2019), the Gilroy Garlic Festival (2019), the Pittsburgh's Tree of Life synagogue (2018), the Charleston Emmanuel church (2015), and others attest, white supremacist websites have become virtual breeding grounds for ideologically motivated violence. In this chapter, we combine the scholarship on emotions in social movements and on interactions in online environments with the preliminary analysis of data we collected on white supremacist websites to examine the links between those websites and ideologically motivated violence. We focus on two interrelated features of these websites that seem especially relevant to understand ideologically motivated violence: they incite violent revenge and induce derealization.

Although most participants of white supremacist websites do not commit acts of domestic terrorism such as ideologically motivated mass shootings, it seems that many perpetrators of such crimes participate in those websites. For example, a recent Brookings Institute report finds that members of the Stormfront website have been tied to one hundred murders (Squire, 2019; see also Chan et al., 2015; Cohen et al., 2014). The mass shooters in Poway, Pittsburgh, Christchurch, and El Paso posted messages on white supremacist websites before committing their crimes (Conway et al., 2019), and some explicitly cited the Christchurch killer's manifesto—which was posted on another white supremacist website—as a source of inspiration (Dearden, 2019). As the mass shootings in Christchurch (New Zealand), Halle (Germany), Oslo (Norway), and others also indicate, the link between participation in white supremacist websites and mass shootings is not limited to the United States, and several white supremacist mass shooters around the world have drawn inspiration from violent acts and rhetoric originating here (Larkin, 2009). On more aggregate levels, research in Germany finds that hate crimes against refugees increase during periods of rising anti-refugee comments on a right-wing social media site (Müller & Schwarz, 2021). Similarly, a UN Human Rights Council fact-finding mission notes that "in Myanmar, military leaders and Buddhist nationalists used social media to slur and demonize the Rohingya Muslim minority ahead of and during a campaign of ethnic cleansing" (Laub, 2019). In the aftermath of the Poway mass shooting, *New York Times* journalist Warzel (2019) concluded:

> It's becoming increasingly difficult to ignore how online hatred and message board screeds are bleeding into the physical world—and how social platforms can act as an accelerant for terroristic behavior. The internet, it seems, has imprinted itself on modern hate crimes, giving its most unstable residents a theater for unspeakable acts—and an amplification system for an ideology of white supremacy that only recently was relegated to the shadows.

White supremacists are certainly neither the sole perpetrators of domestic terrorism nor the only social movement that uses the internet to promote hatred, fear, and sadistic fantasies of revenge. However, the Department of Homeland Security has recently concluded that they pose the most persistent and lethal threat in contemporary America (Swan, 2020). As FBI director Christopher Wray also testified in a congressional hearing, "racially motivated violent extremism, specifically of the sort that advocates for the superiority of the white race, is a persistent, evolving threat" (Bump, 2021).

Rapidly contaminating many societies (Albrecht et al., 2019), the white supremacist ideology has developed multiple strains that, in spite of their local inflections, present a set of core beliefs that meet many of Umberto Eco's fourteen criteria of "eternal fascism" (1995). As Simi and Futrell (2009, p. 92) summarize, participants of the white power supremacist movement:

> see themselves defending the white race from genocide by Jews and their "nonwhite pawns." Their utopian vision is of a racially-exclusive world dominated by Aryans where "nonwhites" are eliminated,

separated, or at least subordinated to Aryan authority.... Many support the vision of Aryan militarist nationalism that requires the creation and defense of an all-white, non-Jewish homeland. They also
abhor homosexuality, interracial sex, marriage, and procreation, and
tend to idealize conservative, traditional, patriarchal family forms and
community relations dominated by Aryan kinship.

White supremacists enforce rigid boundaries between whites and a wide variety of "enemies" whom they dehumanize, demonize, and paint as subhuman, weak, depraved, corrupting, devious, and posing a direct threat to whites
(see also Adams & Roscigno, 2005; Bhatt, 2021; Blee et al., 2017; Ferber & Kimmel, 2000; Jasper, 2011).

The mobilization of social movement participants against a perceived
threat from enemies deemed subhuman and dangerous is worrisome because
under certain conditions, it is more likely to lead to extreme violence (Berbrier, 2000; Simi & Windisch, 2020; Turner, 2009, 2007). For example, having accused imagined enemies of conspiring to engineer the great replacement and perpetrate white genocide (see Friauf & Phillips, this volume) as
well as other heinous crimes, the messages circulating on white supremacist
websites justify and celebrate extreme violence against them. A most infamous expression of this reasoning appeared in the last comment posted on
the white supremacist Gab website by the mass shooter at the Pittsburgh's
Tree of Life synagogue, just before he went on a killing rampage: "HIAS likes
to bring invaders in that kill our people. I can't sit by and watch my people
get slaughtered. Screw your optics, I am going in."[1] In addition, and regardless of the paranoid threats participants evoke to justify hate crimes against
so-called anti-whites, violence is always already prominent in the new Euro-
American fascism because, as Bhatt (2021, p. 47) notes,

Any ideology of organic inequality cannot but be animated by a meta-
physics of violence against those who are considered unequal. The long-
cultivated political ideology of "race war" thus becomes an imperative.... Fascist violence today is not typically directed against the state
or institutions but against people in civil society.

How does participation in white supremacist websites help explain members'
decision to perpetrate ideologically motivated extreme violence? We suggest
that a combination of two features of those websites may offer part of the explanation: they incite violent revenge and they induce derealization.

In psychology, the term *derealization* is often paired with *depersonaliza-
tion*, as both terms refer to a dissociative disorder where individuals perceive
their surroundings, others, objects, and self in distorted ways. Experiencing

a wall, veil, or screen separating them from their surroundings, they feel detached from them. People and objects appear as unreal, lifeless, muted, fake, "wrong," blurry, unnaturally sharp, too big, or too small. Sounds are distorted, too loud, or too soft, and time speeds up, slows down, or stands still (Spiegel, 2021). Here, we use the term *derealization* to refer to the perceptual distortions users experience in online environments. While every website will, by design, induce some degree of derealization in users (see Gottschalk & Fuller, 2021; Gottschalk, 2018), we are interested in the distortions that are unique to white supremacist websites.

The White Supremacist Movement on the Internet

For most of history, individuals have participated in social movements by joining "dense local networks" (Turner, 2007) that consist of physically co-present participants (Simi & Futrell, 2006b). In those networks, members develop frames that explain their predicament, interpret adverse individual experiences as collective victimization (see also Duffy, 2003; Jasper, 2014; Polletta, 1999, 1998), celebrate their slighted identity, paint a likely future, learn to aim their negative emotions on designated targets, and develop plans of action (see Snow & Benford, 1988; Snow et al., 1986).

Today, white supremacists meet, participate, organize, and mobilize also—and especially—online, on websites that form a vast, constantly updated, and hyperconnected network (see Albrecht et al., 2019; Awan, 2014; Bliuc et al., 2019, 2018; Burris et al., 2000; Klein, 2017; Martin, 2014; Simi & Futrell, 2006a, 2006b; Tufekci, 2018, 2017; Vysotsky & McCarthy, 2016, for example). Varying in foci, preferred targets, stridency, criteria for membership, digital architecture, political inflections, and sophistication of arguments, these websites disseminate the fables, frames, and fantasies distinctive of the white supremacist ideology (see Adams & Roscigno, 2005; Duffy, 2003; Gerstenfeld et al., 2003; Glaser et al., 2002). They provide instant and constant access to a growing library of documents in a wide variety of formats. Whenever members want to and wherever they happen to be, they can read, watch, download, listen to, or interact with those documents and purchase commodities that articulate the movement ideology.

Because they exist online, white supremacist websites provide members with new opportunities to literally connect to each other, to the local scene, and to the broader national and international movement. For example, in contrast to physical networks where participants must know about, locate, and access specific places where social movement–related activities occur, websites are accessible to virtually anyone and from virtually everywhere (see Gamson, 1996; Schrock, 2015). Similarly, if the physical places where social movement participants congregate are inevitably limited and limiting in terms of capacity and in terms of participants' needs for invisibility, anonymity, and privacy, those limitations no longer exist on websites. They can accommodate a quasi-infinite number of participants and can exist on a wide and flexible spectrum of visibilities (see Fielitz & Thurston, 2019; Futrell & Simi, 2004). Further, if physical places operate under time constraints (gatherings take place on certain days, during certain hours), websites are always open and across all time zones. These affordances also mean that participants can now be mobilized to gather online *at the same time*, regardless of their respective geographical location. More worrisome, as the 2017 Charlottesville "Unite the Right" rally and the January 6, 2021, U.S. Capitol attack demonstrate, large numbers of isolated participants (and their families) who are scattered across vast geographical areas can be quickly mobilized online to gather in the same physical place, at the same time, and launched against designated targets (see also Allbright, 2017; Schrock, 2015). Additionally, if members of physical social movements can only participate in one activity at a time (attending one particular meeting or another but not both), members of white supremacist websites can participate simultaneously in many activities on different websites, platforms, and devices.

These opportunities for constant and instant access significantly extend the global reach of the white supremacist ideology and increase its salience in participants' minds and lives. Having delegitimized official news channels as propaganda and having accused them of being complicit in truly aberrant conspiracies, the constantly updated texts circulating on white supremacist websites become for many members the exclusive source of information about social reality. Importantly also, constant and instant access to those websites and other members reinforces users' new collective identity, their feelings of community, of solidarity, and of siege. On those websites, individuals once stigmatized for harboring white supremacist beliefs, for claiming a white supremacist identity, or for advancing paranoid conspiracy theories can now feel proud, validated, empowered, and part of a powerful, global, and omnipresent network (Futrell & Simi, 2004; Simi & Futrell, 2006a, 2006b).

As we develop below, white supremacist websites have become much more than virtual spaces that complement participants' activities in physical spaces and that facilitate their access to valued resources. While those websites most certainly fulfill those functions, they also incite violent revenge and induce derealization. In concert, these effects escalate the risk that some members will commit ideologically motivated acts of extreme violence.

Inciting Violent Revenge

Hostile emotions are the main drivers of the violence found in phenomena such as gangbanging, genocide, terrorism (Turner, 2007), suicide bombing

(Brym, 2007), and ideologically motivated mass shootings, and chief among them is the thirst for revenge. Cota-McKinley et al. (2001, p. 344) define revenge as "the infliction of harm in return for perceived injury or insult or as simply getting back at another person" (2001, p. 344). Fueled by the anger, indignation, and hatred associated with perceived injustice, its goals include "righting perceived injustice, restoring the self-worth of the vengeful individual, and deterring future injustice" (Cota-McKinley et al., 2001, p. 344). Scheff (1994) suggests that revenge is often motivated by the experience of shame and the act of revenge seems to be its antidote (see also Scheff, 2000, 1988). Discussing emotions in social movements, Jasper also notes that "if pride for one's group is a central goal, humbling one's enemies is another. Especially after humiliations, revenge can become a primary goal" (2011, p. 290). Obsessive and irrational, revenge increases the risk of violence because *it attaches pleasure to aggression* (Turner, 2007, p. 525; see also TenHouten, 2017; Van Ness & Summers-Effler, 2019).

Like many other websites, white supremacist ones enable participants to interact near synchronously with each other via texts, images, and video clips under conditions of invisibility and anonymity. It is generally established that individuals interacting on text-based platforms that afford anonymity and invisibility tend to be less inhibited than in face-to-face encounters or in more traditional forms of written communication (Gottschalk, 2018). This disinhibition is especially likely to occur on white supremacist websites because they routinely expose participants to messages normalizing hatred and sadistic violence and that, both explicitly and implicitly, incite them to follow suit. Thus, while "you can't link arms and sing 'We Shall Overcome' in cyberspace" (Gamson, 1996, p. 35), participants on white supremacist websites quickly discover that—under the double cloak of anonymity and invisibility—they can publicly express hitherto repressed sadistic fantasies of revenge against dehumanized and demonized culprits (see also Daniels, 2012; Klein, 2017; Tufekci, 2018). As they also realize, this public expression is not just inherently cathartic (Jasper, 2011, p. 296) but is also rewarded with instant and constant positive feedback (Conway et al., 2019; Scrivens et al., 2018) and even pleasurable and potentially addictive neuro-chemical reactions (see Simi et al., 2017). These experiences mend participants' self-esteem by replacing the isolated, self-censoring, and unremarkable individual with a powerful, heroic, and proud (but anonymous) "brother" bound to others by a sacred and righteous mission. Since participants seek self-enhancing feedback, they will naturally be motivated to increase not only the frequency but also the virulence of those negative emotions they convey to each other online.

The infamous 2012 Facebook experiment revealed that unaware users exposed to mild negative posts would quickly contaminate their networks with mild negative emotions (Goel, 2014; Kramer et al., 2014; Waldman, 2014).

Accordingly, one can only imagine the velocity and ferocity with which violent emotions such as revenge can circulate in white supremacist websites. Here, influential members can easily wage subtle but devastating "whispering campaigns" (see Shibutani, 1966, p. 99), propagate various types of "moral shocks" (Jasper, 1998, p. 409), or inject virulent "dread rumors" (Miller, 2004, p. 513) about severe and imminent threats into society's communication stream. More alarmingly, Daniels (2018) finds that algorithms on search engines and social media sites systematically manipulate the likelihood that increasingly extreme posts will circulate more broadly, thereby capturing participants' attention and stirring powerful emotions (see also Fisher & Taub, 2018; Klein, 2018). As the "Stop the Steal" accusation driving the January 6 Capitol riot also makes abundantly clear, a thirst for violent revenge that has been manufactured, circulated, and amplified on white supremacist websites can motivate individuals and organizations to actually organize, mobilize, and attack with deadly consequences.

This incitation to publicly embrace and verbalize vengeful emotions increases the risk that some members will act on them, for at least two reasons. One, because, as we saw above, the very ideology of white supremacist and other fascist ideologies bestows the ultimate honors not to those who talk (or post) but to those who act (see Adams & Roscigno, 2005; Bhatt, 2021; Simi & Windisch, 2020). To wit, on some white supremacist websites, mass shooters are quickly anointed as "saints" and sources of inspiration. Two, because, as we develop in the next section, the accelerating circulation of sadistic fantasies of violent revenge occurs in a virtual context that induces derealization.

Inducing Derealization

Individuals who entertain fantasies of violent revenge seldom act on it. According to sociologist Randall Collins, interpersonal violence rarely occurs because protagonists are typically restrained by the tension/fear barrier:

> For violence to happen, there must be situational conditions which allow at least one side to circumvent the barrier. . . . Contrary to our popular images of violence as something easy for people to do, violent threats most of the time abort—they do not get past the barrier . . . violence is emotionally difficult to carry out, and having a motivation is not enough. (2012a, p. 135)

While the tension/fear barrier includes protagonists' evaluation of the risks they run if they resort to violence (2012a, 2012b), substantial evidence suggests that participation in online environments prompts derealization—distortions in individuals' perceptions of their surroundings, objects, reality, others, and self. For example, as early as 1966, Joseph Weizenbaum—the creator of the crude ELIZA language-processing computer program—was dismayed to find that "extremely short exposures to a relatively simple computer program could induce powerful delusional thinking in quite normal adults" (Carr, 2011, p. 205). Fifty years later, Turkle remarks that the shift to simulation and immersion technologies in advanced sciences "can tempt its users into a lack of fealty to the real" (2009, p. 8; see also Rainie et al., 2017). Over the last five decades, a voluminous scholarship has explored how and what unique features of online environments prompt what kinds of perceptual distortions in users. Among those features that are especially relevant for our discussion, we note: instant and constant access and feedback, the experience of omnipresence, omnipotence, radical ephemerality, personalization, anonymity, invisibility, and the disconnect between gestures and their effects. In combination, these features distort how users experience self, time, space, physical reality, others, and their interrelations (Gottschalk & Fuller, 2021; Gottschalk 2018). As a result, they are logically more likely to assess information, situations, and risks incorrectly. It also bears remembering that the perceptual distortions users routinely experience in online environments do not magically disappear when they shut their computers down. Since interactions with computers can change brain architecture, and can do so relatively quickly (Carr, 2011), the perceptual distortions users experience when they go online and interact with others there can accompany them in—and shape—their face-to-face encounters as well. If, as sociologist Simmel famously noted, the urban environment prompted significant changes in city dwellers' mental and emotional life, there is no reason why we cannot grant online environments a similar effectivity.

Participation on pretty much any website will induce certain types of emotional orientations and intensities. What is distinctive of white supremacist websites and similar ones is a constantly updated logorrhea of messages that warn participants of existential and imminent threats posed by dehumanized culprits, and that celebrate violent revenge fantasies against them. In most social settings, these threats would be considered paranoid and the revenge fantasies would be considered psychopathic or criminal. However, by normalizing this content, by rewarding members who voice it, and by glorifying those who act on it, and by delegitimizing all other sources of information, white supremacist websites supplant the real with the imagined. To wit, some participants can and do "take exemplary acts" (Gamson, 1996) to influence others and publicize the movement. Those exemplary acts in turn go instantly viral, generate instant feedback, and encourage imitation in real life (Lankford & Madfis, 2018; Van der Vegt et al., 2020). Thus, the mass shooter at the El Paso Walmart introduced his manifesto by directly referencing the Christchurch mass shooter's manifesto, which was published on a white supremacist website (Dearden, 2019). Similarly, many Capitol rioters posted live selfies from the riot on social media, and the mass shooters at the Poway and Halle (Germany) synagogues posted live streams of their rampage, thereby merging online and offline domains. More alarmingly, shortly after the Poway synagogue mass shooter posted his manifesto on the 8chan website, users cheered, and the first response encouraged the mass shooter to "get a high score" (Collins & Blankenstein, 2019).

When participants' experiences of online derealization combine fantasies of violent revenge with the fear of an existential and imminent threat, their ability to correctly evaluate the plausibility, severity, and imminence of said threat, their role in the situation, and the real consequences of enacting their revenge fantasies will necessarily be compromised. With the rapid development of deep fakes and social bots, exposure to the violent revenge/derealization combination will likely increase in frequency, and so will the number of attacks and victims. Deep fakes are audio-visual depictions of people and events that never happened but that look compellingly authentic (Knight, 2018, p. 38). However, if the events depicted are fake, the emotions they arouse are all too real. In addition, the contamination of the online environment by messages prompting violent emotions and action will soon no longer require human intervention; social bots will be able to perform this work more precisely and efficiently than human beings. As Ferrara et al. (2016, p. 96) explain, "a social bot is a computer algorithm that automatically produces content and interacts with humans on social media, trying to emulate and possibly alter their behavior." Social bots can engage users in entertaining conversations, comment on their posts, and answer their questions. Others can search networks for influential people and capture their attention. They can infiltrate popular discussions, discern topics, produce responses, and amplify the visibility of misleading information. Others can "'clone' the behavior of legitimate users, by interacting with their friends and posting topically coherent content with similar temporal patterns" (Ferrara et al., 2016, pp. 99–100). While those scenarios sound admittedly farfetched, governments take them seriously (see Wardle & Derakhshan, 2017; Woolley & Howard, 2017).

Conclusions: Digital Limits

The messages circulating on white supremacist websites incite toxic emotions among its participants, especially the urge for violent revenge. Whether participants convert this urge into violent action depends in part on the intensity of their grievances and their evaluations of the threats they believe exist, of the risks they run by resorting to violence, and of the rewards they anticipate for doing so. However, in both content and form, this online environment degrades participants' ability to accurately evaluate the plausibility, imminence, and severity of invented threats, the support for their revenge fantasies, and the concrete consequences of enacting them. In this high-velocity and emotionally volatile environment, the urge for revenge can both "go viral"—as in the January 6 Capitol riot––and be activated in isolated individuals who embrace conspiratorial and apocalyptic orientations (Bhatt, 2021; Vysotsky & McCarthy, 2016) and whose capacities for reality testing have been compromised by overexposure to toxic messages (see Cohen et al., 2014). Those individuals are more likely to enact their violent revenge fantasies when the messages they are overexposed to dehumanize and demonize designated culprits, as such perceptual distortions deny them victim status (Vysotsky & McCarthy, 2016) and thus the possibility of empathy. This risk reaches the detonation point when the perpetrators believe that an existential threat is imminent, as they can now justify extreme violence as self-defense (see Berbrier, 2000; Ware, 2020). As the messages circulating on white supremacist websites also make clear, other participants will reliably celebrate this violence, find it inspiring, and bestow the perpetrators heroic status. Under those conditions, some individuals are more likely to enter what Collins calls the "tunnel of violence." Like derealization, it is defined as "perceptual distortions in the flow of time, vision, sound, and sense of self" (2012a, p. 131) and "an altered state of consciousness" (p. 137). Its entrance is on the computer screen, and its exit is in the street, the department store, the synagogue, the college campus, the mosque, and the church.

During World War II, the French government in exile in London was transmitting radio communiqués to French citizens and Resistance fighters about the course of the war, the landing in Normandy, and other critical information. On their end, the Germans were scrambling these transmissions by broadcasting looping noise signals. The messages that circulate on white supremacist websites and other similar platforms perform the same function as those signals. Here, however, they do not simply disrupt the transmission of important information with a recognizable "noise" signal. They transmit disinformation, accusations, conspiracy theories, and threats that negate the very foundations of the social contract. In contrast to World War II French citizens and Resistance fighters who could easily distinguish between looping noise signals and London communiqués, millions of people in our society can no longer do so—or no longer want to.

In an acceleratingly unstable social environment, one cannot underestimate the risks resulting from the combined effects of contagious vengeful emotions and derealization that are engineered on white supremacist websites. In light of recent hate-motivated mass shootings, COVID-19 disinformation, the January 6, 2021, Capitol riot, and the mounting threat of future ones, it does not seem unreasonable to demand that those websites that contaminate society's communication stream with conspiracy theories, incitation to violence, disinformation, and similar messages be disrupted or shut down. To wit, on November 27, 2018, the French government decided to block all access to the Démocratie Participative website—the French equivalent of the Daily Stormer and other sites of its ilk (Untersinger, 2018). In Germany, new laws impose severe punishments on those who peddle hatred online (Laub, 2019). Such interventions will, of course, not completely eradicate the contamination of society's communication stream by disinformation and incitation to violence. They will also inevitably arouse heated debates, especially in the American context, of First Amendment protections for hate speech. Nevertheless, they might at least disrupt the toxic processes driving the "fascosphere" and contain their destructive effects before it is too late.

NOTE

1. Hebrew Immigrant Aid Society. Founded in 1881 to assist Jews fleeing pogroms in Russia and Eastern Europe, HIAS now provides assistance to all who flee persecution.

REFERENCES

Adams, J., & Roscigno, V. J. (2005). White supremacists, oppositional culture and the world wide web. *Social Forces, 84*(2), 759–778.

Albrecht, S., Fielitz, M., & Thurston, N. (2019). Introduction: The rightward pressure. In M. Fielitz & N. Thurston (Eds.), *Post-Digital cultures of the far right: Online actions and offline consequences in Europe and the US* (pp. 7–24). Verlag.

Allbright, C. (2017, November 1). A Russian Facebook page organized a protest in Texas. A different Russian page launched the counterprotest. *Texas Tribune.* https://www.texastribune.org/2017/11/01/russian-facebook-page-organized-protest-texas-different-russian-page-l/

Awan, I. (2014). Islamophobia and Twitter: A typology of online hate against Muslims on social media. *Policy and Internet, 6*(2), 133–150.

Benford, R. D., & Snow, D. A. (1993). "You could be the hundredth monkey": Collective action frames and vocabularies of motive within the nuclear disarmament movement. *Sociological Quarterly, 34*(2), 195–216.

Benford, R. D., & Snow, D. A. (2000). Framing processes and social movements: An overview and assessment. *Annual Review of Sociology, 26*, 611–639.

Berbrier, M. (2000). The victim ideology of white supremacists and white separatists in the United States. *Sociological Focus, 33*(2), 175–191.

Berbrier, M. (2002). Making minorities: Cultural space, stigma transformation frames, and the categorical status claims of deaf, gay, and white supremacist activists in late twentieth century America. *Sociological Forum, 17*(4), 553–591.

Bhatt, C. (2021). White extinction: Metaphysical elements of contemporary Western fascism. *Theory, Culture & Society, 38*(1), 27–52.

Blee, K., DeMichele, M., Simi, P., & Latif, M. (2017). How racial violence is provoked and channelled. *Socio, 9*, 257–276.

Bliuc, A., Betts, J. Vergani, Iqbal, M., & Dunn, K. (2019). Collective identity changes in far-right online communities: The role of offline intergroup conflict. *New Media & Society, 21*(8), 1770–1786.

Bliuc, A., Faulkner, N., Jakubowicz, A., & McGarty, C. (2018). Online networks of racial hate: A systematic review of 10 years of research on cyber-racism. *Computers in Human Behavior, 87,* 75–86.

Brym, R. J. (2007). Six lessons of suicide bombers. *Contexts, 6*(4): 40–45.

Bump, P. (2021, March 3). FBI Director Wray reconfirms the threat posed by racist extremists. *Washington Post.* https://www.washingtonpost.com/politics/2021/03/02/fbi -director-wray-reconfirms-threat- posed-by-racist-extremists/

Burris, V., Smith, S., & Strahm, S. (2000). White supremacist networks on the internet. *Sociological Focus, 33*(2): 215–235.

Carr, N. (2011). *The Shallows: What the internet is doing to our brains.* New York: W. W. Norton.

Chan, J., Ghose, A., & Seamans, R. (2015). The internet and racial hate crime: Offline spillovers from online access. *Management Information Systems Quarterly, 40*(2), 381–403. NET Institute Working Paper No. 13-02. Available at SSRN: https://ssrn.com/abstract =2335637

Cohen, K., Johansson, F., Kaati, L., & Mork, J. C. (2014). Detecting linguistic markers for radical violence in social media. *Terrorism and political violence, 26*(1), 246–256.

Collins, B., & Blankstein, A. (2019, April 28). *Anti-Semitic open letter posted under name of synagogue shooting suspect.* NBC News. https://www.nbcnews.com/news/us-news /anti-semitic-open-letter-posted-online-under-name-chabad-synagogue-n999211

Collins, R. (2004). *Interaction ritual chains.* Princeton University Press.

Collins, R. (2012a). Entering and leaving the tunnel of violence: Micro-sociological dynamics of emotional entrainment in violent interactions. *Current Sociology, 6*(12), 132–151.

Collins, R. (2012b). *Violence: A micro-sociological theory.* Princeton University Press.

Conway, M., Scrivens, R., & Macnair, L. (2019). Right-wing extremists' persistent online presence: History and contemporary trends. *International Center for Counter-Terrorism,* October. http://www.jstor.com/stable/resrep19623

Cota-McKinley, A. L., Woody, W. D., & Bell, P. A. (2001). Revenge: Effects of gender, age, and religious background. *Aggressive Behavior, 27,* 343–350.

Daniels, J. (2012). Race and racism in internet studies: A review and critique. *New Media and Society, 15*(5), 695–719.

Daniels, J. (2018). The algorithmic rise of the "alt right." *Contexts,* March 28. https://con texts.org/articles/the-algorithmic-rise-of-the-alt-right/

Dearden, L. (2019, August 24). Revered as a saint by online extremists, how Christchurch shooter inspired copycat terrorists around the world. *Independent.* https://www.in dependent.co.uk/news/world/australasia/brenton-tarrant-christchurch-shooter-attack -el-paso-norway-poway-a9076926.html

Duffy, M. E. (2003). Web of hate: A fantasy theme analysis of the rhetorical vision of hate groups online. *Journal of Communication Inquiry, 27*(3), 291–312.

Eco, U. (1995, June 22). Eternal fascism: Fourteen ways of looking at blackshirt. *New York Review of Books,* 12–15. https://interglacial.com/pub/text/Umberto_Eco_-_Eternal _Fascism.html

Ferber, A. L., & Kimmel, M. (2000). Reading the right: The Western tradition in white supremacist discourse. *Sociological Focus, 33*(2), 193–213.

Ferrara, E., Varol, O, Davis, C. Menczer, F., & Flammini, A. (2016). The rise of social bots. *Communications of the Association for Computer Machinery, 59*(7). https://doi.org/10 .1145/2818717

Fielitz, M., & Thurston, N. (Eds.). (2019). *Post-digital cultures of the far right: Online actions and offline consequences in Europe and the US.* Bielefeld: Transcript.

Fisher, M., & Taub, A. (2018, April 25). How everyday social media users become real-world extremists. *New York Times*. https://www.nytimes.com/2018/04/25/world/asia/facebook-extremism.html

Futrell, R., & Simi, P. (2004). Free spaces, collective identity, and the persistence of U.S. white power activism. *Social Problems, 51*(1), 16–42.

Gamson, J. (1996). Safe spaces and social movements. In J. A. Holstein and G. Miller (Eds.), *Perspectives on social problems* (Vol. 8, pp. 27–38). Emerald Group Publishing Limited.

Gerstenfeld, P. B., Grant, D. R., & Chiang, C. P. (2003). Hate online: A content analysis of extremist internet sites. *Analyses of Social Issues and Public Policy, 3*(1), 29–44.

Glaser, J., Dixit, J., & Green, D. P. (2002). Studying hate crime with the Internet: What makes racists advocate racial violence? *Journal of Social Issues, 58*(1), 177–193.

Goel, V. (2014, June 29). Facebook tinkers with users' emotions in news feed experiment, stirring outcry. *New York Times*. https://www.nytimes.com/2014/06/30/technology/facebook-tinkers-with-users-emotions-in- news-feed-experiment-stirring-outcry.html

Gottschalk, S. (2018). *The terminal self: Everyday life in hypermodern times*. Routledge

Gottschalk, S. (2021) Click, validate, and reply: Three paradoxes of the terminal self. In N. Ruiz-Juno, W. Gibson & D. Vom Lehn (Eds.), *The Routledge International Handbook of Interactionism* (pp. 99–111). Routledge.

Gottschalk, S., & Fuller, C. (2021). Derealization and infra-humanization: A symbolic interaction theory with digital technologies. In W. H. Brekhus, T. DeGloma, & W. R. Force (Eds.), *Oxford Handbook of Symbolic Interaction*. Oxford University Press. https://doi.org/10.1093/oxfodhb/9780190082161.013.3

Honneth, A. (1995). *The struggle for recognition: The moral grammar of social conflicts*. Polity Press.

Jasper, J. A. (1998). The emotions of protest: Affective and reactive emotions in and around social movements. *Sociological Forum, 13*(3), 397–424.

Jasper, J. A. (2011). Emotions and social movements: Twenty years of theory and research. *American Review of Sociology, 37*, 285–303.

Jasper, J. A. (2014). Constructing indignation: Anger dynamics in protest movements. *Emotion Review, 6*(3), 208–213.

Klein, A. (2017). *Fanaticism, racism, and rage online: Corrupting the digital sphere*. Palgrave-McMillan.

Knight, W. (2018). Fake America great again. *MIT Technology Review, 121*(5), 36–41.

Kramer, A. D. I., Guillory, J. E., & Hancock, J. T. (2014). Experimental evidence of massive-scale emotional contagion through social networks. *Proceedings of the National Academy of Sciences, 111*(24), 8788–8790. https://doi.org/10.1073/pnas.1320040111

Lankford, A., & Madfis, E. (2018). Media coverage of mass killers: Content, consequences, and solutions. *American Behavioral Scientist, 62*(2), 151–162.

Larkin, R. W. (2009). The Columbine legacy: Rampage shootings as political acts. *American Behavioral Scientist, 52*, 1309–1326.

Laub, Z. (2019, June 7). *Hate speech on social media: Global comparisons*. Council on Foreign Relations. https://www.cfr.org/backgrounder/hate-speech-social-media-global-comparison

Martin, J. A. (2014). Mobile media and political participation: Defining and developing an emerging field. *Mobile Media & Communication, 2*(2), 173–195.

Miller, D. (2004). Rumor: An examination of some stereotypes. *Symbolic Interaction, 28*(4), 505–519.

Müller, K., & Schwarz, C. (2021). Fanning the flames of hate: Social media and hate crime. *Journal of the European Economic Association, 19*(4), 2131–2167.

Mutz, D. (2018). Status threat, not economic hardship, explains the 2016 presidential vote. *Proceedings of the National Academy of Sciences, 115*(19), E4330–E4339. https://doi.org /10.1073/pnas.1718155115

Polletta, F. (1998). "It was like a fever . . ." Narrative and identity in social protest. *Social Problems, 45*(2), 137–159.

Polletta, F. (1999). "Free spaces" in collective action. *Theory and Society, 28*(1), 1–38.

Rainie, L., Anderson, J., & Albright, J. (2017, March). *The future of free speech, trolls, anonymity, and fake news online.* Pew Research Center. http://www.pewinternet.org/2017 /03/29/the-future-of-free-speech-trolls-anonymity-and-fake-news-online/Download ed 6/9/2017

Scheff, T. J. (1988). Shame and conformity: The deference-emotion system. *American Sociological Review, 53*(3), 395–406.

Scheff, T. J. (1994). *Bloody revenge: Emotion, nationalism and war.* Westview Press.

Scheff, T. J. (2000). Shame and the social bond: A sociological theory. *Sociological Theory, 18*(1), 81–99.

Schrock, A. R. (2015). Communicative affordances of mobile media: Portability, availability, locatability, and multimediality. *International Journal of Communication, 9*(0), 1229–1246.

Scrivens, R., Davis, G., & Frank, R. (2018). Searching for sings of extremism on the web: An introduction to sentiment-based identification of radical authors. *Behavioral Sciences of Terrorism and Political Aggression, 10*(1), 39–59.

Shibutani, T. (1966). *Improvised news: A sociological study of rumor.* Bobbs-Merrill.

Simi, P., Blee, K., DeMichele, M., & Windisch, S. (2017). Addicted to hate: Identity residual among former white supremacists. *American Sociological Review, 82*(6), 1167–1187.

Simi, P., & Futrell, R. (2006a). Cyberculture and the endurance of white power activism. *Journal of Political and Military Sociology, 34*(1), 115–142.

Simi, P., & Futrell, R. (2006b, August 1). White power cyberculture: Building a movement. *Political Research Associates.* https://politicalresearch.org/2006/08/01/white-power -cyberculture

Simi, P., & Futrell, R. (2009). Negotiating white power activist stigma. *Social Problems, 5*(1), 89–110.

Simi, P., & Windisch, S. (2020). The culture of violent talk: An interpretive approach. *Social Sciences, 9*(120), 1–16.

Snow, D. A., & Benford, R. D. (1988). Ideology, frame resonance and participant mobilization. *International Social Movement Research, 1*, 197–217.

Snow, D. A., Rochford, E. B., Worden, S. K., & Benford, R. D. (1986). Frame alignment processes, micromobilization, and movement participation. *American Sociological Review, 51*(4), 64–81.

Spiegel, D. (2021). *Depersonalization/derealization disorder.* Merck Manual. https://www .merckmanuals.com/home/mental-health-disorders/dissociative-disorders/deper sonalization-derealization-disorder

Squire, M. (2019, August 7). *How big tech and policymakers miss the mark when fighting online extremism.* Brookings. https://www.brookings.edu/blog/techtank/2019/08/07 /how-big-tech-and-policymakers-miss- the-mark-when-fighting-online-extremism/

Swan, B. R., (2020, September 24). *White supremacists are greatest terror threat* [DHA draft document]. Politico. https://www.politico.com/news/2020/09/04/white-suprem acists-terror-threat-dhs-409236

TenHouten, W. D. (2017). Social dominance, hierarchy, and the pride-shame system. *Journal of Political Power, 10*(1), 94–114.

Tufekci, Z. (2018). The road from Tahir to Trump. *MIT Technology Review, 121*(5), 10–17.

Turkle, S. (2009). *Simulation and its discontents.* MIT Press.

Turner, J. R. (2007). Self, emotions, and extreme violence: Extending symbolic interactionist theorizing. *Symbolic Interaction, 30*(4), 501–530.

Turner, J. R. (2009). The sociology of emotions: Basic theoretical arguments. *Emotion Review, 1*(4), 340–354.

Untersinger, M. (2018, November 27). La justice francaise ordonne le blocage du site raciste Démocratie participative. *Le Monde.* https://www.lemonde.fr/pixels/article/2018/11/27/la-justice-francaise-ordonne-le-blocage-du-site-raciste-democratie-participative_5389364_4408996.html

Van der Vegt, I., Mozes, M., Gill, P., & Kleinberg, B. (2020). Online influence, offline violence: language use on YouTube surrounding the "Unite the Right" rally. *Journal of Computational Social Science, 4*(1), 333–354.

Van Ness, J., & Summers-Effler, E. (2019). Emotions in social movements. In D. A. Snow, S. A. Soule, H. Kriesi & H. J. McCammon (Eds.), *The Wiley-Blackwell companion to social movements* (2nd ed., pp. 411–428). Wiley-Blackwell.

Vysotsky, S., & McCarthy, A. L. (2016). Normalizing cyberracism: A neutralization theory analysis. *Journal of Crime and Justice, 40*(4), 446–461.

Waldman, K. (2014, June 29). *Facebook's unethical experiment.* Slate. http://www.slate.com/articles/health_and_science/science/2014/06/facebook_unethical_experiment_it_made_news_feeds_happier_or_sadder_to_manipulate.html

Wardle, C., & Derakhshan, H. (2017). *Information disorder: Toward an interdisciplinary framework for research and policymaking.* Council of Europe.

Ware, J. (2020). *Testament to murder: The violent far-right's increasing use of terrorist manifestos.* International Centre for Counter-Terrorism. https://icct.nl/publication/testament-to-murder-the-violent-far-rights-increasing-use-of-terrorist-manifestos/

Warzel, C. (2019, March 28). Mass shootings have become a sickening meme. *New York Times.* https://www.nytimes.com/2019/04/28/opinion/

Wilkins, C. L., & Kaiser, C. R. (2014). Racial progress as threat to the status hierarchy: Implications for perceptions of anti-White bias. *Psychological Science, 25*(2), 439–446.

Woolley, S. C., & Howard, P. N. (2017). Computational propaganda worldwide: Executive summary [Working Papers 2017.11]. University of Oxford.

10

Mass Violence, White Empathy

How Media Narratives Shape Public
Sentiment on Mass Shootings

Scott Duxbury

oral panics refer to mass public concern surrounding a social problem perceived to pose a threat to social or moral order (Cohen, 2002). Typically, moral panics involve (1) identifying a new type of social problem; (2) connecting that social problem to a broader cultural, moral, or social issue; and (3) identifying a source of blame (Hier, 2008). Moral panics have appeared throughout history, ranging from Puritan witch hunts (Erikson, 1964) to comic books (Goode & Ben-Yehuda, 1994) and violent crime (Garland, 2008). The media plays a central role in stoking moral panic surrounding crime (Critcher, 2003). With the advent of the twenty-four-hour news cycle came a spike in the amount of news coverage directed toward crime (Enns, 2016; Miller, 2016). As Garland (2001) describes, the rise of crime news media has positioned victims' suffering center stage in public discourse, increasing crime salience and fear. Whereas crime was once regarded as an implied component of any social order, the centrality of victims' suffering drew rigid moral boundaries between "victims" and "offenders." The result is a cultural shift toward understanding criminal offenders as (1) morally inferior to "good citizens" and (2) a threat to moral order (Garland, 1997, 2001; Gottschalk, 2006).

Media coverage of moral panics often centers around the behaviors of a racial or ethnic "folk devil." The folk devil is a caricaturesque representation of a racial or ethnic minority group, portrayed to have different and inferior cultural practices and moral standards. The political or social influence of the folk devil is perceived to erode the moral fabric of a society, largely through the folk devil's involvement in whatever social problem is causing moral panic. Racial folk devils play an important role in moral panics surrounding crime. All the while that media coverage stokes crime fear, the imagery that crime news media circulates portrays black men as the typical perpetrator (Beckett & Sasson, 2004; Russell, 1998). The public thus tends to understand crime as a threat posed by an increasingly aggressive body of racial minorities (Duxbury, 2021; Peffley & Hurwitz, 2007; Quillian & Pager, 2001).

This has been the pattern for crime-based moral panics for much of the twentieth century. Victim suffering is placed center stage; minority offenders are blamed. Yet, mass violence has broken this trend. Despite diversity in the demographic profiles of mass shooters, media coverage of mass shootings overwhelmingly directs attention to white offenders. The prevalence of mass shootings in public consciousness and the historical racialization of moral panics point to a strange paradox. On one hand, moral panics thrive when blame is laid at the feet of a racial folk devil. On the other, the stereotypical image of a mass shooting perpetrator is white.

In this chapter, I argue that the "white folk devil" central to mass shootings results from careful boundary work. Public discourse often treats white mass shooters' motives differently from nonwhite shooters' motives by deploying specific types of media frames that attribute the causes of mass violence to a particular set of psychological strains, while these same frames are deployed less frequently to explain shootings with nonwhite perpetrators (Duxbury et al., 2018). The unique frames commonly used to explain white-involved mass shootings advance two outcomes. First, they cast violent behavior among white offenders as abnormal and in need of exceptional explanations. Second, by denying those same frames to offenders of color, the *absence* of comparable media frames reinforces the criminalization of racial minorities. I discuss policy recommendations for this dilemma that locate two sites of intervention: (1) changing media narratives on race and mass shootings to erase the double-standard; and (2) extending the same types of preventative school shootings policies that are common in affluent districts to address "routine" gun violence in disadvantaged districts.

Whitewashing Mass Shootings

Judgments about what events can be categorized as a mass shooting can be ambiguous. And that ambiguity gives considerable power to claims makers, such as the media and political actors, about the causes of mass shootings as well as which groups are responsible. In the past, debates about types of deviance and appropriate policy responses have often been demarcated along racial lines. Historically, blackness has been associated with criminality from racial tropes surrounding black male hypersexuality (Russell, 1998), distorted crime statistics that inflate racial disparities in offending (Muhammad, 2010), excessive surveillance of black populations that make crime easier to record (Browne, 2015), and media coverage that directs disproportionate coverage to crimes with black offenders (Beckett & Sasson, 2004).

However, while media coverage tends to direct attention to crimes with black perpetrators, mass shootings are typically seen as a white phenomenon. The apparent consensus on the race of mass shooters overstates the homogeneity of offender demographics. Although mass shooters tend to be white, the demographic profile of mass shooting offenders is not much "whiter" than other forms of crime. Lankford (2016), for instance, studies 308 mass murders between 2006 and 2014. He finds that the racial composition of mass homicide is comparable to the racial composition of violent crimes at large. Although the racial profile of *public* mass shooters does tend to skew white, Lankford (2016) reports that even this difference is smaller than suggested by public discourse.

Rather than the racial profile of offenders, one distinguishing feature between mass shootings and other forms of gun violence is how each type of crime is *described* in public discourse. Although coverage of some shootings in the immediate aftermath of the September 11 attacks tended to describe the shootings as domestic terrorism (Altheide, 2009), the long-term effect of the War on Terror was that domestic terrorism was rarely used as a label for later shootings during the twenty-first century.[1] As Maguire et al. (2002) show, although labels of domestic terrorism were common between the car bombings of Timothy McVeigh in 1993 and 9/11, media coverage rarely labeled mass shootings as domestic terrorism after 2003. Schoon and Beck (2021), for instance, recently found that, controlling for variation in tactical repertoires, formal designations by overseeing governments, and ideological leanings of organizations, one of the strongest predictors of whether news media describe militant organizations as terrorists is whether the organization is Islamic. Similar processes have been observed in research on gang violence, where media frames that describe gun violence as gang related tend to be deployed when offenders are black or Latinx (see Linnemann & McClanahan, 2017; Metcalf, 2012). Chen et al. (2015) report experimental evidence consistent with these results, finding that respondents are more likely to attribute mass shootings to mental illness when the race of the shooter is experimentally manipulated to be white as compared to Asian American.

My coauthors and I tested the impact of race on media frames of mass shootings (Duxbury et al., 2018). We compiled a stratified random sample of 433 news stories covering 219 mass shootings between 2013 and 2015, where mass shootings were defined as shootings involving four or more injured or killed victims. We coded each document as either expressing (1) no frame to explain the cause of the shooting; (2) framing the violence as stemming from the perpetrator's mental illness; or (3) stemming from gang violence. Consistent with Chen et al. (2015), we found that white shooters were far more likely to be framed as mentally ill, while black shooters were far more likely to be framed as involved in gang violence. But what was striking was that there was no association between the gang violence and mental illness frames. What this means is that stories that portrayed shooters as mentally ill were no more or less likely to portray the shooting as gang related, and vice versa. Race, rather than gang affiliation, emerged as a key determinant.

This prior research tells us two things about media coverage of mass violence. The first is that disproportionate media coverage of white mass shooters creates a misperception that mass shootings are overwhelmingly white phenomena. While it is true that the recent increase in mass shootings is partly attributable to a resurgence of white supremacist ideology (e.g., Friauf & Phillips, 2022, this volume; Vyotsky, 2022, this volume), the racial profile of mass murderers—when all types of this crime are considered, not only public attackers—is not substantially different from the racial profile of violent crime at large. Second, because media coverage tends to coalesce around singular frames, rather than more complex and multicausal explanations, and because mental illness is typically used to explain white shooters' motivations, media narratives contribute to a rhetorical framework that invokes distinct explanations for white mass shooters' motivations.

The Symbolic Boundaries of Mental Illness

Why is there racial variation in mental illness narratives of mass violence? Although historically mental illness has been stigmatizing and often used to discredit the legitimate political frustrations of marginalized groups, such as women and black people (e.g., Metzl, 2010), medical narratives tend now to be assigned when news coverage emphasizes the *sympathetic characteristics* of the offender. By assigning a mental illness narrative to mass shootings and by using this explanatory frame to distinguish the causes of mass violence from competing explanations—such as gang violence or domestic terrorism[2]—public discourse tends to circulate narratives that cast white mass shooters as empathetic characters, while simultaneously denying similar treatment to offenders of color.

Peter Conrad (2007) first described the medicalization of social problems to explain how certain types of deviance get lumped under the umbrella of medical intervention. A line of research in medicalization has shown that the boundaries of mental illness are particularly slippery and often deployed to competing ends. Although medicalization is sometimes used as a political weapon to discredit minorities (Metzl & MacLeish, 2015), it is generally a weaker form of state oversight than criminalization, largely because medicine is a more autonomous social institution. Further, while mental illness stigma has steadily declined in recent decades (Corrigan & Fong, 2014), criminal stigma has only become more salient and more stigmatizing (Blumstein & Nakamura, 2009; Pager, 2007).

When used to explain the causes of white deviance, mental illness enables more preventative and less punitive responses to crime than is allowed for nonwhite deviance. The most explicit evidence of this dynamic comes from Lindsay and Vuolo's (2021) recent study. Lindsay and Vuolo (2021) examined rhetoric surrounding the crack cocaine epidemic in the 1980s and rhetoric surrounding the current opioid epidemic. They found that public discourse on crack cocaine frequently used racialized rhetoric and a criminal justice lens, while contemporary opioid discourse tends to deploy a public health narrative and use race-neutral sympathetic language. Next, Lindsay and Vuolo (2021) fielded a survey experiment to evaluate whether respondents were more likely to support treatment or criminal justice intervention when the race of the drug offender was experimentally manipulated. Results showed that support for criminal justice intervention increased for black drug offenders, but most respondents preferred treatment-oriented interventions for white drug offenders. Consequently, even after controlling for the *type* of drug in vignettes (crack cocaine or opioids), respondents were more likely to prefer treatment-based interventions for white drug users, while respondents preferred criminal justice interventions for black drug users (see also Hansen & Roberts, 2012).

By promoting mental illness as a causal explanation, media narratives circulate unique types of rhetoric that are typically denied to nonwhite offenders. In fact, when media coverage labels mass shooters as mentally ill, four types of themes tend to emerge: a shooter is described as (1) a victim of society; (2) having a generally good or sympathetic character; (3) the shooting being out of character for the offender; and (4) being from a good environment (Duxbury et al., 2018). What is striking about this type of discourse is how offender centered it is. While crime news coverage tends to be victim-centric—especially when offenders are nonwhite (Beckett & Sasson, 2004; Garland, 2001)—mass shootings coverage directs a surprising amount of attention to offenders' motives and their sympathetic characteristics.

What is even more striking is how this coverage breaks down by race. When we cross-tabulated the frequency of each of these four themes by race (Duxbury et al., 2018), we found that 77 percent of white shooters described as mentally ill were also characterized as victims of society, while another 41 percent of articles offered testimony to their generally good character. In contrast, for black shooters, the only theme expressed was the victim-of-society theme, and it only appeared in one of the six news articles that described a black shooter as suffering from mental illness. Black shooters, when characterized as mentally ill, were never described as having good character, were never presented as though the shooting was out of character, and were never characterized as coming from a good environment. Nor did any of these themes routinely appear in media coverage that attributed a mass shooting to gang behavior, which was the predominant frame in media articles covering mass shootings with black perpetrators.

These results underscore an important point. It is not only that mental illness frames are more commonly applied to shootings with white perpetrators. But when mental illness frames *are* deployed to explain shootings with nonwhite perpetrators, they are typically not associated with explanations that fixate on the exceptional nature of the shooters' motives. Although these findings are evocative, they are not surprising against the backdrop of research on the medicalization of deviance. When deviant behavior is associated with dominant racial groups, whether in the form of drug epidemics or mass violence, mental illness is used as a softer framework for social control than the criminal justice mechanisms and criminalization narratives typically deployed to regulate deviance associated with racial minorities.

Public Perceptions of Race and Mass Violence

How the public understands the causes of mass violence and the groups associated with it carries important implications for public opinion. Omi and Winant (1994) introduce the concept of "racial projects" to describe how various forms of state and public discourse impact collective understandings of race and behaviors associated with racial groups. Media discourse, including frames, narratives, and images circulated through news coverage, provides one of the dominant streams of information that the public obtains about crime and the groups that commit it (Enns, 2016). Media coverage has historically undermined public support for egalitarian racial policies by portraying black populations as underserving of governmental assistance (Kellstedt, 2003). Consequently, by portraying mass violence as abnormal when a perpetrator is white—but routine when an offender is nonwhite—media coverage of mass shootings contributes to broader racial projects that cast minority groups as violent and criminally threatening.

Although mass shootings are rare events, they draw disproportionate media coverage when compared with other forms of gun violence relative to their actual prevalence. Thus, the media narratives and frameworks used to describe mass shootings can impact public attitudes in important ways. Research in policy making describes how collective understandings of the urgency, relevance, and nature of social problems inform the speed with which social problems are handled and the types of policies promoted (Jones & Baumgartner, 2005). Consequently, racial caricatures that portray black people and populations as perpetually violent contribute to crime policies that disproportionately punish black offenders (Duxbury, 2021), increase support for racially disparate crime control (Creighton & Wozniak, 2018; Peffley & Hurwitz, 2007), and contribute to the perception that the mere presence of a black population is indicative of higher crime rates (Pickett et al., 2012; Quillian & Pager, 2001).

An emerging body of literature suggests that collective understandings of white deviance as preventable and nonwhite deviance as routine contribute to racial inequalities in punishment. For instance, Ramey (2016) finds that early childhood misbehavior is much more frequently addressed with counseling and medication among white schoolchildren, while black and Latinx schoolchildren are more frequently punished with suspension and expulsion. Further, Ramey (2016) finds that these early differences in how childhood misbehavior is handled partly mediate social control experiences in adulthood, where white adults are more likely to be involved in counseling while black and Latinx adults are more likely to be incarcerated, in part, because of differences in childhood social control experiences. Hansen and Roberts (2012) similarly argue that the public health orientation of opioid abuse policy and the criminal justice orientation of crack cocaine policy are primarily determined by the racial demographics of substance users.

Applied to the case of school shootings, this literature helps to explain variation in how school districts react to the threat of mass school shootings. Although schools have accelerated trends toward securitization in both affluent and nonaffluent districts since Columbine (Madfis, 2015), securitization in mostly white and affluent districts has been more frequently coupled with preventative measures, such as anti-bullying and bystander awareness programs, while similar preventive approaches are less common in the communities of color that experience so-called routine gun violence much more frequently. However, as many affluent, mostly white districts have poured money into anti-bullying programs, bystander awareness programs, and threat assessment protocols with the goal of preventing mass school shootings, poorer districts with largely nonwhite student bodies tend to be equipped with much more invasive securitization, such as metal detectors, security guards, and routine police presence (Hirschfield, 2008; Rios, 2011). These vulnerable populations are not only further criminalized through excessive securitization and criminal justice oversight (Drake, 2017) but also bear the brunt of community damage from "routine" gun violence, which takes many more lives than school shootings on any given year (Metzl & MacLeish, 2015).

As described by scholars such as Ramey (2016), Lindsay and Vuolo (2021), and Hansen and Roberts (2012), the tendency to address school shootings with preventative measures in predominantly white districts aligns with broader racial projects that cast white deviance as abnormal and preventable and nonwhite deviance as habitual. These collective understandings inform the behaviors of authority figures who mete out sanctions and policy makers who design responses to gun violence on school campuses, as well as contributing to broader public understandings of nonwhites as habitually violent. Although it would be erroneous to attribute the criminalization of black populations and medicalization of white deviance entirely to media coverage of mass violence—or even media coverage alone—the media possess unique influence by providing the public with most of its information about crime. Hence, media coverage plays an important, though often damaging, role in informing public understandings of race, mass violence, and, by extension, the types of policies that should be used to address violent crime and other social problems.

Conclusion

How authority figures, policy makers, and the public understand the prevalence of violence and the groups responsible for it impacts policy. Because mass shootings attract a disproportionate amount of media coverage relative to their prevalence, the media frames that cast white mass violence as abnormal play an important part in contributing to broader understandings of racial involvement in crime, its habitual nature, and how it should be addressed. The lack of emphasis on mental illness in media coverage of nonwhite mass shooters reinforces minority criminalization by carving out a medical exception for a type of violence widely understood to be a white phenomenon. These understandings carry implications for how gun violence is handled in nonwhite school districts and for public attitudes that impact a range of social disparities. Social policies should therefore focus on extending preventive interventions to disadvantaged districts that more frequently suffer from routine gun violence as well as imposing guidelines on how the media can describe mass shooters' intentions.

First, school shootings prevention policies should seek to extend preventative measures to majority nonwhite districts that are more frequently affected by gun violence. Proactive approaches, including anti-bullying and bystander awareness programs, should be broadened to include nonwhite areas under the understanding that such approaches avoid the excessive criminal justice contact that is far too common in predominantly nonwhite districts. By extending preventative interventions to nonwhite districts that are less gripped by fear of school shootings, gun violence policy can more effectively address the types of shootings that receive relatively less media attention while also offering the benefit of providing nonpunitive programs for single-victim school shootings and other forms of gun violence, which are far more common.

Second, policy should seek to impose guidelines on how media coverage can portray the racial demographics of mass shootings and describe shooters' intentions. These rhetorical frameworks shape public understandings of the prevalence of mass shootings, its causes, and how mass shootings should be controlled. They also carry consequences beyond mass shootings policy alone by reinforcing criminal stereotypes about racial minorities that impact a range of social policies (Duxbury, 2021; Kellstedt, 2003). Reforms that require broadcasting agencies to meet evidentiary standards to invoke mental illness explanations may help to combat the view that specific racial groups tend to commit mass violence only when suffering from mental illness. Independent review boards, such as Poynter and the Columbia Journalism School, and media ombudspeople that examine media coverage and attempt to hold media organizations accountable should review what narratives are presented to explain the causes of mass violence and what evidence is available to support those narratives. Third-party review offers an accountability check to validate media coverage against known facts about offenders' mental health and criminal histories and to establish criteria for evaluating when a particular narrative is being invoked in a racially biased manner. Directing attention away from *both* the "exceptional" nature of white mass violence and "routine" nature of nonwhite violence may go a long way toward redressing the criminalization of racial minorities in mass media and its associated impact on public attitudes.

NOTES

1. This may be changing, as white supremacist groups have increasingly committed racially motivated mass shootings in recent years and some media outlets have referred to these shootings as domestic terrorism. Despite this recent shift, the domestic terrorism label continues to be disputed depending on journal outlet, where conservative news sources like Fox News tend to eschew the domestic terrorism label for white supremacist shootings and liberal outlets tend to be more willing to espouse it. This stands in contrast to the mental illness frame described here, which appears regardless of the ideological leanings of news outlets (Duxbury et al., 2018).

2. Another commonly invoked causal narrative for mass violence is gun availability. As Carlson (2020, pp. 93–96) describes, gun culture is often invoked to competing ends: liberal political discourse frequently describes guns as enabling mass violence, whereas conservative political discourse often invokes mental illness narratives to direct political pressure away from gun control.

REFERENCES

Altheide, D. L. (2009). The Columbine shootings and the discourse of fear. *American Behavioral Scientist, 52*(10), 1354–1370.

Beckett, K., & Sasson, T. (2004). *The Politics of injustice: Crime and punishment in America*. Pine Forge Press.

Blumstein, A., & Nakamura, K. (2009). Redemption in the presence of widespread criminal background checks. *Criminology, 47*(2), 327–359.

Browne, S. (2015). *Dark matters: On the surveillance of blackness*. Duke University Press.

Burton, A. L., Pickett, J. T., Jonson, C. L., Cullen, F. T., & Burton Jr., V. S. (2020). Public support for policies to reduce school shoots: A moral-altruistic model. *Journal of Research in Crime and Delinquency, 58*(3), 269–305.

Carlson, J. (2020). *Policing the Second Amendment: Guns, law enforcement, and the politics of race.* Princeton University Press.

Chen, C. Y., Purdie-Vaughns, V., Phelan, J. C., Yu, G., & Yang, L. H. (2015). Racial and mental illness stereotypes and discrimination: Identity-based analysis of the Virginia Tech and Columbine shootings. *Cultural Diversity and Ethnic Minority Psychology, 21*(2), 279–287.

Cohen, S. (2002). *Folk devils and moral panics.* Routledge.

Conrad, P. (2007). *Medicalization of society: On the transformation of human condition into treatable disorder.* John Hopkins University Press.

Corrigan, P. W., & Fong, M. W. M. (2014). Competing perspectives on erasing the stigma of illness: What says the dodo bird? *Social Science Medicine, 103,* 110–117.

Creighton, M. J., & Wozniak, K. H. (2018). Are racial and educational inequities in mass incarceration perceived to be a social problem? Results from an experiment. *Social Problems, 66*(4), 1–18.

Critcher, C. (2003). *Moral panics and the media.* Open University Press.

Drake, S. (2017). *Academic segregation: The criminalization of "mediocrity" and the institutionalization of ethnic capital* [Dissertation]. University of California, Irvine.

Duxbury, S. W. (2021). Fear or loathing in the United States? Public opinion and the rise of racial disparity in mass incarceration, 1978–2015. *Social Forces, 100*(2), 427–453.

Duxbury, S. W., Frizzell, L. C., & Lindsay, S. L. (2018). Mental illness, the media, and the moral politics of mass violence: The role of race in mass shootings coverage. *Journal of Research in Crime and Delinquency, 55*(6), 766–797.

Enns, P. K. (2016). *Incarceration nation: How the United States become the most punitive democracy in the world.* Cambridge University Press.

Erikson, K. (1964). *Wayward puritans: A study in the sociology of deviance.* Wiley.

Frymer, B. (2009). The media spectacle of Columbine: Alienated youth as an object of fear. *American Behavioral Scientist, 52*(10), 1387–1404.

Garland, D. (1997). "Governmentality" and the problem of crime: Foucault, criminology, sociology. *Theoretical Criminology, 1*(2), 173–214.

Garland, D. (2001). *The culture of control: Crime and social order in contemporary society.* University of Chicago Press.

Garland, D. (2008). On the concept of moral panic. *Crime, Media, and Culture: An International Journal, 4*(1), 9–30.

Goffman, E. (1986). *Stigma: Notes on the management of spoiled identity.* Touchstone.

Goode, E., & Ben-Yehuda, N. (1994). Moral panics: Culture, politics, and social construction. *Annual Review of Sociology, 20,* 149–171.

Gottschalk, M. (2006). *The prison and the gallows: The politics of mass incarceration in America.* Cambridge University Press.

Hansen, H., & Roberts, S. K. (2012). Two tiers of biomedicalization: Methadone, buprenorphine, and the racial politics of addiction treatment. In J. N. Bingley (Ed.), *Advances in medical sociology, vol. 14, Critical perspectives on addiction* (pp. 79–102). Emerald Group.

Hier, S. P. (2008). Thinking beyond moral panic: Risk, responsibility, and the politics of moralization. *Theoretical Criminology, 12*(2), 173–190.

Hirschfield, P. J. (2008). Preparing for prison?: The criminalization of school discipline in the USA. *Theoretical Criminology, 12*(1), 79–101.

Jones, B. D., & Baumgartner, F. (2005). *The politics of attention: How government prioritizes problems.* University of Chicago.

Kellstedt, P. M. (2003). *The mass media and the dynamics of American racial attitudes.* Cambridge University Press.

Lankford, A. (2016). Race and mass murder in the United States: A social and behavioral analysis. *Current Sociology, 64*(3), 470–490.

Lindsay, S. L., & Vuolo, M. (2021). Criminalized or medicalized? Examining the role of race in responses to drug use. *Social Problems, 68*(4), 942–963.

Linnemann, T., & McClanahan, B. (2017). From "filth" and "insanity" to "peaceful moral watchdogs": Police, news media, and the gang label. *Crime, Media, and Culture, 13*(3), 295–313.

Madfis, E. (2015). "It's better to overreact": School officials' fear and perceived risk of rampage attacks and the criminalization of American public schools. *Critical Criminology, 24,* 39–55.

Maguire, B., Weatherby, G. A., & Mathers, R. A. (2002). Network news coverage of school shootings. *Social Science Journal, 39*(3), 465–470.

Metcalf, J. (2012). Reviewing "Monsters": The press reception and media constructions of contemporary street gang memoirs. *Crime, Media, and Culture, 8*(3), 333–353.

Metzl, J. M. (2010). *The protest psychosis: How schizophrenia became a black disease.* Beacon Press.

Metzl, J. M., & MacLeish, K. T. (2015). Mental illness, mass shootings, and the politics of American firearms. *American Journal of Public Health, 105*(2), 240–251.

Miller, L. L. (2016). *The myth of mob rule: Violent crime and democratic politics.* Oxford University Press.

Muhammad, K. G. (2010). *The condemnation of blackness: Race, crime, and the making of modern urban America.* Harvard University Press.

Omi, M., & Winant, H. (1994). *Racial formation in the United States.* Taylor & Francis Group.

Pager, D. (2007). *Marked: Race, crime, and finding work in the era of mass incarceration.* Princeton University Press.

Peffley, M., & Hurwitz, J. (2007). Persuasion and resistance: Race and the death penalty in America. *American Journal of Political Science, 51*(4), 996–1012.

Pickett, J. T., Chiricos, T., Golden, K. M., & Gertz, M. (2012). Racial composition and whites' perceptions of victimization risk: Do racial stereotypes matter? *Criminology, 50*(1), 145–186.

Quillian, L., & Pager, D. (2001). Black neighbors, higher crime? The role of racial stereotypes in evaluations of neighborhood crime. *American Journal of Sociology, 107*(3), 717–767.

Ramey, D. M. (2016). The influence of early school punishment and therapy/medication on social control experiences during young adulthood. *Criminology, 54*(1), 113–141.

Rios, V. (2011). *Punished: Policing the lives of black and Latino boys.* New York University Press.

Russell, K. (1998). *The color of crime: Racial hoaxes, white fear, black protectionism, police harassment, and other macroaggressions.* NYU Press.

Schoon, E. W., & Beck, C. J. (2021). Repertoires of terror: News media classification of militant groups, 1970 to 2013. *Socius: Sociological Research for a Dynamic World, 7,* 1–12.

Towers, S., Gomez-Lieven, A., Khan, M., Mubayi, A., & Castillo-Chavez, C. (2015). Contagion in mass killings and school shootings. *PLOS One, 10*(7). https://doi.org/10.1371/journal.pone.0117259

PART IV

Mass Shootings and American
Mass Media and Social Media

11

"I'll See You on National T.V.!"

America's Fame-seeking Mass Shooters
and Their Global Influence

JASON R. SILVA

Introduction

In the United States, fame is viewed as the ultimate marker of success (Gallup, 2019), and a desire for fame—solely for the sake of being famous—is one of the most-valued goals among young people (Twenge, 2014; Uhls & Greenfield, 2012). For those who wish to be famous, the yearning to be visible and valued is the biggest perceived appeal of fame (Greenwood et al., 2013). This pursuit of attention also coincides with a blurred distinction between fame (positive attention) and infamy (negative attention) (Wills & Lankford, 2019). Given the high demand for fame in America, and the comparatively low supply, the desire to be famous can lead to antisocial, deviant, and even violent behavior (Lankford, 2016; Twenge, 2014; Wills & Lankford, 2019). This is because individuals are aware that negative behavior often draws more attention than positive behavior (Lankford, 2018b; Wills & Lankford, 2019). In other words, some individuals would rather elicit a negative response from an audience than be ignored by society.

To this end, scholars illustrate the role of fame and infamy in driving mass shooter motivations. Concerningly, studies identify a rise in fame-seeking mass shooting incidents and casualties in the United States at the turn of the century (Lankford, 2016; Silva & Greene-Colozzi, 2019). To understand this rising threat, this chapter examines current research surrounding fame-seeking mass shooters in America, the potential influence of American media and culture on global mass shootings, and possible strategies for addressing these attacks. This area of mass shooting inquiry is particularly important given Lankford's (2016) predictions that the number of fame-seeking incidents will continue to grow, shooters will attempt to kill more victims than ever before, and they will innovate new ways to garner attention.

Fame-seeking Mass Shooters in the United States

Lankford (2016) conducted perhaps the first study of fame-seeking mass shooters and provided an initial list of perpetrators who sought infamy and glory through killing. Silva and Greene-Colozzi (2019) expand this initial study and highlight four criteria for characterizing and identifying fame-seeking motivations. These offender criteria include (1) direct statements about becoming famous; (2) seeking media notoriety via legacy tokens (e.g., letters or videos sent to the media); (3) posting online before the attack to capitalize on the attention they plan to receive; and (4) idolizing violent role models.[1] With this framework in mind, some notable examples of America's fame-seeking shooters are provided below, along with a discussion of the relationship between shooters and mass media in the United States.

Examples of America's Mass Shooters

A few months before the 2011 Tucson shooting, the offender (who suffered from suicidal ideations) posted on Myspace, "WOW! I'm glad I didn't kill myself. I'll see you on National T.V.!" Fame-seeking shooters sometimes make these explicit statements about their desire to be famous. In his suicide note, the 2007 Westroads Mall shooter stated, "Just think tho, I'm gonna be fuckin famous." The 2014 Isla Vista shooter stated, "Infamy is better than total obscurity . . . I never knew how to gain positive attention, only negative." The 1999 Columbine shooters discussed with one another about how "directors will be fighting over this story" and "whether it would be better if Steven Spielberg or Quentin Tarantino directed the film about them."

Making direct statements about wanting to be famous prior to the shooting can be risky for offenders planning their attack and hoping to avoid being thwarted. As such, offenders may also make statements during or after their attack. During the 2001 Burns security shooting, the offender forced a hostage to film the attack, stating he wanted to "go down in . . . history," he was going to put on "a hell of a show," and the slayings "should be good enough to last about a week on the news. It's time to feed the news media." In jail postattack, the 1992 Simon's Rock College of Bard shooter told other inmates he was "excited that he was getting attention from the news media" and he "hoped to be on television or have a movie made about what happened." These examples illustrate how fame-seeking shooters hope and anticipate that the mass media will tell their story.

American Mass Media Attention for Mass Shooters

Fame-seeking mass shooters and the news media have a symbiotic relationship (Silva & Greene-Colozzi, 2019). Fame-seeking shooters need media attention to fulfill their desire for notoriety. Since these offenders frequently experience social isolation, peer rejection, and general feelings of victimization (Silva & Greene-Colozzi, 2019), they view media attention as rightful recognition from a previously dismissive society (Langman, 2017). Profit-driven media outlets also utilize coverage of fame-seeking shooters to attract a consumer audience fascinated by sensational and violent forms of homicide (Duwe, 2000). While mass shootings receive more media attention than other forms of crime and homicide (Duwe, 2000), not all mass shootings are considered newsworthy (Silva & Capellan, 2019). Studies find characteristics influencing the newsworthiness of mass shootings include younger offenders, school locations, and a greater number of victims (Fox et al., 2021; Silva & Capellan, 2019). Given these characteristics often coincide with fame-seeking shooters, Silva and Greene-Colozzi (2019) find they receive heightened levels of media coverage. As outlined below, Lankford and Madfis (2018) address the consequences of this coverage, finding it (1) increases competition to maximize victim fatalities; (2) gives offenders what they want; and (3) leads to mass shooting contagion and copycat offenders.

First, mass shootings have unfortunately become a routine experience in America. To this end, the newsworthiness of mass shootings is largely dependent on the number of casualties (Fox et al., 2021; Silva & Capellan, 2019). To ensure media attention, fame-seeking shooters planning their attacks recognize they need to incur greater body counts than ever before. As the 2015 Umpqua Community College shooter noted, "Seems the more people you kill, the more you're in the limelight." As mass shooting death tolls continue to rise, it increases competition to maximize casualties and get the highest "score."[2] For instance, the Columbine shooters expressed their desire to cause "the most deaths in U.S. history." Thus, studies identify a rise in fame-seeking mass shooting fatalities at the turn of the century (Lankford, 2016; Silva & Greene-Colozzi, 2019). Ultimately, media attention provides a strong incentive to kill as many victims as possible by rewarding shooters who engage in especially deadly attacks.

Second, many shooters explicitly admit they desire notoriety and/or reach out to news organizations via submitted legacy tokens (Silva & Greene-Colozzi, 2019). For example, the 2007 Virginia Tech shooter sent his self-made video and manifesto to NBC News to draw further attention to himself and his actions. NBC decided to broadcast and publish portions of this material, which received enormous amounts of public attention. While this coverage can be informative for understanding the shooter mindset and overall phenomenon, when media outlets give fame-seeking shooters attention, they are helping them achieve their goals. For instance, the Umpqua Community College shooter discussed the 2015 CBS News shooter's actions in a blogpost, stating, "I have noticed . . . when they spill a little blood, the whole world knows who they are. A man who was known by no one, is now known by everyone. His face splashed across every screen, his name across the lips of every person on the planet, all in the course of one day." Ultimately, the Umpqua Community College shooter decided to carry out a mass shooting just a month after he saw the attention received by the CBS News shooter.

Third, the contagion effect suggests behaviors can "go viral" and spread throughout society like a disease, increasing the likelihood of their occurrence in the short and long term (Lankford & Madfis, 2018, p. 264). In other words, glorified, excessive, and sensationalistic media attention increases the likelihood of subsequent mass shootings and copycat incidents. The copycat effect refers to individuals imitating another shooter's modeled behavior (Lankford & Madfis, 2018). When fame-seeking shooters receive extensive media attention, their celebrity can turn them into role models (Langman, 2017; Wills & Lankford, 2019). The 2012 Sandy Hook shooter noticed this when suggesting, "Just look at how many fans you can find for all different types of mass murderers . . . and beyond these fans are countless more people who can sympathize with them." Impressionable individuals idolizing mass shooters may in turn copy these behaviors and commit their own mass shooting (Follman & Andrews, 2015; Langman, 2018). Langman (2018) suggests the news media publicity given to violent role models legitimizes violence and provides a road map for engaging in an attack. For instance, the Sandy Hook shooter created a spreadsheet detailing hundreds of mass murder incidents and ranking their casualties. This emphasizes his idolization of previous shooters and recognition that casualty counts generate attention. His research of previous shooters also served as a template for engaging in his own mass shooting.

Columbine offers the clearest example of fame-seeking role models, idolization, and copycat shootings. As one of the Columbine shooters predicted, "I know we're gonna have followers." Unfortunately, he was correct, as Columbine has sparked a subculture of "Columbiners" and copycats (Follman & Andrews, 2015; Raitanen & Oksanen, 2018). Follman and Andrews (2015) find the Columbine shooters inspired at least seventy-four copycat cases in the United States between 1999 and 2015; including twenty-one attacks and fifty-three thwarted plots. Peterson and Densley (2021) suggest an important reason for their specific cultural impact: Columbine took place at the advent of twenty-four-hour cable news and during "the year of the net." Unfortunately, it seems these advancements in mass media may also be influencing international fame-seeking mass shooters.

America's Influence on Fame Seeking in Other Countries

The United States has more mass shootings than any other country in the world (Silva, 2022); however, some of the deadliest mass shootings in the last decade occurred internationally, including the 2019 Christchurch mosque shooting in New Zealand, the 2019 Suzano School shooting in Brazil, and the 2011 22 July shooting in Norway. Like American mass shootings, these high-fatality international incidents were perpetrated by fame-seeking shooters. International fame-seeking shooters are a largely understudied area of inquiry. Nonetheless, preliminary findings suggest an international contagion effect brought on by the American media, the rise of the internet, and a growing global cultural desire for celebrity seeking.

The Global Reach of American Media

In our increasingly globalized world, American entertainment and culture have a powerful influence that stretches beyond U.S. borders (Crothers, 2021). For instance, the American-based news outlet CNN was at the forefront of international news, and in 2020, six of the ten most-visited English-language news websites were American media outlets (Majid, 2021). Similarly, the ten highest-grossing films worldwide in 2019 were all American made (Berkowitz, 2019). This mass media attention turns American celebrities into global stars who are recognized and revered around the world.

The rise of personal computers, the internet, and social media also makes it far easier for American culture to influence people around the world, without anyone having to leave the comfort of their own home (Crothers, 2021). American-based social media outlets, such as Facebook, Twitter, and You-Tube, have billions of monthly visits and are tremendously influential worldwide (Routley, 2019). These companies have also given rise to a new form of global celebrity: those who are only famous for doing things related to the internet (Djafarova & Trofimenko, 2019). And as many social media users learn, when people act out provocatively, immorally, or even dangerously, they often garner more attention (Wills & Lankford, 2019).

Unfortunately, the breadth of American media means fame-seeking shooters in the United States are being provided a global platform. After Columbine, the popularity of the internet enabled global online fan communities celebrating mass shooters (Oksanen et al., 2014; Raitanen & Oksanen, 2018). Media accounts of mass shootings fuel this subculture, with members participating in the circulation and re-creation of online media content and giving it new meanings (Raitanen & Oksanen, 2018). Mass shootings also generate "digital waves" of Twitter activity that result in trending topics, incident-specific hashtags, and the posting and sharing of millions of tweets around the world (Harb et al., 2020; Zhang et al., 2019). To this end, Lankford (2016) suggests a concerning prospect: as American media and entertainment culture continues to be exported to foreign countries, it may be accompanied by the idolization of fame and mass shooters, as well as international contagion and copycat effects.

Initial Findings on International Fame-seeking Mass Shooters

Studies find American mass shooters—particularly the fame-seeking Columbine and Virginia Tech school shooters—have inspired international mass shooters since the turn of the century (Langman, 2017, 2018; Larkin, 2009; Polland & Rosenburg, 2011). Larkin (2009) identified school shooters in Argentina, Canada, Finland, and Germany who imitated or referenced Columbine. Langman (2017, 2018) offers examples of international offenders idolizing and modeling previous American mass shooters. The 2011 Tasso da Silveira Municipal School shooter in Brazil idolized the Virginia Tech shooter, referring to him as a "brother"; and suggested that "like [the VT shooter], he was once weak and now is strong and will seek revenge for himself and others who like him were persecuted." The 2002 Gutenberg-Gymnasium School shooter in Germany researched Columbine online, discussed the shooting with friends, and was impressed with the shooters' execution of the attack. The shooter also made his fame-seeking desires particularly explicit when stating, "I'm going to be really big one day . . . [and] Everybody will talk about me." Even after two decades, Columbine is continuing to have a lasting influence on global fame-seeking mass shooters. Evidence indicates the 2019 Suzano School shooters[3] in Brazil were inspired by the Columbine shooters, were fans of Columbine-related American media,[4] and wanted to garner their own celebrity. As suggested by the Sao Paulo civil police director, the shooters "wanted to prove they could act like in Columbine High School, with cruelty, and with a tragic character, so they could be more recognized than even the Columbine killers" (Savarese & Prengaman, 2019).

The limited international fame-seeking mass shooter research that exists has primarily focused on school shootings. However, Lankford (2016) and Langman (2017) identify two nonschool fame-seeking shooters: the 2011 22 July shooter in Norway and the 2016 Olympia Shopping Mall shooter in Germany, who was inspired by the Norway shooter and conducted his attack on the fifth anniversary. Both shooters left behind manifestos (i.e., legacy tokens) that suggest they wanted to receive global attention. These manifestos (and additional evidence) indicate they drew inspiration from American mass shooters and terrorists. In terms of the latter, it is important to point out that they were also both interested in (and motivated by to varying degrees) far-right ideology. Lankford and Madfis (2018) emphasize the link between fame and ideological shooter motivations; both perform violence to gain attention and go viral. While these two shooters hoped to bring attention to their ideological cause, they also sought fame and attention for themselves. The recent 2019 Christchurch mosque shooter in New Zealand illustrates similar interconnected fame and extremist motivations, as well as the influence of American culture on international shootings. The shooter often researched and praised President Trump online and referred to him as a symbol of "renewed white identity" (RCI, 2020). His interest in far-right ideology led him to research the 2011 Norway shooter and the 2017 Quebec City shooter online. The Christchurch shooter came to idolize these attackers, even writing the Quebec City shooter's name on one of his guns, and he ultimately modeled their attacks.

The recent Christchurch mosque shooting offers support for the three predictions Lankford (2016) initially made about fame-seeking mass shooters. As noted, he suggests fame-seeking shooters will do the following: (1) attempt to kill more than past offenders; (2) innovate new ways to get attention; and (3) inspire other shooters, and subsequent shootings will continue to grow. First, the Christchurch shooter killed fifty-one and injured eight victims, and this is currently the third-deadliest mass shooting in the world. Second, the shooter was keenly aware of the power of the internet as an innovative method for furthering his celebrity. Before the attack, the shooter posted on the message board 8chan, stating, "Well lads, it's time to stop shitposting and time to make a real life effort post. I will carry out and attack against the invaders and will even live stream the attack via Facebook" (RCI, 2020). He ultimately offered a seventeen-minute Facebook Live stream of the shooting. The shooter also made his manifesto available online and emailed it to seventy different media outlets. Third, the high casualty count and innovative methods drew enormous media attention. This attention contributed to the Christchurch shooter's role model idolization, as well as global copycat offenders. His streaming of the attacks allowed users to respond in real time with comments such as, "He at least did something, that's respectable," and, "So what's his kill count?" (Wells & Lovett, 2019). The shooting inspired four subsequent copycat shooters in 2019, including two in the United States (California synagogue and Texas Walmart) and two internationally (Norway mosque and Germany synagogue) (Wells & Lovett, 2019). Both international shooters even modeled the Christchurch shooter by live streaming their attacks. Unfortunately, it seems that Lankford's (2016) predications for fame-seeking mass shootings in America also apply to the global phenomenon.

Strategies for Prevention

Traditional consideration for mass shooting prevention often focuses on gun control. However, the contentious nature of gun control in America has pushed scholars to examine alternative approaches for addressing the phenomenon.[5] Current strategies for addressing fame-seeking mass shootings include early identification of dangerous fame seekers and denying shooters attention.

Leakage, Warning Signs, and Threat Assessment

It is a misconception that mass shooters suddenly "snap" and start killing people (Lankford & Silva, 2021). Offenders are often involved in weeks, months, or even years of interest, fantasizing, and planning before committing a mass shooting (Levin & Wiest, 2018; Silver et al., 2018). This suggests there is an extended window of opportunity for threat assessment, intervention, and prevention (Lankford & Silva, 2021). During this time, shooters frequently exhibit identifiable warning signs and leakage of violent intent. Many fame-seeking shooters leak their intentions via concerning internet or social media posts (Wills & Lankford, 2019). Some even post on media platforms right before the attack to capitalize on the interest they plan to receive after the shooting (Lankford, 2016b; Silva & Greene-Colozzi, 2019). For example, the 2017 Pennsylvania supermarket shooter made explicit warnings on Twitter two weeks prior to the shooting and provided the details of his intended targets in a YouTube video. Identifying leakage appears to be a promising avenue for prevention. Silva's (2021) examination of foiled mass shootings finds one-third of offenders had fame-seeking motivations. In the pursuit of fame, they often leaked information about their plans, and their shooting plots were subsequently thwarted. For example, the 2018 Walter Johnson High School shooting plot was foiled after the offender posted an image of himself online with a gun stating, "Ha, ha, I'm going to shoot up the school." This emphasizes the value of promoting the FBI's "See Something, Say Something" campaign for preventing future shootings (Silver et al., 2018).

Leakage and warning signs do not always involve direct threats of a shooting plot. The use of the internet and social media to seek fame or attention has also become so prevalent in America that it may be difficult to know when intervention is necessary (Wills & Lankford, 2019). In other words, it is hard to differentiate "howlers" (those verbalizing threats without underlying intent) from "hunters" (those developing an actual plan to commit violence) (Calhoun & Weston, 2015; Silva & Greene-Colozzi, 2021). Nonetheless, Wills and Lankford (2019) illustrate potential warnings signs that can help identify those at risk of actually engaging in an attack, including making explicit statements, showing implicit signs of narcissism, loneliness, abandonment/

rejection, depression, suicide, conflict with family members, failure with love/romance/sex, anger against members of society, and having violent role models. While having at least one characteristic is common for many members of society who will never engage in a mass shooting, counting the number of warning signs for a concerning individual offers a method for gauging the likelihood a person poses a legitimate threat (Wills & Lankford, 2019). Future warning sign campaigns may want to highlight these characteristics as potential indicators of dangerous individuals. In general, research on threat assessment indicate threats that are more detailed, direct, developed, and actionable should be taken seriously (Calhoun & Weston, 2015; Madfis, 2020).

Denying Attention

Efforts to avoid shooter glorification and prevent future fame-seeking mass shootings often emphasize the importance of denying shooters attention in news and social media. To deny shooters their desired attention, Lankford and Madfis (2018) propose that news media outlets should stop publishing the names and photos of mass shooters. In other words, "Don't Name Them, Don't Show Them, But Report Everything Else." The No Notoriety movement and Don't Name Them campaign offer similar approaches to avoiding fame-seeking shooter glorification. The No Notoriety campaign suggests limiting the use of the shooter's name to once per article (as a reference point), and the name should never be in the story headline. They also suggest media outlets should refuse to broadcast or publish self-serving statements, photos, videos, and manifestos made by the shooter. Importantly, this altered reporting may deter future offenders from engaging in a mass shooting after recognizing they will not receive any attention.

Future research should continue examining strategies for avoiding offender glorification in the news media. Research should also consider the effectiveness of certain changes in coverage for reducing the fame-seeking problem. Mass shooting scholars largely rely on media coverage (a form of "open-source data") to examine the problem. Removing the offender's name, background, and contextual information from coverage may impact the extent of information scholars have at their disposal for investigating and addressing the phenomenon. Additionally, given the value of warning signs and leakage for thwarting fame-seeking shooter plots, eliminating coverage detailing offenders' lives could reduce the chances that those close to potential shooters would recognize similar warning signs and report them. Changes in media coverage need to ensure a balance between avoiding fame-seeking offender glorification and informing scholars and the public (Fox et al., 2021).

With the advent of the internet and social media, mass shooters can also make it difficult to keep their identities and self-serving content from spreading (Howells et al., 2022). Like most people in the modern age, shooters make social media accounts and message board posts that the public can directly access. As noted, some offenders specifically use the internet and social media to generate more attention to themselves and their actions. To address this concern, social media companies could assist efforts for denying attention by quickly disabling their accounts and removing their posts (Lankford & Madfis, 2018). Densley and Peterson (2019) suggest every violent message and image leaves a "digital fingerprint," and over time, internet algorithms should aim to flag mass shooter materials as they are uploaded to prevent them from being reposted. To further these efforts, some governments have even created legislation making it illegal to distribute videos of attacks and attackers. After the Christchurch shooting, New Zealand and Australia made it illegal to post the shooter's recorded live stream of the attack (RCI, 2020). Since then, numerous individuals have been arrested, charged, and imprisoned for distributing the video.

Using artificial intelligence to filter out banned internet content is not always effective, and potential regulations in the United States will be limited by the First Amendment. As such, the Don't Name Them campaign has extended beyond denying news media and social media attention, with calls for avoiding the offender's name and focus in political discourse. This approach received global recognition, with many government and law enforcement officials expressing their desire to deny mass shooters fame. After the 2016 Orlando nightclub shooting, the FBI director stated, "You will notice that I'm not using the killer's name. . . . Part of what motivates sick people to do this kind of thing is some twisted notion of fame or glory. And I don't want to be part of that . . . so that other twisted minds don't think that this is a path to fame and recognition" (Lankford & Madfis, 2018). After the Christchurch mosque shooting, the prime minister of New Zealand stated, "He sought many things from his act of terror, but one was notoriety—that is why you will never hear me mention his name" (RCI, 2020).

In conclusion, potential fame-seeking offenders planning a mass shooting may see the media and public notoriety given to previous offenders, which subsequently bolsters their own drive and motivations. However, scholars suggest planning a mass shooting plot is akin to daydreaming, and the enjoyment from premeditated mass violence often occurs during planning and preparation (Levin & Wiest, 2018; Silva & Greene-Colozzi, 2022). Levin and Wiest (2018) propose that for some shooters, "that dream ends the moment the event begins, and the reality is almost never as fulfilling as the fantasy" (p. 7). For example, the 2009 Larose-Cut Off Middle School shooter idolized the Columbine shooters, and he dreamed of engaging in a similar copycat shooting, developing detailed plans for his attack. But after firing one shot, he seemed to recognize the reality of his fantasized plan and committed suicide (Silva & Greene-Colozzi, 2022). Similarly, a 2012 offender planned to kill "at least 70 students" at the Waller High School's pep rally, with the goal of becoming the "biggest mass murderer in history." He had a fascination with mass shootings (particularly Columbine), he would "rank killers," and he fantasized about "some sort of violent act" nearly every day. He initially killed his family to spare them from dealing with the aftermath of his actions. However, the event became "all too real," and he gave up on his planned school attack, instead writing on the wall of his family home, "I will never forgive myself, I don't know why I did this." These incidents highlight the unique role media outlets can play in preventing potential fame-seeking shooters by forcing those daydreaming and planning a mass shooting to face this reality *before they attack*. The No Notoriety campaign suggests that instead of focusing on the offenders, the media should focus on the victims' names and backgrounds, as well as their tragic experiences and heroic actions during the attack. This altered form of coverage sends the message to potential shooters that victims' lives are more valued than shooters' actions.

NOTES

1. Comprehensive lists of fame-seeking offenders and their methods for garnering notoriety can be identified in four primary sources: Lankford (2016), Langman (2017), Silva and Greene-Colozzi (2019), and Wills and Lankford (2019). Unless referenced otherwise, all direct quotes from shooters in this chapter derived from these sources.

2. In online mass shooting forums like 8chan, users regularly refer to the death count in mass shootings as the *score* (Ailworth et al., 2019).

3. Like Columbine, the Suzano shooting involved co-offenders.

4. Initial reports suggest they were fans of the film *Elephant* (a fictional film loosely based on Columbine) and the *American Horror Story* television series (which features an episode inspired by Columbine).

5. Additionally, fame-seeking offenders often use illegal means for obtaining firearms (Silva & Greene-Colozzi, 2019). This suggests they may not be deterred by legislation limiting legal firearms sales.

REFERENCES

Ailworth, E., Wells, G., & Lovett, I. (2019, August 8). Lost in life, El Paso suspect found a dark world online. *Wall Street Journal*. https://www.wsj.com/articles/lost-in-life-el -paso-suspect-found-a-dark-world-online-11565308783

Berkowitz, J. (2019, December 16). Disney's dominance of the 2019 box office means its takeover of movies is complete. *Fast Company*. https://www.fastcompany.com/9044 3668/disneys-dominance-of-the-2019-box-office-means-its-takeover-of-movies-is -complete

Calhoun, F. S., & Weston, S. W. (2015). Perspectives on threat management. *Journal of Threat Assessment and Management, 2*(3–4), 258–267.

Crothers, L. (2021). *Globalization and American popular culture*. Rowman & Littlefield.

Densley, J., & Peterson, J. (2019, March 18). Terrorism is a performance. *Star Tribune*. https://www.startribune.com/terrorism-is-a-performance-don-t-watch/507322442/

Djafarova, E., & Trofimenko, O. (2019). "Instafamous"—credibility and self-presentation of micro-celebrities on social media. *Information, Communication & Society, 22*(10), 1432–1446.

Duwe, G. (2000). Body-count journalism: The presentation of mass murder in the news media. *Homicide Studies, 4*(4), 364–399.

Follman, M., & Andrews, B. (2015, October 5). How Columbine spawned dozens of copycats. *Mother Jones*. https://www.motherjones.com/politics/2015/10/columbine-effect-mass-shootings-copycat-data/

Fox, J. A., Gerdes, M., Duwe, G., & Rocque, M. (2021). The newsworthiness of mass public shootings: What factors impact the extent of coverage? *Homicide Studies, 25*(3), 239–255.

Gallup. (2019). *Success index.* https://populace.org/research

Greenwood, D., Long, C. R., & Dal Cin, S. (2013). Fame and the social self: The need to belong, narcissism, and relatedness predict the appeal of fame. *Personality and Individual Differences, 55*(5), 490–495.

Harb, J. G., Ebeling, R., & Becker, K. (2020). A framework to analyze the emotional reactions to mass violent events on Twitter and influential factors. *Information Processing & Management, 57*(6), 102372.

Howells, S., Parnaby, P., & Broll, R. (2022). Is No Notoriety enough?: Attaining micro-fame beyond the mass media. *All American massacre: The tragic role of American culture and society in mass shootings*. Temple University Press.

Langman, P. (2017). *Role models, contagions, and copycats: An exploration of the influence of prior killers on subsequent attacks.* School Shooters, Info. https://schoolshooters.info

Langman, P. (2018). Different types of role model influence and fame seeking among mass killers and copycat offenders. *American Behavioral Scientist, 62*(2), 210–228.

Lankford, A. (2016). Fame-seeking rampage shooters: Initial findings and empirical predictions. *Aggression and Violent Behavior, 27*(2), 122–129.

Lankford, A. (2018a). Do the media unintentionally make mass killers into celebrities? An assessment of free advertising and earned media value. *Celebrity Studies, 9*(3), 340–354.

Lankford, A. (2018b). Identifying potential mass shooters and suicide terrorists with warning signs of suicide, perceived victimization, and desires for attention or fame. *Journal of Personality Assessment, 100*(5), 471–482.

Lankford, A., & Madfis, E. (2018). Don't name them, don't show them, but report everything else: A pragmatic proposal for denying mass killers the attention they seek and deterring future offenders. *American Behavioral Scientist, 62*(2), 260–279.

Lankford, A., & Silva, J. R. (2021). The timing of opportunities to prevent mass shootings: A study of mental health contacts, work and school problems, and firearms acquisition. *International Review of Psychiatry, 33*(7), 638–652.

Larkin, R. W. (2009). The Columbine legacy: Rampage shootings as political acts. *American Behavioral Scientist, 52*(9), 1309–1326.

Levin, J., & Wiest, J. B. (2018). *The allure of premeditated murder: Why some people plan to kill.* Rowman & Littlefield.

Madfis, E. (2020). *How to stop school rampage killing: Lessons from averted mass shootings and bombings.* Palgrave Macmillan.

Majid, A. (2021, January 27). Top 50 largest news websites in the world. *Press Gazette.* https://www.pressgazette.co.uk/top-50-largest-news-websites-in-the-world-right-wing-outlets-see-biggest-growth/

Oksanen, A., Hawdon, J., & Räsänen, P. (2014). Glamorizing rampage online: School shooting fan communities on YouTube. *Technology in Society, 39*(1), 55–67.

Peterson, J., & Densley, J. (2021). *The violence project: How to stop a mass shooting epidemic.* Abrams Press.

Polland, S., & Rosenburg, S. (2011). Brazilian school shooting mirrors school violence lessons from around the world. *Communique, 40*(3), 12–13.

Raitanen, J., & Oksanen, A. (2018). Global online subculture surrounding school shootings. *American Behavioral Scientist, 62*(2), 195–209.

Routley, N. (2019). *Ranking the top 100 websites in the word.* Visual Capitalist. https://www .visualcapitalist.com/ranking-the-top-100-websites-in-the-world/

Royal Commission of Inquiry (RCI). (2020). *Royal Commission of Inquiry into the terrorist attack on Christchurch masjidain.* https://christchurchattack.royalcommission.nz/

Savarese, M., & Prengaman, P. (2019, March 14). Brazil police: school attackers imitating Columbine massacre. *ABC News.* https://abcnews.go.com/International/wireStory /brazil-wonders-school-shooters-kill-61671742

Silva, J. R. (2021). A comparative analysis of foiled and completed mass shootings. *American Journal of Criminal Justice, 46*(2), 187–208.

Silva, J. R. (2022). Global mass shootings: Comparing the United States against developed and developing countries. *International Journal of Comparative and Applied Criminal Justice.* https://doi.org/10.1080/01924036.2022.2052126

Silva, J. R., & Capellan, J. A. (2019). The media's coverage of mass public shootings in America: Fifty years of newsworthiness. *International Journal of Comparative and Applied Criminal Justice, 43*(1), 77–97.

Silva, J. R., & Greene-Colozzi, E. A. (2019). Fame-seeking mass shooters in America: Severity, characteristics, and media coverage. *Aggression and Violent Behavior, 48*(5), 24–35.

Silva, J. R., & Greene-Colozzi, E. A. (2021). Mass shootings and routine activities theory: The impact of motivation, target suitability, and capable guardianship on fatalities and injuries. *Victims and Offenders, 16*(4), 565–586.

Silva, J. R., & Greene-Colozzi, E. A. (2022). An exploratory study of failed mass shootings in America. *Security Journal, 35*(2), 367–399.

Silver, J., Simons, A., & Craun, S. (2018). *A study of the pre-attack behaviors of active shooters in the United States between 2000–2013.* Federal Bureau of Investigation.

Twenge, J. (2014). *Generation me—revised and updated: Why today's young Americans are more confident, assertive, entitled—and more miserable than ever before.* Atria.

Uhls, Y. T., & Greenfield, P. M. (2012). The value of fame: Preadolescent perceptions of popular media and their relationship to future aspirations. *Developmental Psychology, 48*(2), 315–326.

Wells, G., & Lovett, I. (2019). "So what's his kill count?": The toxic online world where mass shooters thrive. *Wall Street Journal.* https://www.wsj.com/articles/inside-the-toxic -online-world-where-mass-shooters-thrive-11567608631

Wills, A., & Lankford, A. (2019). Indicators of unhealthy fame-seeking and attention-seeking among public mass shooters and active shooters. *Journal of Campus Behavioral Intervention, 7*(1), 34–45.

Zhang, Y., Shah, D., Foley, J., Abhishek, A., Lukito, J., Suk, J., Kim, S. J., Sun, Z., Pevehouse, J., & Garlough, C. (2019). Whose lives matter? Mass shootings and social media discourses of sympathy and policy, 2012–2014. *Journal of Computer-Mediated Communication, 24*(4), 182–202.

12

Is No Notoriety Enough?

Attaining Micro-Fame beyond the Mass Media

Stephanie Howells, Ryan Broll,
and Patrick F. Parnaby

On May 3, 1999, *Time* magazine ran with "The Monsters Next Door: What Made Them Do It?" emblazoned across the cover. This question is posed underneath two large, colorful photos of the Columbine shooters. Bordering the photos of the killers are smaller black-and-white images of the thirteen people killed in the Columbine shooting. At the time, this cover was typical of reporting on mass killings like rampage school shootings, with a focus on the killers, the carnage, and the extreme violence. But, as research has demonstrated, this extensive focus on the killers and the details of their heinous crimes fueled their fame and led to copycat shootings (see, e.g., Meindl & Ivy, 2017).

The recognition that many mass killers desire fame has led to campaigns encouraging media to focus less on the killers themselves while highlighting the victims instead. Initiatives such as No Notoriety point out that infamy can arise from undue focus on the killers. No Notoriety thus calls for the mass media to "eliminate the gratuitous use of the name and likeness of rampage mass killers, and to shift the focus to the victims, heroes and survivors" (No Notoriety, n.d.a), arguing that the attention media provide serves as a call to action and that instead, the only message media outlets should be sending is that *"you will not receive fame in this way any more"* (italics in original; No Notoriety, n.d.a).

No Notoriety and other initiatives such as the FBI's Don't Name Them campaign have led to some positive changes in media reporting. Some mass media outlets, like *Time* magazine, have released covers highlighting the survivors of mass shootings without mention of those who perpetrated the killings. For example, on April 2, 2018, the cover of *Time* magazine featured a large image of five survivors of the Marjory Stoneman Douglas shooting in Parkland, Florida, and March for Our Lives Organizers. On top of the image of the five survivors, it says, "ENOUGH." The word *enough*—again in all caps, with a period at the end—was also featured on the cover of *Time* magazine in August 2019; this time the backdrop did not involve the perpetrator or the victims but instead was an artist's rendering of the locations of 253 mass shootings that had taken place in the United States to date that year (Felsenthal, 2019).

Time magazine's use of the term *enough* is a call for change because there has been more than enough gun violence, enough death, and enough terror. However, we wonder whether the push to remove information from the mainstream mass media through movements like No Notoriety is *enough* to deny mass shooters the fame that they often seek. Initiatives like No Notoriety are a laudable attempt to reduce media-inspired fame in mass media outlets, but they do not address the fame created on social media outlets. No Notoriety does acknowledge that "anyone can post anything, including themselves on the internet," yet their goal is to stop these killers from being highlighted with the mainstream mass media (No Notoriety, n.d.a). Given the plethora of alternative outlets that are coming to dominate the modern media landscape, focusing exclusively on legacy media, and not on social media, may not be sufficient to achieve the initiative's objectives.

Fame and celebrity can be established through venues other than the mainstream news media, including a variety of social media outlets such as Facebook, YouTube, Twitter, Snapchat, Instagram, Reddit, Tumblr, TikTok, and so on. And even if the killers themselves are not the ones posting the information or explicitly seeking fame (or infamy) through their actions, the very nature of social media and the global expansion of the internet allows for the information to be shared quickly and on a worldwide scale regardless of whether and how traditional news media report on the story.

In this chapter, we argue that a reduction in widespread fame through changes to news media reporting does not preclude mass shooters from acquiring micro-fame via social media. Similarly, we argue that those who are motivated to commit a mass shooting may seek out role models regardless of reporting changes within the mass media. We address the challenges associated with attempting to regulate social media content, especially in the American culture where the right to free speech is frequently touted. Finally, we provide recommendations for the future in the hopes of reducing the fame and celebrity of mass shooters on a global scale.

Micro-Fame and Contemporary Celebrity

The American problem of fame seeking, celebrity culture, and narcissism has been widely documented (see, for example, Bushman, 2017; Greenwood et al., 2013; Lankford, 2016). Some seek fame with the intention of influencing others—for worthy or unworthy reasons—and the media's free advertising makes this social influence possible (Lankford, 2018). America's ubiquitous desire for fame and celebrity status (see, Gamson, 1994; Lankford, 2016; Parnaby & Sacco, 2004) has been, in a sense, mapping itself onto a new set of structural conditions for more than two decades. During the late 1990s and early 2000s, the internet began to destabilize legacy media's gatekeeping role vis-à-vis fame and celebrity status (Marshall, 2020; Serazio, 2010). As new information technologies made content development and its networked dissemination cheaper and easier, mediatization and celebritization became individualized processes driven not entirely by the centralized and professionalized print, radio, television, and film industries but also by decentralized and enterprising amateurs (Khamis et al., 2017).

With user-generated content at its core, it was the arrival of Web 2.0, and social media platforms such as YouTube, Twitter, Facebook, and Instagram in particular, that set the stage for widespread "micro-celebrity" practices whereby users could stimulate their own popularity (i.e., their own "brand") through rigorous self-promotion (Giles, 2018; Khamis et al., 2017; Marwick & Boyd, 2010).[1] The potential audience is now nothing short of staggering, with sites like Facebook and YouTube boasting more than two billion active monthly users.[2] That represents more than one-quarter of the entire global population. Micro-fame is fame that is generated through the mediatization and celebritization processes on and through social media platforms. Thus, people can aspire to achieve online celebrity through their own self-promotion, but others may have micro-fame bestowed upon them even without their own social media accounts or direct involvement.

This new fame apparatus, now two decades into its evolution, allows for the acquisition of micro-fame by well-intentioned and industrious social media users but also by those with nefarious intentions. It is now well documented that in the past, mass shooters have sought to secure fame and notoriety, in part, by sharing their intentions, ideologies, and related manifestos with *legacy* media outlets before their crimes (see Lankford, 2016; Schildkraut & Elsass, 2016; Serazio, 2010). Mass shooters have explicitly shared their desire to be famous, often using the killing as their means to that end (Lankford, 2016). Some of these killers have directly reached out to media organizations, and some have attempted to increase the number killed or injured to garner media attention (Lankford, 2016; Lankford & Madfis, 2018).

As online fame and celebrity become more normalized, and as the news media engage in more responsible media coverage as called for by No Notoriety—such as by elevating the names of victims, limiting the name of the perpetrator, refusing to publish manifestos or other creations by the assailant, and so on—mass shooters have turned to social media to generate their own celebrity. For example, prior to killing seventeen people at Marjory Stoneman Douglas Highschool in Parkland, Florida, the assailant posted photos of himself with weapons and proclaimed that he wanted to be a "professional school shooter" (McLaughlin & Park, 2018) and that "you'll all know who I am" (CNN Wires, 2018). Similarly, prior to killing twenty in a rampage shooting at a Walmart in El Paso, Texas, in 2019, the killer posted his 2,300-word manifesto online (Arango et al., 2019). Also in 2019, the assailant in the New Zealand mosque shooting that killed fifty-one and left forty additional injured had posted his manifesto on Twitter (Jaffe, 2020) and then used a helmet-mounted camera to stream his rampage via Facebook Live. In fact, Peterson and Densley (2021) claim that fame-seeking perpetrators have increased since 2015, and their data demonstrate that since 1999, forty-four mass shooters engaged in social media use related to the shooting. Although legacy media may be the ultimate opportunity for mass shooters to achieve their desired "capital F fame: to have their names and faces featured everywhere and known to everyone" (Lankford & Madfis, 2018, p. 270), the use of social media prior to (or during) the shooting may allow mass shooters to reach their own audiences directly and achieve some measure of attention (Lankford, 2016; Silva & Greene-Colozzi, 2019b; Silva, 2022, this book).

But there is a second dimension of micro-fame and notoriety that is, in a sense, *bestowed* upon many mass shooters, sometimes within hours of their initial attack. Unconstrained by geographic boundaries, social media users converge in cyberspace to construct the perpetrator(s) in ways that suggest admiration, empathy, and sometimes romanticized heroism (Schildkraut & Elsass, 2016; Raitanen & Oksanen, 2018). As Gamson (1994) notes, "The publicity machine focuses attention on the worthy and unworthy alike, churning out many admired commodities called celebrities, famous because they have been made to be" (pp. 15–16).

Indeed, several fan communities exist on social media platforms that bring together those with a shared interest in mass shootings or other heinous events. These dark fandoms, or "communities of fans who identify with or otherwise celebrate those who have committed heinous acts, such as mass or serial murderers" (Broll, 2020, p. 795), are widespread online. Many of these online groups have formed after mass shootings. The No Notoriety initiative began after the 2012 Aurora, Colorado, movie theater shooting, when the father of one of the victims issued a challenge to Anderson Cooper to stop naming the killers (No Notoriety, n.d.b), yet an online community (referred to as "Holmies") exists, dedicated to the killer. Broll (2020) studied a "Columbiner" community (subreddit) on Reddit comprised of more than three thousand members who posted more than seven hundred comments over a three-month period. As of early 2022, a similar mass shooting subreddit (r/MassShooting) has about 1,300 members, a subreddit centered on posting and sharing crime scene photos (r/CrimeScene) has more than 207,000 members, and a serial killer dark fandom (r/serialkillers) boasts more than 529,000 members.

What was once left solely to journalists to decide whether and how to report is now also a challenge for the average citizen. Social media provides fame-seeking mass shooters a variety of outlets to share their manifestos and live streams with the opportunity to not only reach more people but also reach them much faster than traditional media outlets ever could. Users continue to "share," "like," "retweet," or otherwise engage with the posts and disseminate them further; mass killers in the twenty-first century may no longer need to rely exclusively upon legacy media outlets to share their names, images, or details of the shooting for them to garner fame.

No Notoriety and Social Media

The Challenge of Regulating Content on Social Media

If encouraging the mainstream media to adhere to the tenets of No Notoriety is difficult, then the task is exponentially more challenging on the internet and social media. Content posted on social media platforms is regulated by those platforms' "community guidelines," with content that violates those guidelines being removed (Hooker, 2019). For example, mainstream platforms prohibit the posting of hateful content, posts intended to harass others, and illegal materials (e.g., extremism, child pornography). Some, such as Twitter, also prohibit the "promotion of weapons and weapon accessories,"[3] and others, such as YouTube, prohibit instructing "viewers on how to make firearms, ammunition, and certain accessories."[4] Content posted by some mass shooters—or, posted by others who glorify the shooters' violence—may violate such policies. As Twitter's community guidelines note: "Glorifying violent acts could inspire others to take part in similar acts of violence."[5] Generally, social media companies have had success using artificial intelligence (AI) to detect and remove content that violates their policies—most videos removed from YouTube are taken down automatically, and nearly three-quarters are removed before they are seen by even a single user (Lapowski, 2019). Still, critics have charged that community use guidelines are applied arbitrarily, and there are countless examples of social media companies reversing their decisions to permit or remove content following public backlash (Hooker, 2019).

Beyond consistently enforcing their community guidelines, several other challenges exist when attempting to regulate social media content in the aftermath of mass shootings. First, whereas AI is largely successful at removing static content, it currently struggles to moderate live streams. When AI cannot resolve an issue that users have reported, it is usually turned over to human moderators to process, but this takes some time (Lapowski, 2019).

Second, in many ways, the success of social media platforms has yielded its own challenges. Originally intended to facilitate social interactions among friends and acquaintances, social media now fills many roles. For example, journalists track and disseminate information on Twitter, Facebook has become a popular news source, and former U.S. President Donald Trump regularly turned to social media to make official policy announcements while in office (Hooker, 2019). As such, the community use guidelines of internet giants like Facebook and Google include exceptions for newsworthy content (Lapowski, 2019). Robertson (2021) explains:

> Videos of murder have created a quandary for social network moderators who are tasked with distinguishing between meaningful journalism and content that could inspire copycat attacks or play into a killer's search for publicity. Platforms like Facebook and YouTube have scrambled to remove video directly recorded by mass shooters. . . . But, they've also been criticized for removing video documenting newsworthy events like police shootings.

Third, social media companies often disagree on the newsworthiness of content, and their community use guidelines permit and prohibit different materials. For example, within about twenty-four hours of the 2021 mass shooting at a Boulder, Colorado, supermarket, Facebook's companies had removed the profiles of the shooter (Matthews, 2021). Conversely, YouTube refused to take down live streams of the shooting posted by a bystander, arguing that the videos fell within its exceptions for news and documentaries (Robertson, 2021). At its peak, the live stream on YouTube had about thirty thousand viewers, and the video was seen by more than five hundred thousand people within twenty-four hours of the shooting (Robertson, 2021).

Even when accounts are disabled and violent content is quickly removed, it may have been visible to countless others, downloaded, reposted, or otherwise shared in the meantime. The 2019 New Zealand mosque shooting demonstrates this challenge. Alongside social media posts suggesting a violent attack was imminent, the shooter streamed the attack via Facebook Live.

Within the first twenty-four hours after the shooting, Facebook reported removing 1.5 million videos and blocking 1.2 million videos at upload; still, an additional three hundred thousand videos remained (Pham et al., 2019). In a WIRED article, Lapowski (2019) reports, "Almost immediately, people copied and reposted versions of the video across the internet, including on Reddit, Twitter, and YouTube." Each of these distinct sites has its own policies for removing violent content, which one can expect will have been posted elsewhere while the site reviews it. Indeed, Surette (2015) contends that whereas print and broadcast media serve broad audiences limited by time and place, in contrast, access to social media is "unbounded to their digital nature" (p. 197).

An additional challenge comes from "prosumers"—people who create new online material from existing material. Cheap and easy-to-use digital editing software makes it possible for people to quickly create new media, often including information from the shooters' original posting, and making it more difficult to track and take down (Schildkraut & Elsass, 2016). In fact, after the shooting in El Paso, Texas, in 2019, social media users encouraged others to create original content of the shooting footage, which would make it easier to distribute without detection and removal from moderators (Harwell, 2019).

Fourth, not all content that affords mass shooters notoriety violates community guidelines. For example, Broll (2020) found that the Columbiner community on Reddit allows for rampant discussions of the shooters, their motives, and the outcome of their actions as permissible on the social media platform. Although overt support or sympathy for the shooters violated informal established norms within the Columbiner community, such comments were policed internally by members and moderators without formal reprimand or removal by the platform itself.

Some of the material posted by mass shooters is still active on social media platforms years after the events, perpetuating micro-fame as the material continues to be viewed and shared easily with others. News media outlets also use this information in their own reporting, helping the shooters to achieve the "capital F fame" they desire.

Opportunities for Minimizing Notoriety

Notwithstanding the challenges of regulating content on social media platforms, there may be several avenues to reduce the notoriety of mass shooters in such domains. First, as advancements in AI continue to be made, it is likely that platforms will become more effective at removing harmful posts. Beyond removing content, several platforms have moved to display public service announcements (PSAs) or warnings when users seek out potentially harmful content. For example, since 2012, Instagram, Pinterest, and Tumblr have attempted to moderate pro–eating disorder content by displaying pop-up PSAs when users search for hashtags like #proana (pro-anorexia) or #thin-spiration (Gerrard, 2018). Although this solution is imperfect (Gerrard, 2018), applying similar PSAs to content related to mass shootings may give pause to casual consumers and could decrease the number of people who view live streams or material that social media platforms deem newsworthy. Such cautions may also be advantageous for minimizing the reach of fan communities that do not violate a platform's community guidelines but nevertheless facilitate content that may bring notoriety to mass shooters.

Second, some jurisdictions have moved to criminalize the distribution of content related to specific incidents. For example, in New Zealand, sharing videos of the mosque shooting is a criminal offense, and stiff sentences have been delivered to those who have violated this law (BBC, 2019). Such a move may be more difficult to implement in the United States given the frequent claims of those whose posts are merely restricted that social media platforms are violating their First Amendment right to free speech—even though the First Amendment does not apply to censorship decisions made by private corporations (Hooker, 2019).[6]

Third, and perhaps most effectively, Hooker (2019) argues that consumer and brand pressure may be effective in pressuring social media platforms to conform to normative expectations. Public pressure has been impactful in the No Notoriety movement, with mainstream media outlets, such as NPR, acknowledging that shifting consumer expectations and public pressure has shaped their editorial decisions and policies (McBride, 2021). Public pressure has also helped to shape the community guidelines of social media platforms. For example, in 2018, public pressure resulted in Facebook improving the transparency of its community guidelines; similar pressure contributed to YouTube's 2019 decision to redouble its efforts to remove hateful content. Because many of the largest social media companies are publicly traded,[7] such pressure may be particularly powerful if these corporations become concerned that their stock values may suffer. Although the reach of social media platforms is several orders of magnitude greater than that of mainstream media outlets, they remain susceptible to public pressure and consumer demand— "social media and the internet may raise questions, but the answers are not new, and the answers need not be radical" (Hooker, 2019, p. 38).

To be sure, not all social media platforms are amenable to such pressures— especially those not publicly traded or that perceive themselves as being countercultural and rebellious. An unintended consequence of removing content from one site is that it may be driven deeper into the depths of the internet and toward more problematic sites (Rogers, 2020). For example, although Reddit has recently taken steps to regulate some content, particularly in the manosphere,[8] by removing hateful and misogynistic subreddits, many impacted users simply left Reddit for less regulated spaces, like independent websites and forums or controversial spaces like 4chan (Copland, 2020). As Copland (2020) notes, restricting content on one platform "does not necessarily mean however that the quarantine reduced the levels of misogyny and other hateful material on the web overall" (p. 21). Still, if an objective is to minimize the notoriety of mass shooters, then making content difficult to stumble across is a positive step.

Conclusion

Initiatives such as No Notoriety are an important step to ensuring that fame (or infamy) is not given to those who seek it through nefarious means. Not naming them, not sharing gory details, and not showing the perpetrators in the mainstream media has the potential to stop the killers from becoming household names. But is it enough to stop copycat killings? Is it enough to stop those who yearn to be famous? We do not believe it is. We do believe that responsible media coverage, as No Notoriety recommends, has the potential to reduce copycat shootings and not glorify a culture of violence. We also believe that a similar approach to improving social media reporting is necessary and could have similar positive effects.

Those who wish to seek out such content will inevitably find a way to do so in the internet age, and fandoms will continue to exist that may afford shooters a degree of micro-fame. Of additional concern is the significant influence that social media can generate; individuals not explicitly seeking out this material may come across it, engage with it, and continue to generate micro-fame for the shooter. The social and cultural influence of social media cannot be downplayed. Thus, while it is important to minimize the notoriety and fame generated to the extent possible, it is also exceptionally important to ensure that they do not acquire notoriety through popular platforms with audiences that, in most cases, are much larger than those of the mainstream media.

NOTES

1. Although self-promotion has long existed, it has been made easier, cheaper, and more efficient via the internet and the ever-increasing number of social media platforms.

2. See https://www.statista.com/statistics/272014/global-social-networks-ranked-by-number-of-users/.

3. See https://business.twitter.com/en/help/ads-policies/ads-content-policies/weapons-and-weapon-accessories.html.

4. See https://support.google.com/youtube/answer/7667605?hl=en.

5. See https://help.twitter.com/en/rules-and-policies/glorification-of-violence.

6. For example, U.S. Rep. Marjorie Taylor Greene, whose Twitter account has been suspended multiple times for posting false or misleading content, has decried that the social media platform is "violating my freedom of speech" (Molina, 2021).

7. For example, Facebook (FB) and Twitter (TWTR) are publicly traded, as are the parent companies of Snapchat (Snap Inc.; SNAP) and YouTube (Alphabet Inc.; GOOG).

8. The "manosphere" consists of groups such as men's rights activists (MRAs), pick-up artists, MGOW (men going their own way), and incels (involuntary celibates) who believe that feminist values have come to dominate society and they must rebel to protect their own existence (see Marwick & Caplan, 2018).

REFERENCES

Arango, T., Bogel-Burroughs, N., & Benner, K. (2019, August 3). Minutes before El Paso killing, hate-filled manifesto appears online. *New York Times.* https://www.nytimes.com/2019/08/03/us/patrick-crusius-el-paso-shooter-manifesto.html

BBC. (2019, June 18). *New Zealand man jailed for 21 months for sharing Christchurch shooting video.* https://www.bbc.com/news/world-asia-48671837

Broll, R. (2020). Dark fandoms: An introduction and case study. *Deviant Behavior, 41.* https://doi.org/10.1080/01639625.2019.1596453

Bushman, B. J. (2017). Narcissism, fame seeking, and mass shootings. *American Behavioral Scientist, 62*(2), 229–241.

CNN Wires. (2018, May 30). *Parkland shooter on cellphone video: "You'll all know who I am."* https://fox2now.com/news/parkland-shooter-on-cellphone-video-youll-all-know-who-i-am/

Copland, S. (2020). Reddit quarantined: Can changing platform affordances reduce hateful material online? *Internet Policy Review, 9*(4), 1–26.

Felsenthal, E. (2019, August 7). The story behind TIME's's gun violence cover. *Time.* https://time.com/5646854/time-cover-enough-shootings/

Gamson, J. (1994). *Claims to fame: Celebrity in contemporary America.* Berkeley: University of California Press.

Gerrard, Y. (2018). Beyond the hashtag: Circumventing content moderation on social media. *New Media & Society, 20*(12), 4492–4511.

Giles, David C. (2018). *Twenty-first century celebrity: Fame in digital culture.* Bingley: Emerald Publishing.

Greenwood, D., Long, C. R., & Dal Cin, S. (2013). Fame and the social self: The need to belong, narcissism and relatedness predict the appeal of fame. *Personality and Individual Differences, 55*(5), 490–495.

Harwell, D. (2019, August 4). Three mass shootings this year began with a hateful screed on 8chan. Its founder calls it a terrorist refuge in plain sight. *Washington Post.* https://www.washingtonpost.com/technology/2019/08/04/three-mass-shootings-this-year-began-with-hateful-screed-chan-its-founder-calls-it-terrorist-refuge-plain-sight/

Hooker, M. P. (2019). Censorship, free speech, and Facebook: Applying the First Amendment to social media platforms via the public function exception. *Washington Journal of Law, Technology & Arts, 15*(1), 36–73.

Jaffe, E. M. (2020). From terrorists to trolls. Expanding web host liability for live-streaming, swatting, and cyberbullying. *Boston University Journal of Science and Technology Law, 26*(1), 51–66.

Khamis, S., Ang, L., & Welling, R. (2017). Self-branding, "micro-celebrity" and the rise of Social Media Influencers. *Celebrity Studies, 8*(2), 191–208.

Lankford, A. (2016). Fame-seeking rampage shooters: Initial findings and empirical predictions. *Aggression and Violent Behavior, 27*, 122–129.

Lankford, A. (2018). Do the media unintentionally make mass killers into celebrities? An assessment of free advertising and earned media value. *Celebrity Studies, 9*(3), 340–354.

Lankford, A., & Madfis, E. (2018). Don't name them, don't show them, but report everything else: A pragmatic proposal for denying mass killers the attention they seek and deterring future offenders. *American Behavioral Scientist, 62*(2), 260–279.

Lapowski, I. (2019, March 15). Why tech didn't stop the New Zealand attack from going viral. *WIRED.* https://www.wired.com/story/new-zealand-shooting-video-social-media/

Marshall, D. P. (2020). Celebrity, politics, and new media: an essay on the implications of pandemic fame and persona. *International Journal of Politics, Culture, and Society, 33*, 89–104.

Marwick A. E., & Boyd, D. (2010). I tweet honestly, I tweet passionately: Twitter users, context collapse, and the imagined audience. *New Media & Society, 13*(1), 114–133.

Marwick, A. E., & Caplan, R. (2018). Drinking male tears: Language, the manosphere, and networked harassment. *Feminist Media Studies, 18*(4), 543–559.

Matthews, D. (2021, March 23). Facebook removes profiles of alleged Boulder shooter. *Daily News.* https://www.nydailynews.com/news/national/ny-facebook-remove-pro file-alleged-boulder-shooter-ahmad-alissa-20210323-au6qwovrofbjfly32ocrx5kcva -story.html

McBride, K. (2021, March 25). *NPR standards need more clarity around when to name a mass shooter.* NPR. https://www.npr.org/sections/publiceditor/2021/03/25/981170871 /npr-standards-need-more-clarity-around-when-to-name-a-mass-shooter

McLaughlin, E. C., & Park, M. (2018, February 15). *Social media paints picture of racist "professional school shooter."* CNN. https://www.cnn.com/2018/02/14/us/nikolas-cruz -florida-shooting-suspect/index.html

Meindl, J. N., & Ivy, J. W. (2017). Mass shootings: The role of the media in promoting generalized imitation. *American Journal of Public Health, 107*(3), 368–370.

Molina, B. (2021, August 10). Twitter suspends Marjorie Taylor Greene—again—for "misleading" COVID-19 tweet. *USA Today.* https://www.usatoday.com/story/tech/2021/08 /10/marjorie-taylor-greene-twitter-suspension-covid-vaccine-tweet-misleading/5550 685001/

No Notoriety. (n.d.a). *Q&A with our founders.* https://nonotoriety.com/about/

No Notoriety. (n.d.b). *No name. No photo. No notoriety.* https://nonotoriety.com/

Parnaby, P. F., & Sacco, V. F. (2004). Fame and strain: The contributions of Mertonian deviance theory to an understanding of the relationship between celebrity and deviant behavior. *Deviant Behavior, 25*(1), 1–26. https://doi.org/10.1080/01639620490253992

Peterson, J., & Densley, J. (2021). *The Violence Project database of mass shootings in the United States, 1966–2020.* The Violence Project. https://www.theviolenceproject.org

Pham, S., O'Sullivan, D., & Meyersohn, N. (2019, March 18). *Facebook has removed 1.5 million copies of the mosque attack video. New Zealand says it needs to do more.* CNN Business. https://www.cnn.com/2019/03/17/business/facebook-youtube-twitter-new -zealand-shooting/index.html

Raitanen, J., & Oksanen, A. (2018). Global online subculture surrounding school shootings. *American Behavioral Scientist, 62*(2), 195–209.

Robertson, A. (2021, March 23). YouTube won't remove a three-hour live-streamed video of the mass shooting in Boulder. *The Verge.* https://www.theverge.com/2021/3/23/223 46465/boulder-mass-shooting-live-stream-youtube-moderation

Rogers, R. (2020). Deplatforming: Following extreme internet celebrities to Telegram and alternative social media. *European Journal of Communication, 35*(3), 213–229.

Schildkraut, J., & Elsass, J. (2016). *Mass shootings: Media, myths, and realities*. Denver, CO: Praeger.

Serazio, M. (2010). Shooting for fame: Spectacular youth, Web 2.0 dystopia, and the celebrity anarchy of Generation Mash-Up. *Communication, Culture & Critique, 3*(3), 416–434.

Silva, J. (2022). "I'll see you on national T.V.!" Understanding and addressing the fame-seeking mass shooter problem. *All American massacre*. Temple University Press.

Silva, J., & Greene-Colozzi, E. A. (2019a). Fame-seeking mass shooters in America: Severity, characteristics, and media coverage. *Aggression and Violent Behavior, 48*, 24–35.

Silva, J., & Greene-Colozzi, E. A. (2019b). Mass shootings and routine activities theory: The impact of motivation, target suitability, and capable guardianship on fatalities and injuries. *Victims and Offenders, 16*(4), 565–586.

Surette, R. (2015). Performance crime and justice. *Current Issues in Criminal Justice, 27*(2), 195–216.

13

"And What Are All These People Watching?"

The American Celebrity Industry, Genre, and
Film Adaptations of School Shootings

LINDSAY STEENBERG

Trends in School Shootings

n April 1999, an episode of the teen program *Buffy the Vampire Slayer* was pulled from broadcast because its plot regarding an averted school shooting painfully resonated with those at Columbine High School, which had been struck the week before. Perhaps in alignment with the contagion warnings championed by the World Health Organization regarding representations and news coverage of suicide, the WB network chose not to air the episode until later that year. Certainly, the WB's decision was not unique, as many programmers redesigned their schedules with mindful attention to the recent Columbine massacre.

At one point in the episode, the main characters discuss the threat of a school shooting, with Xander admitting he struggles with the thought that another teenager would gun people down without a reason. With trademark sarcasm, his classmate Cordelia replies, "Yeah, because that never happens in American high schools." Another character chimes in, "It's bordering on trendy at this point."

This exchange, in the typically irreverent tone of the series, provides evidence that even prior to the Columbine shootings, when this episode was filmed, school shootings were already perceived to be on the rise in the United States. In framing high school shootings as "trendy," the series also taps into one of the leading discourses about American school shooters: the entanglement between celebrity as cultural background and as a perpetrator motivation. This chapter is an investigation of the way the school shootings are fictionalized in the context of the American celebrity industries. I argue that in fictional television and, in particular, film, the notoriety of the school shooter is filtered through the lens of popular genres and mapped onto a mythologized space of the American high school, relying on celebrity as a structuring narrative force, thematic concern, and industrial reality. This *Buffy* episode folds threats of school shootings into the language of the fantasy and teen genres and wraps up with the perpetrator contained, mass shooting and suicide averted, and a humorous kinship deepened among its ensemble cast. This resolution and the episode's last-minute removal from broadcasting schedules is illustrative of narrative media's somewhat paradoxical attempts to sensitively tell stories of mass shootings even as they sensationalize and commodify them.

This article focuses on three American narrative films released after Columbine that dramatize school shootings in different ways: *Zero Day* (Coccio, 2002), *We Need to Talk about Kevin* (Ramsay, 2011), and *Run Hide Fight* (Rankin, 2020). Each of these films constructs its story out of a complex combination of fact and (genre) fiction and encourages a kind of archetypal or imaginatively metonymic reading. My analysis builds on Jason Silva's (2019) thought-provoking analysis of films about mass shootings and his proposal that cinematic fiction and news media work with the same "image bank" in their visualizations. My main avenue of investigation is the ways stories of school shootings are framed using the language of genre filmmaking and rely on celebrity to shape their narratives, characters, and moral systems.

Serial and Mass Shooter Celebrity

Films about mass shootings are relatively rare, although, as Silva proves, the fame-seeking perpetrator is the most commonly represented (2019, p. 248). The rarity of these types of cinematic killers is striking when compared with the similar mediated figure of the serial killer. There are a tremendous number of stories about serial murder appearing across mainstream popular culture from television shows such as *Criminal Minds* (CBS, 2005–2020) and *Mindhunter* (Netflix, 2017–2019) to films such as *The Silence of the Lambs* (Demme, 1991) and *Seven* (Fincher, 1995), just to name a few. In the true crime genre, the serial killer achieves a level of notoriety that few mass shooters are able to attain. I would argue that this is due, in part, to the sexualized nature of serial murder and the way stories about serial killers, and the experts who hunt them, has so successfully mobilized popular psychology and psychoanalysis (with its evocative vocabulary). The mass shooter inspires less narrative flourish.

The nature of the infamy of the serial murderer and the mass shooter is also different. Arie Croitoru et al. (2020) argue that school shootings often receive a glut of media attention at the moment of the crime, often focused on their local community. Building on this, I would argue that the terms *mass* and *serial* might be useful to understand the types of celebrity that the hyper-mediation of these divergent crimes produce. Infamous mass shooters usually attack in a single incident, so they have a brief and intense rise to public visibility, followed by a relatively quick drop-off in interest and cultural currency in a similar manner as the microcelebrity or "celetoid" of social media. Conversely, the celebrity serial killer is distinguished by recurring spikes in recognizability and cultural fascination. These spikes are contingent on the mystery associated with serial murder, which by its very definition must remain unsolved for some time. The compelling nature of the unsolved puzzle should not be underestimated, as it raises both the stakes and the drama of the crime. Mass shootings are typically over in a matter of minutes, with the perpetrator identified, but a serial killer's crimes can continue unpunished for years. Serial killers are thus perfectly suited to the logic of the sequel or long-form serial television, like the many fictions featuring Hannibal Lector. It is worth briefly pointing out that the etymology of the term *serial killer* is tied to film serials and "indirectly belongs to cinema" (Jarvis, 2007, p. 328). This connection is generally attributed to celebrity profiler Robert Ressler, who claims he coined the term based on childhood memories of film serials (Steenberg, 2013). The celebrity of the mass shooter is marked by an urgent intensity that diffuses quickly and resolves with finality that is difficult to expand into cinematic storytelling. Alternatively, the serial killer's embodiment of a recurring and nuanced formulation of celebrity is ideally suited to media exploitation.

The "media effects" debate, which attempts to answer the fundamental question of whether watching violent media makes people more likely to engage in violence, is one of the most contentious topics in media studies. This broader debate is still raging and can be set aside here. In the case of school shooters, there are explicit links between the violent act of mass shooting, the fame-seeking motivation of many perpetrators, and the mass media that both covers and contributes to the problem (Lankford, 2016). Likewise, there is firm evidence of copycat crimes, particularly with Columbine as a key reference point (Larkin, 2009). Fame or infamy is a proven motivation for mass shootings and many of the perpetrators themselves have openly admitted that they seek it. Mass shootings are thus built out of, and into, celebrity culture and the celebrity industries. Films that dramatize school shootings bear a heavy representational burden. Several social scientists and criminologists have flagged the intertwined nature of celebrity and the fame-seeking mass shooter. However, the way that this fits into the wider American media landscape, including fictional adaptations and the networked celebrity industry, remains underexamined. Similarly, scholarly studies on celebrity have tended to avoid discussions on notoriety, with a few notable exceptions (e.g., Penfold-Mounce, 2009). This chapter represents one small step to fill this gap, making some initial interdisciplinary connections about how the language of film genres is mobilized in stories of American school shootings, which might provide insights into the specific mechanisms of celebrity that underpin mass shootings or at least the cultural mythologies circulating around them.

In this I must be clear: I am a film and television scholar whose expertise lies in interrogating representation and how it fits into (and is built out of) culture and creative production. While many of the contributors to this volume have expertise in real crimes and criminals, mine lies with the cultural mythology that surrounds such crimes. They are not interchangeable, of course, but they are interdependent in complex ways. I would argue that the spaces in which films reference an event such as Columbine are perfect sites for examining those interdependencies to understand some part of the relationship between the violent quest for notoriety and the stories we tell ourselves about it.

Double Framing and Cinematic School Shootings

Stories about these crimes unfold in mediated public places just as the crimes themselves require public spaces and audiences (Silva, 2019). In adaptations of events like the Columbine shooting, the publicly facing nature is doubled, as the violence unfolds in the mass media (or the public movie theater) as well as the fictional high school on screen. Each of my key case study films is self-aware about this double framing, as each firmly implicates the cinema viewer in the process of constructing violent celebrity.

While I argue that the nature and sharpness of the critique varies depending on the film's genre and mode of address, the three films I use as illustrative case studies all feature a defining moment in which the perpetrators address the audience both on screen and in the cinema. This jarring direct address does not quite break the fourth wall, as it is doubly framed and mediated through onscreen TV broadcast, home video, or live stream. These moments showcase the perpetrator as the embodiment of the film's message, and sometimes even its core lesson, on the entanglement of fame and violence.

We Need to Talk about Kevin and the Art Cinema Mode

The titular character in *We Need to Talk about Kevin* (hereafter, *Kevin*) appears on television after he has been captured for shooting his classmates, sister, and father with a bow and arrow. He broadcasts a chilling message about the complex feedback loop between violence, celebrity, and the media: "It's got so bad that half the time the people on TV, inside the TV, they're watching

TV. And what are all these people watching? Huh? People like me. I mean what are all you doing right now but watching me? You don't think you would have changed the channel right now if all I did was get an A in geometry."

Lynne Ramsay's *Kevin* is based on the best-selling novel by Lionel Shriver and tells the story of a school shooting by following the troubling and troubled childhood of the eponymous character through the point of view of his struggling mother. The film uses many of the techniques associated with the art cinema, as outlined by David Bordwell's (1979) seminal work, including a loosened nonlinear narrative, which makes it unclear when events are taking place. Eva Khatchadourian, played with off-putting nuance by Tilda Swinton, is an unlikeable protagonist who lacks direction and exists in a traumatized present that is interrupted by disorienting flashbacks.

Ramsay's strategy for dramatizing the school shooting is to accuse her audience of complicity in the sensationalism that might produce such an act (via Kevin's monologue) but also to employ the ambiguity and distanciation techniques of the art cinema to force those spectators to sit with their guilt and discomfort, offering them no heroic or investigative characters to orient them or frame the story. This is an effective tactic, and the film is difficult to view. Gus Van Sant's Columbine-inspired *Elephant* is similarly unsettling in its use of art cinema conventions, such as the long tracking shot following students through the doomed high school, making spectators part of the space and the violence that they know will inevitably erupt. Both films take advantage of the ability of art cinema to confront their spectators with the act of school shooting intellectually and ethically, rather than exclusively emotionally or melodramatically.

Zero Day and the Found Footage Mockumentary

As with the cinéma verité associations of *Elephant*, the mockumentary *Zero Day* plays with documentary modes and their associations of realism. And like *Kevin*, the film features the perpetrators' direct address to an onscreen camera: in this case, Andre and Cal are filming themselves in the lead-up to a planned school shooting, which is framed through CCTV footage at the film's climax. In one sequence, they are burning books and CDs, including William Golding's *Lord of the Flies*, which I would suggest functions here as a kind of cultural shorthand, signaling the atavistic and violent nature of boyhood as well as a unifying curriculum-led object for Americans who also studied the book in high school. In fact, Cal admits that he "thought it kicked ass actually." As the books burn in the background, the boys address the camera: "We didn't get this from any videogames, books, movies, or CDs. This was *our* idea and nobody else's . . . fuck the reasons. There are none."

However, Andre then goes on to explain how he was bullied and called gay by classmates, thereby negating the video's insistence on a lack of reasons for the shootings. Through several moments where homosexuality is used as an insult or suggested between the two young men (as an "army of two"), there are resonances to the way that the Columbine shooters were framed and to homophobic insults reported by school shooters (Kimmel & Mahler, 2003). Van Sant's *Elephant* suggests a queer disruption in its formulation of the intense partnership between the school shooters that defies clear categorization.

Peter Turner's study of found footage horror films argues that the mockumentary aesthetic of *Zero Day*, and its use of the perpetrators' direct address to the camera, promotes an intimacy with the characters made all the more terrifying by the found footage device's association with realism (2019, p. 172). Released after the unprecedented success of *The Blair Witch Project* (Myrick and Sánchez, 1999), *Zero Day* plays with this notion of realism and intimacy through the shaky handheld camera, double framing (using CCTV), and presenting a series of confessional videos that recall the "basement tapes" that were left by the Columbine shooters. Here the cinema viewers can rest easier in their role as forensic viewer or archaeologist rather than voyeur. The format of the found footage mockumentary is able to offer this reassurance even as it heightens feelings of horror by a combination of banal scenarios (prom, dentist, family birthday) and the countdown to inevitable brutality.

Run Hide Fight and the Action Film

Kyle Rankin's 2020 *Run Hide Fight* is the most recent film, distributed by the conservative *Daily Wire* and telling the story of a school shooting through the point of view of Zoe Hull, a troubled female student who violently fights back against the perpetrators. Like both my previous examples, the film features its perpetrator directly addressing an onscreen camera. Zoe interrupts the live stream to speak directly to both perpetrator and viewers, insisting that she will be hijacking his notoriety by rewriting it as her own celebrity heroism: "Isn't it ironic that after all your goddamn hard work, people aren't going to remember you. . . . No. They're going to remember me."

This is the perpetrator's ultimate punishment, perhaps more than his slow death at Zoe's hands: not a dismantling of the system of celebrity attached to the school shooting, but a generic adaptation from a killer's violent manifesto into a hero-led action narrative. If *Zero Day* gives us uncanny access to the killers' minds and points of view, *Run Hide Fight* comprehensively villainizes its central fame-hungry perpetrator by juxtaposing him against an empowered teenaged action heroine, recalling archetypal characters such as Sarah Connor in *Terminator 2* (Cameron, 1991).

I would argue *Kevin*'s speech is the most unsettling, as it leaves the audience not with a hero to suture their point of view and live out a kind of fantasy of resistance nor even with the project of forensic recovery of the found footage tapes. Rather, it suggests that the audiences (at home and in the film) are perpetuating the celebrity system that prompted such violence; simply by looking, by paying attention, by "buying into" this as a pathway to celebrity, they are making such a pathway possible. Furthermore, where *Run Hide Fight* offers us the point of view of a young girl desperate to protect her friend and recover from the pain of her mother's death, *Kevin* leaves us only with Kevin's mother, Eva—unlikeable, doomed, and just as frightened and confused as we are over Kevin's pathology.

Each film represents a different way of working through the cultural trauma of the school shooting through fiction. Moreover, each film uses the well-worn pathways of a different cinematic genre—and this is an undertheorized aspect of school shooters' stories. Ramsay's *Kevin* uses the disjointed, non-linear narrative and ambiguous oneiric plotting of the art cinema to disorient and alienate its viewers. *Zero Day* similarly uses conventions of indie or independent cinema, including the inventive use of "found footage" and the casting of nonprofessional actors who were encouraged to improvise. The realism associated with the video format and their largely quotidian content heightens the horror of the violence while developing the forensic gaze of the spectator at a time when there was a boom in interest in forensic science stemming from the success of television shows like *CSI* (CBS, 2000–2015).

Run Hide Fight relies on the pacing, spectacles, and iconography of the action cinema (particularly in its vengeance-seeking mode, recalling such big-budget hits as *Taken* or the earlier *Death Wish* series). In the action scenario, violence is not the issue, as it can be either criminal *or* heroic and remains the main spectacle on offer in a genre that glamorizes firearms in particular. The action hero enacts legitimized violence and, indeed, embodies *legitimized* celebrity that comes with the spectacular performance of such violence. This is further reinforced by Zoe's journey from female victim to empowered action heroine who fights back (as evident in the film's title).

News reports of school shootings often use the language of the action cinema to frame heroic victims, as in the case of Kendrick Castillo, Brendan Bialy, and Joshua Jones, who fought the shooters in the Highlands Ranch suburb of Denver in 2019 (Sky News, 2019), and the framing of Columbine High School teacher and coach William David Sanders as heroically protecting students (Leavy & Maloney, 2009). The action hero scenario provides compelling evidence that conventions of genre films about school shooters have a deep investment in, and influence on, how these events are reported. This conflation has become *hyperreal*, a term used to describe an indistinguishable combination between real and simulation that is accepted as even more authentic than reality. The hyperreal school shooting can be attributed to specific social problems (such as gun control, homophobia, bullying) even as it can be sewn into the universalizing conventions of several genres, providing evidence of both its power and its flexibility. Examples include *Run Hide Fight*'s action hero narrative, *Zero Day*'s found footage–based authenticity, and *Kevin*'s bewildering nonlinear narrative.

The Structuring Absences of Notoriety

These ways of exploiting or resisting the celebrity-seeking pathways of the school shooter resonate with the No Notoriety and Don't Name Them campaigns suggested by scholars such as Lankford and Madfis (2018) and Meindl and Ivy (2017) as ways the media might prevent fame-seeking shooter attacks. Erasing the identity of the school shooters like those at Columbine is a logical and promising tactic to frustrate the desire of those perpetrators and their potential imitators. However, they remain as structuring absences in all stories about their crimes. Even without their names as labels, the footprint of their celebrity grows but manifests with different orientations.

Ramsay's strategy in *Kevin* is to refocus the school shooter's story through the lens of the perpetrator's grieving and alienated mother—his notoriety becomes hers. The film uses alienation and blankness as an antidote to the glamour of celebrity or fanatical adolescent zeal that marks the personalities of Cal and Andre of *Zero Day*, who record seemingly endless hours of themselves on video. Kevin keeps notebooks that are disturbingly blank—reflecting and commenting on the structuring absence of the unnamed school shooter and the network of victimization that ripples outward from their acts and the echo effect of notoriety that can be projected from a blank source or an absent presence.

Celebrity Crime Scenes

As No Notoriety campaigns work toward subverting the fame-seeking shooter and potential copycats, many school shootings tend to achieve visibility and celebrity not by the perpetrators' names, but by the geographical location of the crime. I would argue that Columbine holds more public recognition and cultural currency than the names of the shooters themselves. While the substitution of place for perpetrator is not universal, particularly for shootings that happen in large urban centers such as Atlanta, it does represent a pattern of celebrity, as in Sandy Hook or Virginia Tech, which provides a productive site for investigating what underpins such celebrity.

Elsewhere, I have examined the intersection between celebrity and crime (Steenberg, 2017) and the ways this has been studied. I have proposed a serviceable taxonomy to categorize the types of crimes, criminals, and victims most frequently framed in the media and adapted into fictional narratives, including the celebrity crime (e.g., Jack the Ripper murders), celebrity criminal (e.g., Ted Bundy), celebrity victim (e.g., Elizabeth Short, aka the Black Dahlia), victimized celebrity (e.g., John Lennon), and celebrity expert (e.g., Sherlock Holmes or Patricia Cornwell). To describe and analyze the particular formulation of celebrity motivated by the school shooter, I propose another, geographically dependent, category: the celebrity crime scene. Here the celebrity crime scene is the American high school, a near mythic space in globalized popular culture and determinate of its own genre (the teen film). The American high school as a potent and hyperreal combination of hierarchical, angst-ridden adolescent hell and nostalgic paradise is a celebrity space in itself. This is layered when the space becomes the site of intense violence.

In many ways, this article is not only a brief investigation of films about school shootings, but a map of the interconnections between mediation, school shooters, and a form of celebrity that is rooted in place as much as in the body of the attacker. The celebrity crime scene is a heterotopic map that resists clear stratification or excavation. It encourages, even requires, a forensic gaze that looks to answer the ritual question asked around school killings, "How could this happen here?" The forensic gaze activated here throws into relief issues around the politics of class, race, and gender in a constant desire to suture social issues (such as gun control, bullying, patriarchal misogyny, eroding influences of celebrity culture) to the celebrity crime scene. Columbine is particularly relevant here as a nationalized and illustrative event, or a "landmark incident" (Silva, 2019, p. 239), rather than representations, for example, of the contrasting case of the West Nickel Mines school shooting, which occurred in an Amish community (see Birkland & Lawrence, 2009).

Michael Moore's documentary *Bowling for Columbine* is one of the most vocal manifestations of the geographically contingent forensic gaze, whose purpose is to contextualize the Columbine shootings (here by discussing them as a part of a wider culture of gun violence in America). His film highlights place as central to his search for answers about Columbine, as he spends considerable time talking about Littleton as a typical white middle-class suburb and making connections to his home state of Michigan and the small town of Oscoda, where one of the Columbine shooters lived for some years. In his mission to answer the question of "How could this happen here?" Moore considers several angles, rejecting, for instance, that the shooters were influenced by the music of Marilyn Manson, who is framed as articulate and insightful particularly when contrasted against the bombast of NRA champion Charlton Heston. The film is deftly constructed through insider or confrontational interviews and crosscut scenes that are used as evidence for the cause-and-effect relationship between school shootings like Columbine and the lack of gun control in the United States.

Moore's cognitive map or geographic profile of the Columbine event sees Littleton as typical, even axiomatic, because his film addresses viewers who live in similar places and belong to similar demographics (white, middle-class, educated) as those families who sent their children to Columbine High School. I would argue that such an orientation marks the mode of address of many films and reports of school shootings, which elides readings that might connect race and class tensions or toxic masculinity to the shootings. This underexamined connection is discussed in several chapters in this volume (e.g., Bridges et al., 2022; Gascón, 2022) with regards to incidents of U.S. mass shootings.

In his desire to map the literal and motivational geography of Columbine and the fame-seeking shooters who would follow in other places, Michael Moore has, ironically perhaps, made himself famous—as forensic investigator, crusader, and cartographer of social problems. I would suggest that Michael Moore fits the category of so-called celebrity expert that I proposed as part of the taxonomy of celebrity and crime mentioned earlier. Such an expert becomes a safety net or alibi for audiences that might feel uncomfortable with their desire to watch the spectacle of a school shooting in a manner similar to *Zero Day*'s tactic of showing the shooting only on CCTV, thus both insisting on immediacy and (hyper)realism. By viewing Moore's cinematic map of the celebrity crime scene, viewers are offered a forensic framing device that is ostensibly educational and diffuses the charges of prurience leveled by Ramsay's film and its title character. The celebrity crime scene map is disorienting when it lacks an expert, a reliable narrator, or a tour guide figure, such as Michael Moore.

Dark Tourism and Dark Fandom

Because mediations of school shootings are fixed in place, they can become the focal point of the practice of dark tourism and related practices of dark fandom, which proliferate with ease and anonymity online. Philip L. Stone (2013) defines *dark tourism* as the practice of visiting places associated with death and violence, which exist on a spectrum of darkness from the death camps at Auschwitz and Dachau to ghost tours of New York. Columbine High School has become a site of dark tourism or, in some cases, a kind of uncanny pilgrimage. The differences in these labels may well be academic, as the line that divides the dark tourist from the grieving pilgrim may be difficult to locate and may be contingent on the tourist's/pilgrim's relationship to the victims of the violence—this is exemplified in the epilogue to *Zero Day*,

184 / Lindsay Steenberg

where unnamed teenagers burn the memorial crosses dedicated to Cal and Andre.

The shootings at Columbine happened just as digital technologies were expanding to provide new ephemeral and diffuse spaces for dark tourism and for the related communities of dark fandom, which Ryan Broll defines as those "who identify with or otherwise celebrate those who have committed heinous acts, such as mass or serial murders" (2020, p. 795). Broll investigates the notoriety-fueled dark fandom circulating around the Columbine shooting and its perpetrators on spaces such as Reddit, where some self-identify as "Columbiners" (see also Daggett, 2015; Oksanen et al., 2014). These studies suggest that the digital communities forming around notorious criminals are similar to other online celebrity-based groups.

I would suggest that the celebrity sought and granted to school shooters via dark tourism and fandom relies on an industry that spans many mediated spaces. Graeme Turner suggests that "America . . . has the most developed version of the celebrity industry" (2013, p. 199). He insists that we think in terms of a celebrity industry rather than an entertainment or film industry that depends upon celebrity. Turner defines the celebrity industry as a hypercommercialized space that feeds the symbiotic needs of contributors, be they publicists, journalists, or the celebrities themselves, who represent both the product and contributing producers. He suggests that "these interdependencies are, in my view, deliberately mystified" (2013, p. 202).

There is a symbiotic economic and ideological relationship between the celebrity industry (and its many subindustries, such as film or news media) and the spaces and practices of dark tourism and fandom. In my analytical descriptions of filmmakers such as Michael Moore and Lynne Ramsay, I am arguing that their works on school shootings can, and do, simultaneously critique and contribute to the celebrity industries and the notoriety they produce, albeit on genre-contingent registers. I have, furthermore, suggested that independent or art cinema's mode of address presents the most compelling and unsettling tactics to dismantle or bypass the celebrity industries.

Film as an Active Shooter Drill in a Risk-attuned Culture

In his analysis of media coverage of the Columbine shooting, Benjamin Frymer argues the following:

> [The shooters] were transformed from complex teenagers into concrete identifiable objects for the public to fear, to hate, and to consume. These hyper real objects disguised the fact that, in significant ways, there was no ultimate Reality or Truth underneath the crime or their

alienation—it largely mirrored the media world itself as [they] turned their crime and themselves into a spectacle. (2009, p. 1390)

Films based on school shootings since Columbine have recirculated these hyperreal celebrity objects, which does more than merely bolster the violent celebrity apparatus or encourage future fame-seeking mass killers. They can be more nuanced in their framing, interpretations, and adaptations. They can be ways to publicly work through the horror of the act of mass killing. To push this further, they may function as mediated active shooter drills, allowing spectators to grieve (if only vicariously) by prompting them to revisit their media memories or work through how such violence might be avoided or, in the case of some stories, combated or punished in the future. The act of viewing these films permits a graphic, but safely framed, spectacle of violence and near incomprehensible motivations in the context of a culture deeply attuned to risk.

Where *Run Hide Fight* can offer the fantasy of an active shooter drill that resolves itself through violent resistance and the conventions of the action genre, the art cinema–inflected *Kevin* and *Elephant* suggest that our efforts of working through grief in such cinematic active shooter drills is superficial if not impossible. They present nonlinear, illogical, dreamlike reflections of anguish and alienation. *Zero Day* promises a countdown but offers a crime scene—its format mimics the evidence locker as its edited hours of found footage video testimony and CCTV footage formulates a type of simulated true crime for armchair detectives. It allows the viewer privileged and troubling access to the subjectivities and POV of the perpetrators. Where the viewer may have an appetite for the action narrative (and box office figures and franchise production confirm that this is true), the tactic of refusing resolution may be more in keeping with the mandate of No Notoriety and may, through a lingering sense of unease, actively resist the celebrity or notoriety industry. *Zero Day* and, in particular, *We Need to Talk about Kevin* are films that do not allow their perpetrators a clearly defined story arc. They are fragmentary, ambiguous, and they use provocative framing devices (video tapes, CCTV, a mother's traumatized flashbacks). Through these mechanisms, Kevin, Cal, and Andre are denied the spotlight they are so desperately seeking. They are always at one remove, relegated to ghostly traces rather than celebrity criminals. Conversely, the teenaged shooters of *Run Hide Fight* are painted as iconic and one-dimensional villains, much like Hans Gruber in *Die Hard*. This genre-based route toward infamy makes the shooters more recognizable, if less complex. It is clear that feature films contribute to our shared vocabulary of crime and celebrity. Building on this assumption, I would argue that Lynn Ramsay's *We Need to Talk about Kevin* is a film of such unsettling ambiguity and victim-centered nuance that it can intervene and refuse the pathways of notoriety craved by mass shooters.

ACKNOWLEDGMENT

The author would like to acknowledge the invaluable contribution of her research assistant, Simon McFadden.

REFERENCES

Birkland, T. A., & Lawrence, R. G. (2009). Media framing and policy change after Columbine. *American Behavioral Scientist, 52*(10), 1406–1425.

Bordwell, D. (1979). The art cinema as a mode of film practice. *Film Criticism, 4*(1), 56–64.

Bridges, T., Tober, T. L., & Brazzell, M. (2022). Mass shootings and American masculinity. In E. Madfis and A. Lankford (Eds.), *All American massacre: The tragic role of American culture and society in mass shootings*. Temple University Press.

Broll, R. (2020). Dark fandoms: An introduction and case study. *Deviant Behavior, 41*(6), 792–804.

Croitoru, A., Kien, S., Mahabir, R., Radzikowski, J., Crooks, A., Schuchard, R., Begay, T., Lee, A., Bettios, A., Stefanidis, A. (2020). Responses to mass shooting events: The interplay between the media and the public. *Criminology & Public Policy, 19*(1), 335–360.

Daggett, C. (2015). Eric Harris and Dylan Klebold: Antiheroes for outcasts. *Participations Journal of Audience and Reception Studies, 12*(1), 46–77.

Frymer, B. (2009). The media spectacle of Columbine: Alienated youth as an object of fear. *American Behavioral Scientist, 52*(10), 1387–1404.

Gascón, D. (2022). Structural strain, intersectionality, and mass murder: A case study of the Isla Vista shooting. In E. Madfis and A. Lankford (Eds.), *All American massacre: The tragic role of American culture and society in mass shootings*. Temple University Press.

Jarvis, B. (2007). Monsters inc.: Serial killers and consumer culture. *Crime, Media, Culture: An International Journal, 3*(3), 326–344.

Kimmel, M. S., & Mahler, M. (2003). Adolescent masculinity, homophobia, and violence. *American Behavioral Scientist, 46*, 1439–1458.

Lankford, A. (2016). Fame-seeking rampage shooters: Initial findings and empirical predictions. *Aggression and Violent Behavior, 27*, 122–129.

Lankford, A., & Madfis, E. (2018). Don't name them, don't show them, but report everything else: A pragmatic proposal for denying mass shooters the attention they seek and deterring future offenders. *American Behavioral Scientist, 62*(2), 260–279.

Lankford, A., & Silver, J. (2020). Why have public mass shootings become more deadly?: Assessing how perpetrators' motives and methods have changed over time. *Criminology & Public Policy, 19*(1), 37–60.

Larkin, R. (2009). The Columbine legacy: Rampage shootings as political acts. *American Behavioral Scientist, 52*(9), 1309–1326.

Leavy, P., & Maloney, K. P. (2009). American reporting of school violence and "people like us": A comparison of newspaper coverage of the Columbine and Red Lake school shootings. *Critical Sociology, 35*(2), 273–292.

Malkki, L. (2014). Political elements in post-Columbine school shootings in Europe and North America. *Terrorism and Political Violence, 26*(1), 185–210.

Meindl, J. N., & Ivy, J. W. (2017). Mass shootings: The role of the media in promoting generalized imitation. *American Journal of Public Health, 107*(3), 368–370.

Oksanen, A., Hawdon, J., & Räsänen, P. (2014). Glamorizing rampage online: School shooting fan communities on Youtube. *Technology in Society, 39*, 55–67.

Penfold-Mounce, R. (2009). *Celebrity culture and crime: The joy of transgression.* Palgrave Macmillan.

Silva, J. R. (2019). Mass shooting films: Myths, academic knowledge, and popular criminology. *Victims & Offenders, 14*(2), 239–264.

Sky News. (2019, September 13). *Denver school shooting: Hero student tackled gunman and died to protect his friends.* https://news.sky.com/story/denver-school-shooting-hero -student-tackled-gunman-and-died-to-protect-his-friends-11714992

Steenberg, L. (2013). *Forensic science in contemporary American popular culture: Gender, crime, science.* Routledge.

Steenberg, L. (2017). *Crime and celebrity.* Oxford Research Encyclopedia of Criminology and Criminal Justice. http://criminology.oxfordre.com/view/10.1093/acrefore/97801 90264079.001.0001/acrefore-9780190264079-e-26?rskey=h1XcHf&result=1

Stone, P. (2013). Dark tourism scholarship: A critical review. *International Journal of Culture, Tourism, and Hospitality Research, 7*(3), 307–318.

Turner, G. (2013). The economy of celebrity. In S. Redmond & S. Holmes (Eds.), *Stardom and celebrity: A reader* (pp. 193–205). Sage Publications.

Turner, P. (2019). *Found footage horror films: A cognitive approach.* Routledge.

PART V

Mass Shootings and American Politics

14

The American Politics of Mass Shootings

Sun Tzu, Clausewitz, and the Unicorn

Tom Diaz

The deadliest public mass shooting in the United States to date was on October 1, 2017 (Diaz, 2019). The gunman fired on an open-air music festival from a Las Vegas hotel's upper floor. Using modified assault rifles, the shooter killed fifty-eight people and wounded more than four hundred within ten minutes. Two of the wounded later died, bringing the death toll to sixty.

At a briefing the next day, White House press secretary Sarah Huckabee Sanders affected to fence off "political debate" (Bump, 2017). "Today is a day for consoling the survivors and mourning those we lost," she said. "Our thoughts and prayers are certainly with all of those individuals. There's a time and place for a political debate, but now is the time to unite as a country." Sanders crossed her own boundary by then arguing that "we don't want to . . . try to create laws that won't stop these types of things from happening." Trying "to create laws" and arguing against a given type of laws are inherently political debate.

The "too soon" argument's premise is that it is unseemly to advocate for changes in law or policy in the wake of such shootings. Whatever its merits, it is almost never observed in practice. But the argument raises three questions about attempts to achieve a reduction in public mass shootings through political means—that is, changes in law and government policy.

What is *politics*? What measures success in politics? And how successfully have gun violence reduction advocates and their opponents practiced politics to achieve the end of stopping public mass shootings and reducing their lethality?

Given that most legislative and policy changes proposed for preventing public mass shootings and reducing their lethality require federal action, this chapter focuses on national politics. It proposes that the leadership of the two sides of the gun violence reduction debate follow fundamentally different models of practical politics. Gun violence reduction advocates have followed a partisan party model. Gun rights advocates have pursued a cultural struggle model. The chapter argues that the cultural struggle model has been more effective in an era of increasing cultural and political polarization and that the partisan party model has been counterproductive. Guns and gun rights are not merely subjects of policy disagreement between parties. They drive cultural division and political polarization. Finally, maxims from leading analysts of war strategy are examined to suggest perspectives on why gun rights advocates have been more effective in the politics of the so-called culture war.

Political Models

Heywood (2019) describes two broad approaches to defining politics. One sees politics as an arena. The other views politics as a process. Leftwich (2004) states that the arena approach focuses narrowly on the formal institutions of government and assumes that politics is about governments and how they make policies and decisions binding on society. The process approach sees politics as much broader, happening not only in government institutions but wherever questions of power, control, and resources are contested at any level of human society.

Political science scholarship contains many elaborations on and variations of these basic approaches (Heywood, 2019). Spitzer (2015), for example, defines gun control politics as the making of "social regulatory policy" by governments (i.e., arena) and describes in detail the actions of partisans on both sides of the issue (i.e., process).

In this chapter, I draw on my personal experience as a staff lawyer working on gun control legislation for the Crime Subcommittee of the U.S. House of Representatives, a subsequent fifteen years as senior policy analyst for a gun violence reduction organization in Washington, as well as research and writing I have done for three books about guns, the gun industry, and the gun violence problem in America, including public mass shootings. I integrate the two broad conceptual approaches to politics with my experience by proposing in this chapter two models of practical politics that I call the *partisan party model* and the *cultural struggle model*.

Partisan Party Model

The partisan party model frames politics as the pursuit of policy goals by partisan organizations in the arena of government—the activities of political parties. In this model, politics lies in the actions of elected or appointed officials from different parties and their factions. Viewed primarily as a contest between parties and their leaders in Washington, politics is treated as a top-down phenomenon.

In my experience, the news media report partisan party politics as if it were a horse race. A win for one party's agenda is seen as a defeat for the other party. Congressional leaders are perceived by advocates and news media as powerful, virtually autonomous players in Washington's government arena. Along with the president, they are expected to set national agendas and implement them by whipping votes in Congress, enacting laws, and setting national policies by executive action. An advocate's priority in the partisan party model is logically to influence key players in Congress, the White House, and the executive branch.

Cultural Struggle Model

The cultural struggle model frames politics as a process that begins at the bottom and weaves upward in a complex web of advocacy. This model treats politics as a broader struggle than the battles of parties in Washington's partisan arena. The contest engages all of society and all of the means of influence available to advocates at every level.

Those means of influence go far beyond political parties. "Political" and "nonpolitical" institutions interact in important ways that shape government decisions (Leftwich, 2004). Economic institutions shape the markets in which guns are sold and advocate for freedom from regulation (Diaz, 1999). Legal institutions shape the laws that define the permissible scope of executive and legislative action (McClurg & Denning, 2016). They do this by publishing scholarly works, influencing judicial appointments, and engaging in strategic litigation to set constitutional norms (Teles, 2008).

In my view of the cultural struggle model, national elected and appointed party players are less autonomous than in the partisan party model. An advocate's priority in the cultural struggle model is developing and motivating strong grass roots, integrating them upward into activist organizations, and allying them with economic and legal interests

Practical politics is not an either-or choice, and advocates did not necessarily explicitly choose from these notional models. Rather, combinations of their decisions and complex societal forces have led each side to construct an apparatus that fits into one of the models.

Measures of Success

Measures of success in practical politics are elusive. This chapter measures success using the principal goals for which the opposing sides have advocated with respect to national law and policy intended to prevent or reduce the lethality of public mass shootings. Three major goals consistently cited on the gun violence reduction side have been banning the sale or transfer of so-called assault weapons, limiting firearm magazine capacity, and revamping federal background checks, both in scope and the definitions of prohibited classes of persons they identify (Webster & Vernick, 2013). These measures, in theory, would weed out persons inclined to commit public mass shootings and reduce the firepower, and thus lethality, of firearms that they might use.

Gun rights advocates have sought to expand the right of citizens to carry concealed firearms in public and use them defensively, prevent bans on the sale of so-called modern sporting rifles and limits on magazine capacity, and roll back existing controls, such as those restricting the sale of machine guns and suppressors ("silencers") (Diaz, 2013). Aside from the issue of constitutional gun rights, they argue that stricter criminal penalties and a well-armed citizenry are the most effective ways to stop public mass shootings. In the words of NRA Executive Vice President Wayne LaPierre, "It takes a good guy with a gun to stop a bad guy with a gun" (Overby, 2012).

It is important to note that effectiveness in reducing the incidence of public mass shootings or their lethality is a different question from effectiveness in passing legislation or effecting policy changes. The former question—a complex one involving causality and correlation—is not addressed in this chapter.

Gun Rights Advocates: Hunting Votes

Gun rights advocates hunt for votes at the grass roots. Those district-by-district votes ultimately determine outcomes in Congress, memorialized in the maxim that "all politics is local."

The gun rights movement first grappled with the increasingly polarized nature of American culture and political life in 1977, when a faction of hard-liner gun rights advocates seized control of the National Rifle Association (NRA) at its annual convention in Cincinnati. Known thereafter as the "Revolt at Cincinnati," this pivotal moment stopped in its tracks the previous NRA leadership's plan to abandon gun rights advocacy in favor of promoting shooting sports. Those plans included moving the NRA's headquarters from Washington to a sports center in Colorado Springs. The hard-liners reversed course and began an aggressive program of expanding Second Amendment rights (Melzer, 2009).

The "Silent Revolution"

The Cincinnati revolt was not an isolated event. It was an early skirmish in the polarization that Inglehart (1977) suggests began with a "silent revolution" in the two decades after World War II. By the twenty-first century, the American people, not merely political elites, were deeply divided, polarized over cultural and thus political issues (Abramowitz, 2018).

Inglehart (1977) proposed that unprecedented levels of economic and physical security after the war upended values held since the Industrial Revolution. The shift was from the materialist "survival values" of economic and physical security to postmaterialist "self-expression values" of individual autonomy and self-expression (Inglehart et al., 2018). The rise of postmaterialist values led to social and political movements advocating for such causes as environmental protection, gender equality and identity, and accommodation to immigration. Gun control also rose to the political fore, embodied in the Federal Gun Control Act of 1968 (Spitzer, 2015).

One person's self-expression is another's heresy. The silent revolution sparked a silent counterrevolution. A culture war ensued. Bishop (2009) argues that the clash fundamentally changed American politics. Voters stopped simply following party bosses and party agendas. Instead, they sorted themselves according to personal values. Party loyalty plummeted during the summer of 1965. Significantly, popular trust in government programs also cratered, replaced by doubt and skepticism (Bishop, 2009).

Although voters eventually returned to political parties, the parties and their agendas were thoroughly realigned. What it meant to be a Democrat or a Republican changed. "Moderate Republicans" and "yellow dog Democrats" faded out of existence.

The Culture War

The 1977 NRA coup was an early clash in the broader culture war. Leadership at the top of a powerful national organization was toppled by a wave from below, gun owners and gun rights advocates who held different cultural values and political views than did their erstwhile leaders (Diaz, 2019).

The event was a significant victory for the silent counterrevolution. Yet it was barely noticed outside of the NRA. Its significance was by no means apparent or widely understood. But it was deep change made manifest, the growing power of ordinary people sorting themselves by personal values and abandoning passive conformity to agendas handed down from above.

The Cincinnati revolt was both genesis and foundation of the cultural struggle model followed ever since by gun rights advocates. A vast body of gun owners, potential gun owners, and others sympathetic to gun ownership—perhaps two-thirds of the electorate (Parker et al., 2017)—morphed into the gun rights movement of today, with a hard core of determined advocates and a softer core of persons who own or are willing to own guns.

Two forces beyond the personal values of gun enthusiasts fueled this cultural movement. One was economic; the other, legal.

Market Economics

The hundreds of millions of Americans open to gun ownership make up the last great gun market in the world, called by the late gun industry leader Bill Ruger "a little money-making machine" (Diaz, 1999). The power of that market led to another landmark in the struggle: the welding together of the gun rights political movement with the worldwide gun industry's business interests in the 1990s.

The marriage of these interests grew out of the shock to gun consumers and the gun industry alike with passage of the 1994 Federal Assault Weapons Ban. The ban itself was easily evaded and doomed to expiration after a ten-year "sunset" period (Diaz, 2013). But it signaled the potential power of politicians in Washington to wipe out the only growing market the gun industry had—semiautomatic assault rifles (or "modern sporting rifles") and high-capacity pistols. Moreover, it was clear that the power of federal law to ban firearms by design type could obliterate a strategy vital to the industry's very survival—that is, continuous design innovation and marketing of new types and models of guns to attract new buyers and motivate owners to buy again (Diaz, 1999).

Prior to the mid-1990s, the NRA and the gun industry had a friendly but not significantly politically collaborative relationship, characterized primarily by advertising and glowing reciprocal product reviews in NRA publications. In the course of my research as a policy analyst and author, I have observed the changing tone and content of NRA publications from the late 1960s to the present, the public statements of its leaders, and the backgrounds of its more prominent board members. I have also studied gun industry advertising and the industry's own analyses of its markets and their prospects. In my opinion, before the 1990s, the NRA's leaders could, as they often did, plausibly say that the organization represented gun owners, not the gun industry, arguing that the National Shooting Sports Foundation (NSSF) represented the industry. That increasingly changed after passage of the 1994 ban. Industry leaders and the NRA have gradually formed a de facto coalition, the parallel objectives of which have been defense of the industry and expansion of gun rights. Individual rights and personal liberty (as opposed to hunting and other sporting uses) are now central themes in industry advertising and gun rights advocacy literature. Concurrently, the gun industry is often cast as indispensable to American liberty.

Legal Strategy

The Cincinnati revolt was one point in a larger matrix. In the mid-1970s, historically separate cadres of conservatives—religious fundamentalists, free market capitalists, libertarians, and intellectuals—were creating new working alliances on a range of culture-driven issues. None of this mobilization has been more important to gun rights advocacy than the conservative legal movement, embodied in public interest law firms, law school teaching, scholarly articles, judicial appointments, and "strategic litigation" (Teles, 2008).

This nominally nonpolitical legal activity is integral to the cultural struggle model. Judicial votes are at least as powerful as congressional votes. Judicial rulings fence in political options. Recent gun rights victories in the Supreme Court such as D.C. v. Heller and McDonald v. Chicago happened because conservative lawyers shaped key litigation aimed at winning favorable judicial rulings (Doherty, 2008).

This is not partisan party politics. This is cultural struggle politics.

Gun Violence Reduction Advocates: Hunting the Unicorn

Gun violence reduction advocates have historically sought leadership from the White House and favorable votes in Congress. For at least three decades, they have sought a moderate, bipartisan alliance to pass so-called common-sense federal legislation.

Until recently, America's gun control organizations were a handful of small, competing entities headquartered in a few major cities. Funded by charitable foundations and direct mail, these advocates never came together in a unified, deeply rooted coalition. During the battle for the 1994 crime bill, for example, I was directed by a frustrated superior to call representatives of the groups to a meeting and try to get them to work more closely together. That and many other of my experiences within the movement lead me to confirm Goss's argument that "the nation has never witnessed a vigorous, nation-spanning social movement to control access to firearms" in large part because the leading gun control advocates "have chosen political strategies that are anathema to movement building" (Goss, 2006, p. 28).

On a Rational Sandbar

Goss called the gun control strategy "rational national." The movement's leaders deliberately eschewed the grassroots mobilization essential to the cultural struggle model of politics, preferring a model in which elite leaders and experts pursued comprehensive federal legislation in Washington. "By choice and circumstance, gun control was a top-down political campaign without a bottom-up social movement" (Goss, 2006, p. 194). Spitzer recounts a number of instances when these leaders rejected incremental measures in favor of the comprehensive ideal (Spitzer, 2015). This strategy stranded gun control advocacy on the sandbar of an idyllic period of "compromise and tempered ideology" that bloomed in the mid-1960s but began to wither in the mid-1970s (Bishop, 2009).

Over this decade, abandonment of parties at the grass roots gave Washington's politicians freedom to act autonomously. Partisanship waned as the electorate split its votes between parties. This seemed ideal for national party politics. Bipartisan political elites enacted ambitious government initiatives, including the Federal Gun Control Act of 1968. This era was the so-called normal to which many American politicians long to return.

But the silent counterrevolution was smoldering beneath this tranquil bipartisan surface. Its partisans no longer believed that Washington could solve their problems, were angry about intrusions on their personal values, and were poised to tear down and rebuild party structures and platforms to conform to those values. It burst forth in 1994 when the Democrats lost control of the House of Representatives for the first time since 1952. Sometimes called "the Republican Revolution," the election surprised and shocked political elites and pundits—much as did Donald Trump's victory in 2016.

Gun control advocates have nonetheless continued to pursue their elitist, rational national strategy—the partisan party model of politics (Karni, 2021; White House, 2021; Diaz, 2019).

The Public Health Model

The focus of action and intellectual core of rational national advocacy has been the public health approach to reducing death and injury. Successful in combating contagious diseases—at least until the cultural blowback of the COVID-19 pandemic—the public health approach relies on science and reasoned argument to persuade politicians to implement policies that reduce death and injury and citizens to cooperate with those policies (Hemenway, 2017). Gun rights advocates denounce public health analysis relating to firearms as disguised "anti-gun advocacy" (Ouimet, 2022).

The approach has four steps in the case of violence reduction (Centers for Disease Control and Prevention, n.d.). Step one defines the problem by analyzing data about a given kind of violence. In the case of public mass shootings, the universe of data would include anything that can be known and quantified about shooters, weapons, circumstances, and personal and institutional histories.

Step two uses scientific research methods to identify "risk factors," the things and conditions that increase the risk of violence. These might include the relative lethality of different configurations of firearms (e.g., weapons using high-capacity magazines) and early signals of shooters' proclivities or intents (e.g., a history of interpersonal violence, social media posts).

Step three uses scientific methods to develop and test strategies to moderate the risk factors and prevent violence. Examples of strategies include banning specific types of firearms and accessories and prohibiting persons with certain histories from possessing any firearms.

Step four disseminates the developed strategies in hopes of their being enacted into law or implemented by government units that deal with violence, such as law enforcement and the courts.

The rational national approach has expended substantial resources on the first three of these steps, the scholarly production of moderated "evidence-based" studies identifying the causes of gun violence in general, public mass shootings in particular, and developing strategic solutions. Some of these studies have been translated from the arcane statistical calculations and neutral language of professional journals into the plain English of advocacy and then disseminated by gun control organizations. Some advocates also publish lay reports based on anecdotal accounts.

It is the fourth step—getting strategic policies implemented—that eludes the rational national elite. The strategic premise appears to be that there is a body of unengaged or undecided opinion in the public and Congress that can be swayed by scholarly reports demonstrating that guns kill people and that lots of guns, particularly military-style guns, kill lots of people (Stolberg, 2021). This approach is aimed at middle-of-the-road voters and politicians who, if only they can be persuaded, will swing elections and stand up and be counted in congressional votes for the correct side of the gun control fight. It relies heavily on lobbying presidents to take strong positions and Congress to enact comprehensive legislation.

The rational national model may have worked in the era of the sandbar, when liberals dominated government and progressive forces won big in courts, independent regulatory agencies, and a compromise-friendly Congress. But many argue that even in that era, success in Washington depended on years of grassroots organizing and bottom-up advocacy. In any case, the model has flatly failed since the fleeting and illusory victories of the 1993 Brady Law and the 1994 Federal Assault Weapons Ban.

A prime reason is that the unicorn of a rational middle open to persuasion probably does not exist. In the words of a former chief of staff to House Speaker Nancy Pelosi, bipartisanship "has become the Sasquatch of American politics: rarely seen but fervently sought" (Lawrence, 2021). There are almost no open-minded survivors in the no-man's-land between cultural trenches. True, some people call themselves independents. But Abramowitz argues that the independent label is merely appropriated as a badge of intellectual integrity by many who are in practice partisan. The few true independents have little interest in voting or politics.

Winners and Losers

Almost all major victories in gun control laws at both the federal and state levels since 1994 have been won by the gun rights side—ranging from liberalized state firearm carry laws to expanded rights to carry firearms on federal public land (Diaz, 2013). The industry won protection from most civil lawsuits in the 2005 Protection of Lawful Commerce in Arms Act (PLCAA). As in the anti-mask and anti-vaccination campaigns and the takeover of the Capitol on January 6, 2021, cultural forces—not academic wisdom—have prevailed.

Clausewitz, Sun Tzu, and the Nature of Warfare

Culture war seems so different from armed conflict that principles of the latter do not apply to the former. But contemporary politics is peppered with talk about "weaponized" issues (Goldiner, 2021; Foxx & Luetkemeyer, 2021).

Given the combative nature of the culture war, several maxims about successful armed conflict promulgated by scholars of warfare like Gen. Carl von Clausewitz and Chinese scholar Sun Tzu seem remarkably apt for assessing the politics of public mass shootings as described above (Felter, 2014; Tzu et al., n.d.). I submit that these maxims suggest measures by which to assess the efforts of political opponents struggling over cultural terrain. As moderately paraphrased by me into present-day language, they are as follows: (1) know yourself and know your opponent—do not project your perspective onto your opponent (Sun Tzu); (2) fit objectives to the means available—do not pursue unrealistic or counterproductive goals (Clausewitz); (3) know that things change over time—actions cause reactions (Sun Tzu); and (4) defense has an advantage over offense—change is hard (Clausewitz).

Applying the Maxims

Ticking through the maxims of warfare provides perspective on the politics of gun control over recent decades.

Know yourself and know your opponent—do not project your perspective onto your opponent.

Gun control advocates have consistently misjudged the nature and extent of the American gun culture and its opposition to gun control laws (Parker et al., 2017; Yamane, 2017; Wright, 1995).

The phrase *commonsense gun laws* illustrates one dimension of this problem. The *common* assumes that there is a consensus that need only be activated to implement obvious solutions. Once the scales fall from Americans' eyes, they will see the *common sense* of the leading gun control proposals.

This projected commonsense consensus assumes that most Americans—like most gun violence reduction advocates—do not like guns and would prefer to see them gone. But there is strong evidence to the contrary. Most Americans either own guns or are open to gun ownership.

According to recent polling by the Pew Research Center, 30 percent of Americans say that they own a gun. In a population estimated to be about 330 million in 2018, that would mean that roughly 99 million Americans own a gun. An additional 36 percent say that they are open to owning a gun in the future—about 118 million Americans. Taken together, therefore, there are about 217 million Americans—two-thirds of the population—who are not opposed to gun ownership (Parker et al., 2017). The number may be even higher given that recent critiques of issue polling have shown underreporting by conservative respondents on gun ownership questions (Urbatsch, 2019). This openness to guns is reflected in the burst of gun sales reported in 2020 and 2021 (Walsh, 2021).

These facts about Americans and their attitudes toward guns raise a related problem. That is the tendency of gun violence reduction advocates to cite strict gun regulation in other countries—Canada, Japan, Australia, for instance—as models for the United States (Diaz, 2019). This approach fails to recognize that for broad historical reasons, the United States is different from these countries, its culture is different from them, and thus its politics is different (Kopel, 1992). The United States is not Scotland, Australia, or Japan. Projecting their gun cultures and gun control regimens onto America simply does not work.

Finally, the role and nature of the NRA is largely misunderstood. It is often cast as "the problem," with the primary explanation that the NRA buys politicians through its donations and thus blocks political action. The facts are that the NRA contributes only to politicians who have already proven their allegiance to the gun rights agenda, and the sums that it contributes are a relatively small proportion of those raised by these politicians (Diaz, 2019; Rushe, 2018). It is more useful to understand that the NRA has a "highly motivated mass membership and the ability to bring pressure to bear from that membership" (Spitzer, 2015). It is instructive to peruse the NRA's publications and its website to grasp the scope of its ties to the American gun culture beyond its membership and overt gun rights advocacy, such as ubiquitous firearms instruction, sporting competitions, and publishing directories of popular gun shows.

Fit objectives to the means available—do not pursue unrealistic or counterproductive goals.

As we have seen, the two sides have followed different political models, used different means, and sought different goals. This chapter argues that the rational national, partisan party politics model has proven unrealistic both in means and goals. But beyond the question of winning votes in Washington, the rational national model has actually been counterproductive and even self-defeating. This is apparent in subtle but real ways.

First, politicians do not like expending political capital on losing propositions. Politicians in Washington do not like being asked repeatedly to embrace legislation for which advocates cannot produce enough popular support in their constituencies to make that embrace politically wise. For the last thirty years, gun control advocates have presented Washington politicians with a standard menu of policies that have repeatedly failed to be enacted or only been passed in a piecemeal or temporary manner (e.g., banning assault weapons, limiting ammunition magazine capacity, expanding background checks). They have failed because—no matter what national polling favoring stricter gun laws purportedly shows—gun control advocates have failed to deliver bottom-up pressure from individual constituencies. I have observed that lobbyists may speak for a movement's goals, but the strength or weakness of the cultural web behind them is what ultimately influences political leaders. Personal conversations I have had about the prospects for gun control legislation with senior staff members working in Congress (as recently as 2021) confirm this view. And more than one member of Congress told me directly when I was a staff member that they would personally have liked to vote for gun control legislation, but the pressures they got from their districts were heavily against it.

Second, three decades of ambitious rhetoric and failed delivery have created a political vacuum into which gun rights advocates have rushed. As empty as the rhetoric of banning guns has been in fact, its threats provide a steady stream of inflammatory propaganda for the gun rights cultural model, which is well wired down to the precinct level.

If the minds of the population are to be changed, it is likely not by commonsense mandates from Washington but from grassroots organization and a web of cultural activism—the hard, day-to-day, precinct-level work and alliances in which other more successful movements have engaged over long periods of time as a condition precedent to success in Washington.

Gun control organizations have in varying ways and degrees recently attempted to create grassroots organizations to build action from the ground up. One example is March for Our Lives, a social action network created by student survivors of the public mass shooting at the Marjory Stoneman Douglas High School in Parkland, Florida, on February 14, 2018. Marches and rallies marked the early days of the movement, but its leaders have subsequently focused on building a long-term structure to inspire activists and activate voters. They are said to have some three hundred local chapters and have published an overall strategy to stop public mass shootings or lessen their lethality. That strategy endorses a familiar menu of bans on assault weapons and high-capacity magazines and expanding the scope and effect of background checks. In the future, whether gun control organizations attempt to leverage social movements through a cultural struggle model—and whether they will be successful—remains to be seen.

Know that things change over time—actions cause reactions.

The civilian gun market and profiles of gun owners have changed over the last thirty years. Many gun control advocates seem unaware of the breadth and depth of this change.

One change obviously relevant to the public mass shooting problem is the industry's successful militarization of the civilian gun market. I regularly visit gun stores, gun sales websites, and nearby shooting ranges; review advertising and popular gun enthusiast literature; and examine industry sales data. I talk to gun owners and gun store staff. What I see, hear, and read clearly demonstrates this militarization. Semiautomatic assault rifles (modern sporting rifles), high-capacity semiautomatic pistols, and hybrid designs blending the two ("assault pistols") dominate the market today (Diaz, 2013, 2019). New shooting sports have been organized around these guns, and hybrid models featuring a range of calibers have undercut the old argument that "no one hunts with an assault rifle."

Ownership of these firearms is not limited to a few hundred potential mass shooters. Nor are they owned only by men compensating for sexual inadequacy (as suggested by some gun control advocates). Tens of millions of ordinary gun enthusiast Americans—of all races, ethnicities, and genders—own them and like them. No one knows exactly how many AR-15 type rifles are owned in America, but a conservative projection from data provided in federal court by the NSSF in 2017 suggests that at least twenty million such rifles are in private hands in America (Curcuruto, 2017).

As unpleasant as this reality may be, the political dynamic of 2022 is vastly different from that of 1994, when the Federal Assault Weapons Ban was enacted (Diaz, 1999, 2013). This type of gun was relatively new to the civilian market in the early 1990s. Its place in that market was questioned, even by some writers for NRA magazines. Many law enforcement organizations opposed their sale to civilians. That has all changed. The political lift in Washington to ban specific types of guns or accessories is more difficult today by an order of magnitude.

Defense has the advantage over offense—change is hard.

As Spitzer (2015) points out, it is as a rule more difficult to enact new laws than to block them, and one of the NRA's most effective strategies has been to keep gun control legislation bottled up in committees to avoid floor discussion and votes. Gun rights advocacy in Washington need not win new ground. It need only hold its ground while working to expand its terrain at the state and local levels and in the courts. The NRA and the gun industry need only wait out the rational national strategy's repeated charges up Capitol Hill.

Endgame

As with other fronts in America's culture war, there is no easy endgame, no foreseeably achievable political action in either model of politics that will resolve once and for all the problem of public mass shootings. The most one can reasonably expect is a series of inconclusive half victories unless and until the gun violence reduction movement changes its basic political model and develops serious nationwide muscle from the grass roots upward.

REFERENCES

Abramowitz, A. (2018). *The great alignment: Race, party transformation, and the rise of Donald Trump.* Yale University Press.

Bishop, B. (2009). *The big sort: Why the clustering of like-minded America is tearing us apart.* Mariner Books.

Bump, P. (2017, November 1). For Trump, October's two mass killings lead to very different responses. *Washington Post.* https://www.washingtonpost.com/news/politics/wp/2017/11/01/for-trump-octobers-two-mass-killings-lead-to-very-different-responses/

Centers for Disease Control and Prevention. (n.d.). *The public health approach to violence prevention.* https://www.cdc.gov/violenceprevention/about/publichealthapproach.html

Curcuruto, J. (2017). Declaration of James Curcuruto in support of plaintiffs' motion for preliminary injunction. Rapp v. Bercerra, U.S. District Court for the Central District of California, Southern Division, Case No.: 8:17-c-00746-JLS-JDE\ (filed November 10, 2017).

D.C. v. Heller, 554 U.S. 570 (2008).

Diaz, T. (1999). *Making a killing: The business of guns in America.* The New Press.

Diaz, T. (2013). *The last gun: How changes in the gun industry are killing Americans and what it will take to stop it.* The New Press.

Diaz, T. (2019). *Tragedy in Aurora: The culture of mass shootings in America.* Rowman & Littlefield.

Doherty, B. (2008). *Gun control on trial: Inside the Supreme Court battle over the Second Amendment.* Cato Institute.

Felter, J. (2014, December 19). *Know the enemy and the nature of the conflict we face.* Hoover Institution. https://www.hoover.org/research/know-enemy-and-nature-conflict-we-face

Foxx, V., & Luetkemeyer, B. (2021, December 22). Democrats want to weaponize OSHA against small businesses. *FOX Business.* https://www.foxbusiness.com/politics/democrats-osha-small-businesses

Goldiner, D. (2021, December 15). Trump accuses N.Y. Attorney General James of "weaponizing" her office to persecute him. *New York Daily News.* https://www.nydailynews.com/news/politics/us-elections-government/ny-trump-lashes-out-new-york-attorney-general-james-20211215-mlg53mjm3fg3pmaslrkr6qb53y-story.html

Goss, K. (2006). *Disarmed: The missing movement for gun control in America.* Princeton University Press.

Hemenway, D. (2017). *Private guns, public health.* University of Michigan Press.

Heywood, A. (2019). *Politics.* Red Globe Press.

Inglehart, R. (1977). *The silent revolution: Changing values and political styles among Western publics.* Princeton University Press.

Inglehart, R., Miller, J., & Woods, L. (2018). *The silent revolution in reverse: Trump and the xenophobic authoritarian populist parties.* Paper presented at American Political Science Association Meeting.

Karni, A. (2021, March 26). Supporters of gun control assail Biden over delay on action. *New York Times.* https://www.nytimes.com/2021/03/26/us/politics/gun-control-biden-mass-shootings.html

Kopel, D. (1992). *The samurai, the mountie, and the cowboy: Should America adopt the gun controls of other democracies?* Prometheus Books.

Lawrence, J. (2021, April 28). You don't actually need to reach across the aisle, Mr. Biden. *New York Times.* https://www.nytimes.com/2021/04/28/opinion/joe-biden-bipartisanship.html

Leftwich, A. (2004). *What is politics?—The activity and its study.* Polity Press.

McClurg, A. J., & Denning, B. P. (2016). *Guns and the law.* Carolina Academic Press.

McDonald v. Chicago, 561 U.S. 742 (2010).

Melzer, S. (2009). *Gun crusaders: The NRA's culture war.* New York University Press.

Ouimet, J. (2022, January). CDC statements resurrect concerns over agency's past anti-gun advocacy. *American Rifleman.*

Overby, P. (2012, December 21). NRA: "Only thing that stops a bad guy with a gun is a good guy with a gun." NPR. https://www.npr.org/2012/12/21/167824766/nra-only-thing-that-stops-a-bad-guy-with-a-gun-is-a-good-guy-with-a-gun

Parker, K., Horowitz, J. M., Igielnik, R., Baxter Oliphant, J., & Brown, A. (2017, June 22). *America's complex relationship with guns.* Pew Research Center. https://www.pewresearch.org/social-trends/2017/06/22/americas-complex-relationship-with-guns/

Rushe, D. (2018, May 4). Why is the National Rifle Association so powerful? *The Guardian.* https://www.theguardian.com/us-news/2017/nov/17/nra-gun-lobby-gun-control-congress

Spitzer, R. (2015). *The politics of gun control* (6th ed.). Paradigm Publishers.

Stolberg, S. (2021, March 27). Can new gun violence research find a path around the political stalemate? *New York Times.* https://www.nytimes.com/2021/03/27/us/politics/gun-violence-research-cdc.html

Teles, S. (2008). *The rise of the conservative legal movement: The battle for control of the law.* Princeton University Press.

Tzu, Sun, Clausewitz, C., & Machiavelli, N. (n.d.). *The art of war: Trilogy.* Amazon Kindle Edition.

Urbatsch, R. (2019). Gun-shy: Refusal to answer questions about firearm ownership. *Social Science Journal, 56*(2), 189–195. https://doi.org/10.1016/j.soscij.2018.04.003

Walsh, J. (2021, December 1). Gun sales near record levels as U.S. grapples with another school shooting. *Forbes.* https://www.forbes.com/sites/joewalsh/2021/12/01/gun-sales-near-record-levels-as-us-grapples-with-another-school-shooting

Webster, D. W., & Vernick, J. S. (2013). *Reducing gun violence in America: informing policy with evidence and analysis.* The Johns Hopkins University Press.

White House. (2021, February 10). *Readout of the White House's meeting with gun violence prevention advocates.* https://www.whitehouse.gov/briefing-room/statements-releases/2021/02/10/readout-of-the-white-houses-meeting-with-gun-violence-prevention-advocacy-groups-2/

Wright, J. D. (1995). Ten essential observations on guns in America. *Society, 32,* 63–68. https://doi.org/10.1007/BF02693310

Yamane, D. (2017). The sociology of U.S. gun culture. *Sociology Compass, 11*(7). https://doi.org/10.1111/soc4.12497

15

Heated Partisan Rhetoric

An Important Factor in Mass Shootings That
Involve Political Figures in the United States

MARK R. JOSLYN

ndiscriminate violence against ordinary Americans is one of the truly frightening characteristics of mass shootings. From schoolchildren, FedEx employees, and supermarket workers, to church congregations and music festival fans, mass shooters usually kill or injure common folk. The range of
victims can, in fact, make it difficult to determine the causes of violence.

However, for a very small number of shootings, gunmen target well-known
political figures. And in two recent cases, the alleged cause of violence was
harsh political imagery and heated rhetoric. In other words, politics may have
provoked the shooter.

In 2011, Gabrielle Giffords, a House Democrat from Arizona, was shot
and suffered a serious brain injury. Six years later, Steve Scalise, a House Republican from Louisiana, was shot and sustained severe bone and organ injuries.

These two shootings offer a useful context to examine the public's beliefs
about a connection between gun violence and politics. Democrats have consistently regarded mass shootings as a reflection of broader problems in society—as having systemic causes (Joslyn & Haider-Markel, 2012). For example,
after the mass shooting at Virginia Tech, Democrats typically implicated institutional shortcomings regarding gun laws and lack of mental health care.

By contrast, Republicans generally advance more narrowly tailored causal attributions. Mass shootings are thought to be isolated events (Joslyn &
Haider-Markel, 2012). According to this manner of thinking, people make

choices, and their actions cannot be sufficiently explained by prevailing social and political milieus—the perpetrator acted, and ultimately the causes of those actions are found within the individual.[1]

The attempted assassinations of Giffords and Scalise test the stability of these partisan attributions. When Democratic leaders are the target of violence—and Republican rhetoric may have influenced the shooter—it would be self-serving for both sides to maintain their perspectives. Democrats may blame broader social and political causes, such as inflammatory rhetoric and partisan polarization, while Republicans may blame the individual alone and claim the shooting was an isolated incident.

But what about when the victims are reversed? When Republican elected officials are the target of violence—and Democrat rhetoric is considered the source of provocation—will GOP members abandon attributions focused primarily on the shooter and adopt broader causes originating from the political environment? And in this scenario, will Democrats revise their causal attributions and focus narrowly on the shooter?

The empirical evidence demonstrates that partisan-motivated mass shootings can alter typical attributional patterns. In particular, the Scalise shooting influenced the attributions of Republicans—from blaming the shooter to pointing the finger at Democrats. However, Democrats' attributions were largely unchanged regardless of which party leaders the violence struck. In addition, both Democrats *and* Republicans who believed the Giffords and Scalise shootings were primarily motivated by partisan hostilities (external attributions) exhibited increased support for stricter gun policies to prevent future attacks. However, among partisans that did not connect rhetoric to gun violence, comparatively few supported tougher gun restrictions.

Results thus strongly suggest that in the wake of politically motivated shootings—especially those involving a Republican elected official—policy makers can expect an unusually supportive attitudinal environment for gun control regulations.

Motivated to Kill an Elected Official

Tucson Shooting

In 2011, Arizona's Democrat House representative Gabrielle Giffords barely survived an attempt on her life. Giffords was shot in Tucson and suffered a serious brain injury. Six people died, including a U.S. district judge and a nine-year-old child; thirteen others were wounded.

Even before the identity of the shooter was known, liberal commentators blamed the attack on violent imagery and inflammatory rhetoric of Tea Party candidates and conservatives during the 2010 midterm elections. Observers recounted Giffords's Tea Party opponent's fundraiser at a shooting range where he invited supporters to "help remove Gabrielle Giffords from office" before shooting an M16 rifle (Gold, 2011). Liberals also referenced callous campaign imagery, notably from Sarah Palin's PAC, which featured stylized crosshairs targeting Giffords. Local Pima County Sheriff Clarence Dupnik linked conservative rhetoric to violence:

> When you look at unbalanced people, how they respond to the vitriol that comes out of certain mouths about tearing down the government. The anger, the hatred, the bigotry that goes on in this country is getting to be outrageous. (Somashekhar, 2011)

Before being shot, Giffords had expressed similar concerns and specifically mentioned the Tea Party and Palin's use of crosshairs that targeted her congressional seat:

> We're in Sarah Palin's "targeted" list, but the thing is that the way she has it depicted, we're in the cross-hairs of a gun sight over our district. When people do that, they've got to realize that there are consequences to that action. (Quinn & Gallagher, 2011)

Former Democratic senator and presidential candidate Gary Hart was more direct. He stated:

> We all know that there are unstable and potentially dangerous people among us. To repeatedly appeal to their basic instincts is to invite and welcome their predictable violence. (Gold, 2011)

The perpetrator had met Giffords three years earlier and had become obsessed with her. He suffered from paranoid schizophrenia and regularly posted anti-government views on social media, though reports suggested he did not have a clear and coherent political motivation (Montopoli, 2011).

Alexandria Shooting

In the summer of 2017, a gunman shot House Majority Republican Whip Steve Scalise and several others during a morning practice of the congressional Republicans' baseball team. The assailant died after a ten-minute shootout with law enforcement. Scalise suffered critical bone and organ injuries and underwent several surgeries.

Just hours after the shooting, political accusations started. Republicans blamed Democrats, pointing to relentless anti-Trump rhetoric that created a climate of violence that inspired the shooter. On Fox News, Newt Gingrich argued:

> You've had a series of things, which sends signals that tell people that it's OK to hate Trump. It's OK to think of Trump in violent terms. It's OK to consider assassinating Trump and then . . . suddenly we're supposed to rise above it—until next time. (Seitz-Wald, 2017)

Republicans also cited the controversial play in New York called *Shakespeare in the Park* as an example of the troubling signal Gingrich referenced (Wilkinson, 2017). The production portrayed Julius Caesar as Trump. A blond Julius Caesar was assassinated, brutally stabbed to death by women and minorities (Beckett, 2017). In another example, Republicans denounced comedian Kathy Griffin posing with a fake severed and bloodied Trump head.

The local police were familiar with the shooter. They had responded to several complaints from his neighbors and extended family. The shooter was a member of several Facebook groups that were strongly anti-Republican, raged regularly on social media about destroying the president, volunteered for Bernie Sanders's 2016 presidential campaign in Iowa, and wrote nearly thirty letters to the editor expressing his anti-Republican feelings. In the shooter's pocket, the FBI found a list of names of Republican congressmen.

In many ways, Republican criticisms were a reversal of Democrats after the Giffords shootings. Both parties were quick to point fingers at each other, drawing a direct line between gun violence and partisan rhetoric. One important difference concerns the gunman's motivation. While the Tucson shooter seemed focused on Giffords, the Alexandria gunman concentrated more broadly on Republican legislators.

Causal Attributions

Attribution theory examines the causes people assign for behaviors or events. In Fritz Heider's (1958) original formulation, people attribute behavior to internal/dispositional factors or to environmental/external factors. Once causes are identified, policy alternatives that seek to eliminate the problem can be discussed and thoroughly considered. Stone's (1997, p. 189) classic thesis on the formation of policy agendas underscores the importance of causal understanding: "Causal stories are essential political instruments for shaping alliances and for settling the distribution of benefits and costs." The public's understanding of the causes of mass shootings is therefore vital to constructing political alliances and foundational to the policy agenda process.

Internal vs. External

For internal attributions, the causes of the behavior are within the individual. For external attributions, the environment or social/political context is responsible. For example, citizens understandably want to know why a gunman would shoot a congresswoman. The violent act can be explained as dispositional. The gunman is mentally ill, fundamentally evil, or lacks proper moral restraint and respect for human life. Simply, bad people do bad things.

Alternatively, the causes of the shooting could be environmental—traumatic childhood experiences, poor upbringing, permissive gun laws, or even strong partisan rancor and inflammatory imagery. The social and political milieu shapes life's choices and abets violent behaviors.

The causes of mass shootings are complicated, and the details often escape media scrutiny. In such circumstances, some people lean on their political predispositions to make sense of the violence. Causal attributions, in fact, often justify political identities—particularly party identification. Partisan motivations and sentiment are especially important factors in constructing causal attributions.

Motivation and Attribution

A range of motivations influence attributions, including enhancing self-esteem (Zuckerman, 1979), creating favorable impressions (Bradley, 1978), and preserving political beliefs. These drives can be folded under the larger umbrella of motivated reasoning (Kunda, 1990; Lodge & Taber, 2013). Strong dispositions—social and political—produce defensive and biased cognition. People selectively process information, challenge discordant information, and fashion judgments in ways that align with their prior beliefs. Information processing will therefore suit a specific purpose and yield a desired conclusion.

Consider research on party identification. Partisan motivations directly influence the choice of attributions (Iyengar, 1991). For example, Democrats typically view poor people as casualties of an unjust economic and political system. Systemic powers limit or remove individual agency. Therefore, Democrats generally do not hold the poor responsible for their circumstances. This causal reasoning fits well with Democrat values and justifies government intervention.

By contrast, Republicans are more likely to blame the poor. They point to insufficient drive and poor decisions. They argue that people can and do prosper with proper motivation. This internal attribution for poverty warrants a more limited view of government intervention.

Partisans, in fact, disagree about the causes of many issues, including crime (Carroll et al., 1987), obesity (Joslyn & Haider-Markel, 2019), blame after natural disasters (Malhotra & Kuo, 2008), and the origins of homosexuality (Haider-Markel & Joslyn, 2008; Suhay & Jayaratne, 2013).

More relevant for mass shootings is that Democrats often implicate external causes, believing gun violence stems from larger institutional shortcomings—specifically, weak gun laws. Republicans infer the causes as internal, focusing largely on assailant characteristics (Joslyn & Haider-Markel, 2012). In addition, after a shooting, different representations (frames) of potential causes influence people's attributions of blame (Haider-Markel & Joslyn, 2001). In other words, partisans can be primed to adopt alternative causes of mass shootings. The news media characterization of a mass shooting is therefore an important determinant of citizens' causal reasoning.

Finally, the type of causal attribution leads to distinctive beliefs about the regularity of shootings and favored policy responses. If shootings are caused by the environment, then the violence will likely happen again, and government intervention is needed. On the other hand, if mass shootings are isolated and specific to troubled individuals, not much can be done about them.

Expectations

The literature shows partisans prefer causal explanations that align with their party values (Suhay & Jayaratne, 2013). For most issues, including mass shootings, Democrats tend to believe larger environmental factors are responsible (Joslyn & Haider-Markel, 2012). Mass shootings reflect broader problems in society—such as inadequate gun laws. Democrats then will advance government solutions as a remedy for problems they believe are systemic. Blaming the system creates momentum to change that system.

Republicans tend to fault individuals. They do not cast blame as widely as Democrats and maintain a limited view of government intervention. Mass shootings are tragic but isolated. Condemning perpetrators preserves the status quo.

However, the unusual circumstances of partisan-inspired mass shootings would be expected to alter these patterns. Partisans are aware that their own party blames the opposition party's inflammatory rhetoric for the shooting. In our age of extreme partisan animosity and negative partisanship (Abramowitz, 2018), this attribution strikes a chord. In other words, the opposition caused the tragedy.

Accordingly, after the Giffords shootings, both parties would be expected to maintain their attributions. Democrats may blame broader problems in society—sharp partisan rhetoric aimed at Giffords—and Republicans may fault the shooter. However, for the Scalise shooting, I expect Republicans to cast aside their inclination for internal attributions and embrace the partisan rhetoric cause. And, just like Democrats, for Republicans who believe partisan rhetoric caused political violence, I expect support for stricter gun laws.

Data and Methods

To test expectations, I utilized several national surveys conducted following the Tucson shooting and a national survey fielded by the University of Kansas Political Science Department after the Alexandria shooting.

Just three days after Giffords was shot, Gallup (Jones, 2011) asked people the following question: "Just your best guess, do you think the heated language used in politics today was or was not a factor influencing the Arizona shooter to commit the attack?—Major factor, minor factor, not a factor." Overall, 21 percent thought heated language was a major factor, 21 percent believed it was a minor factor, and 47 percent said it was a nonfactor.

The question separates partisans in the expected manner. Forty percent of Democrats identified heated language as a major factor, while only 10 percent of Republicans did.[2] As expected, Democrats were more willing than Republicans to identify an external cause—heated language—and believe it was a major factor. Only about a quarter of Republicans recognized language as a factor, and of that fraction, most considered it a minor one.

Pew Research Center (2011) asked people to choose between an external or internal causal attribution for the shooting: "Thinking about the shooting in Tucson, Arizona last week, do you think this shooting reflects broader problems in American society, or are things like this just the isolated acts of troubled individuals?"

In comparison to other high-profile shootings, the response for broader problems was notably lower. About a third of the sample thought Tucson reflected broader problems in society, and nearly 60 percent isolated acts of troubled individuals. By comparison, after the Virginia Tech shooting, approximately 50 percent thought the tragedy reflected broader problems.

The difference likely turns on the unusual nature of the Tucson shooting. While school shootings are relatively common—implying systemic influence—shootings that target elected officials are not.

Nevertheless, 45 percent of Democrats considered Tucson a reflection of broader problems, but less than a quarter of Republicans (23 percent) did. In short, the partisan patterns were predictable. Democrats favored external attributions—broader problems and heated language a factor—while Republicans favored internal attributions—isolated acts and heated language a nonfactor.

After the Alexandria shooting, the Kansas University Political Science Survey asked a random sample of U.S. adults the identical question about heated language except referenced the Virginia shooter. Compared to Gallup's Tucson survey, a significantly higher percentage of the sample considered heated political language a major factor—37 percent—or a minor factor—46 percent. About the same proportion of Democrats thought heated language was a major factor, but, as anticipated, a notably higher percentage of Republicans, 34 percent, also considered rhetoric a major factor.

After the Tucson shooting, party polarization and hostilities intensified and expanded considerably with Donald Trump's campaign and unexpected 2016 victory. The Alexandria shooting thus took place during unprecedented partisan rancor. Accordingly, more people justifiably considered the Alexandria shooting as a symptom of a larger political conflict (60 percent) and thought Alexandria reflected broader problems in society. In fact, a majority of both parties said the shooting was a reflection of broader problems in society.

This change is important. The Alexandria attack prompted Republicans to identify the cause for mass shooting much like Democrats do. The typical partisan divide narrowed as a significantly greater percentage of Republicans identified political language as the major cause of the shooting. The percentage more than tripled from 10 percent to 34 percent—see Figure 15.1.

The key question now is whether the beliefs about partisan rhetoric causing mass shootings influence support for stricter gun regulations. If so, the Alexandria shooting would be notable for its impact on Republican support for gun control.

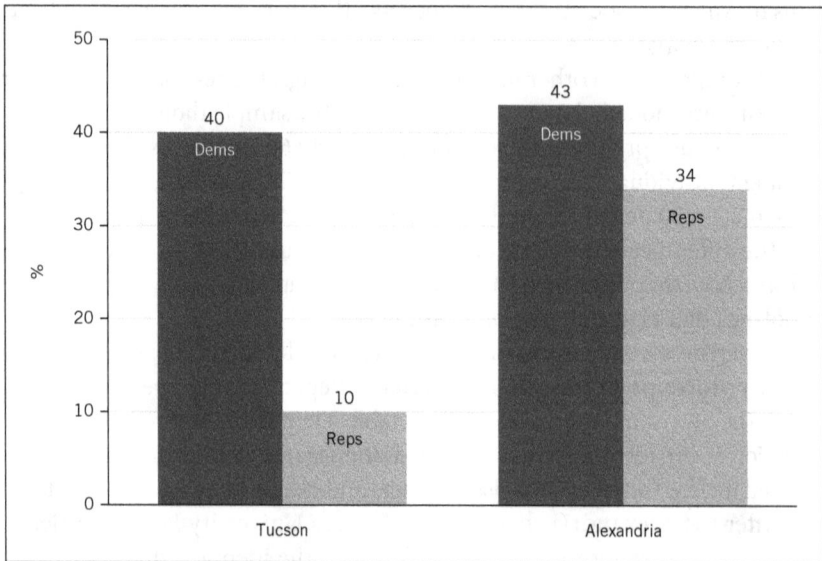

Figure 15.1 Percentage of Respondents Who Believed Heated Political Language Was a Major Factor in Each Shooting. (*Source: Gallup and Kansas Political Science Surveys*)

Support for Gun Regulation

After high-profile mass shootings, political debate centers on gun access. Democrats typically argue for stronger gun laws, while Republicans support gun rights. The positions are consistent with each party's conventional causal reasoning. If mass shootings are isolated incidents by disturbed individuals—as many GOP believe—then changing gun laws makes no sense. Individuals are the problem, not guns. On the other hand, if mass shootings are a symptom of broader social problems (including political hostilities)—as many Democrats think—then gun control may be the solution.

For the Giffords' tragedy, Gallup asked the following question about gun policy:

> Next, as you may know, this past weekend six people were killed and others including a member of Congress were wounded in a shooting in Tucson, Arizona. From what you know about the shootings, do you think—This tragedy would have been prevented if the state of Arizona had stricter gun laws, (or) This tragedy would have occurred even if the state of Arizona had stricter gun laws.

Almost a quarter of the sample thought stricter gun laws could have prevented the tragedy. However, very few Republicans (7 percent) subscribed to this view, while over 40 percent of Democrats endorsed it.

The Kansas University survey asked respondents a similar question:

> Have the shootings in Virginia made you more likely to support stricter gun control laws, less likely to support stricter gun control laws, or has your opinion on gun laws stayed the same?

About a third of respondents said more likely. This time, more than double the percentage of Republicans supported stricter gun laws, and about the same percentage of Democrats did. In addition, for both tragedies, there is a significant relationship between beliefs about heated rhetoric and beliefs about gun control laws.

Figure 15.2 depicts logistic modeling estimates of various predictor variables on support for stricter gun laws in Arizona. Education typically increases the probability of support for gun control laws, and it does for this question as well (+0.05). Similarly, members of the Democratic party (+0.12) and females (+0.05) show a greater likelihood of support for stricter gun regulations. Republicans, however, were less likely than Democrats to think gun laws were responsible for the Gifford shooting (−0.11).

Importantly, even after controlling for these demographic characteristics, heated language was the most impactful variable, exerting twice the effect

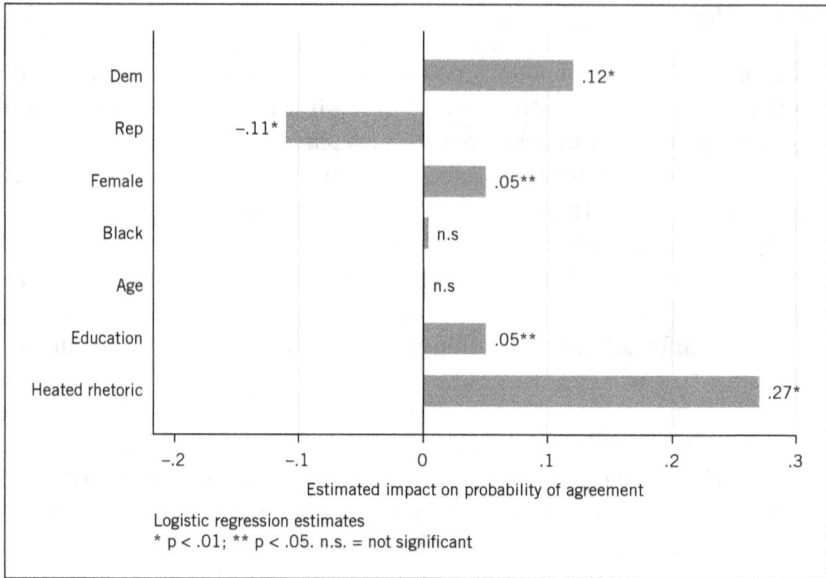

Figure 15.2 Estimated Impact on Probability of Agreement That the Tucson Tragedy Could Have Been Prevented if AZ Had Stricter Gun Regulations.

of party identification on beliefs about gun regulations (+0.27). Causal attributions for mass shootings are thus strong predictors of people's attitudes about gun regulations. An identical model for the Alexandria shooting returned the same patterns of association.

Figures 15.3 and 15.4 display predicted probabilities for stricter gun laws across the three response categories for heated rhetoric. People who did not consider inflammatory language a factor were largely unmoved. Gun law attitudes were not impacted in a significant way. However, for people who identified political rhetoric as a minor or major factor, their probabilities of believing guns could have prevented the Tucson tragedy, or of supporting stricter gun laws after Alexandra, increased substantially. Overall, those who attributed the Giffords and Scalise shootings to partisan language were far more supportive of stricter gun laws.

To this point, the statistical models controlled for the impact of other predictor variables, including party identification, and estimated the impacts of attributions (heated rhetoric) on gun regulation attitudes. Now, for a final test, I examine whether the attribution impacted Republicans' and Democrats' gun regulation attitudes. In other words, do Republicans and Democrats who attributed the cause of the mass shootings to heated rhetoric exhibit increased support for gun regulations?

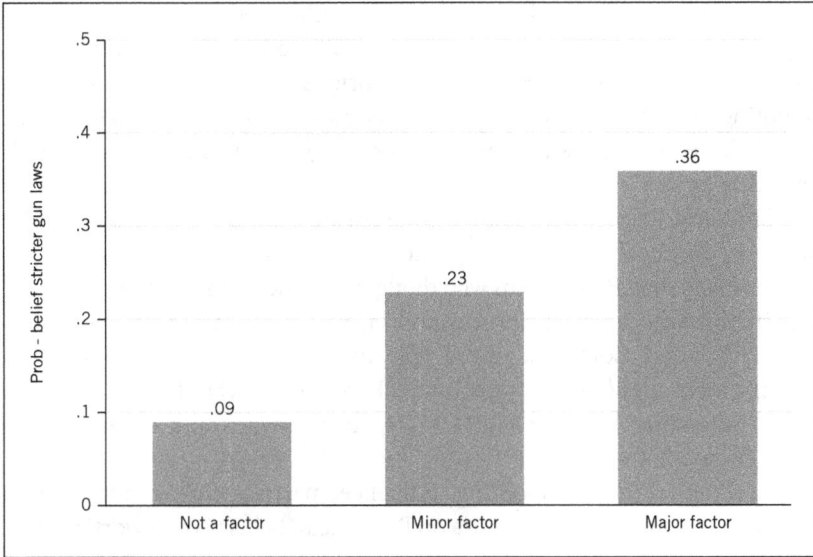

Figure 15.3 Impact of Heated Partisan Rhetoric on Probabilities of Believing That Stricter Gun Laws in AR Could Have Prevented the Tragedy. (*Source: Gallup Data*)

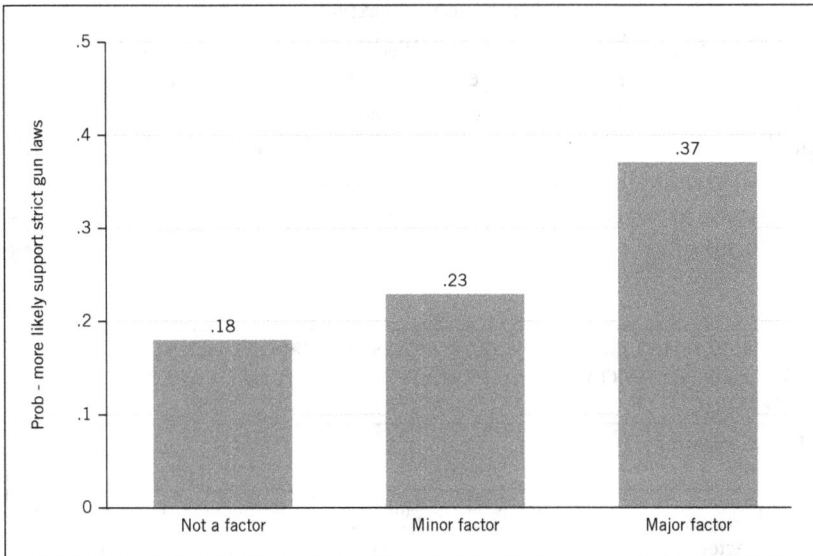

Figure 15.4 Impact of Heated Partisan Rhetoric on Likelihood of Supporting Stricter Gun Control Laws after Alexandria Shooting. (*Source: University of Kansas Survey*)

The data show the attribution positively influenced both Republican and Democrat support for stricter gun laws (see Table 15.1). For example, Democrats who identified heated political rhetoric as a major factor in the Tucson shooting were more likely to support stricter gun laws (0.57) than Democrats who believed rhetoric was a minor factor (0.21). The pattern appears for Alexandria as well.

Similarly, Republicans who identified heated political rhetoric as a major factor in the Tucson shooting were more likely to support stricter gun regulations (0.09) than Republicans who thought rhetoric was a minor factor (0.03). Again, the pattern repeats for Alexandria, but the estimated effects are substantially larger. Compare, for example, the estimated probabilities of supporting stricter gun regulations among Republicans who think rhetoric is a major factor after Alexandria (0.24) to Republicans who think it a major factor after Tucson (0.09).

In short, while both shootings influenced partisan support for gun regulations, the impact of Alexandria on Republican beliefs is noteworthy. First, substantially more Republicans attributed the shootings to heated political rhetoric. And second, that attribution produced a stronger impact on Republicans' support for stricter gun regulations than did the Tucson shooting.

Conclusions

This chapter applied attribution theory to explain causal explanations for mass shootings of political figures. According to the theory, people generally construe the causes of events by referencing external or internal factors. Democrats typically attribute shootings to broader problems in society, while Republicans consider shootings isolated incidents. However, in the Alexandria case, where the shooter targeted a Republican elected official—a significant proportion of Republicans adopted Democrats' penchant for external causes. Specifically, Republicans blamed incendiary Democrat rhetoric for inspiring

TABLE 15.1   ESTIMATED PROBABILITIES OF SUPPORT FOR STRICTER GUN LAWS BY PARTY ID AND PERCEIVED IMPACT OF HEATED POLITICAL RHETORIC

Heated Political Rhetoric	Tucson		Alexandria	
	Democrats	Republicans	Democrats	Republicans
Not a factor	0.21	0.03	0.36	0.08
Minor factor	0.37	0.11	0.37	0.11
Major factor	0.57	0.09	0.51	0.24
Note: Entries are estimated probabilities drawn from full models.				

the shooter. In addition, like Democrats, Republicans who attributed the shooting to harsh partisan rhetoric exhibited greater support for stricter gun laws.

Keeping in mind the limitations of a two-case analysis, the empirical findings lead to several conclusions. First, the evidence supports Heider's (1958) original theory that people identify external or internal attributions to explain events—in this case, politically motivated gun shootings. Likewise, the empirical results confirm prior research on mass shootings that shows Democrats prefer external attributions while Republicans favor internal ones (Joslyn & Haider-Markel, 2012).

Second, the data also demonstrate the importance of political context. The details of the shootings—especially the targets of the gunmen—shape reasoning about the causes of the shootings. This is apparent among Republicans who increased blame on partisan rhetoric when a Republican leader was the target of violence.

Third, increased political polarization in American culture may change attribution as well. This study showed that partisans are willing to link opposition party activities to the violent behavior of mass shooters. In other words, a significant number of partisans believe the other party was the main cause of gun violence, at least in these incidents. This speaks to the level of antipathy and distrust between the two parties.

Finally, among both parties, beliefs that harsh partisan language inspired the shooter translated into support for stricter gun laws. This connection suggests a "policy window" (Kingdon, 1984) whereby shifts in public attention and attitudes increase the likelihood that lawmakers could act on gun violence.

While federal responses to mass shootings remain modest and fail to produce meaningful change (Schildkraut & Carr, 2020), state responses include gun restrictions as well as the loosening of gun regulations (Luca et al., 2020). For mass shootings involving political figures—an important but small subset of mass shootings—the data point to a boost in partisan support for gun regulations. In this regard, it is perhaps not a coincidence that the only major federal gun control laws in the past fifty years were prompted by violence. For example, the assassinations of John F. Kennedy, Robert Kennedy, and Martin Luther King Jr. led to the Federal Gun Control Act of 1968, the attempted assassination of Ronald Reagan led to the Brady Bill of 1993, and several mass shootings inspired the Federal Assault Weapons Ban in 1994. No one hopes for more tragic violence, but meaningful policy changes may become more feasible in the aftermath of such incidents.

NOTES

This chapter is an expanded version of a guest blog post at Political Violence at a Glance, "Inciting to Violence? Attributions for Political Violence Have a Partisan Bent."

1. In the past, Republicans/conservatives have broadly blamed violent media, poor parenting, declining morality, and mental illness.

2. CBS asked a similar question, and a familiar partisan split emerged: "Some people have said that the harsh political tone of recent political campaigns has encouraged violence. What do you think? Do you think the recent harsh political tone has anything to do with the Arizona shootings, or not?" Overall, 41 percent thought harsh political tone was a factor—57 percent of Democrats and 23 percent Republicans. The *Wall Street Journal* also asked a similar question: "Thinking about the shootings of a Member of Congress, a Federal judge and others in Tucson, Arizona last weekend, do you feel the extreme political rhetoric used by some in the media and by political leaders was an important contributor to the incident, or do you feel this is more of an isolated incident by a disturbed person that occurs from time to time?" Overall, 25 percent felt extreme political rhetoric led to the shooting—38 percent of Democrats and 12 percent of Republicans (Joslyn & Haider-Markel, 2012).

REFERENCES

Abramowitz, A. I. (2018). *The great alignment*. New Haven: Yale University Press.

Beckett, L. (2017, June 12). Trump as Julius Caesar: Anger over play misses Shakespeare's point, says scholar. *The Guardian*. https://www.theguardian.com/culture/2017/jun/12/donald-trump-shakespeare-play-julius-caesar-new-york

Bradley, G. W. (1978). Self-serving biases in the attribution process: A reexamination of the fact or fiction question. *Journal of Personality and Social Psychology, 34*(2), 978–989.

Carroll, J., Perkowitz, W. T., Lurigio, A. J., & Weaver, F. M. (1987). Sentencing goals, causal attributions, ideology, and personality. *Journal of Personality and Social Psychology, 52*(1), 107–118.

Gold, M. (2011, January 8). In Gabrielle Giffords shooting, many on left quick to lay blame. *Los Angeles Times*. https://www.latimes.com/archives/la-xpm-2011-jan-08-la-na-giffords-shooting-media-20110109-story.html

Haider-Markel, D. P., & Joslyn, M.R. (2001). Gun policy, opinion, tragedy, and blame attribution: The conditional influence of issue frames. *Journal of Politics, 63*(2), 520–543.

Haider-Markel, D. P., & Joslyn, M.R. (2008). Beliefs about homosexuality and support for gay rights: An empirical test of attribution theory. *Public Opinion Quarterly, 72*(2), 291–310.

Heider, F. (1958). *The psychology of interpersonal relations*. New York: Wiley.

Iyengar, S. (1991). *Is anyone responsible? How television frames political issues*. Chicago: University of Chicago Press.

Jones, J. M. (2011, January 12). *Most doubt political rhetoric a major factor in Arizona shootings*. Gallup. https://news.gallup.com/poll/145556/doubt-political-rhetoric-major-factor-ariz-shootings.aspx

Joslyn, M. R., & Haider-Markel, D.P. (2012). The politics of causes: Mass shootings and the cases of the Virginia Tech and Tucson tragedies. *Social Science Quarterly, 94*(2), 410–423.

Joslyn, M. R., & Haider-Markel, D. P. (2019). Perceived causes of obesity, emotions, and attitudes about discrimination policy. *Social Science & Medicine, 223*(1), 97–103.

Kingdon, J. W. (1984). *Agendas, alternatives, and public policies*. New York: Harper Collins.

Kunda, Z. (1990). The case for motivated reasoning. *Psychological Bulletin, 108*(3), 480–498.

Lodge, M., & Taber, C. (2013). *The rationalizing voter.* Cambridge, U.K.: Cambridge University Press.

Luca, M., Malhotra, D., & Polquin, C. (2020). The impact of mass shootings on gun policy. *Journal of Public Economics, 181*(2), 1–20.

Malhotra, N., & Kuo, A.G. (2008). Attributing blame: The public's response to hurricane Katrina. *Journal of Politics, 70*(1), 120–135.

Montopoli, B. (2011, January 10). *What does Jared Lee Loughner believe?* CBS News. https://www.cbsnews.com/news/what-does-jared-lee-loughner-believe/

Pew Research Center. (2011, January 19). *No shift toward gun control after Tucson shootings.* Pew Research Center. https://www.pewresearch.org/politics/2011/01/19/no-shift-toward-gun-control-after-tucson-shootings/

Quinn, B., & Gallagher, P. (2011, January 9). US congresswoman Gabrielle Giffords shot as six die in Arizona massacre. *The Guardian.* https://www.theguardian.com/world/2011/jan/08/gabrielle-giffords-shot-tucson-arizona

Schildkraut, J., & Carr, C. M. (2020). Mass shooting, legislative responses, and public policy: An endless cycle of inaction. *Emory Law Journal, 69*(5), 1045–1071.

Seitz-Wald, A. (2011, June 14). After shooting, some in GOP blame incitement by Democrats. *NBC News.* https://www.nbcnews.com/politics/congress/after-shooting-some-gop-blame-incitement-democrats-n772586

Somashekhar, S. (2011, January 9). Sheriff Dupnik's criticism of political "vitriol" resonates with public. *Washington Post.* http://voices.washingtonpost.com/44/2011/01/sheriff-dupniks-criticism-of-p.html

Stone, D. A. (1997). *Policy paradox: The art of political decision making.* New York: Norton.

Suhay, E., & Jayaratne, T. E. (2013). Does biology justify ideology? The politics of genetic attribution. *Public Opinion Quarterly, 77*(2), 497–521.

Wilkinson, A. (2017, June 19). *Why outrage over Shakespeare in the park's Trump-like Julius Caesar is so misplaced.* Vox. https://www.vox.com/culture/2017/6/12/15780692/julius-caesar-shakespeare-in-park-trump-public-theater-outrage

Zuckerman, M. (1979). Attribution of success and failure revisited, or: The motivational bias is alive and well in attribution theory. *Journal of Personality, 47,* 245–287.

16

Support for Gun Rights

*Group Identities, Perceptions of Safety, and Attitudes about
Responses to Mass Shootings in the United States*

DONALD P. HAIDER-MARKEL, ABIGAIL VEGTER,
AND PATRICK J. GAUDING

O n an annual basis, mass shootings tend to make up a small percentage
of all gun violence deaths in the United States. In fact, for most recent
years, suicides with guns constitute a majority of gun-caused deaths.
However, debate over gun regulation often revolves around mass shootings.
In part, this is because mass shootings increase the salience of gun violence
due to the national attention they receive, even if only for a few days after each
high-profile incident (García-Montoya et al., 2021).

Indeed, mass shootings have become the focal point for proponents of gun
regulations, as well as for gun rights activists. Since the Columbine High School
mass shooting in April 1999, gun owners and gun organizations have consistently argued that guns make individuals and society safer and that government intervention will do little to stop mass shootings. Significant portions
of the public, including many Republicans and conservatives, have adopted
this point of view as well. In addition, although the public is polarized on many
gun policy issues, recent expansions of concealed carry laws and stand your
ground policies make it clear that many policy makers on the ideological right
are following the talking points emanating from gun culture.

Our research seeks to understand the social and psychological roots of
divergent attitudes on these issues. First, we explore changes in aggregate opinion on guns and mass shootings and track the literature about opinion changes after highly publicized mass shootings. Second, we argue that politicized
group identities motivate beliefs about guns, safety, and effective government
response to mass shootings. These identities lead their adherents to engage

in a form of motivated reasoning that results in preferences and beliefs that protect self-interests—here, a desire to protect gun ownership from restrictions and increasingly expand gun access and ownership. In this case, we expect gun owners, especially those with a strong gun owner identity, to adhere to a belief that guns make society safer and that government can do little to stop mass shootings.[1] Meanwhile, non-gun-owning Republicans and conservatives, having aligned themselves with gun owners as members of a common in-group, are expected to engage in similar motivated reasoning toward protecting the self-interest of their in-group and adopt the arguments made in gun culture about safety and mass shootings.

We test several hypotheses with analysis of several recent national surveys of American adults. Our results support the notion that motivated self-interest drives some groups to believe that guns make us safer and that government intervention, especially increased gun regulation, will not reduce mass shootings. The finding holds for gun owners, but also those who have adopted gun owners as part of their in-group. We believe our findings support the notion that gun owners adhere to rugged individualism as a means to face a dangerous world, generating a worldview that is broadly in line with those of Republicans and conservatives, and that this view shapes their perception of viable responses to mass shootings. We discuss the implications of our findings for the future of the gun debate and public policy in America.

Mass Shootings and Public Opinion

Each large-casualty mass shooting event in the United States turns the world's attention to America's particularized problem of gun violence. Each event brings forward now-common narratives that we have been exposed to since the 1990s. Gun restriction advocates call for new gun restrictions, while gun rights advocates speak of not politicizing tragedy or even use the occasion to advocate for expansions of gun rights, arguing that such attacks could have been stopped by a "good guy with a gun." However, significant bipartisan portions of the public do support some new gun restrictions (Miller, 2017), as well as other government interventions meant to address gun violence (Van Green, 2021). In addition, general support for stricter gun regulations tends to spike following mass shootings, increasing as much as 15 percentage points (Cohn & Sanger-Katz, 2019).

However, what many observers seem to ignore is just how dramatically public comfort with guns and a broader gun culture have grown. For example, according to national polls, it appears many Americans have changed their attitudes on whether guns make us safer or less safe. In the 1990s, most American adults believed that guns make us less safe, but by 2014, a solid majority was now believing that guns make us safer.[2] At the same time, Americans appear to have grown increasingly doubtful about the ability of government to address mass shootings or gun violence generally. A few examples are merited. First, a majority of Americans are now more likely to believe that increased gun regulation will do little or nothing to reduce violence in the country (61 percent), while only 39 percent believe that gun regulation will decrease violence. In the 1990s, the public was evenly divided on this question.[3]

Indeed, a 2017 Gallup poll found that 58 percent of adults believe that new gun regulations would have little or no impact on the number of mass shootings (Newport, 2021). Polls by the Pew Research Center in 2017, 2018, and 2021 found that just under 50 percent of adults believed that new gun regulations would decrease mass shootings, while about 42 percent said they would make no difference and about 9 percent said there would be more mass shootings (Schaeffer, 2021).

Second, for most of the last twenty years, a majority of the public came to believe that government action will not be effective in preventing mass shootings (see Figure 16.1). The question asks, "Which of the following statements come closer to your overall view?" (1) "Shootings like the one in . . . [location] . . . will happen again regardless of what action is taken by government and society"; or (2) "Government and society can take action that will be effective in stopping mass shootings from happening again." The majority of people selected the first answer.

School shootings can sometimes be an exception to this trend. Most notably, after the 2018 shooting deaths of seventeen schoolchildren in Parkland, Florida, there was a large uptick in those believing that the government and society can do something to reduce mass shootings (up to 64 percent). How-

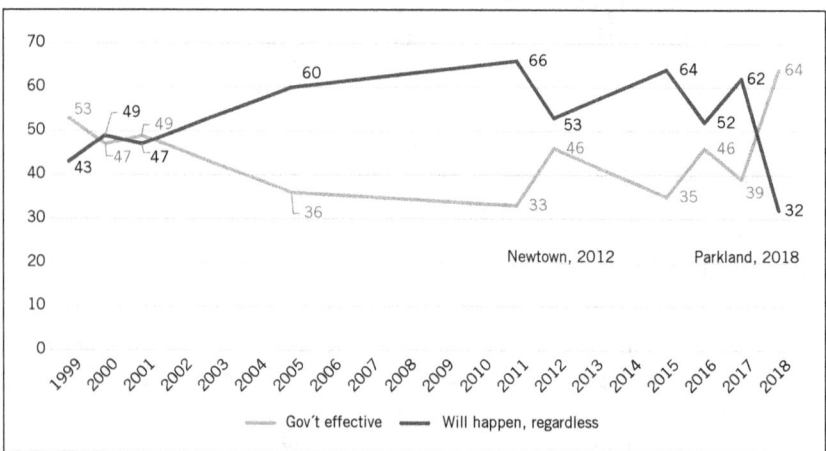

Figure 16.1 Can Government and Society Take Action That Will Be Effective in Preventing Mass Shootings? (*Adapted from CNN and CBS/New York Times Polls*)

ever, other mass shootings also produced increases in the percentages indicating something could be done, only to see that decline in subsequent surveys. Similar questions have not been reported in more recent surveys, but it is likely that the percentage indicating nothing can be done has again increased.

The data trends do suggest that many Americans no longer believe that we can do much to prevent mass shootings, including adopting stricter gun regulations. This shift in attitudes since the 1990s coincides with an increasing acceptance of gun rights and gun culture in American society. In the same time period, many states have increasingly expanded the rights of gun owners to carry concealed weapons, with a majority now allowing for concealed carry with few or no restrictions (Malone & Steidley, 2019). In addition, thirty states have adopted so-called stand your ground laws, which have significantly expanded the rights of individuals to use deadly force when they feel threatened outside of their own property (*Stand Your Ground*, 2021).

The trend of expanding gun rights runs in tandem with the development of a politicized social identity around gun ownership. This identity was fostered by the National Rifle Association (NRA) and the Republican Party's wholesale incorporation of the NRA's perspective on gun rights that began in the 1970s and 1980s (Joslyn et al., 2017; Lacombe, 2019; 2021; Lacombe et al., 2019).

In short, we contend that elite conservatives' and Republicans' wholesale endorsement of gun rights had led more Americans to adopt gun owners' views on mass shootings. Specifically, we argue that gun owners have a motivated self-interest to argue that guns make us safer, that gun regulations will not reduce mass shootings, and that government can do little to reduce mass shootings—and that this perspective has now been embraced by Republicans and conservatives overall.

Gun Owners, Identity, and Motivated Reasoning

To understand how gun owners and their allies hold distinct opinions about guns in society and mass shootings compared with other adults, we must first turn to a deeper look at attitudes about mass shootings. The influence of mass shootings on public opinion has become a contentious focus of social science debate, with some studies suggesting that attitudes about guns or gun regulations do not change in the wake of a mass shooting (Barney & Schaffner, 2019; Rogowski & Tucker, 2019) or that mass shootings might generate backlash toward gun regulation (Jang, 2019; Kantack & Paschall, 2020). Other research suggests that geographic proximity to mass shootings can influence attitudes, with those living in closer proximity to attacks becoming more supportive of gun regulation (Newman & Hartman, 2019). Indeed, Barney and Schaffner (2019) find that Democrats living in closer proximity to mass shootings became supportive of increased gun regulation, while similarly situated Republicans became less supportive. Furthermore, there is some evidence that following mass shootings, issue framing around gun safety (Haider-Markel & Joslyn, 2001) and emotional reactions (Joslyn & Haider-Markel, 2018) can shift attitudes.

At minimum, the evidence concerning attitudes following mass shootings suggests that different groups of people could have different attitudinal responses to the shootings—that the event is filtered through perceptual predispositions. Our attention is focused on how and why the attitudes of gun owners, Republicans, and conservatives might align following mass shootings given these groups' alliance and overlap in recent decades.

Following mass shootings, observers often posit a given set of causal attributions focused on individual factors or systemic factors, and they may be deemed controllable or uncontrollable (Haider-Markel & Joslyn, 2001; Joslyn & Haider-Markel, 2017). When there is no obvious recipient of blame, causal attributions are "more likely to be influenced by an individual's own perspective and favor social psychological needs" (Joslyn & Haider-Markel, 2017, p. 431). Attributions for shootings often place blame on violence in popular culture, the availability of guns, poor parenting, lack of morality in society, mental health issues, or the individual shooter (Haider-Markel & Joslyn, 2001; Joslyn & Haider-Markel, 2017).

Different groups are predisposed to attribute different causes to mass shootings. Partisanship has been shown to influence attributions regarding the 1999 mass shooting at Columbine High School, with Republicans being more likely to blame violence in the media and Democrats being more likely to blame gun laws (Haider-Markel & Joslyn, 2001). Relatedly, ideology influenced attributions for the 2016 Orlando shooting, with conservatives blaming terrorism and liberals blaming guns (Joslyn & Haider-Markel, 2018).

Like Republicans and conservatives, gun owners are also less likely to blame guns or lax gun regulation for mass shootings (Joslyn & Haider-Markel, 2017). As such, it is worthwhile to unpack these attitudes. Gun owners, Republicans, and conservatives tend to subscribe to principles of individual freedom and individual self-sufficiency. These groups' predispositions tend to motivate them away from seeing government intervention as desirable or necessary for addressing problems in society (Groenendyk & Krupnikov, 2021). Thus, in the case of mass shootings, placing blame on the lack of government regulation of guns seems unlikely.

In addition, gun owners have a motivated self-interest concerning the regulation of guns (Joslyn & Haider-Markel, 2017). Kunda (1987, 1990) argues that attitudes stem from reasoning that is motivated by our biases, emotions, beliefs, and attachments. Even when provided with contradicting information, individuals are biased by their preconceived beliefs and engage in motivated reasoning (Groenendyk & Krupnikov, 2021; Taber & Lodge, 2006). For gun owners, calls for increased gun regulation potentially pose a threat to their interests as gun owners and, for some, even to their own sense of identity. Gun owners participate in motivated reasoning at the very onset of their gun ownership, utilizing it to justify their purchase in the first place (Strobe et al., 2017). This reasoning is also reenforced by American pro-gun interest groups such as the NRA through membership communications and training programs. Lacombe (2019) shows gun rights supporters use similar frames—largely of identity and threatened self-interest—when discussing gun regulation.

Meanwhile, even if they are not gun owners, Republicans and conservatives have aligned themselves with gun owners and the rights of gun owners (Joslyn et al., 2017). This alliance allows Republicans and conservatives to see themselves as part of a larger in-group that includes gun owners as fellow travelers. Subsequently, like gun owners, Republicans and conservatives may engage in a similar pattern of motivated reasoning about mass shootings, making them more likely to suggest that there is nothing the government can do to prevent them (Groenendyk & Krupnikov, 2021). In short, we expect gun owners, Republicans, and conservatives to be less likely to indicate that the government can be effective in preventing mass shootings. We plot what this overlap in attitudes might look like in Figure 16.2, noting that a subset of gun owners is not Republican or conservative, just as not all Republicans are conservatives or gun owners.

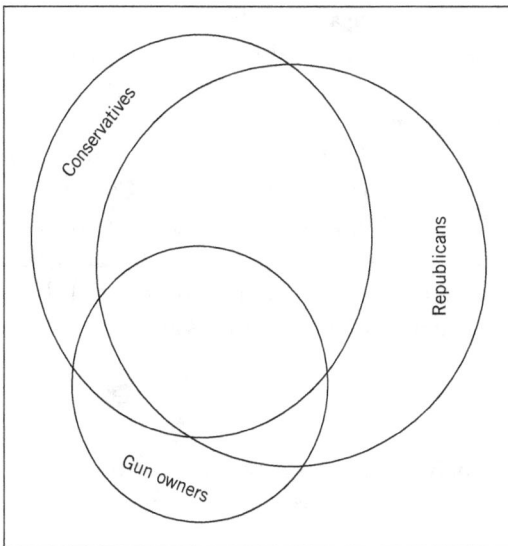

Figure 16.2 Group Identity and Overlap.

Data and Methodology

We utilized several datasets based on national surveys of American adults in order to explore the influence of gun ownership, partisanship, and ideology on mass shooting prevention attitudes. Our data come from several points in time, covering eighteen years, allowing us to assess how attitudes, and some determinants of those attitudes, have shifted over time. First, we utilized survey data from an April 7–9, 2000, nationally representative probability sample survey conducted by Gallup (for CNN and *USA Today*) of 1,006 of American adults. The second dataset includes a nationally representative sample of 620 American adults conducted December 17–18, 2012, by the Opinion Research Corporation (for CNN). Third, we use a unique nationally representative sample of 2,091 American adults fielded June 28–July 1, 2017, by Survey Sample International (SSI) for the authors. Lastly, we use data from a nationally representative survey conducted by SSI (for the authors) in August 2018, with a total of 2,543 American adults. Both SSI surveys contain an oversample of gun owners. All four surveys were conducted just after highly publicized mass shootings. As such, we expect that the respondents have been primed by the recent mass shootings to think about what, if anything, can be done about them.

Dependent Variable

Our general dependent variable of interest is mass shooting prevention opinion. All four datasets use nearly identical language to measure prevention views, allowing us to compare across datasets. The options vary slightly by dataset, as the year allowed the survey to reference a mass shooting that occurred around the time of the survey. The questions ask, "Which of the following statements come closer to your overall view? Government and society can take action that will be effective in preventing shootings like the one [in Colorado (2000), in Connecticut (2012), in general (2017), or in Texas (2018)] from happening again, or Shootings like the one [in Colorado (2000), in Connecticut (2012), in general (2017), or in Texas (2018)] will happen again regardless of what action is taken by government and society." Responses indicating that the government and society can do something are coded as 1, and those indicating that shootings will keep happening regardless are coded as 0.

Independent Variables

Our chief independent variables of interest are gun ownership, partisanship, and ideology. For the 2017 and 2018 datasets, we code gun ownership on a scale, with personal gun ownership coded as 2, gun present in the home as 1, and no form of gun ownership as 0. For 2000 and 2012, gun ownership was measured dichotomously, with a gun in the home coded as 1 and no guns in the home coded as 0. We measure partisanship on a five-point scale for 2000 and 2012 and a seven-point scale for 2017 and 2018 from strong Democrat to strong Republican. We measure ideology on a five-point scale ranging from very liberal to very conservative. Our control variables are derived from the literature (Barney & Schaffner, 2019; Felson & Pare, 2010; Joslyn & Haider-Markel, 2013, 2017) as common predictors of public opinion related to guns: gender (measured dichotomously with female coded as 1), race (measured dichotomously with white coded as 1), residential context (Midwest in 2000 and 2012 and urban-rural continuum for 2017 and 2018), age (measured in years), and education (measured on a scale from less than high school degree to advanced degree).

Results

We utilized logistic regression to investigate the influence of gun ownership, partisanship, and ideology on belief about the ability of government to prevent mass shootings. Our results are displayed in Table 16.1. All four models utilize the question on mass shooting prevention as the dependent variable.

Overall, the results suggest people who are younger, male, gun owners, conservatives, Republicans, and/or less educated express less confidence in the American government's ability to prevent mass shootings. However, there were some changes over time that can be seen across Models 1–4. Model 1 displays our results from the analysis of survey data from 2000, measuring respondents' opinion on government's ability to reduce mass shootings. As shown, gun ownership has a statistically significant negative relationship with views on mass shooting prevention (b = −0.477, p < 0.01), suggesting that gun owners are less likely to believe that government action can prevent mass shootings.[4] This finding is consistent with our contention that gun owners engage in a form of motivated reasoning toward their self-interest following mass shootings. In addition, conservatives are less likely to believe that the government can stop mass shootings (b = −0.221, p < 0.01), and although Republicans appear to be less likely to believe we can do anything about mass shootings, the coefficient is not statistically significant.

We plot the marginal effect coefficients for each variable to show the change in prevention opinion when predictor variables move from their minimum to their maximum. This allows us to trace the size of each variable's impact. The impact of a variable is larger the further away its marginal effect is from zero, with zero being delineated by the horizontal line in the middle of each figure. Additionally, the result is statistically significant if the variable's confidence interval, the bracket around the data point itself, does not cross zero.

TABLE 16.1   THE DETERMINANTS OF BELIEF IN GOVERNMENT'S ABILITY
TO PREVENT MASS SHOOTINGS

	Model 1: 2000	Model 2: 2012	Model 3: 2017	Model 4: 2018
Independent Variables				
Gun owner	−.477**	−.486**	−.200**	−.204**
	(.141)	(.190)	(.052)	(.055)
Female	.400*	.449*	−.044	.054**
	(.160)	(.160)	(.095)	(.010)
White	−.234	−.059	−.158	−.006
	(.198)	(.238)	(.118)	(.124)
Ideology ^ conservative	−.221**	−.370**	−.123**	−.087**
	(.084)	(.105)	(.036)	(.031)
Party ID ^ Republican	−.043	−.249**	−.087**	−.171**
	(.045)	(.066)	(.029)	(.025)
Residence ^ rural	−.075	−.100	−.027	--------
	(.160)	(.224)	(.032)	
Education	.099*	.257**	.115**	.069*
	(.045)	(.101)	(.034)	(.034)
Age	−.201**	−.085	−.019**	−.011**
	(.072)	(.088)	(.003)	(.004)
Constant	.936	1.237	−.378	.367
	(.428)	(.523)	(.591)	(.586)
Pseudo R square	.06	.12	.06	.06
Number of cases	925	577	2084	1814

Notes: Coefficients are logistic regression coefficients; standard errors are in parentheses. ** $p < .01$; * $p < .05$.

The marginal effects of variables from Model 1 are presented in Figure 16.3, Panel 1, below. As shown, gun ownership appears to be the largest negative predictor of attitudes about the government's ability to end mass shootings.

Model 2 displays the results of our data analysis of 2012 survey data on mass shooting prevention. Once again, gun ownership is strongly associated with being less likely to believe the government can do anything to stop mass shootings (b = −0.486, p < 0.01). In addition, by 2012, both partisanship (b = −0.249, p < 0.01) and ideology (b = −0.370, p < 0.01) predict attitudes, with Republicans and conservatives being less likely to indicate that government can take action to prevent mass shootings. Gender and education are statistically significant and positive, suggesting that women and the more educated are more likely to believe that government and society can prevent mass shootings. We calculate the marginal effects of variables in the model, shown in Figure 16.3, Panel 2, with gun ownership and partisanship appearing to have similarly sized effects on prevention opinion.

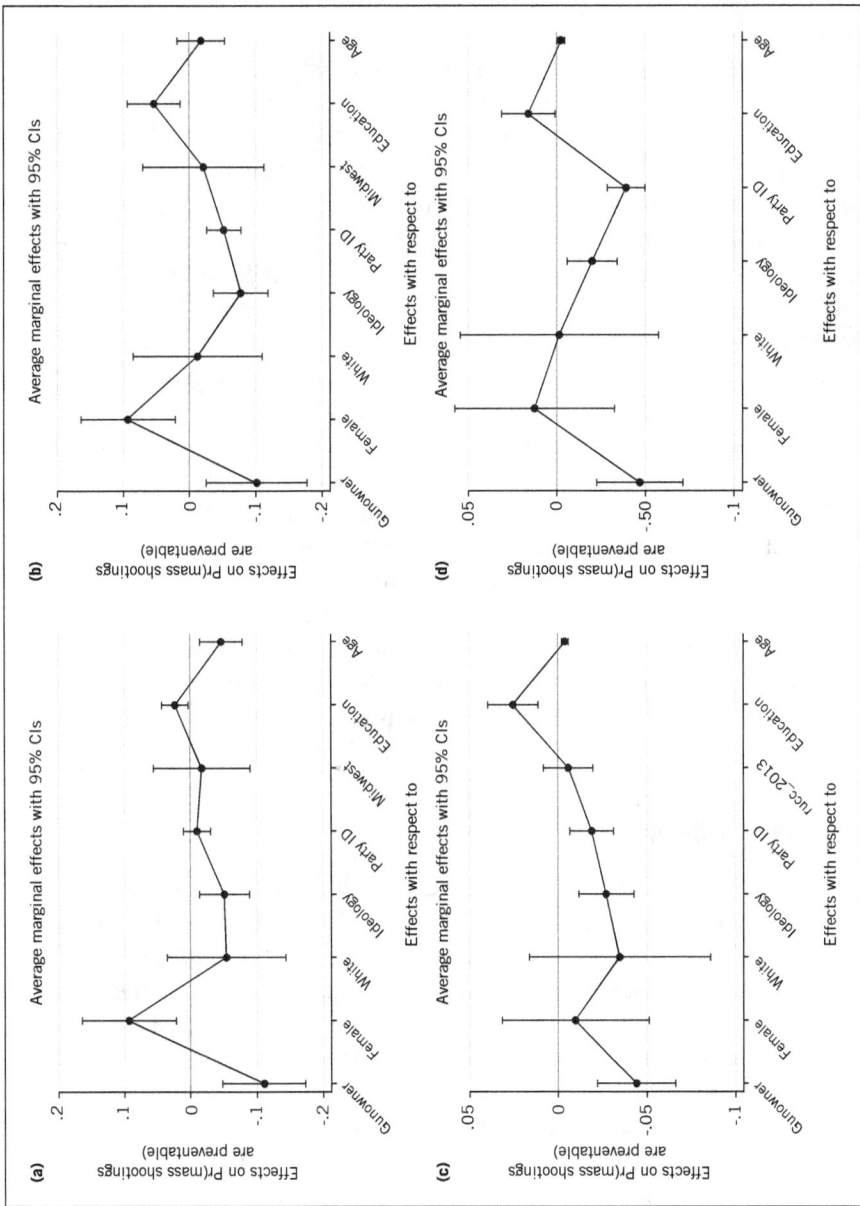

Figure 16.3 Marginal Effects of Predictor Variables across the Models.; **16.3a** Model 1, Data from 2000.; **16.3b** Model 2, Data from 2012.; **16.3c** Model 3, Data from 2017.; **16.3d** Model 4, Data from 2018.

Model 3 presents the results of our analysis of the 2017 survey data. Gun owners (here measured on a three-point scale) were significantly less likely to indicate that the government could do something about mass shootings (b = −0.200, p < 0.001). Likewise, Republicans (b = −0.087, p < 0.01) and conservatives (b = −0.123, p < 0.001) were significantly less likely to indicate that the government or society could do something to stop mass shootings. The marginal effects are shown in Figure 16.3, Panel 3, with gun ownership having the strongest impact on attitudes.

The final model, Model 4, displays results from our analysis of the 2018 survey data. In this model, the effects of gun ownership remain negative and statistically significant (b = −0.204, p < 0.001). Additionally, partisanship (b = −0.171, p < 0.001) and ideology (b = 0.087, p < 0.01) are negative and statistically significant, with Republicans and conservatives being less likely to indicate that the government can prevent mass shootings. The marginal effects are shown in Figure 16.3, Panel 4, and display the strength of gun ownership, partisanship, and ideology as powerful predictor variables.

Across all our models and over time, gun ownership is the most consistent predictor of attitudes, with gun owners being more likely to indicate that the government can do little to prevent mass shootings. This set of findings is consistent with our argument that gun owners engage in a form of self-interested motivated reasoning when considering government interventions to stop mass shootings. Likewise, since at least 2012, Republicans and conservatives, who see gun owners as part of their in-group, appear to exhibit similar attitudes following mass shootings. The evidence supports the notion that these groups are engaged in motivated reasoning about efforts to stop mass shootings.

Concluding Thoughts

Relative to all other wealthy Western democracies, the United States is a uniquely violent country (Messner & Rosenfeld, 2012). Mass shootings are a salient reminder of this problem. However, the public's attitudes about guns and mass shootings have not shifted long term toward more gun regulation for the purpose of increased public safety and reducing mass shootings. Instead, the trends suggest that a large portion of the public has increasingly come to see guns as providing more safety, and those individuals are less likely to believe that government and society can do anything to reduce mass shootings in the United States. Recent changes in some public attitudes may foretell a future change, but the longer-term trends have been steady.

Our project sought to understand these shifts in attitudes by examining the social and psychological predictors of attitudes. We examined changes in aggregate opinion on guns and mass shootings and explored the literature about attitudes following mass shootings. Next, we argued that politicized group identities motivate beliefs about guns, safety, and effective government responses to mass shootings. We contend that these politicized identities lead their adherents to engage in a form of motivated reasoning that results in preferences and beliefs that protect self-interests—here, a desire to protect gun ownership from increased restrictions.

We focused our attention on the coalition of gun owners, Republicans, and conservatives, arguing that members of these overlapping groups have come to view themselves as fellow travelers. With Republicans and conservatives seeing gun owners as members of their in-group, this coalition has been able to expand gun rights in the U.S. states and enhance aggregate positive attitudes about guns providing safety and negative views of the government's ability to stop mass shootings. We illustrate this point by examining the determinants of believing that government can do little to stop mass shootings in four public opinion polls from 2000 to 2018. Our analysis allows us to draw several important conclusions.

First, the coalition of gun owners, Republicans, and conservatives has been able to effectively shift the narrative around guns and increase perceptions that they increase safety rather than decrease it.[5] In addition, this coalition has now convinced a majority of states to expand the rights of gun owners through the adoption of concealed carry laws and stand your ground laws. Some state and local governments have taken this further and adopted constitutionally questionable laws that are designed to prevent local law enforcement officials from assisting in the enforcement of federal gun regulations (Kuang, 2021).

Second, our analysis suggests that since at least 2012, gun owners, Republicans, and conservatives have been more likely to indicate that there is nothing the government can do to prevent mass shootings. This finding is consistent with our argument that members of this allied group are incentivized to engage in motivated reasoning to protect their self-interests. In this case, the protected self-interest is to resist increased gun regulation by the government. These results expand upon existing literature that has suggested that gun owners are motivated to form self-serving attitudes around guns and extend that logic to allied groups of Republicans and conservatives, including those who might not be gun owners.

Third, the impact of gun ownership on attitudes about preventing mass shootings is greater than the influence of any other factors in our models, including education and gender. The influence of partisanship and ideology is nearly as strong in most models, but gun ownership is the single most important predictor from 2000 to 2018.

Finally, our results hold meaningful implications for the debate over guns going forward. As the beliefs of gun owners and a broader gun culture become increasingly embedded in Republican and conservative ideological camps, we might expect public beliefs about guns and mass shootings to tilt in favor of gun rights. Indeed, as more of the public has come to view government action as futile for stopping mass shootings, it is increasingly less likely to see national legislators support new gun laws or regulations meant to reduce mass shootings. However, demographically, Americans are less likely to identify as Republican or conservative (Pew Research Center, 2020), perhaps pointing toward a more polarized future on gun issues where gun rights activists are a minority. Of course, if Republican efforts in the states to gerrymander majorities (FiveThirtyEight, 2021) and insert partisan bias into election administration (Kerson, 2021) continues, Republican minority rule at the state level may freeze any progress toward regulating guns as a means for reducing gun violence. Thus, in the short term, we are unlikely to see significant declines in gun violence, including mass shootings, that stem from changes in public opinion or new firearms legislation.

NOTES

1. The evidence increasingly suggests that there are measures that can be taken to reduce gun violence and mass shootings (Smart & Schell, 2021).

2. Data trends are based on national polls conducted for Gallup, the Pew Research Center, and NBC News and the *Wall Street Journal*. The question wording varies but are similar to this: "Do you think that gun ownership in this country does more to (1) protect people from becoming victims of crime, or (2) put people's safety at risk?"

3. Data trends are based on national polls conducted for Gallup, the Pew Research Center, and NBC News and the *Wall Street Journal*. The 1989–2015 question wording varies but is similar to this: "Can stricter gun control laws reduce violence in this country?: yes, gun control will reduce violence, or no, gun control will not reduce violence."

4. Using the variance inflation factor (VIF) test for each of our models, there is multicollinearity among the gun owner, party identification, and ideology variables (as suggested by Figure 16.2). However, separately removing each of these variables from the models does not substantively change the performance of other variables in the models.

5. Refer to note 2.

REFERENCES

Barney, D. J., & Schaffner, B. F. (2019). Reexamining the effect of mass shootings on public support for gun control. *British Journal of Political Science, 49*(4), 1555–1565.

Celinska, K. (2007). Individualism and collectivism in America: the case of gun ownership and attitudes toward gun control. *Sociological Perspectives, 50*(2), 229–247.

Cohn, N., & Sanger-Katz, M. (2019, August 10). On guns, public opinion and public policy often diverge. *New York Times.* https://www.nytimes.com/2019/08/10/upshot/gun-control-polling-policies.html

Felson, R. B., & Pare, P. P. (2010). Gun cultures or honor cultures? Explaining regional and race differences in weapon carrying. *Social Forces, 88*(3), 1357–1378.

FiveThirtyEight. (2021, November 23). *There won't be many competitive districts left after this round of Gerrymandering.* https://fivethirtyeight.com/videos/there-wont-be-many-competitive-districts-left-after-this-round-of-gerrymandering/

García-Montoya, L., Arjona, A., & Lacombe, M. (2021). Violence and voting in the United States: How school shootings affect elections. *American Political Science Review*. Early view, https://doi.org/10.1017/S0003055421001179

Groenendyk, E., & Krupnikov, Y. (2021). What motivates reasoning? A theory of goal-dependent political evaluation. *American Journal of Political Science*, 65(1), 180–196.

Haider-Markel, D. P., & Joslyn, M. R. (2001). Gun policy, opinion, tragedy, and blame attribution: the conditional influence of issue frames. *Journal of Politics*, 63(2), 520–543.

Jang, S. M. (2019). Mass shootings backfire: The boomerang effects of death concerns on policy attitudes. *Media Psychology*, 22(2), 298–322.

Joslyn, M. R. (2020). *The gun gap: The influence of gun ownership on political behavior and attitudes*. New York: Oxford University Press.

Joslyn, M. R., & Haider-Markel, D. P. (2013). The politics of causes: mass shootings and the cases of the Virginia Tech and Tucson tragedies. *Social Science Quarterly*, 94(2), 410–423.

Joslyn, M. R., Haider-Markel, D. P., Baggs, M., & Bilbo, A. (2017). Emerging political identities? Gun ownership and voting in presidential elections. *Social Science Quarterly*, 98(2), 382–396.

Joslyn, M. R., & Haider-Markel, D. P. (2017). Gun ownership and self-serving attributions for mass shooting tragedies. *Social Science Quarterly*, 98(2), 429–442.

Joslyn, M. R., & Haider-Markel, D. P. (2018). The direct and moderating effects of mass shooting anxiety on political and policy attitudes. *Research & Politics*, 5(3), 1–9.

Kantack, B. R., & Paschall, C. E. (2020). Does politicizing gun violence increase support for gun control? Experimental evidence from the Las Vegas shooting. *Social Science Quarterly*, 101(2), 893–908.

Kerson, Roger. (2021, December 3). Meet the Trump fanatics who have taken over elections in a critical swing state. *Slate*. https://slate.com/news-and-politics/2021/12/trump-fanatics-michigan-election-officials.html?via=rss

Kuang, J. (2021, November 22). Missouri police ask Republican legislators to amend act blocking federal gun laws. *Kansas City Star*. https://www.kansascity.com/news/politics-government/article255973367.html

Kunda, Z. (1987). Motivated inference: Self-serving generation and evaluation of causal theories. *Journal of Personality and Social Psychology*, 53(4), 636–647.

Kunda, Z. (1990). The case for motivated reasoning. *Psychological Bulletin*, 108(3), 480–498.

Lacombe, M. J. (2019). The political weaponization of gun owners: The National Rifle Association's cultivation, dissemination, and use of a group social identity. *Journal of Politics*, 81(4), 1342–1356.

Lacombe, M. J. (2021). *Firepower: How the NRA turned gun owners into a political force*. Princeton, NJ: Princeton University Press.

Lacombe, M. J., Howat, A. J., & Rothschild, J. E. (2019). Gun ownership as a social identity: Estimating behavioral and attitudinal relationships. *Social Science Quarterly*, 100(6), 2408–2424.

Malone, C. A., & Steidley, T. (2019). Determinants of variation in state concealed carry laws, 1970–2016. *Sociological Forum*, 34(2), 434–457.

Messner, S. F., & Rosenfeld, R. (2012). *Crime and the American dream*. Boston, MA: Cengage Learning.

Miller, S. V. (2017, October 3). Lots of Republicans actually support gun control. *Washington Post: Monkey Cage*. https://www.washingtonpost.com/news/monkey-cage/wp/2017/10/03/lots-of-republicans-actually-support-gun-control/

Newman, B. J., & Hartman, T. K. (2017). Mass shootings and public support for gun control. *British Journal of Political Science*, *49*(4), 1527–1553.

Newport, F. (2021, April 2). *American public opinion and gun violence*. Gallup: Polling Matters. https://news.gallup.com/opinion/polling-matters/343649/american-public-opinion-gun-violence.aspx

Parker, K., Horowitz, J., Igielnik, R., Oliphant, B., & Brown, A. (2017). *America's complex relationship with guns*. Washington, DC: Pew Research Center. http://assets.pewresearch.org/wp-content/uploads/sites/3/2017/06/06151541/Guns-Report-FOR-WEBSITE-PDF-6-21.pdf

Pew Research Center. (2020, June 2). *The changing composition of the electorate and partisan coalitions*. Pew Research Center. https://www.pewresearch.org/politics/2020/06/02/the-changing-composition-of-the-electorate-and-partisan-coalitions/

Rogowski, J. C., & Tucker, P. D. (2019). Critical events and attitude change: support for gun control after mass shootings. *Political Science Research and Methods*, *7*(4), 903–911.

Schaeffer, K. (2021, May 11). *Key facts about Americans and guns*. Pew Research Center. https://www.pewresearch.org/fact-tank/2021/05/11/key-facts-about-americans-and-guns/

Shootings, guns and public opinion. (2015). Roper Center for Public Opinion Research. https://ropercenter.cornell.edu/shootings-guns-and-public-opinion

Smart, R., & Schell, T. L. (2021). *Mass shootings in the United States*. Rand Corporation. https://www.rand.org/research/gun-policy/analysis/essays/mass-shootings.html

Stand Your Ground. (2021). Giffords Law Center to Prevent Gun Violence. https://giffords.org/lawcenter/gun-laws/policy-areas/guns-in-public/stand-your-ground-laws/

Stroebe, W., Leander, N. P., & Kruglanski, A. W. (2017). The impact of the Orlando mass shooting on fear of victimization and gun-purchasing intentions: Not what one might expect. *PloS one*, *12*(8), e0182408. https://doi.org/10.1371/journal.pone.0182408

Taber, C. S., & Lodge, M. (2006). Motivated skepticism in the evaluation of political beliefs. *American Journal of Political Science*, *50*(3), 755–769.

Van Green, T. (2021, August 4). *Wide differences on most gun policies between gun owners and non-owners but also some agreement*. Pew Research Center. https://www.pewresearch.org/fact-tank/2021/08/04/wide-differences-on-most-gun-policies-between-gun-owners-and-non-owners-but-also-some-agreement/

PART VI

Mass Shootings and American Education

17

A Case of American Exceptionalism

The Influence of Super Controllers in Mass School Shootings

Brooke Miller Gialopsos, Cheryl Lero Jonson,
Melissa M. Moon, and William A. Stadler

Mass school shootings have an undeniable effect on Americans' psyche, with the majority of teens and parents experiencing stress and worry about these incidents (American Psychological Association, 2018). This rare form of violence has contributed to a deep moral panic across the United States (Burns & Crawford, 1999). Despite other countries experiencing mass school shootings, the sheer number of these incidents occurring on American soil is a case of American exceptionalism (Lankford, 2016). Understanding why the United States is unique in this regard not only helps explain these tragic incidents but can also offer avenues to develop and implement successful prevention measures.

Within this context, this chapter explores mass school shootings in America from an environmental criminological lens. We propose American schools create a unique opportunity structure that increases the likelihood of mass shootings. Although a handful of researchers have considered how routine activity theory (RAT) may explain mass shootings generally (Schildkraut et al., 2019; Silva & Greene-Colozzi, 2020) and how opportunity perspectives have guided offenders' target selection in prominent school shootings (Gialopsos & Carter, 2015), here we utilize Sampson et al.'s (2010) idea of super controllers to explain how the opportunity structure in American schools is inherently different from other countries. In doing so, we first provide an overview of key theoretical concepts, including RAT, the crime triangle, controllers, and super controllers, and their application to mass school shootings. Next, we discuss how super controllers use incentives and disincentives to influence crime prevention efforts. We suggest the composition of super controllers, both individually and collectively, is uniquely American. We end with a call for evidence-based practices in our educational settings, arguing that each of these factors has the ability to alter the opportunity structure in our schools and potentially prevent future mass school shootings in America (Silva & Greene-Colozzi, 2020).

Routine Activity Theory

Cohen and Felson's (1979) RAT proposes the spatial and temporal intersection of (1) motivated offenders and (2) suitable targets in the absence of (3) capable guardianship increases the likelihood of crime. This convergence of key elements—the opportunity for crime—occurs during the routine activities of individuals. Unlike many criminological theories, this approach holds motivation as a constant, assuming there will always be potentially motivated offenders.[1] With that assumption, crime prevention strategies do not attempt to target the root causes of criminality but instead focus on changing the opportunity structure in which crime occurs. Simply, if the three elements do not converge, then crime is not possible (Sampson et al., 2010).

To illustrate the importance of opportunity in mass school shooting prevention, the COVID-19 pandemic provides an example. In places where schools were shut down and classes were delivered virtually/remotely, there were zero school shootings. During this period, there is no reason to suspect a potential offender's motivation changed—and, in fact, strain and other motivating factors likely increased. Instead, the opportunity structure was drastically altered—with schoolhouses empty and students at home, there were no targets for a mass school shooting converging in time and space with motivated offenders. Using this logic, it becomes clear why mass shootings also are less likely to occur during school breaks, as the opportunity structure does not allow for the convergence of targets and offenders.

When attempting to understand why mass school shootings occur more frequently in the United States, it is important to remember motivated offenders exist all over the world. Although research has found America has far more than its share of incidents (Lankford, 2016), there are examples of school shooters in other countries. Furthermore, the number who commit these attacks is only a portion of people with that motive: some are thwarted or decide not to attack (NTAC, 2021). This suggests that while many nations have individuals who may want to commit mass school shootings, some countries may be better at preventing them.

Thus, we argue efforts to prevent mass school shootings can be directed toward altering the opportunity structure for this type of criminal behavior. To be clear, knowing the motivations for and causes of mass shootings are important endeavors that should be empirically explored; however, theoretically and practically speaking, this is not the only way to examine and prevent these incidents. As discussed below, understanding and changing the opportunity structure through the use of controllers, super controllers, and empirically informed incentives presents additional pathways to more fully understand and potentially prevent these tragedies.

Routine Activity Theory Extended

Often depicted by the crime triangle, RAT focuses on three key elements of a crime—offender, target, and place—and views each one as crucial to understanding why crime occurs. These elements comprise the innermost triangle (Figure 17.1). However, there are factors that influence the actions and behaviors of inner triangle inhabitants. Theoretically, these serve a critical purpose in that they influence—or exercise control over—a required element or condition for crime (Sampson et al., 2010). For example, when viewing the second layer of the triangle, a guardian, or protector of targets, can provide aid to a potential target and reduce its likelihood of victimization. This can include formal guardians (e.g., police) and informal guardians (e.g., parents) who are close to potential victims. A handler, or a person who is influential in a potential offender's life (e.g., coach), can decrease the likelihood of an offender engaging in crime by offering support, supervision, or assistance

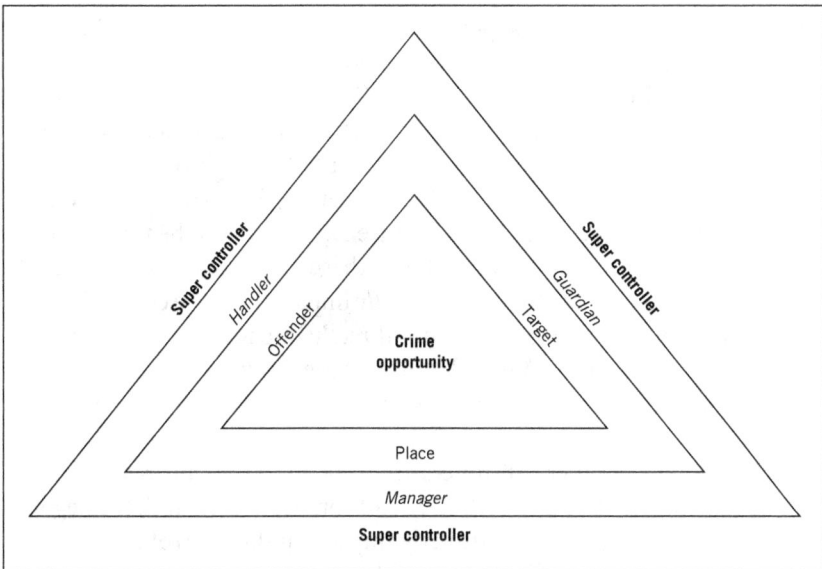

Figure 17.1 Three Layers of the Crime Triangle. (*Adapted from Sampson et al., 2010*)

(Felson, 1986), while managers, or those who control behavior in certain places (e.g., owners), have the ability to increase or decrease the occurrence of crime at a place by setting rules/regulations (Eck, 1994; Eck & Weisburd, 1995).

Applying RAT to school shootings, a guardian could be a teacher who protects the school; a handler could be a friend, parent, or coach whose actions keep the potential offender from offending; and a manager could be any staff member (e.g., administrator) who wants to prevent crime and disruptions at school. Thus, the second triangle in Figure 17.1 represents the three controllers—guardians, handlers, and managers—who directly influence the targets, offenders, and places, respectively. Theoretically, mass school shootings provide a unique application of this theory as one person—a singular teacher, coach, or counselor—has the capability to serve as multiple controllers—they can guard targets, handle offenders, and manage places.

Consequently, crime results when controllers are unsuccessful. When a mass school shooting occurs, at least one type of controller was unsuccessful. A handler (e.g., parent) may have failed to help the offender cope with emotional problems or violent impulses and was unable to intervene. Or a manager (e.g., school administrator) may have failed to respond to the warning signs and growing threat an at-risk student posed. Or a school guardian (e.g., teacher) may have been unable to prevent the attack by not reporting concerning behavior.

Note, this second layer of the triangle is not uniquely American. Rather, the absence or ineffectiveness of guardians, handlers, and/or managers is present in any mass school shooting in the world. However, we argue it is the next concept, or the third layer—super controllers—that contributes to America's exceptionalism regarding mass school shootings.

More than fifteen years after Felson's (1986) and Eck's (1994) additions, Sampson et al. (2010) further extended RAT by offering a theoretical rationale for why many crime prevention measures fail by exploring who controls the controllers (i.e., guardians, handlers, managers). Known as super controllers, the crime triangle's third layer (Figure 17.1) regulates the three controllers through incentives and disincentives. These super controllers are people, organizations, and institutions who *directly* impact the three controllers (i.e., guardians, handlers, managers) and *indirectly* impact the target, offender, and place. Sampson et al. (2010) identified three categories of super controllers—formal, diffuse, and personal—with ten total types of super controllers (Table 17.1).

All ten types of super controllers are relevant to the causes and prevention of mass school shootings. Although all countries have similar categories and types of super controllers directly impacting the controllers and indirectly affecting targets, offenders, and places, the nuance of each category, as well as the specific types and roles of super controllers, are country spe-

TABLE 17.1   SUPER CONTROLLER TYPOLOGY AND MASS SCHOOL SHOOTINGS

Category	Type	Examples
Formal	Organizational	School boards/districts; boards of trustees
	Contractual	SROs
	Financial	Federal/state funding; insurance
	Regulatory	Department of Education; lack of gun regulations
	Courts	Lawsuits following shootings
Diffuse	Political	Second Amendment; NRA
	Market	Oversaturated, unregulated gun market; school security industry
	Media	Sensationalized news coverage; reporting policies; social/entertainment media
Personal	Groups	Peer code of silence; peer pressure; parental influence
	Family	Gun exposure/safety/education; access to mental health care

cific. Furthermore, the power and reach of super controllers to incentivize or disincentivize controllers and influence one another varies drastically across countries.

Super Controllers' Influence on Controllers

Super controllers directly influence controllers through incentives and disincentives (Sampson et al., 2010). Many unsuccessful crime prevention efforts can be attributed to super controllers' inability to incentivize prevention efforts of the controllers. The ability of super controllers to influence controllers lies within other environmental criminological theories, namely, rational choice theory (Cornish & Clarke, 1986) and situational crime prevention (Cornish & Clarke, 2003). Sampson et al. (2010) argue the same five mechanisms used to impact offenders' decision-making are used by super controllers to influence controllers, through the manipulation of effort, risk, rewards, excuses, and provocations. Importantly, super controllers also may influence one or more of these mechanisms.

According to Sampson et al. (2010), super controllers can impact the *effort* needed for controllers to participate in crime prevention efforts. By making it easier and/or less expensive, controllers will be more likely to engage in preventative actions or less able to avoid intervention efforts. For instance, the family could impact the effort needed for a potential offender to obtain a firearm. Second, super controllers can influence the *risk* of penalties controllers face. These negative consequences could be criminal justice–related penalties (i.e., lawsuits) but also other equally powerful incentives like fear of crime, financial loss, criticism, and bad publicity (i.e., media). These serve as disincentives for controllers. Third, super controllers can change, increase, or create new *rewards* that incentivize prevention efforts. These serve as positive incentives for controllers. To illustrate, governmental funding could influence if a district has a dedicated school nurse or psychologist. Fourth, super controllers can use incentives in a way that *remove excuses* from controllers for not engaging in prevention efforts. For example, armed assailant trainings remove the excuse of not knowing what to do in crisis situations. Finally, super controllers can *remove provocations* (e.g., factors that precipitate or induce crime) that may impact controllers' ability or desire to adopt crime prevention efforts (Sampson et al., 2010). Organizational school policies may limit grievances and stress by adopting inclusionary rather than exclusionary disciplinary policies.

Using this super controller framework, it is possible to speculate why America experiences more mass school shootings. Unlike our European counterparts, the United States has fortified schools and responds to concerning behaviors with exclusionary (e.g., zero tolerance, suspensions, expulsions, arrests) rather than inclusive means, further isolating potentially dangerous individuals. Additionally, access to mental health services in America is unobtainable to many due to its cost-prohibitive nature, limiting avenues of help for schools and parents. These factors combined with the saturation of firearms and a political system that is unable or unwilling to limit access to guns creates a perfect storm that may partially explain America's exceptionalism in enduring these tragedies. Below we elaborate on how each of the ten types of super controllers uniquely contribute to mass school shootings in America.

Formal Super Controllers

The first category is formal super controllers. The five types of super controllers in this category rely on "formal social, legal, or financial authority to alter controllers' behavior" (Sampson et al., 2010, p. 41). First, *organizational* super controllers influence controllers within their specific organization. School districts, school boards, and boards of trustees are examples. These entities make decisions regarding school policies that influence and are enforced by teachers, staff, and administrators. In America, many of these policies involve zero-tolerance procedures that have effectively created a school-to-prison pipeline (Gottfredson et al., 2020). These organizational policies also mandate the removal of students from schools, potentially increasing the grievances against the school, which is a known precursor to many targeted school attacks (Lankford & Silva, 2021; United States Government Accountability Office, 2020). These policies differ from the holistic and inclusive responses to school violence—focusing on victims *and* offenders—often utilized in many European countries (Council of Europe, 2021).

Second, *contractual* super controllers utilize contracts to exert control over people and organizations (Sampson et al., 2010). For schools, this could include school resource officers (SROs), which involve contractual arrangements between local police or sheriff's departments to place sworn law enforcement in schools. The contractual arrangement directly dictates the policies for SROs and indirectly impacts the response of other school personnel and students. Despite the mixed research in terms of their impact on and/ or responses to crime, America has an exceedingly high number of law enforcement officials inside our schools compared with other countries (Gottfredson et al., 2020; Pigott et al., 2018). As a result, these contractual arrangements impact the opportunity structure of mass shootings. The presence of SROs influences organizational super controllers through the increased use of exclusionary, rather than inclusionary, disciplinary practices, including arrests (Fisher & Hennessy, 2016; Pigott et al., 2018). This formal, and often criminal justice, response to issues in school may increase grievances against classmates, teachers, or the school itself and isolate motivated offenders, which are known risk factors for targeted school violence (NTAC, 2019).

Third, *financial* super controllers impact the behavior of controllers. Consistent with Sampson et al.'s (2010) examples, school districts are provided governmental funding to ensure safe schools. In America, school safety funding is often earmarked for targeting hardening measures (e.g., access control) and increasing police presence rather than expanding access to mental health assistance. The American Civil Liberties Union (2021, p. 39) indicates there are "14 million students in schools with police but no counselor, nurse, psychologist, or social worker" despite increased mental health issues facing our nation's youth. As mentioned, zero tolerance and fortification of schools may contribute to rather than attenuate the likelihood of mass violence in schools (Madfis, 2020).

This lack of mental health access is further exacerbated in the United States, where Americans are more likely than Europeans to report they are unable to obtain or cannot afford professional mental health care (Tikkanen et al., 2020). Counter this with France, which offers ten free sessions with a psychologist for youths under age seventeen (Associated Press, 2021). Thus, financial super controllers in the United States seem to focus on less effective and potentially iatrogenic means to addressing mass school shootings compared with other countries.

Fourth, *regulatory* super controllers include government regulatory agencies that create rules for institutions and staff (Sampson et al., 2010). In America, this includes the Department of Education as well as FERPA and HIPAA for information-sharing purposes. These regulations may influence how teachers respond to certain behaviors or discussions with students. Although all countries have rules schools must follow, many regulations that American schools must adhere to come from state and local levels rather than the federal government due to the Tenth Amendment. This localized power and decision-making creates variation across states, translating into policy differences in schools across America. This also contributes to America's lack of national school violence prevention standards, which results in variation in prevention measures across the country.

Finally, Sampson et al. (2010) identify *courts*, both civil and criminal, as impactful on controllers. The United States is a highly litigious country where threats of lawsuits carry enormous weight. Litigation geared toward educational institutions following prior mass school shootings can impact school administrators and their decision-making process. Also, school districts may adopt certain policies out of fear of lawsuits, directly impacting how school personnel (e.g., teachers) respond in the event of a shooting. Furthermore, since American courts are courts of precedent, these judge-made decisions have long-lasting impacts. Other countries have judiciaries that are rooted in common law and/or are relatively litigious, but other factors come into play in America. In the United States, group litigation (i.e., class action lawsuits) are commonplace and contingent fees are allowed, leading to more lawsuits as well as ones with greater risk (Rubin, 2010).

After the shooting in Parkland, Florida, parents were awarded $25 million from Broward County Public Schools for negligence (Allen, 2021), and lawsuits were filed within ten days of the Oxford High School shooting (Goldstein, 2021). Additionally, in the two years following the deaths of seventeen people at Marjory Stoneman Douglas High School, police in Florida schools nearly doubled (Curran, 2020), and, in Oxford, zero-tolerance policies concerning threats and the addition of security guards were quickly implemented after the shooting (62 CBS Detroit, 2021). These policies, implemented partly to lessen liability and prevent litigation concerning negligence, often have iatrogenic, rather than protective, effects, contributing to factors related to mass school shootings. This is in contrast to countries where these events bring discussions and action on gun control rather than school fortification (Noack, 2018).

Diffuse Super Controllers

The second category of super controllers are identified as diffuse. Rather than being single entities, institutions, or individuals, the three types of diffuse super controllers—political, markets, and media—are collections (Sampson et al., 2010). Their reach is significant and wide reaching and often unintentionally impact the controllers. Diffuse super controllers also impact all other super controllers in important ways.

Political super controllers "can provide incentives and disincentives for controllers to prevent crime" (Sampson et al., 2010, p. 43). This category is exceptionally influential in America. Politically, the United States holds a unique position as one of only three countries constitutionally protecting the right to bear arms (Weiss & Pasley, 2019). As the Second Amendment is woven into the nation's fabric, for many Americans, gun ownership becomes central to their identity (Parker et al., 2017). This results in gun control legislation being met with fierce political debate (Conley, 2019). Although gun control supporters encompass a larger group of people, gun rights supporters, spearheaded by the NRA, are "more intense, better organized, and more willing to base their vote solely on a candidate's gun control stance" (Schutten et al., 2021, p. 2). American politicians, unlike their international counterparts, are often reluctant to pass gun control legislation, despite wide public support. This results in fewer restrictions on who can obtain firearms and on the types of firearms available, increasing the likelihood one may have access to a gun.

Relatedly, *markets* represent a type of diffuse super controller that influences controllers (Sampson et al., 2010). The primary link to mass shootings is the oversaturated gun market, with the United States home to almost half the supply of civilian-owned guns in the world (Fox, 2018). Therefore, motivated offenders have more tools at their disposal than elsewhere. Furthermore, the American gun market is relatively unregulated with little oversight. Other countries have limited their gun markets in response to mass school shootings (Every-Palmer et al., 2021), whereas America, rooted in tradition, is hesitant to limit access to firearms. Political super controllers have substantial influence on the market due to the reluctance to pass gun control legislation (Schildkraut & Hernandez, 2014).

Another market—the school security industry—plays a powerful role in school shootings and, in doing so, directly impacts the policy decisions of controllers (Cornell, 2006). This $3 billion market (Ma, 2018) sells the latest technological advancements that harden targets, strengthen access control, increase surveillance, and identify threats. Created as a response to mass school shootings, this market—in magnitude and scope—is a uniquely American phenomenon. This type of super controller influences other super controllers, including organizational, financial, and contractual.

The third type of diffuse super controller is media. Publicity, both positive and negative, impacts controllers and prevention strategies (Sampson et al., 2010). Although media is tasked with information sharing following mass shootings, there have been significant changes to how media cover these tragedies to potentially reduce copycat crimes (Lankford & Madfis, 2018). Even with these modifications, American media conglomerates must still make a profit, pressuring them to be first to break the news and to portray the event in a dramatic manner to attract more viewers or readers. Additionally, entertainment and social media regularly portray mass shootings and often do so in a sensationalized fashion. It is likely America's First Amendment protections may contribute to harm and misinformation surrounding mass shootings. Media spread fear, create moral panic (Burns & Crawford, 1999), and increase individuals' perceived risk of mass shootings. As a result, media impact what controllers do and how other super controllers respond. For example, social media movements in response to U.S. school shootings exert influence over political super controllers and are exceptionally American. Fear cultivated in media also results in organizational super controllers (e.g., school districts) overestimating their risk of a shooting and implementing potentially iatrogenic policies (Madfis, 2016).

Personal Super Controllers

The final category is personal super controllers. These are individuals or small networks that are more informal in nature yet impact the behavior of controllers (Sampson et al., 2010). The first type is *groups*, which include peer groups and neighbors. Examples of their influence include peer pressure, bystander intervention, and the culture around intervening, including the code of silence, or "don't snitch" mentality, of students (Madfis, 2014). Peer pressure impacts all facets of adolescence and influences students' willingness to intervene, share information, and comply with school policies. Although other countries have similar issues, these peer-related norms are part of a larger culture, and American culture is unique in many ways. Because the United States has the most guns per capita, the presence and/or threat of guns among peers is just one more item on the list of things not to "snitch" about. Also, America's individualistic culture is preoccupied with success and self-reliance rather than the well-being of others. It is possible this cultural predisposition factors into the code of silence for American youth.

Additionally, Sampson et al. (2010) explain how groups of parents influence the parenting of other parents. Most schools have social media groups for parents to share information, which may influence other parents' decision-making. Parent Teacher Associations (PTAs) and small groups of parents can push schools to remove existing safety measures (e.g., active assailant trainings) or expand evidence-based prevention programs (e.g., bystander intervention, restorative practices, bullying/suicide prevention), which impact the opportunity structure for these events.

Family represents the final type of super controller. According to Sampson et al. (2010), this group can affect how other family members "intervene to prevent crime" (p. 45). Family plays a central role in discussions of and education regarding guns, gun safety, and exposure and access to guns, as well as mental health and suicidality. Due to the large number of gun-owning families and research that shows prior school shooters tend to obtain guns from their homes (NTAC, 2019), American families play a large role when it comes to influencing handlers, guardians, and managers. This was illustrated after the Oxford High School shooting, where the perpetrator's parents purchased the firearm used and were aware of his concerning behaviors but failed to intervene (Williams & White, 2021).

Moving Forward

Current American policies have created a unique opportunity structure for mass shootings to occur in our nation's schoolhouses. Unfortunately, many strategies used are not achieving their goal of preventing tragedy (Gottfredson et al., 2020; Madfis, 2020), and many incentives are misguided. By expanding RAT to consider both controllers and super controllers, not only are more layers of prevention identified but also there is an ability to explain more fully the distinctive nature of American mass school shootings.

Efforts to prevent crime often entail strengthening or mobilizing controllers in different ways (Sampson et al., 2010). By utilizing environmental criminological perspectives and concepts such as situational crime prevention, rational choice theory, and crime pattern theory (Gialopsos & Carter, 2015; Schildkraut et al., 2019), we can embed school shooting prevention efforts within the robust crime prevention literature. American schools need and deserve theoretically based programs to drive school safety policies. We need to understand how factors both within and outside the school—controllers *and* super controllers—can impact the likelihood of a shooting occurring. Doing so allows for a multifaceted examination of mass school shootings and provides more thorough explanations for this uniquely American phenomenon, as well as more avenues to prevent these tragic events.

ACKNOWLEDGMENT

We thank John Eck for his invaluable insight on this chapter.

NOTE

1. The presence of motivated offenders as a constant is a criticism of RAT (see Gialopsos & Carter, 2015), as evidenced in other chapters of this volume. However, remaining true to RAT, we assume motivation is constant and explore other components of the criminal opportunity structure to explain American mass school shootings.

REFERENCES

Allen, G. (2021, October 19). *A Florida school district will pay $25 million to the families of Parkland victims.* NPR. https://www.npr.org/2021/10/18/1047153012/parkland-families-lawsuit-25-million-settlement-broward-county

American Civil Liberties Union. (2021). *Cops and no counselors: How the lack of school mental health staff is harming students.* https://www.aclu.org/report/cops-and-no-counselors

American Psychological Association. (2018, October). *Stress in America generation Z.* https://www.apa.org/news/press/releases/stress/2018/stress-gen-z.pdf

Associated Press. (2021, April 14). *France fights kids' mental health woes with free counseling.* ABC News. https://abcnews.go.com/Health/wireStory/france-fights-kids-mental-health-woes-free-counseling-77072669

Burns, R., & Crawford, C. (1999). School shootings, the media, and public fear: Ingredients for moral panic. *Crime, Law, and Social Change, 32*(2), 147–168.

Cohen, L. E., & Felson, M. (1979). Social change and crime rate trends: A routine activity approach. *American Sociological Review, 44*(4), 588–605.

Conley, M. A. (2019). Asymmetric issue evolution in the American gun rights debate. *Social Science Research, 84*, 1–8.

Cornell, D. G. (2006). *School violence: Fear versus facts.* Routledge.

Cornish, D., & Clarke, R. V. (Eds.). (1986). *The reasoning criminal: Rational choice perspectives on offending.* Springer-Verlag.

Cornish, D., & Clarke, R. V. (2003). Opportunities, precipitators and criminal decisions: A reply to Wortley's critique of situational crime prevention. In M. J. Smith & D. B. Cornish (Eds.), *Theory for practice in situational crime prevention* (pp. 41–96). Criminal Justice Press.

Council of Europe. (2021). *Violence in Schools.* https://www.coe.int/en/web/children/violence-in-schools

Curran, F. C. (2020). *The expanding presence of law enforcement in Florida schools.* University of Florida Education Policy Research Center.

Eck, J. E. (1994). *Drug markets and drug places: A case-control study of the spatial structure of illicit drug dealing* [Ph.D. dissertation]. University of Maryland.

Eck, J. E., & Weisburd, D. (1995). Crime places in crime theory. In J. E. Eck & D. Weisburd (Eds.), *Crime and place, Number 4 in crime prevention studies series* (pp. 1–33). Criminal Justice Press.

Every-Palmer, S., Cunningham, R., Jenkins, M., & Bell, E. (2021). The Christchurch mosque shooting, the media, and subsequent gun control reform in New Zealand: A descriptive analysis. *Psychiatry, Psychology and Law, 28*(2), 274–285.

Felson, M. (1986). Linking criminal choices, routine activities, informal control, and criminal outcomes. In D. B. Cornish & R. V. Clarke (Eds.), *The reasoning criminal: Rational choice perspectives on offending* (pp. 119–128). Springer-Verlag.

Fisher, B. W., & Hennessy, E. A. (2016). School resource officers and exclusionary discipline in U.S. high schools: A systematic review and meta-analysis. *Adolescent Research Review, 1*(3), 217–233.

Fox, K. (2018, March 9). *How US gun culture compares with the world in five charts.* CNN. https://www.cnn.com/2017/10/03/americas/us-gun-statistics/index.html

Gialopsos, B., M., & Carter, J. W., II. (2015). Offender searches and crime events. *Journal of Contemporary Criminal Justice, 31*(1), 53–70.

Goldstein, D. (2021, December 9). In Michigan, first lawsuit is filed. *New York Times.* https://www.nytimes.com/2021/12/09/us/michigan-school-shooting-lawsuits-oxford.html

Gottfredson, D. C., Crosse, S., Tang, Z., Bauer, E. L., Harmon, M. A., Hagen, C. A., & Green, A. D. (2020). Effects of school resource officers on school crime and responses to school crime. *Criminology & Public Policy, 19*(3), 905–940.

Lankford, A. (2016). Are American's public mass shooters unique? A comparative analysis of offenders in the United States and other countries. *International Journal of Comparative and Applied Criminal Justice, 40*(2), 171–183.

Lankford, A., & Madfis, E. (2018). Don't name them, don't show them, but report everything else: A pragmatic proposal for denying mass killers the attention they seek and deterring future offenders. *American Behavioral Scientist, 62*(2), 260–279.

Lankford, A., & Silva, J. (2021). The timing of opportunities to prevent mass shootings: A study of mental health contacts, work and school problems, and firearms acquisition. *International Review of Psychiatry, 33*(7), 638–652.

Ma, A. 2018. *Anxiety over shootings bolsters $2.7 billion school security industry.* Marketplace. https://www.marketplace.org/2018/05/08/anxiety-over-shootings-bolsters-27-billion-school-security-industry/

Madfis, E. (2014). Averting school rampage: Student intervention amid a persistent code of silence. *Youth Violence and Juvenile Justice, 12*(3), 229–249.

Madfis, E. (2016). "It's better to overreact": School officials' fear and perceived risk of rampage attacks and the criminalization of American public schools. *Critical Criminology, 24*(1), 39–55.

Madfis, E. (2020). *How to stop school rampage killing: Lessons from averted mass shootings and bombings.* Palgrave Macmillan.

National Threat Assessment Center (NTAC). (2019). *Protecting America's schools: A U.S. Secret Service analysis of targeted school violence.* U.S. Secret Service, Department of Homeland Security.

National Threat Assessment Center (NTAC). (2021). *Averting targeted school violence: A U.S. Secret Service analysis of plots against schools.* U.S. Secret Service, Department of Homeland Security.

Noack, R. (2018, February 15). Europe had school shootings, too. Then they did something. *Washington Post.* https://www.washingtonpost.com/news/worldviews/wp/2018/02/15/europe-had-school-shootings-too-then-they-did-something-about-it/

Parker, K., Horowitz, J., Igielnik, R., Oliphant, B., & Brown, A. (2017). *America's complex relationship with guns: An in-depth look at the attitudes and experiences of U.S. adults.* Pew Research Center.

Pigott, C., Stearns, A. E., & Khey, D. N. (2018). School resource officers and the school to prison pipeline: Discovering trends of expulsions in public schools. *American Journal of Criminal Justice, 43*(1), 120–138.

Rubin, P. H. (2010, November 16). More money into bad suits. *New York Times.* https://www.nytimes.com/roomfordebate/2010/11/15/investing-in-someone-elses-lawsuit/more-money-into-bad-suits

Sampson, R., Eck, J. E., & Dunham, J. (2010). Super controllers and crime prevention: A routine activity explanation of crime prevention success and failure. *Security Journal, 23*(1), 37–51.

Schildkraut, J., & Hernandez, T. C. (2014). Laws that bit the bullet: A review of legislative responses to school shootings. *American Journal of Criminal Justice, 39*(2), 358–374.

Schildkraut, J., Naman, B. M., & Stafford, M. C. (2019). Advancing responses to mass shootings using a routine activity approach. *Crime Prevention and Community Safety, 21*(4), 346–361.

Schutten, N. M., Pickett, J. T., Burton, A. L., Jonson, C. L., Cullen, F. T., Burton, Jr., V. S. (2021). Are guns the new dog whistle? Gun control, racial resentment, and vote choice. *Criminology, 60*(6), 90–123.

Silva, J. R., & Greene-Colozzi, E. A. (2020). Mass shootings and routine activities theory: The impact of motivation, target suitability, and capable guardianship on fatalities and injuries. *Victims & Offenders, 16*(4), 565–586.

62 CBS Detroit. (2021, December 15). *Oxford School District sets new safety plan after shooting.* https://detroit.cbslocal.com/2021/12/15/oxford-school-district-sets-new-safety-plan-after-shooting/

Tikkanen, R., Fields, K., Williams, R. D., II, & Abrams, M. K. (2020). *Mental health conditions and substance use: Comparing U.S. needs and treatment capacity with those in other high-income countries.* The Commonwealth Fund. https://www.commonwealthfund.org/publications/issue-briefs/2020/may/mental-health-conditions-substance-use-comparing-us-other-countries

United States Government Accountability Office. (2020). *K–12 education: Characteristics of school shootings.* https://www.gao.gov/assets/gao-20-455.pdf

Weiss, B., & Pasley, B. (2019). Only 3 countries in the world protect the right to bear arms in their constitutions: The US, Mexico, and Guatemala. *Business Insider.* https://www.businessinsider.com/2nd-amendment-countries-constitutional-right-bear-arms-2017-10

Williams, C., & White, E. (2021, December 4). *Parents of Michigan boy charged in Oxford school shooting.* ABC News. https://abcnews.go.com/US/wireStory/charging-decision-due-parents-oxford-high-shooting-81538316

18

Perceptions of Blame for Gun Violence in U.S. Schools

Media Coverage of the Stoneman Douglas High School Shooting

AARON KUPCHIK, BENJAMIN W. FISHER,
F. CHRIS CURRAN, AND SALVATORE D'ANGELO

Since the 1999 tragedy at Columbine High School, gun violence in schools—particularly incidents involving mass casualties—have been a focus both of fear over students' safety and of school security practices. These incidents have helped accelerate the trend toward securitization of schools through practices such as the use of school resource officers (SROs), increased surveillance, shooting response drills, and others (Addington, 2009; Jonson, 2017). Critics, however, have noted that schools often respond to incidents of gun violence in ways that are ineffective or even harmful to students (Fisher et al., 2018).

Various frames can be used to make sense of horrific school tragedies and that offer different perspectives of who is at fault for the incident and what sort of responses might best prevent future such tragedies. For example, do policy makers and the public see the problem as one of mental health, availability of guns, weak school security, or something else entirely (see Lee et al., 2020)? What solutions are proposed to reduce risk of future attacks? These frames, or ways of discussing and understanding school gun violence, influence policy debates about how best to educate and protect students. With this in mind, our goal in this chapter is to better understand common perceptions of and responses to gun violence in schools—how the problem of school gun violence and potential responses to it are understood within American society.

We perform an exploratory analysis of how one of the most recent large-scale incidents of school gun violence—the 2018 tragedy at Marjory Stoneman Douglas High School in Parkland, Florida—was discussed by major news outlets. We analyze samples of news articles from the *New York Times*, *Wall Street Journal*, and *USA Today*. Our analyses offer hypotheses for future investigation into how schools, policy makers, and the public understand school gun violence and conceptualize appropriate responses to it. As we discuss below, news media portrayals suggest that views of the Parkland incident and responses to it are heavily influenced by an ethos of individualism and the political quagmire of gun control debate, each of which is characteristic of the American context.

Description of the Incident

Marjory Stoneman Douglas High School in Parkland, Florida, is located in an affluent suburb within the Miami metropolitan area. On February 14, 2018, around two thirty in the afternoon, a nineteen-year-old white male and former student entered the school with an AR-15-style semiautomatic rifle, which he legally purchased in the state of Florida at the age of eighteen (Rogers, 2018). There were multiple warning signs that this individual would engage in this behavior, but those warning signs went unheeded by law enforcement (Kelly, 2018; *USA Today* Editorial Board, 2018).

Upon entering one of the school's buildings, the shooter began firing indiscriminately at anyone in the hallways in front of him. When the hallways had cleared, he targeted those sheltering in multiple locked classrooms. An armed SRO on-site remained outside the building and did not attempt to engage the shooter during the incident. In total, the shooting lasted for about six minutes, after which the shooter put down his gun and fled the scene by blending into a crowd of fleeing students (Turkewitz & Hartocolis, 2018). After being identified, he was soon apprehended by law enforcement. The shooting at Stoneman Douglas High School was a national tragedy leaving seventeen dead and seventeen injured.

Background

Although school violence has been declining since the 1990s (Irwin et al., 2021), gun violence in schools is common enough and provokes enough trauma that it occupies a large part of the public imagination and demands great media attention. Since Columbine, over a quarter of a million students in the United States have been in a school where a shooting has occurred (Cox et al., 2021). Researchers have understood gun violence in schools as a moral panic, in which the high emotional salience but very low level of risk of death by gun violence in schools has a large impact on public policy and practice (Burns & Crawford, 1999). In this vein, interviews with school leaders reveal that, when making decisions about school security practices, they keep gun violence at the forefront of their minds, doing whatever possible to avoid these rare but tragic events (Madfis, 2016). As such, understanding how the media covers high-profile incidents of gun violence in schools is useful for understanding the policy response and public narrative (see Lee et al., 2020).

Prior research suggests that media coverage of violence in schools is varied but demonstrates a few consistent themes. For example, one study analyzed the content of news stories about school violence from 2000 through 2006, finding that the articles portrayed school crime as worsening, focused on a constant threat of tragedy, and eschewed statistical data on school crime in favor of emotional responses from individuals (Kupchik & Bracy, 2009). This may explain in part why, as mentioned above, school leaders are so preoccupied with gun violence in schools. Moreover, it is important to note that media narratives about high-profile incidents of gun violence may shift over time as new information comes to light and the response to the incident begins to actualize (Muschert, 2009; Muschert & Carr, 2006); the sort of media coverage that happens immediately after an incident is often different from the coverage days, weeks, and months later. Thus, examining how news stories evolve is useful when analyzing the media coverage.

Theoretical Framework

Our analysis is guided by the multiple streams theoretical framework (MSF; see Kingdon, 1984), commonly used in the field of public policy, as a mechanism for understanding national conversations that followed the Parkland tragedy. An idealized perspective on policy change assumes that decisions, be they national or local, are driven by a linear and rational process in which a problem is identified, solutions are considered, and a decision is arrived at through rational debate and consideration of the alternative best aligned to address the problem (Bardach & Patashnik, 2019; Feldman & Khademian, 2008). Yet, alternative theories and empirical studies suggest a much more complex and dynamic process in which problem definitions as well as potential solutions are in competition with each other within a context of political pressures and individual and group advocacy (McLendon & Cohen-Vogel, 2008).

Kingdon's (1984) multiple streams framework provides a model for understanding how problem definitions and policy responses may come to be coupled during a window of political opportunity following specific events (Kingdon, 1984). MSF suggests that there are three distinct "streams": one for problems, one for policy solutions, and one for politics. These streams exist over time separately but can become coupled during a window of opportunity, such as a mass school shooting (Kingdon, 1984).

As has been the case with previous school shootings (Viano et al., 2021), the Parkland shooting opened a window for policy makers, advocates, and the public more generally to couple existing problem streams with existing solutions. MSF predicts that, rather than approaching the tragedy at Parkland systematically by identifying and agreeing on a problem, comparing potential policy solutions using evidence, and pursuing the optimal solution that addresses the problem, the period following the Parkland tragedy would instead by characterized by "chaos" and "ambiguity" in which various stakeholders put forward competing definitions of the problem and competing solutions (Kingdon, 1984). What is more, MSF suggests that the coupling of a policy solution to a problem may reflect the political context and the success of particular policy advocates to elevate their definition of the problem and preferred policy solutions.

We focus our study, then, on understanding how the national conversation unfolded within major media outlets following the Parkland tragedy. In particular, we focus on portrayals of the problem (i.e., who or what the blame lies with), policy or practice solutions put forward, and the political actors (policy makers, advocates, and the broader public) who emerged as key voices in the discussions. Based on MSF, we expect these streams to be disorganized, ambiguous, and characterized by competing voices and ideas both for definitions and solutions.

Method

Data

The data from this study consist of ninety news articles, including thirty from each of three news sources: *New York Times*, *USA Today*, and *Wall Street Journal*. We use these sources because they each have a national readership and have a range of reputations in regard to political partisanship. To identify the sample of articles, we conducted an electronic search in ProQuest over a six-month span beginning on the date of the Parkland tragedy (i.e., February 14, 2018, through August 13, 2018) using the following search term: pub(new york times) AND "Stoneman Douglas" AND "shooting" (note that we changed the "pub" phrase of the search term for each of the three news sources). This yielded a total of 435 articles from the *New York Times*, 253 from *USA Today*, and 127 from the *Wall Street Journal*. Next, we conducted systematic random sampling where we retained every nth article, where n was the total number of articles divided by thirty and rounded down to the nearest whole number. When a sampled news article was completely off topic, it was replaced with another article that was adjacent on the list.

Analytic Strategy

The data analysis proceeded in multiple stages. First, each member of the research team skimmed through roughly twenty articles to get a sense of the type of content contained in the articles. Second, the research team met to devise a coding scheme based on this first round of observations from the articles that would be applied to each sampled article. This initial coding scheme was divided into categories according to various types of information that would be collected from each article: (1) sources of blame (e.g., lax gun laws, perpetrator); (2) proposed solutions (e.g., increased security, gun law reform); (3) source of information (e.g., police officer, student, political); and (4) characteristics of the article itself, including whether it was an op-ed and the month of publication. Third, this coding scheme was applied to the articles with an eye toward adding codes as needed. This process yielded a few additional codes that fell within each of the four categories. Fourth, after adding these codes, the research team conducted a line-by-line coding of all ninety articles, tagging relevant sections of text with any and all applicable codes. This coding process generally followed the constant comparative method, where coders looked for consistency between the code's definition and the various segments of text that had been given the same code (Glaser, 1965). Fifth, each coder wrote a memo summarizing the main themes they had noted in their set of articles. These memos contained observations about which codes were applied most frequently, how the narrative shifted over time, and any other relevant information that might not have been captured in the codes themselves. The research team met to discuss their coding and came to a consensus on the most salient themes across the ninety articles.

Results

As suggested by the MSF framework, the period following the Parkland shooting was characterized by competing voices and narratives about the cause and proper response to the tragedy. In the days immediately after the shooting, the sheriff and others mentioned uncertainty as to the motive of the shooter. The Florida governor, Republican Rick Scott, noted that he would "do everything I can to make sure this never happens again" and, when pressed on gun control, said, "Everything is on the table" (Fausset & Kovaleski, 2018).[1] Over the weeks following Parkland, however, this "chaos" began to give way to emergent discourses around the causes of the shooting and the potential responses. For example, the SRO's reaction would be characterized as a failure, and students would become vocal advocates for broader gun control. These problem and policy streams were intertwined with a political stream—throughout the time period examined, politicians were one of the most dominant voices in the media reports on the shooting. Accordingly, we observed that the problem and policy streams that gained the most traction often were shaped by the emergent politics of the discourse. For example, as student advocates pushed an agenda of gun control, many politicians shifted to proposals for school security and armed personnel—despite the apparent failure of the armed officer who was present.

In the sections that follow, we discuss these discourses organized around several broad categories and against the backdrop of the multiple streams framework. We find that overall, the discourses tended to focus on an individualization of both the problem as well as potential policy solutions. This individualization, combined with or perhaps as result of the political elements of the issue, resulted in decoupling in some cases between problem and proposed solution as various actors competed to control the discourse and coupling of problems and solutions.

School Security Policy and Personnel

We found that where school security was criticized, it was done so in a way that individualized the failures of security personnel rather than problematizing the security policies and practices. In the days following the shooting, a number of politicians and law enforcement officials publicly praised the bravery and response of law enforcement. As details of the inadequate response by the school's SRO and other first responders emerged, the narrative quickly shifted into one of individualized blame. Trump, who had previously praised law enforcement's response, said, in reference to the SRO (who failed to enter the school building during the shooting), "He [the SRO] heard it right from the beginning. So he certainly did a poor job, but that's a case where somebody was outside, they're trained, they didn't act properly under pressure, or they were a coward" (Davis, 2018). Others as well focused on the individual failures of the SRO to act in this instance rather than addressing the effectiveness of SRO programs generally, thus implying that SROs are effective if they act properly.

Similar critiques were leveraged against law enforcement and other social service agencies more broadly. As it became apparent that the FBI, the Department of Children and Families, and the school district had received tips and/or investigated the perpetrator at several points throughout the prior years, criticism against these organizations emerged. In this case, however, the criticism largely focused on individualized shortfalls—failures to properly investigate or act on a tip—rather than critiques of the organizational structures. As a result of individualized criticisms, the SRO and several other deputies were either fired or disciplined for their perceived lack of action. After further investigation of law enforcement response, the Broward Sheriff's Office Deputies Association took a no-confidence vote for the sheriff, citing both a number of long-standing issues and the sheriff's handling of the Parkland shooting (Hayes, 2018a). At the state level, the governor called on the FBI director to resign (Rogers, 2018).

As the discourse progressed to conversations around solutions or policy responses, the individualized focus of blame for the event combined with the political environment would shape the proposed policy responses. Student advocates and others focused on broad-based gun control. While some politicians initially indicated that gun control legislation was a possibility, their narrative quickly shifted to one focused on school security, likely in part due to political considerations. As would be expected, the gun rights lobby suggested that "the emotional reaction to the Parkland shooting shouldn't lead to laws that deprive responsible gun owners of their rights. A better response, they say, is greater attention to mental health, school-security funding, and enforcement of existing gun laws" (Hackman, 2018). *USA Today* reported survey results suggesting that a majority of respondents supported police in schools and other security measures (Page & Icsman, 2018).

Politically, then, proposals to expand school security were able to gain traction. The *New York Times* framed these proposals as an attempt by Republican legislators to turn "away from significant gun control legislation" to "quell public uproar over the recent massacre in Parkland" (Stolberg & Green, 2018). In some cases, such as in Florida, where gun control legislation was signed into law—raising the minimum age to buy firearms, increasing wait time when purchasing a firearm, and banning bump stocks—the legislation was coupled with provisions that allowed for the arming of school staff and increased funding for school resource officers (Campo-Flores, 2018).

The individualization of the problem of school security allowed for the coupling of policy solutions that otherwise may not have fit with the problem. Instead of viewing SROs or other armed individuals as ineffective at preventing shootings, as research has suggested (Livingston et al., 2019), the individualization of the problem of the SRO's response allowed legislation to expand SROs and arm teachers. Coupled with political support, increases in school security, particularly the arming of individuals, emerged as a salient solution to a problem of individualized failures in school security.

Gun Control

After the initial reporting about the details of the shooting had subsided, the three media sources then turned to discussions of gun control as a potential response. Student survivors and Democratic politicians loudly pressed for a ban on deadly assault weapons, like the AR-15 semiautomatic rifle used by the Stoneman Douglas shooter (Bacon, 2018). However, such proposals failed to attract Republican support. In a motion that failed along party lines, the Florida House rejected a Democrat bill banning assault rifles (Turkewitz & Hartocolis, 2018).

As we discuss below, news articles also reported on calls for "red flag" laws, which grant judges the ability to remove weapons from individuals deemed dangerous (Turkewitz & Hartocolis, 2018) and strengthening background checks on gun buyers (Kelly, 2018). Even President Trump was among those supporting such measures early on (Turkewitz & Hartocolis, 2018). But in general, the media coverage of the issue of gun control was shallow, with very few specifics of how states or the federal government ought to address this thorny issue. The national conversation stagnated with Democrats favoring broad gun control proposals that stood little chance of passing without Republican support and Republicans, including President Trump, successfully framing the debate around school security and target-hardening proposals such as arming teachers (Stolberg & Green, 2018). During this phase of media coverage, articles discussed gun control events, such as the student-led March for Our Lives event in Washington, DC; these stories paid lip service to the commendable student activism without seriously engaging with the gun control message they were pushing. For example, consider this excerpt from *USA Today*:

> "Lawmakers and politicians will scream guns are not the issue," the Parkland, Fla., survivor said passionately. She then got choked up during her next sentence and stopped to throw up on stage. Live stream cameras cutaway from Fuentes. After she regained her composure and received cheers from the crowd, Fuentes exclaimed, "I just threw up on international television, and it feels great!" (Miller, 2018)

Rather than reporting on the message of the Parkland survivor's speech, the spectacle of her vomiting on stage is given precedence. Often the message articles conveyed when gun control was mentioned was that current gun laws did not make sense and that something needed to be done in relation to gun control, but details of specific proposals and gun control–styled solutions were few and far between.

When specifics of gun control proposals were discussed in the news media, these stories described a very individualized approach to gun control. There are many ways one could approach gun control; different approaches might target availability of weapons or general ease of purchase, capacity of the weapons themselves, requirements of weapon technology that make them safer (e.g., fingerprint identification that prohibits a stolen gun from operating), access to ammunition, or gun culture in general, among others. The coverage of discussions of gun control showed a different path, however; discussions among policy makers showed that their vision of gun control was to limit the ability of "dangerous" people, like the Parkland shooter, to have guns. In other words, most of the news coverage did not focus on sale of guns, guns themselves, or gun culture as targets of the solutions. Instead, the news media primarily saw the problem in individualized terms as one of dangerous people in that guns were not problematic unless they were in the hands of dangerous people. President Trump, for example, suggested that the minimum age of purchasing a gun ought to be raised to twenty-one and that background checks should be used because "he doesn't want 'mentally ill people to be having guns'" (Jackson et al., 2018). Others proposed red flag laws that allow judges to confiscate guns from individuals they deem dangerous. In the political rhetoric covered by all three newspapers, dangerous people were primarily those who had mental illness or young people. Consider, for example, this excerpt from an article in the *New York Times*:

> Kathy Fox, who was helping at a booth with collectible Winchester rifles exhibited upright on a turntable, said she was pleased that Representative Brian Mast, a Republican and Army veteran, who represents her district in Florida, had called for a ban on future sales of tactical rifles. But she added that "there's nothing wrong with guns" and that "there are nuts everywhere." (Hsu, 2018)

Thus, even supporters of gun rights and those who earn a living off of gun sales acknowledged that guns should not be in the hands of individuals deemed dangerous.

By framing the problem of guns as one of dangerous people, not the guns themselves or gun culture, politicians individualized the problem in a way that fits with preexisting political themes and a particularly American culture of individualism (e.g., Hauhart, 2015).

Mental Health and Related Supports

Another salient theme throughout the articles was mental health and support for maintaining mental health. The first way that this theme appeared was in regard to the perpetrator. Soon after the incident, several articles gave detailed descriptions of the perpetrator, often focusing on his mental illness as a source of blame for carrying out gun violence. In fact, some articles even mentioned how someone had reported his behavior and threatening comments to the FBI, which they alleged did not follow up adequately on the tip. In this sense, the news articles blamed the perpetrator's mental illness, implying that the incident never would have happened if the perpetrator was in a better state of mental health. This perspective was common among multiple different sources, but it was particularly pronounced among politicians. For example, one *USA Today* article from less than a week after the incident stated:

> Trump, who has cited claims about the suspect's mental health problems and criticized the FBI for failing to follow up on a tip about the shooter, has been reluctant to back gun control after past school shootings. So have Republican members of Congress, many of whom have received contributions from the National Rifle Association and other groups who say the focus should be on mental health and tighter school security measures. (Jackson, 2018)

Similarly, a *Wall Street Journal* article published on the same day explained, "As for mass shootings, almost all of them have involved mentally ill young men. Some used pistols, some used rifles, some had both—but as with street crime, people who shouldn't have weapons got them" (Carlson, 2018).

In addition to blaming individuals' mental illness for causing the incident, the articles also conveyed that a possible solution was to better address mental health needs. This suggestion generally took two forms. The first form consisted of vague mentions of improving access to mental health resources. Articles used language like "greater attention to mental health" and "boosting funding for . . . mental health" (Hackman, 2018), as well as "tackle mental-illness issues" (Hayes, 2018b), but they did not provide more concrete descriptions of what types of mental health issues were relevant or what practical solutions could be offered. The articles—and the sources quoted in them—seemed only to address increasing support for mental health in vague and abstract terms.

The second form that this solution-oriented theme took was restricting gun access for people with mental illness, as we discuss above. This potential solution was described in a highly individualized way that sought not to treat the perceived problems of people but to restrict their rights. One article about the partisan divide among potential solutions noted:

> Republicans are more likely than Democrats to support a ban on firearms for those who have been treated for mental illness, a proposal also backed overwhelmingly by Democrats and independents. "Everyone who commits a mass shooting has a mental issue," says John Shaw, 60, of Madison, Wisconsin. "Preventing them from getting the gun is the most important thing." (Page & Icsman, 2018)

In this quote, the solution to curbing gun violence is mental health—not through offering more expansive treatment options or to promote a broader culture of wellness but through identifying individuals facing mental illness and denying them access to guns. In fact, one proposed method for making this happen (i.e., mandated reporting of individuals who received treatment for mental illness to a centralized repository) would actually punish individuals for seeking treatment. Had they not sought treatment, they would still be allowed access to guns.

To contextualize this framing, we note that prior research has found that around two-thirds of perpetrators of mass shootings, including school shootings, exhibited prior signs of or had formal diagnoses of mental health issues (National Threat Assessment Center, 2019; Vossekuel et al., 2004). More recent research, however, suggests that these may be underestimates due in part to data limitations and because almost all perpetrators of mass shootings may have underlying mental health issues (Lankford & Cowan, 2020). Importantly, however, the opposite is not true; the vast majority of individuals with mental health conditions are not violent and pose little risk of violence. While mental health issues, then, are likely a common characteristic of school shooters, a sole focus on mental health is unlikely to accurately identify individuals at risk of perpetrating school violence. As Lankford and Cowan (2020) suggest, mental health may be assessed in conjunction with other risk factors but should be done in a way that avoids stigmatizing individuals.

Discussion

Our analyses of mainstream news media coverage of the tragedy at Parkland show very individualized coverage of the problem, including its causes and the potential responses to it. The problem itself was framed as a mentally ill individual, without any critical thought to broader issues that might have led to the perpetrator's alienation from the school and society, such as lack of community integration, a hostile school climate, or insufficient community supports. While gun control was discussed as a potential response, coverage of gun control was relatively shallow; the few gun control proposals that the media did cover focused on limiting the ability of dangerous *individuals* (i.e., mentally ill and young) to possess weapons. Other proposed responses included target-hardening approaches, such as arming teachers or increasing school security, intended to deter individuals from committing violence at schools.

These responses illustrate the MSF framework well. Rather than being a linear response to the facts of the case and evidence of best practices, they offer context-driven proposals that resonate with politicians' previously established platforms. Politicians like Trump responded to the event by discussing gun control and mental health, but by limiting these discussions to an individualized framework that saw deviant and mentally ill people as the problem, they could avoid alienating the gun rights lobby or siding with more progressive policy makers who might wish for community supports. These responses also resonate with a uniquely American notion of individualism (e.g., Hauhart, 2015), demonstrating how broad cultural scripts inform perceptions of events and proposed responses.

Our analyses are exploratory only, and as such, they are limited. Our findings are based on relatively small samples of three newspapers' accounts of a single event, and thus they may not represent all coverage of this event or of other events. It is, of course, also difficult to determine whether our findings pick up the agendas of policy makers, news outlets, or both. Nevertheless, our findings are important for demonstrating that responses to mass school violence can be influenced by policy streams more so than evidence on best practices (Lee et al., 2020). For example, there was little focus on strategies shown to mitigate school violence, such as a positive school climate (Steffgen et al., 2013; Turanovic et al., 2020), fair and consistently enforced school rules (Gottfredson, 2000), cognitive-behavioral interventions (Wilson et al., 2001), and other related strategies. Similarly, the focus on gun control waned after the beginning weeks of coverage, perhaps inappropriately; reduced gun ownership has been linked to less homicide (Hepburn & Hemenway, 2004). Hopefully, future research can continue to analyze this trend with the hope that news outlets and policy makers might respond to future events by considering evidence on effectiveness of school security, community-based mental health supports, inclusive school climates, and other ways of conceptualizing violence and responding to it.

NOTE

1. In this chapter, we include citations for sampled articles that we quote or refer to directly. A list of other sampled articles is available upon request.

REFERENCES

Addington, L. A. (2009). Cops and cameras: Public school security as a policy response to Columbine. *American Behavioral Scientist, 52*(10), 1426–1446.

Bacon, J. (2018, March 25). Day after March for Our Lives, Pope Francis uses Palm Sunday sermon to urge youths to lead. *USA Today.* https://www.usatoday.com/story/news/world/2018/03/25/pope-palm-sunday-march-our-lives-youth/456761002/

Bardach, E., & Patashnik, E. M. (2019). *A practical guide for policy analysis: The eightfold path to more effective problem solving.* CQ Press.

Burns, R., & Crawford, C. (1999). School shootings, the media, and public fear: Ingredients for a moral panic. *Crime, Law and Social Change, 32*(2), 147–168.

Campo-Flores, A. (2018, March 9). Florida Gov. Scott signs gun-control, school-safety bill; State raises gun-purchase age to 21 in wake of Parkland school shooting. *Wall Street Journal.* https://www.wsj.com/articles/florida-gov-scott-signs-gun-control-school-safety-bill-1520627652

Carlson, J. (2018, February 20). Real solutions for curtailing gun violence; Toughen penalties for theft of firearms, and seriously enforce illegal-possession and straw-purchase laws. *Wall Street Journal*. https://www.wsj.com/articles/real-solutions-for-curtailing -gun-violence-1519168921

Cohen, M. D., March, J. G., & Olsen, J. P. (1972). A garbage can model of organizational choice. *Administrative Science Quarterly, 17*(1), 1–25.

Cox, J. W., Rich, S., Chiu, A., Muyskens, J., & Ulmanu, M. (2021). Database: How many children have experienced school shootings in America? *Washington Post*. https:// www.washingtonpost.com/graphics/2018/local/school-shootings-database/

Davis, J. H. (2018, February 23). Trump condemns Florida officer who didn't act; Sticks by plan to arm teachers. *New York Times*. https://www.nytimes.com/2018/02/23/us /politics/trump-cpac-guns-school-shooting.html

Fausset, R., & Kovaleski, S. F. (2018, February 15). Nikolas Cruz, Florida shooting suspect, showed "every red flag." *New York Times*. https://www.nytimes.com/2018/02/15/us /nikolas-cruz-florida-shooting.html

Feldman, M. S., & Khademian, A. M. (2008). The continuous process of policy formation. In K. Ahmed & E. Sánchez-Triana (Eds.), *Strategic environmental assessment for policies: An instrument for good governance* (p. 37). The World Bank.

Fisher, B. W., Mowen, T. J., & Boman, IV, J. H. (2018). School security measures and longitudinal trends in adolescents' experiences of victimization. *Journal of Youth and Adolescence, 47*, 1221–1237.

Glaser, B. G. (1965). The constant comparative method of qualitative analysis. *Social Problems, 12*(4), 436–445.

Gottfredson, D. C. (2000). *Schools and delinquency*. Cambridge University Press.

Hackman, M. (2018, March 22). Congress plans to allow gun-violence research; Lawmakers agree to partially alter 1996 ban, clearing way for CDC to study gun violence. *Wall Street Journal*. https://www.wsj.com/articles/congress-plans-to-reverse-ban-on-gun -violence-research-1521668911

Hauhart, R. C. (2015). American sociology's investigations of the American Dream: Retrospect and prospect. *American Sociologist, 46*, 65–98.

Hayes, C. (2018a, April 26). After Parkland school shooting mishaps, Broward deputies say they have "no confidence" in sheriff. *USA Today*. https://www.usatoday.com/story /news/2018/04/26/after-parkland-school-shooting-mishaps-broward-deputies-say-they -have-no-confidence-sheriff/555671002/

Hayes C. (2018b, February 18). Students plan to walk out of schools to protest gun laws. *USA Today*. https://www.usatoday.com/story/news/2018/02/17/students-teachers-plan ning-nationwide-walkout-protest-gun-control-inaction-students-fed-up-they-plan /348752002/

Hepburn, L. M., & Hemenway, D. (2004). Firearm availability and homicide: A review of the literature. *Aggression and Violent Behavior, 9*(4). 417–440. https://doi.org/10 .1016/S1359-1789(03)00044-2

Hsu, T. (2018, February 25). Lines out the door and strong sales at Tampa gun show. *New York Times*. https://www.nytimes.com/2018/02/25/business/gun-show-tampa-park land.html

Irwin, V., Wang, K., Cui, J., Zhang, J., and Thompson, A. (2021). *Report on indicators of school crime and safety: 2020* (NCES 2021-092/NCJ 300772). National Center for Education Statistics, U.S. Department of Education, and Bureau of Justice Statistics, Office of Justice Programs, U.S. Department of Justice. Washington, DC. https://nces.ed .gov/pubsearch/pubsinfo.asp?pubid=2021092

Jackson, D. (2018, February 20). Trump controls. *USA Today*, A1.

Jackson, D., Shesgreen, D., & Gaudiano, N. (2018, February 28). Trump says take guns first and worry about "due process second" in White House gun meeting. *USA Today*. https://www.usatoday.com/story/news/politics/2018/02/28/trump-says-take-guns-first-and-worry-due-process-second-white-house-gun-meeting/381145002/

Jonson, C. L. (2017). Preventing school shootings: The effectiveness of safety measures. *Victims & Offenders*, *12*(6), 956–973.

Kelly, E. (2018, February 19). Some Republicans support tighter background checks. *USA Today*, A2.

Kingdon, J. W. (1984). *Agendas, alternatives, and public policies*. Little, Brown.

Kupchik, A., & Bracy, N. L. (2009). The news media on school crime and violence: Constructing dangerousness and fueling fear. *Youth Violence and Juvenile Justice*, *7*(2), 136–155.

Lankford, A., & Cowan, R. G. (2020) Has the role of mental health problems in mass shootings been significantly underestimated? *Journal of Threat Assessment and Management*, *7*(3–4), 135–156.

Lee, H., Pickett, J. T., Burton, A. L, Cullen, F. T., Jonson, C. L., & Burton Jr., V. S. (2020). Attributions as anchors: How the public explains school shootings and why it matters. *Justice Quarterly*. Online first, https://doi.org/10.1080/07418825.2020.1769710

Livingston, M. D., Rossheim, M. E., & Hall, K. S. (2019). A descriptive analysis of school and school shooter characteristics and the severity of school shootings in the United States, 1999–2018. *Journal of Adolescent Health*, *64*(6), 797–799.

Madfis, E. (2016). "It's better to overreact": School officials' fear and perceived risk of rampage attacks and the criminalization of American public schools. *Critical Criminology*, *24*(1), 39–55.

McLendon, M. K., & Cohen-Vogel, L. (2008). Understanding education policy change in the American states: Lessons from political science. In B. S. Cooper, J. G. Cibulka, & L. D. Fusarelli (Eds.), *Handbook of Education Politics and Policy* (pp. 30–51). Routledge.

Miller, R. W. (2018). Parkland survivor throws up, continues "incredible speech" at March for Our Lives. *USA Today*. https://www.usatoday.com/story/news/nation/2018/03/24/parkland-survivor-throws-up-during-march-our-lives-speech-then-continued-her-incredible-speech-like/456064002/

Muschert, G. W. (2009). Frame-changing in the media coverage of a school shooting: The rise of Columbine as a national concern. *Social Science Journal*, *46*(1), 164–170.

Muschert, G. W., & Carr, D. (2006). Media salience and frame changing across events: Coverage of nine school shootings, 1997–2001. *Journalism & Mass Communication Quarterly*, *83*(4), 747–766.

National Threat Assessment Center. (2019) *Mass attacks in public spaces—2018*. U.S. Secret Service, Department of Homeland Security.

Page, S., & Icsman, M. (2018, February 25). Poll: Americans support tougher gun laws, don't expect Congress to act. *USA Today*. https://www.usatoday.com/story/news/2018/02/25/poll-americans-support-tougher-gun-laws-dont-expect-congress-act/371104002/

Rogers, K. (2018, February 16). Trump visits Florida hospital that treated school shooting victims. *New York Times*. https://www.nytimes.com/2018/02/16/us/politics/trump-parkland.html

Steffgen, G., Recchia, S., & Viechtbauer, W. (2013). The link between school climate and violence in school: A meta-analytic review. *Aggression and Violent Behavior*, *18*(2), 300–309.

Stolberg, S. G., & Green, E. L. (2018, March 8). Not gun control, but alarms, cameras and bulletproof doors. *New York Times*, A14.

Turanovic, J., Pratt, T., Kulig, T., & Cullen, F. (2020). *Individual, institutional, and community sources of school violence: A meta-analysis.* Justice Information Center. https://ncvc.dspacedirect.org/handle/20.500.11990/1850

Turkewitz, J., & Hartocolis, A. (2018, February 20). Highlights: Students call for action across nation; Florida lawmakers fail to take up assault rifle bill. *New York Times*. https://www.nytimes.com/2018/02/20/us/gun-control-florida-shooting.html

USA Today Editorial Board (2018, February 16). Now's the time for more than thoughts and prayers. *USA* Today, A5.

Viano, S., Curran, F. C., & Fisher, B. W. (2021). Kindergarten cop: A case study of how a coalition between school districts and law enforcement led to school resource officers in elementary schools. *Educational Evaluation and Policy Analysis, 43*(2), 253–279.

Wilson, D. B., Gottfredson, D. C., & Najaka, S. S. (2001). School-based prevention of problem behaviors: A meta-analysis. *Journal of Quantitative Criminology, 17*(3), 247–272.

19

Preventing School Shootings and Healing America's Bootstrap Trauma with Compassionate and Cooperative Schools

JESSIE KLEIN

From Aristotle through Rousseau and beyond, great thinkers write that being social is fundamental to being human, an instinctual animal drive and/or a prerequisite to thriving and living in peace. Yet, the United States does not organize schools and society in ways that foster cooperative and compassionate relationships. Instead, this socially disconnected "civilization" creates conditions that breed loneliness, entrench trauma, and foster school shootings. However, schools can build the empathy and collaboration necessary to help people connect with one another and spearhead a more compassionate and less violent society.

In America, escalating rates of youths suffer alone and are then reproached, ostracized, and otherwise bullied as a result of their widely stigmatized depression and anxiety (Sweeting et al., 2006; McConnico et al., 2016; Klein, 2019). According to Stopbullying.gov (n.d.), 20 percent of students in grades nine through twelve are bullied, and approximately 30 percent of young people admit to bullying others. This twenty-first-century tragedy is further alarming, as many school shooters plan their attack because they feel bullied, persecuted, and/or threatened. It is within this historical context that school shootings became a common atrocity (Klein, 2012a).

In the three decades from 1979 to 2008, 148 American school shootings took place (Klein, 2012b). In the next ten years, there were almost double that number (254); and in the *two* school years from 2018 through 2020, there were already 150, or almost 60 percent of the number in the previous decade (NCES, 2021).

These shootings have been growing in number as the emotional landscape in the United States has become bleaker. Since the 1980s, social isolation tripled (McPherson et al., 2006), and depression and anxiety afflict youths at increasingly younger ages and in higher numbers (Twenge, 2006; Hidaka, 2012). Almost 50 percent of the adult population suffers from a behavior or substance addiction disorder (Sussman et al., 2011); children with ADHD rose to 10 percent (Danielson et al., 2018); empathy and trust significantly decreased (Perry & Szalavitz, 2010); and rage plagues one out of ten men (Okuda et al., 2015). Since 2019, suicide rates increased 33 percent (CDC, 2021).

These statistics parallel the Centers for Disease Control's (CDC) description of trauma, including "having difficulty concentrating," being "frequently angry and irritable," struggling with "anxiety, shame, and self-blame," "withdrawing from others," "feeling sad, or depressed," "engaging in addictive behaviors," and becoming more vulnerable to being "victims and perpetrators of violence" (CDC, 2013; CDC, 2020). As such, many in the United States are grappling with systemic trauma.

While trauma expert Bessel Van der Kolk (2015) explains that in order to heal, people require empathy, acceptance, and social support, the United States is organized around an economic and social system founded on extreme competition, self-reliance, and individualism, with corresponding attacks: people are judged for not being the "winners," blamed for being unable to overcome challenging circumstances on their own, and shamed for how these so-called limitations reflect on their character (Messner & Rosenfeld, 1994; Klein, 2012a). When people are emotionally challenged, they are expected to "get over it" by themselves; they are often shamed if they are stuck, and the pain can then set deeper in the psyche (Crumb et al., 2019).

In this context, it is harder to ask for help for fear of being perceived as weak or otherwise inadequate. Support for basic human needs, including financial assistance, social connection, and/or aid with homework or other projects, is too often avoided (Olds & Schwartz, 2010). This hyper-self-reliance value is founded in the common U.S. maxim: "Pull yourself up by your bootstraps," suggesting that via sheer willpower, people should be able to accomplish everything without help regardless of economic or social position (Bologna, 2018).

This American perspective, reflected in iconic films like *High Noon*, also glamorizes the idea that people do everything alone; and yet as research in books like *The Pursuit of Loneliness* (1970), *Bowling Alone: America's Declining Social Capital* (1995), and *The Lonely American* (2009) attest—the more isolated, the less well people become and the more likely they are devastated, and sometimes paralyzed, by depression, anxiety, and violence.

This social isolation associated with hyper self-reliance pressures is compounded and complicated by the U.S. obsession with economic success—so much so that people are routinely assessed in terms of their "worth." On a series of barometers, people view themselves and others according to their value associated with attributes such as their wealth, social relationships, and bodies.

Taken together, the United States is in the midst of what I call "bootstrap trauma": suffering perpetuated by a cutthroat economic and social system that overemphasizes independence (rather than collaborative interdependence) and an individual's "worth" (rather than accepting and appreciating themselves and each other more unconditionally). These distorted values undermine relationships, supports, and empathy, critical for surviving and thriving.

One horrific manifestation of this value system occurs when bullied students perceived to be "losers," because they are seen as "not measuring up," get the message that they should "stand up" and handle their troubles "on their own." Too often they pick up guns to do just that (Klein, 2012a, 2019).

The Culpability of Capitalism

The despair with which people in the United States are grappling recalls old insights. Classic thinkers have illuminated how socio-economic systems can perpetuate contemporary pain—for instance, through sociological concepts of anomie (Emile Durkheim) and alienation (Karl Marx)—and how this anguish drives violence against oneself and others.

Durkheim's *Suicide* (1897) illustrates how high rates of misery are symptoms of dysfunctional social-economic systems and not necessarily individual and familial pathologies. Social isolation develops in societies where there is little that tethers us together and too much that sets us apart. This low integration manifests today in a lack of community, or "weak ties" such as in relationships with store keepers and neighbors, and in the typical combative and judgmental social environments, shrouded in exclusion, cyber harassment, and technologically mediated interactions, that are unfortunate hallmarks of school and workplace bully societies (Klein, 2012a). Steeped in "low integration," people are prey to what Durkheim calls "egoistic suicide."

This society also contends with what Durkheim refers to as "low regulation." Decreases in economic limits since the 1980s means that rather than benefit from progressive taxation that can provide universal health care and other basic needs as provided in many social democracies, people in the United States are encouraged to make and spend as much money as possible while paying as little as possible in taxes that could help address social and environmental problems. Despite overwhelming evidence on the need for progress, the U.S. government places too few controls on greenhouse gases that portend the end of human life (Liu & Yang, 2018) and few limitations on the corporate greed that fuels gross inequality, wage stagnation, and poverty (Crotty et al., 1998). "Anomic suicide" develops from the incompatibility between stoking unlimited desire, and meeting basic needs, which today includes the survival of humanity and other species.

Low integration and regulation combined with extreme individualism and isolation predict the depression, anxiety, suicide, and homicide rates with which people contend. In schools where there also tends to be little community, coupled with high expectations for students to get perfect grades and be successful in sports, extracurricular activities, and around popularity contests, youths tend to feel overwhelmed. Across demographics, many come from families where adults feel similarly inadequate. Discontent develops from systemic demands to acquire and achieve, coupled with limited access to a community of caring others.

Marx writes that alienation develops from replacing the human need to contribute personal creative resources to directly serve the well-being of others with the capitalist imperative to acquire a monetary wage for self-preservation and luxury resources. Since what people create belongs to the owners of production, a given company or corporation, rather than to the worker/creator, people cannot give of themselves freely to others. They are prevented from the human connection that develops when individuals give and the others receives that is so fundamental to living interdependently. As such, people are alienated from themselves, their work, each other, and the essence of being human (1844, 1867).

In schools, students are similarly separated as they prepare for roles in a capitalist society. Rather than work collaboratively to support one another's education and to exchange research, ideas, and discoveries, students are trained to compete, to get the highest grades and to be at the top of the class. When grades are on a curve, students can only do well to the extent that others do badly, undermining the potential for working together to maximize learning. This race tends to create a cheating culture, where students and teachers, judged by their individual achievements, are driven to do whatever it takes (Callahan, 2004). Social environments are similarly structured, where students vie for popularity and social influence. Rather than developing caring friendships, those who make it into the most influential cliques, often have to fight to stay included and can be made into a pariah by a random whim. Schools do little, if anything, to help students build supportive relationships with one another. Pernicious "popularity" contests reflect and reproduce the alienated relationships endemic to capitalism and leave many students depressed and/or enraged.

Acquiring Capital

In this toxic social environment, students assess themselves and one another as value-laden commodities. Early in school careers, they are taught formally and informally to acquire capital. Rather than relate authentically with one

272 / Jessie Klein

another, they find that they need to become what their school rates most highly. They are evaluated according to perceived value. The toxicity of these social norms contributes to "bootstrap trauma" symptoms such as depression and aggression.

To meet needs for acceptance, for instance, individuals require *cultural capital*, valued activities, such as football or cheerleading; *economic capital*, measured by a family's financial worth; *social capital*, associated with who they know; and *symbolic capital*, resources available that confer prestige, for instance, as leader of school government, on sports teams, or in highly visible social cliques. More common today is also pressure to build *body capital*: physical forms deemed most attractive in a given historical moment. Tragically, eating disorders are routinely used to add value, including anorexia (compulsion to lose weight) and bigorexia (obsession with developing muscle).

Males, in particular, are expected to build *masculinity capital*, including expectations to seem dominant over others, invulnerable, powerful, and violent; often via sexual harassing and gay bashing others. This capital is often reduced if associated with low cultural, economic, body, social, and/or symbolic capital. Similarly, different races and ethnicities are perceived to have more or less *race capital*. Being white in America still confers privileges and therefore value.

Worth measured in capital can be quickly acquired or lost, and this figures in the many school shootings where bullied, isolated, and/or marginalized students seemed to believe that their crimes would compensate for their low capital. Many boys have discovered the American recipe: to increase masculinity capital, the trump card is violence. Boys perceived to be feminine, and therefore gay, and/or who were thought to be unsuccessful heterosexually or not sufficiently dominating, felt driven to make up for their diminished value. For instance, the Health High School shooter in Kentucky said he was bullied first because he was "too nice" to girls (Newman, 2002, p. 27). As with many other shooters, he used violence to increase his worth. Proving he was no longer "too nice to girls," he killed three females, wounded three others, and also injured two boys. After the shooting, he said that he "was feeling proud, good, and more respected." He said he thought the shooting would make him more "popular." Even from prison, he said that he felt "more respected now" (Klein, 2012b).

Many school shooters killed girls who rejected them, and/or boys who called them gay, thereby also compensating for lost masculinity capital. For example, the 1998 Westside Middle School shooter in Arkansas targeted a girl after she broke up with him. He threatened to kill another girl for talking about the breakup. He shot two other girls who refused his advances. His partner in the shooting also shot and killed his ex-girlfriend. The shooter at

Parker Middle School in Edinboro, Pennsylvania, targeted his ex-girlfriend, whom he threatened when she broke up with him. He went after another girl who laughed at him when he invited her to the dance where his shooting took place. The 1996 Moses Lake, Washington, school shooter was called a "fag" in algebra class by the popular athlete he later killed, and the aforementioned Heath High School shooter killed a girl who did not return his affections and said he said he targeted the "preps and jocks" who called him "gay" and other homosexual slurs (Klein, 2012b).

Based on my research, nearly 50 percent of shootings between 1979 and 2009 reflect perpetrators' reactions to masculinity challenges (Klein, 2012b). Almost 10 percent were direct responses to the shooter being called homosexual (Klein, 2012b). Premeditated violence against girls was a motive in over 20 percent of these shootings, and almost 15 percent related to dating or domestic violence (Klein, 2012b). Attacks on manhood, as defined by contemporary expectations, led these boys to increase their "masculinity capital" through violence.

When commodified, students need help to meet needs for connection and respect. In the absence of support and guidance, they often fight, in one way or another, to increase their value instead. As masculinity capital is bestowed for appearing strong and powerful, those who bully tend to be rewarded for increasing their "worth" as a result of these behaviors (Thunfors & Cornell, 2008; Garandeau et al., 2014). Students find that hurting others increases coveted popularity, even as their needs for connection and respect continue to go unmet.

The lethal cycle of being bullied and bullying, symptoms of bootstrap trauma, often develops in schools, workplaces, and the larger society where such conditions undermine human connections. Studies show that inequality and hierarchy predict violence (Crochík, 2016), including in academia (Twale & DeLuca, 2008; Strandmark & Rahm, 2014), nursing (Rocker, 2008), and against other care workers (Romero, 2013; Romero & Pérez, 2016), and the more economic inequality in a country, the more bullying (Elgar et al., 2013). Other forms of status hierarchy also predict bullying, including prejudice based on "lookism," where students are valued more or less according to their assessed attractiveness (Chancer, 2019).

American bullying and reactive school shootings also look a lot like the prescriptions in *The Nazi Primer: Official Handbook for Schooling the Hitler Youth* (Hitler & Murphy, 1938), where young Nazis were expected to be "perfect physically," "white," and "an Aryan" (xxvi) with traditional gender qualities: "The boy must be strong, the girl beautiful" (xx). Hitler Youth propaganda circulated in schools idealized Nordic people from Germany, England, Denmark, the Netherlands, Sweden, and Norway—people with tall stature, long faces, narrow and straight noses, lean builds, straight light hair, light eyes, and fair skin (Werner, 1934).

In many schools, youth are bullied because they deviate from these same prescriptions. In addition to students who do not have traditional gender and/ or sexual expression, and those whose bodies are perceived to have too much or too little weight, students are assaulted because they are short or because they have other kinds of race or ethnic features, just as *The Nazi Primer* disparaged people who were "short and large-boned" and if their nose was "sunk low" (32). Many school shooting perpetrators committed their shootings following harassment around lacking such "body capital." For example, the Thurston High School shooter in Oregon killed two students who he said tormented him "for being small," while the Pearl High School shooter in Mississippi was teased and excluded for being a "short little fat boy" (Klein, 2012b).

Much U.S. bullying, then, parallels historic white supremacy, which is also reflected in many school shooters' motives. The mostly white victims-turned-victors did not receive the same white patriarchal dividend (race and masculinity capital) as those who had more Nordic features; these boys found that being white and male was not enough. They were also expected to be tall and able-bodied, have lean builds, be wealthy, and have cisgender qualities. Failing to reflect the Nazi Aryan prototype, the shooters' lack of hegemonic male attributes decreased their worth, rendering their whiteness and masculinity less valuable. References to fascist mass murder serves, then, as a fast track to acquiring capital associated with masculinity.

Many explicitly mentioned Hitler and Nazis to declare their supremacy—including the Mississippi perpetrator, who named his social group "Third Reich" and was also bullied because he was "poor"; the Columbine High School killers, who were known to scream, "Heil Hitler," and were called "gay"; and the Red Lake Senior High School shooter, who referred to himself as "pro-Nazi" and was bullied for being "heavy" (Klein, 2012b). Nazi ideology and paraphernalia were also found in the wake of other school shootings, including the massacre at Stoneman Douglas High School in Florida.

Measuring people in terms of their "worth," takes a heavy toll and manifests in multiple versions of violence against others and oneself. The cost to humanity and mental health as a result of bootstrap trauma, with high rates of suicide, homicide, and mass murder, grows from a focus on capital hyper-independence, and cries for a more connected and compassionate social system. Twenge et al. (2010, p. 153) concurred that "over time, American culture has increasingly shifted toward an environment in which more and more young people experience poor mental health and psychopathology, possibly due to an increased focus on money, appearance, and status rather than on community and close relationships."

"Good Society" Schools

Schools can build more accepting and supportive social environments where students are helped to actualize their potential and directly give their joy and creativity to others, much like Marx and Durkheim envision.

Recent research also reveals the life-serving benefits of empathetically serving others and the detrimental impact that can develop from self-serving emphases. In fact, common recommendations to recover from depression include helping others and practicing random acts of kindness (Seligman, 2004). And yet, instead of affirming and serving one another as a fundamental facet of social organization, such volunteering is prescribed as an "extra-curricular" to heal from the discontent and depression created by the current economic system.

In their study measuring depression and anxiety, Erickson et al. (2018, p. 608) find that "participants reported higher conflict and symptoms on days that they most pursued self [focused] goals, but noted higher perceived support and lower symptoms when pursuing compassionate goals." Likewise, Santini et al. (2019, p. 255) conclude that "volunteering is an activity that not only benefits society but is also associated with optimal mental health in the general population." Giving to others is considered such a powerful formula for improving mental health that one study found that people who gave their organs to those in need experienced comparable emotional well-being benefits to those whose lives they saved (Cohen & Hoffner, 2013). Evidence-based school programs also suggest that helping others, building interdependence, and enhancing social cohesion serves academic, emotional, and developmental growth (e.g., McConnico et al., 2016). Research also suggests that when schools create social cohesion and expectations that students support one another, bullying, so often the impetus for deadly shootings, stops (Ahmed, 2008; Padget & Notar, 2013).

Given this, schools can become leaders in shifting consciousness and behavior away from the system's competitive, hyper-independent, and assessment focus that breeds bootstrap trauma toward more collaborative, accepting, interdependent, and compassionate relationships that help people thrive. Since students from these social microcosms become future leaders, such education can begin to shift socio-political-economic structures that otherwise co-opt relationships and reproduce judging, blaming, and shaming. Students would then be more likely to support rather than stigmatize and reproach one another. They could connect authentically, instead of competing to acquire higher valued (cultural, social, economic, body, masculinity, race) capital; and they could build a socially cohesive and caring society by actualizing their creative potential in the service of others.

Authentic Social Connections

A growing trauma-informed school movement recognizes that students' difficult behaviors may be a response to adverse childhood experiences (ACEs) aggravated by a society that does little to support struggling people. Before turning four years old, an estimated 26 percent of youth experience ACEs related to various forms of abuse, stressful family difficulties, and witnessing or experiencing violence. ACEs are an especially high risk for those from economically challenged neighborhoods, for racial/ethnic minorities, and for others who are disadvantaged (CDC, 2019).

In trauma-sensitive schools, staff from the principal to the janitor are trained to respond to students and to one another with compassion. These schools raise awareness that an everyday occurrence can trigger post-traumatic stress responses. People begin to heal with different forms of unconditional acceptance (Redford et al., 2015). Some examples include those recommended on a Stopbullying.gov fact sheet (2017), including talking circles, social-emotional learning, mindfulness, and restorative justice. Talking circles are discussions where students share something in response to a prompt that helps them see each other's humanity, such as an experience when you felt that you did not fit in. It is difficult to see each other as capital-focused commodities when community members regularly share their vulnerabilities in intimate groups. Social-emotional learning can take many forms. Across the world, schools teach Marshall Rosenberg's nonviolent communication (NVC), which focuses on identifying feelings and finding the most effective and least costly strategy for meeting everyone's needs (Rosenberg, 2015). Building status and making money are often ineffectual strategies for meeting needs for respect and connection, for instance, and students are helped to find more effective paths. Meditation helps to heal overstressed autonomic nervous systems using various forms of mindfulness and breath practices. This helps people feel calmer, more empathetic, and more open to connecting and bonding with one another (Brown & Gerbarg, 2012). Restorative justice programs help to repair harm and social connectedness. When conflicts occur, everyone impacted is invited to a circle. Together the discussions focus on how amends can be made and relationships restored.

In *How to Stop School Rampage Killing*, Eric Madfis (2020, p. 29) shows the efficacy of restorative justice and other "broad-based mental health services, systematic mentoring and support structures, as well as conflict resolution, group conferencing, peer meditation, and anti-bullying school programs." Schools need to decrease punitive responses and create safe spaces for students to break their "code of silence" in trusting relationships with one another and with school staff. Such restorative circles could preempt violence, since in over 80 percent of school shooting cases, someone had prior knowledge of the threat (Madfis, 2020, p. 105). When people believe a situation will be handled appropriately, and that they are appreciated and part of a caring community, tragedies have a better chance of being averted.

To develop these critical relationships, schools can raise awareness about the toxic impact of perceiving one another in terms of capital. Educational films, such as *The Mask You Live In* (2013), *Killing Us Softly* (2014), *The Hunting Ground* (2015), *The Corporation* (2003), and *Thirteenth* (2016), are a handful of documentaries that schools can use to undo prejudice related to gender, sexuality, class, and race.

Conclusion

The competitive, hyper-independent, and quick-to-shame American culture incites misery and produces reactive violence in schools. Shootings in response to poor grades, shaming, or being punitively disciplined also increased dramatically from 1979 through 2008, during the same time when school policies moved toward zero tolerance with an increasing emphasis on high-stakes test scores and grades (Klein, 2012b). These kinds of reactive mass murders beg for new models of justice in response to school violence, as well as alternative educational priorities. Where Colorado led the country in zero-tolerance policies following the shooting at Columbine, for instance, the state has since become one of the first to spearhead restorative justice models instead (PBS NewsHour, 2014).

Without such concerted efforts, students and school staff will continue to suffer with the rest of the population. Stuck in a cycle of competitive judging, self-reliance-focused blaming, and individualist-oriented shaming, depression, anxiety, and other mental health challenges are triggered again and again. The too-common "get over it" perspective only makes the pain more humiliating and more likely to explode in violence. Schools can lead the shift away from the systemic bootstrap trauma plaguing so many and toward a more compassionate and healing society.

Educational institutions can start by removing mental health challenge stigmas, helping community members bond with one another, and creating opportunities for people to contribute directly to one another's well-being. It is through these types of practices that schools can build the kind of "good society" that can decrease violence, increase peace, and promote personal and social thriving—what writers for hundreds of years, from Aristotle through Marx and beyond, have been trying to help us imagine and create.

REFERENCES

Ahmed, E. (2008, December). "Stop it, that's enough": Bystander intervention and its relationship to school connectedness and the shame management. *Vulnerable Chil-*

dren and Youth Studies, 3(3), 203–213. https://www.tandfonline.com/doi/abs/10.1080/17450120802002548

American Psychological Association (APA). (2020). Stress in America 2020: A national mental health crisis. https://www.apa.org/news/press/releases/stress/2020/report-october

Bologna, C. (2018, August 9). Why the phrase "pull yourself up by your bootstraps" is nonsense. *HuffPost.* https://www.huffpost.com/entry/pull-yourself-up-by-your-bootstraps-nonsense_n_5b1ed024e4b0bbb7a0e037d4

Brown, R. P., & Gerbarg, P. L. (2012). *The healing power of the breath: Simple techniques to reduce stress and anxiety, enhance concentration, and balance your emotions.* Shambhala.

Callahan, D. (2004). *The cheating culture: Why more Americans are doing wrong to get ahead.* Harcourt.

Centers for Disease Control (CDC). (2013, December 20). *Traumatic incident stress.* https://www.cdc.gov/niosh/topics/traumaticincident/default.html

Centers for Disease Control (CDC). (2019, November 5). *Vital signs, adverse childhood experiences (ACES): Preventing early trauma to improve adult health.* https://www.cdc.gov/vitalsigns/aces/index.html

Centers for Disease Control (CDC). (2020, February 20). *Leading causes of death reports 1981–2019.* https://webappa.cdc.gov/sasweb/ncipc/leadcause.html

Centers for Disease Control (CDC). (2021, August 30). *Suicide prevention: Facts about suicide.* https://www.cdc.gov/suicide/facts/index.html

Chancer, L. (2019). Bullying and looksism. In J. Klein (Ed.), *Bullying: A reference handbook* (pp. 177–179). ABC-CLIO.

Cohen, E. L., & Hoffner, C. (2013, January 19). Gifts of giving: The role of empathy and perceived benefits to others and self in young adults' decisions to become organ donors. *Journal of Health Psychology, 1,* 128–38.

Crochík, J. L. (2016). Hierarchy, violence and bullying among students of public middle schools. *Paidéia (Ribeirão Preto), 26*(65): 307–315. http://www.scielo.br/scielo.php?script=sci_arttext

Crotty, J., Epstein G., & Kelly, P. (1998). Multinational corps in neo-liberal regime. In D. Baker, G. Epstein, & R. Pollin (Eds.), *Globalization and progressive economic policy* (pp. 1–25). Cambridge University Press.

Crumb, L., Mingo, T. M., & Crowe, A. (2019). "Get over it and move on": The impact of mental illness stigma in rural, low-income United States populations. *Mental Health & Prevention, 13,* 143–148.

Danielson, M. L., Bitsko, R. H., Ghandour, R. M., Holbrook, J. R., Kogan, M. D., & Blumberg, S. J. (2018). Prevalence of parent-reported ADHD diagnosis and associated treatment among U.S. children and adolescents. *Journal of Clinical Child & Adolescent Psychology, 47*(2), 199–212. https://doi.org/10.1080/15374416.2017.1417860

Durkheim, E. (1897). *Suicide, a study in sociology* (1951 ed., J. A. Spaulding, & G. Simpson, Trans.). Routledge.

Durkheim, E. (1912). *The elementary forms of religious life* (Introduction by K. E. Fields, Trans., 1995 ed.). The Free Press.

Elgar, F. J., Pickett, K. E., Pickett, W., Craig, W., Molcho, M., Hurrelmann, K., & Lenzi, M. (2013 April). School bullying, homicide and income inequality: A cross-national pooled time series analysis. *International Journal of Public Health, 58*(2), 237–245. https://www.ncbi.nlm.nih.gov/pubmed/22714137

Erickson, T. M., Granillo, M. T., Crocker, J., & Abelson, J. L. (2018, April). Compassion-ate and self-image goals as interpersonal maintenance factors in clinical depression and anxiety. *Journal of Clinical Psychology, 74*(4), 608–625.

Fine, M. (1997). *Off white: Reading on race, power, and society*. Routledge.

Garandeau, C. F., Lee, I. A., & Salmivalli, C. (2014). Inequality matters: Classroom status hierarchy and adolescents' bullying. *Journal of Youth Adolescence, 43*, 1123–1133. https://doi.org/10.1007/s10964-013-0040-4

Hidaka B. H. (2012). Depression as a disease of modernity: Explanations for increasing prevalence. *Journal of Affective Disorders, 140*(3), 205–214.

Hitler, A., & Murphy, J. V. (1938). *The Nazi primer: Official handbook for schooling the Hitler Youth* (H. L. Childs, Trans.). Harper & Brothers.

Jonsson, P. (2020, December). 2020's murder increase is "unprecedented." But is it a blip? *Christian Science Monitor*. https://www.csmonitor.com/USA/Justice/2020/1214/2020-s-murder-increase-is-unprecedented.-But-is-it-a-blip

Klein, J. (2012a). *The bully society: School shootings and the crisis of bullying in America's schools*. NYU Press.

Klein, J. (2012b). *For educators: The bully society: School shootings and the crisis of bullying in America's schools*. https://nyupress.org/resources/for-educators/; jessieklein.com

Klein, J. (2019). *Bullying: A reference handbook*. ABC-CLIO.

Levula, A., Harré, M., & Wilson, A. (2017). Social network factors as mediators of men-tal health and psychological distress. *International Journal of Social Psychiatry, 63*(3), 235–243.

Liu, Y. S., & Yang, J. H. (2018). A longitudinal analysis of corporate greenhouse gas dis-closure strategy. Corporate Governance. *The International Journal of Business in Soci-ety, 18*(2), 317–330.

Madfis, E. (2020). *How to stop school rampage killing: Lessons from averted mass shootings and bombings*. Palgrave MacMillan.

Marx, K. (1844, 1972). Economic and philosophical manuscripts with Comments on James Mill (M. Milligan, Trans.). In R. C. Tucker (Ed.), *The Marx-Engels reader*. W. W. Nor-ton. https://www.marxists.org/archive/marx/works/1844/james-mill/

Marx, K. (1867). *Capital: A critical analysis of capitalist production*. Cosimo.

McConnico, N., Boynton-Jarrett, R., Bailey, C., & Nandi, M. (2016). A framework for trau-ma-sensitive schools. *Zero to Three, 36*(5), 36–44.

McPherson, M., Smith-Lovin, L., & Brashears, M. E. (2006). Social isolation in America: Changes in core discussion networks over two decades. *American Sociological Review, 71*(3), 353–375. https://doi.org/10.1177/000312240607100301

Messner, S. F., & Rosenfeld, R. (1994). *Crime and the American dream*. Wadsworth.

The National Center for Analysis of Violent Crime (NCAVC). (1999–2002). *The school shooter: A quick reference guide*. U.S. FBI. http://www.fbi.gov

National Center for Education Statistics (NCES). (2021, May). *Violent deaths at school and away from school and school shootings*. https://nces.ed.gov/programs/coe/indicator/a01

Napoletano, A., Elgar, F. J., Saul, G., Dirks, M., & Craig, W. (2016). The view from the bot-tom: Relative deprivation and bullying victimization in Canadian adolescents. *Jour-nal of Interpersonal Violence, 31*(20), 3443–3463.

Newman, K. S. (2002). *Rampage: The social roots of school shootings*. Basic Books.

Okuda, M., Picazo, J., Olfson, M., Hasin, D. S., Liu, S. M., Bernardi, S., & Blanco, C. (2015). Prevalence and correlates of anger in the community: results from a national survey. *CNS Spectrums, 20*(2), 130–139.

Olds, J., & Schwartz, R. S. (2010). *The lonely American: Drifting apart in the twenty-first century*. Beacon Press.

Padgett, S., & Notar, C. E. (2013). Bystanders are the key to stopping bullying. *Universal Journal of Educational Research*, 1(2), 33–41.

PBS NewsHour. (2014). *Colorado high school replaces punishment with "talking circles."* https://www.youtube.com/watch?v=g8_94O4ExSA

Perry, B. D., & Szalavitz, M. (2010). *Born for love: Why empathy is essential—and endangered*. William Morrow.

Redford, J., Pritzker, K., Norwood, T., Boekelheide, T., & Bradwell, J. (2015). *Paper tigers* [Film]. KPJR Films.

Ritzer, G. (2005). The "new" means of consumption: A postmodern analysis. In P. Kivisto (Ed.), *Illuminating social life* (3rd ed., pp. 280–298). Pine Forge Press.

Rocker, C. (2008, August). Addressing nurse-to-nurse bullying to promote nurse retention. *Online Journal of Issues in Nursing*, 13(3). http://ojin.nursingworld.org/MainMenuCategories/ANAMarketplace/ANAPeriodicals/OJIN/TableofContents/vol132008/No3Sept08/ArticlePreviousTopic/NursetoNurseBullying.html

Romero, M. (2013, April). Nanny diaries and other stories: Immigrant women's labor in the social reproduction of American families. *Revista De Estudios Sociales*, 45(45): 186–197. https://www.researchgate.net/publication/262515330_Nanny_Diaries_and_Other_Stories_Immigrant_Women's_Labor_in_the_Social_Reproduction_of_American_Families

Romero, M., & Pérez, N. (2016). Conceptualizing the foundation of inequalities in care work. *American Behavioral Scientist*, 60(2): 172–188. https://journals.sagepub.com/doi/abs/10.1177/0002764215607572

Rosenberg, M. (2015). *Nonviolent communication: A language of life*. Puddledancer Press.

Santini, Z. I., Meilstrup, C., Hinrichsen, C., Nielsen, L., Koyanagi, A., Krokstad, S., Keyes, C. L. M., & Koushede, V. (2019). Formal volunteer activity and psychological flourishing in Scandinavia: Findings from two cross-sectional rounds of the European Social Survey. *Social Currents*, 6(3), 255–269. https://doi.org/10.1177/2329496518815868

Seligman, M. E. P. (2004). *Authentic happiness: Using the new positive psychology to realize your potential for lasting fulfillment* (1st trade pbk. ed.). Free Press.

Stopbullying.gov. (n.d.). *Facts about bullying*. https://www.stopbullying.gov/resources/facts#_Fast_Facts

Stopbullying.gov. (2017, August). *Bullying as an adverse childhood experience (ACE)*. https://www.stopbullying.gov/sites/default/files/2017-10/bullying-as-an-ace-fact-sheet.pdf

Strandmark, M., & Rahm, G. (2014). Development, implementation and evaluation of a process to prevent and combat workplace bullying. *Scandinavian Journal of Public Health*, 42(15), 66–73. https://journals.sagepub.com/doi/full/10.1177/1403494814549494

Sussman, S., Lisha, N., & Griffiths, M. (2011). Prevalence of the addictions: A problem of the majority or the minority? *Evaluation & the Health Professions*, 34(1), 3–56.

Sweeting, H., Young, R., West, P., & Der, G. (2006). Peer victimization and depression in early-mid adolescence: A longitudinal study. *British Journal of Educational Psychology*, 76, 577–594. https://doi.org/10.1348/000709905X49890

Thunfors, P., & Cornell, D. (2008). The popularity of middle school bullies. *Journal of School Violence*, 7(1), 65–82. https://doi.org/10.1300/J202v07n01_05

Twale, D. J., & De Luca, B. M. (2008). *Faculty incivility: the rise of the academic bully culture and what to do about it*. Jossey-Bass.

Twenge, J. M. (2006). *Generation Me: Why today's young Americans are more confident, assertive, entitled—and more miserable than ever before.* Free Press.

Twenge, J. M., Gentile, B., DeWall, C. N., Ma, D., Lacefield, K., & Schurtz, D. R. (2010). Birth cohort increases in increases in psychopathology among young Americans, 1938–2007: A cross-temporal meta-analysis of the MMPI. *Clinical Psychology Review, 30*(2), 145–154. https://doi.org/10.1016/j.cpr.2009.10.005

Van der Kolk, B. A. (2015). *The body keeps the score: brain, mind, and body in the healing of trauma.* Penguin Books.

Werner, M. (1934). *Deutscher National-Katechismus* (2nd ed.). Verlag von Heinrich Handel; (1938) H. L. Childs (Trans.), *The Nazi primer.* Harper & Brothers Publishers.

PART VII

Mass Shootings, Firearms,
and Mental Health in America

20

The Precarious Relationship between Firearm Access and Mass Shootings in the United States

Logically Obvious but Analytically Evasive

PAUL REEPING

Logically Obvious

What Is a Cause?

Epidemiology, at is core, is a science that seeks to understand the underlying causes of disease and other health-related outcomes. Epidemiology really is a science of causal inference. According to *Modern Epidemiology*, a primary text for budding and experienced epidemiologists, a cause can be defined as "an event, condition, or characteristic that preceded the disease onset and that, had the event, condition, or characteristic been different in a specified way, the disease either would not have occurred at all or would not have occurred until some later time" (Rothman et al., 2008).

Using this definition, it appears as if gun access would be an obvious cause of mass shootings: without access to a gun, the mass shooting would not have occurred or would not have occurred until some later time (when a gun was accessible). However, it is important to note that causes are often impossible to formally prove as fact. There are different methods and statistics that epidemiologists believe come close to proving causation, but in many cases the only true way to prove that something is a cause would be to travel back in time and change a specific variable (and only that variable) and see if the outcome of interest was subsequently prevented from occurring. For this reason, scientists can be a bit cautious in their use of the word *cause*, but there are circumstances where the use has seemed to be universally accepted. Most are comfortable in stating that smoking is a cause of lung cancer or that vitamin C deficiency is a cause of scurvy. I argue that gun access in relation to mass shootings is another circumstance where it is appropriate to label gun access as a cause, as it is logically obvious.

Causes as Pies

To understand why gun access should be labeled a cause of mass shootings, it is important to understand that many epidemiologists conceptualize causes as pies, where each piece of the pie contributes to producing the disease or outcome. Importantly, the outcome does not occur until the pie is "filled." This is because it is rare (and perhaps impossible) for a single cause to be sufficient for producing disease. Take heart disease, for example. A poor diet is unlikely to be the only cause of a heart attack; instead, it is more probable that it is a combination of factors that result in a heart attack, including poor diet, but also lack of exercise, genetic predisposition, stress levels, and other environmental factors (or other combinations of causes).

This is also evident in terms of gun access and mass shootings. For example, over the years, there has been great debate as to whether mass shootings are caused by firearms or mental health problems. In reality, it is likely often a combination of both gun access and a mental health crisis (plus other causes) that results in a mass shooting. Take Figure 20.1, for example. Only when the causal pie is completely filled—a person with homicidal intent and perhaps social marginalization experiences a mental health and personal crisis and gains access to a firearm (plus additional, perhaps unknown, circum-

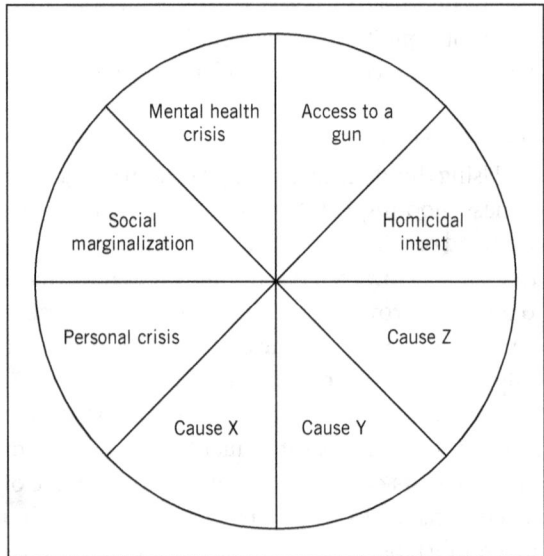

Figure 20.1 A Simple Illustration of a Causal Pie Representing the Different Causes that Might Be Required to Produce a Specific Mass Shooting.

stances contribute to the causal pie)—would a mass shooting subsequently occur. Importantly, every time a mass shooting occurs, there may be a different set of components that causes the event, resulting in an infinite number of possible combinations of components in pies. Much like the uniqueness of a snowflake, every mass shooting is the result of its own unique pie of causes. For example, a mental health crisis may be a cause in one pie, but with a different set of circumstances, a mental health crisis may not be required to cause the mass shooting to occur.

Necessary Causes

However, one cause always needs to be present for a mass shooting to occur: gun access. In epidemiology, a cause that always needs to be present is called a *necessary cause*, as it is a necessary component to the pie. Well-known necessary causes are present mostly in infectious disease epidemiology—*Variola* virus for smallpox disease, HIV for AIDS—but they are rarer outside of infectious disease. For example, while smoking is a major cause of lung cancer, it is not necessary, as there have been plenty of cases of lung cancer where the individual had never smoked. But because smoking is present so often, eliminating smoking would substantially decrease lung cancer. This is because the more individual pies a cause (like smoking, bad diet, or gun access) is a part of, the greater the impact the elimination of that cause would have in reducing the outcome. The causal pie for mass shootings contains gun access in 100 percent of cases; the causal pie for lung cancer contains smoking often, but not always. When something is a necessary cause, however, the elimination of it would result in the elimination of the disease or outcome as a whole. Smallpox disease no longer exists because the *Variola* virus has been eradicated. Another (noninfectious) example is scurvy. While some people may be more or less susceptible to scurvy due to their genetics and other lifestyle choices, supplementing everyone on a pirate ship with lemons to prevent vitamin C deficiency totally eliminates the disease, regardless of what the other causes in the pie may be.

The same would be true for mass shootings if gun access were eliminated. The other causes of mass shootings: mental health problems, personal crises, extremist indoctrination, etc., could all occur, but without access to a firearm, the mass shooting would never come to be. Importantly, gun access is not sufficient to produce the outcome, as it still requires the other components of the pie. Nevertheless, it is still an important variable to intervene upon.

Some might argue that without gun access, the perpetrator would just substitute some other weapon, such a knife or bomb. While this could theoretically occur, the outcome would not be a mass shooting, of course; it would be a knife attack or bombing. These outcomes have their own specific causal pies for occurring and are fundamentally different. For example, it is much more difficult to produce mass death with a knife than with a gun, and it is much more difficult to buy or make a bomb than a gun (Madfis & Levin, 2013). Firearm access therefore must be present in some form for a *mass shooting* to occur; it is a necessary cause.

Analytically Evasive

While gun access is both theoretically and logically a necessary cause of mass shootings, there has been limited *analytical* evidence to support this claim on the multiple levels in which it has been studied.

Does having more firearms cause the United States to have more mass shootings than other countries?

The first study to look exclusively at the relationship between gun access and mass shootings was conducted on the international level. This influential study concluded that countries with high firearm ownership were statistically more likely also to have higher levels of mass shootings (Lankford, 2016). Specifically, it found that the United States, a country with the highest rate of gun ownership, accounted for 31 percent of all public mass shooters, despite only making up 5 percent of the global population (Lankford, 2016). However, even when created carefully and intentionally, international comparisons prove to have issues of confounding due to the vast differences in the cultures, economies, and laws of different countries.

Importantly, this study was also cross-sectional, meaning that the exposure (gun ownership) and outcome (mass shootings) were collected at the same time. This presents another major hurdle to analytically proving that gun access is a cause of mass shootings on any level of analysis: reverse causation. Reverse causation is a phenomenon that occurs when the association you are studying actually occurs in the reverse of what you assumed. This is dangerous because statistically, it is difficult to parse out the direction of an effect. For example, while the hypothesis may be that gun ownership increases mass shootings, it is also reasonable to suggest that mass shootings may increase gun ownership, as individuals arms themselves in fear of these attacks (see Wallace, 2022, this volume). In fact, there is evidence that some Americans may be more likely to purchase or carry firearms due to their fear of mass shootings. Both could be true: easy firearms access may increase mass shootings, and mass shootings may lead people to want more access to firearms. But it is challenging to prove whether gun ownership is a cause of mass shootings on the international level, even when there is a strong association or correlation between the two variables.

Does having more firearms cause some U.S. states to have more mass shootings than others?

Only two studies have set out to determine if gun ownership is associated with mass shootings on the state level. A study published in 2019 concluded that a 10 percent increase in state gun ownership was associated with a 35.1 percent increase in mass shootings, but its authors avoid the use of the word *cause* and instead call on better data collection and study methods to establish causation more accurately (Reeping et al., 2019). The most recent U.S.-focused study on this relationship found that states with the lowest levels of gun ownership (two standard deviations below the mean) experienced a mass shooting (on average) every 4.67 years; states with average household gun ownership experienced a mass shooting every 2.41 years, and the states with the highest level (two standard deviations above the mean) of household gun ownership only had 1.25 years between each mass shooting (Fridel, 2021). The author concludes that household gun ownership was associated with a significant 53.5 percent increase in mass shooting incidence rate but again carefully avoids using the word *cause* throughout the manuscript (Fridel, 2021). This hesitation to use causal language, by both teams of authors, is partially due to the limitations in the collection of data on the topic.

One of the major issues is the lack of data on gun ownership, even on the state level. In the United States, gun ownership cannot be obtained from administrative records; only six states and Washington, DC, require the registration of some types of (not necessarily all) firearms. In contrast, eight states prohibit registries of an any type of firearm, and on the federal level, it is illegal to use the National Instant Criminal Back Check System to create a registry of firearm ownership (*Registration*, 2021). An alternative to registries would be representative surveys of the population. However, when these surveys have been employed, they are spotty and inconsistent in their questioning (Kleck, 2004). Researchers have therefore been left with the use of proxies—such as hunting licenses, gun-related magazine subscriptions—to estimate true gun ownership. The most common proxy is the percentage of suicides committed with a firearm, which has been found to be superior to the other proxies (Kleck, 2004). This measure is calculated simply by dividing the number of individuals who died by firearm suicide over the total number of suicide deaths; however, it has only been found to be valid on the state (or region) level and not valid on smaller units of observation, like the county or city. Furthermore, even though it has been extensively validated, it is often criticized for using a gun violence–related outcome—suicide—in the calculation. (Of note, this proxy is created out of the established theory that gun access is a cause of gun deaths—even if the same researchers avoid outwardly admitting it.)

In recent years, other proxies have been created, including the newly developed state-level estimates of household gun ownership database by RAND

Corporation (Schell et al., 2020), which combines many of the former proxies into one and applies some statistical modeling. Nevertheless, a true measure of gun ownership on the state level remains elusive and limits researchers' ability to study the effect of gun access on mass shootings (or other types of gun deaths). It is therefore difficult to decisively prove that gun ownership is a cause of mass shootings on the state level given that a proxy for gun ownership is used.

Even if scientists had perfect measures of gun ownership on the state level, it would still be difficult to establish causation due to colinearity. For example, more permissive gun laws in a state are associated with more mass shootings (Reeping et al., 2019; Webster et al., 2020). States with more permissive gun laws are also more likely to have higher levels of gun ownership; and the two are highly correlated (Pearson's r = 0.79) (Reeping et al., 2019). Since permissive laws and high gun ownership occur so often together, the inclusion of both in the same statistical models can mask the true relationship of one of the variables or, in some cases, both. If Americans want to know which "causes" the country's mass shooting problem—weak gun laws or too many guns— that would be difficult to answer because these variables exist in a feedback loop. When gun ownership increases in a state, the voters who own those guns (and their political representatives) may push for more permissive gun laws. More permissive gun laws then lead to higher gun ownership and easier gun access, continuing the cycle. How does a researcher fully disentangle these variables? It is difficult and reduces the possibility that researchers will be able to analytically establish causality.

Does owning a firearm (or owning many firearms) cause Americans to be more likely to want to commit mass shootings?

Study design greatly limits the ability to study the effect of an American owning a firearm on their desire to commit a mass shooting. Randomized controlled trials (RCTs) are often considered the gold standard for establishing causality. But conducting an RCT, where individuals in the trial are randomly assigned the exposure of interest, is not possible when the exposure is firearm access. Handing out firearms to a study's participants, simply so researchers could study them, would never be deemed ethical. (Incidentally, this relates back to the first section of this chapter: it is logically obvious that firearms are dangerous. If they were nonthreatening or protective, like Band-Aids or winter coats, the random assignment of them to the populace would not spark fear about increased risks.) Nevertheless, this greatly hampers researchers' ability to claim causality—so much so that the *Journal of the American Medical Association* (JAMA) editors express that they will only permit the word *cause* in their published manuscripts if the study is an RCT (Ruich, 2017).

Even cohort studies, the "second-best" study design for causal inference, are also extremely difficult to conduct when the exposure variable is firearm access and the outcome is mass shootings. Because mass shootings are so incredibly rare, an investigator would need to enroll an impossible number of people to be able to have enough power to determine an effect. For these reasons, most studies on mass shootings on the individual level end up being case-control or cross-sectional studies, which are less than ideal for establishing causation due to both issues of reverse causation and confounding.

Nevertheless, two cross-sectional studies have provided some clues to the relationship between individual gun ownership and mass shootings. For instance, compared to the general population in the United States, perpetrators were not more likely to be gun owners (Lankford et al., 2021). In fact, only 21 percent of mass shooters had owned guns for more than three years before the attack (Lankford & Silva, 2021). This suggests that gun access, not just the mere act of owning a firearm, may be a more important cause of Americans committing mass shootings. Indeed, half the mass shooters studied obtained their first firearm within the final year before the attack (Lankford & Silva, 2021). Overall, however, the limitations in study design make it difficult to impossible for researchers to claim that gun ownership is (or is not) a cause of any individual's desire to commit a mass shooting.

Does easy access to firearms cause Americans to be more likely to want to commit mass shootings?

Individual gun ownership has not yet been found to be a direct cause of an individual's desire to commit a mass shooting. However, that does not preclude individual gun *access* from being a cause of a mass shooting. Certainly, it is conceivable to think of scenarios in which an individual could obtain a gun outside the home quickly and easily via a friend or acquaintance. Indeed, in some cases, a locked firearm that resides in one's home may even be less accessible than a gun that is readily accessible from a friend.

The importance of distinguishing gun ownership from gun access in relation to an individual's desire to commit a mass shooting is especially important because of the nature in which mass shootings occur. Several studies have found that gun ownership is associated with higher levels of other types of gun violence, including gun homicide and suicide (Anglemyer et al., 2014; Kellerman et al., 1993; Wiebe, 2003). However, gun homicide and suicides are often acts of passion, so much so that the presence of a firearm during a domestic violence incident increases the probability that a woman will be shot by 500 percent (Campbell et al., 2002). In contrast, mass shootings are often planned well in advance, suggesting that the ability for an individual to access or obtain a gun is more influential than if a firearm is owned in the household.

But what is gun access? Theoretically, it is the ability for someone to obtain a firearm. But on the practical level, exactly what constitutes access becomes less apparent. For example, how quickly does someone need to be able to access a firearm to say that they have access to one? An hour? A day? A month? A year? Most adults in the United States could probably get their hands on a gun, legally or illegally, given enough time. Also, on what level is gun access measured? Does an individual owning a gun matter, or does the general ability for society to obtain or buy a gun have a larger impact? What about the permissiveness of gun laws and amount of money or effort required for an individual to obtain a firearm? These variables all represent important components of gun access and could be measured in different ways. The lack of a clear measure of gun access—or even a meaningful, agreed-upon definition—makes it more challenging to determine if easy access to firearms causes Americans to be more likely to commit mass shootings.

Conclusion

These are just some of the limitations in establishing causality between gun access and mass shootings, and there are certainly other limitations not mentioned. Some of these constraints, like study design and issues of reverse causation and colinearity, are not able to be easily remedied by epidemiologists, although some study designs and analytical techniques, such as difference in differences, synthetic controls, and other advanced methods, have made progress in this realm. Other limitations, like determining accurate measures of gun access (or even ownership), would require incredible political will and substantial changes in reporting and systems across the United States. Furthermore, the inability to have a registry for firearms and the lack of federal databases are at least on some level meant to *prevent* researchers from obtaining the data they need to make informed academic conclusions on the effects of gun ownership. For example, in 1996, the Dickey Amendment was added as a provision to the annual appropriations legislation (Rostron, 2018) after research was released that linked household gun ownership to higher rates of gun homicide in the home (Kellerman et al., 1993). It prohibited "the use of federal funds to advocate or promote gun control," and while new language has been expressed that permits the studying of causes of gun violence in the United States, it still resulted in a chilling effect of gun violence research for decades (Rostron, 2018). It becomes far more difficult to study whether firearms cause mass shootings when there appear to be large segments of the United States government and population that do not want that question closely examined, let alone answered. It will therefore be a long time, if ever, that the analytical burden of proof will be enough to confidently declare gun access a cause of mass shootings.

Thus, here lies the dilemma. Researchers may never *analytically* prove gun access is a cause of mass shootings in the way that mathematical relationships, like the Pythagorean theorem, have been formally proven. However, it is also *logically* apparent that gun access is a cause of mass shootings on any level. If guns did not exist in a country or state, would this have an impact on how many mass shootings occur within its borders? Of course it would. Similarly, an individual without access to a gun is unable to perpetrate a mass shooting. So, is it necessary to analytically establish that gun access is a cause to be able to call gun access a *cause* of mass shootings? No. We know this to be true logically. Epidemiologists, scientists, public health policy makers, and politicians should not shy away from this word. Gun access is a necessary cause of mass shootings, making it a perfect variable to intervene upon. While there are other causes of mass shootings, such as a mental health crisis, they are not always present in every situation—or causal pie—like gun access is.

It is true that researchers will not (and may not ever) know the exact effects that gun access, especially when conceptualized on the population level, has on the occurrence of mass shootings. But policymakers and researchers do not need to know the exact magnitude of the association to advocate for change now. As long as researchers are diluting their language by declining to call gun access a *cause*, they are also diluting their ability to make meaningful policy recommendations, especially when opponents to reducing gun access are so vocal and clear about their own beliefs. Researchers should not allow limitations in their methods or data to prevent them from telling the obvious truth about guns: they are an important cause of mass shootings.

REFERENCES

Anglemyer, A., Horvath, T., & Rutherford, G. (2014). The accessibility of firearms and risk for suicide and homicide victimization among household members: a systematic review and meta-analysis. *Annals of Internal Medicine, 160*(2), 101–110.

Campbell, J. C., Koziol-McLain, J., Webster, D., Block, C. R., Campbell, D., McFarlane, J., Sachs, C., Sharps, P., Ulrich, Y., & Wilt, S. A. (2002). Research results from a national study of intimate partner femicide: The danger assessment instrument. *Violence Against Women and Family Violence: Developments in Research, Practice, and Policy.*

Fridel, E. E. (2021). Comparing the impact of household gun ownership and concealed carry legislation on the frequency of mass shootings and firearms homicide. *Justice Quarterly, 38*(5), 892–915.

Kellerman, A. L., Rivara, F. P., Ruthforth, N. B., Banton, J. G., Reay, D. T., Francisco, J. T., Locci, A. B., Prodzinski, J., Hackman, B. B., & Somes, G. (1993). Gun ownership as risk factor for homicide in the home. *New England Journal of Medicine, 329*(15), 1084–1091. https://doi.org/10.1056/NEJM199309303291401

Kleck, G. (2004). Measures of gun ownership levels for macro-level crime and violence research. *Journal of Research in Crime and Delinquency, 41*(1), 3–36. https://doi.org/10.1177/0022427803256229

Lankford, A. (2016). Public mass shooters and firearms: A cross-national study of 171 countries. *Violence and Victims, 31*(2), 187–199. https://doi.org/10.1891/0886-6708.VV-D-15-00093

Lankford, A., & Silva, J. R. (2021). The timing of opportunities to prevent mass shootings: A study of mental health contacts, work and school problems, and firearms acquisition. *International Review of Psychiatry, 33*(7), 638–652.

Lankford, A., Silver, J., & Cox, J. (2021). An epidemiological analysis of public mass shooters and active shooters: Quantifying key differences between perpetrators and the general population, homicide offenders, and people who die by suicide. *Journal of Threat Assessment and Management, 8*(4), 125–144.

Madfis, E., & Levin, J. (2013). School rampage in international perspective: The salience of cumulative strain theory. In N. Böckler, T. Seeger, P. Sitzer, & W. Heitmeyer (Eds.), *School shootings* (pp. 79–104). Springer.

Reeping, P. M., Cerdá, M., Kalesan, B., Wiebe, D. J., Galea, S., & Branas, C. C. (2019). State gun laws, gun ownership, and mass shootings in the US: Cross sectional time series. *BMJ (Online), 364*. https://doi.org/10.1136/bmj.l542

Registration. (2021). Giffords Law Center. https://giffords.org/lawcenter/gun-laws/policy-areas/owner-responsibilities/registration/

Rostron, A. (2018). The Dickey amendment on federal funding for research on gun violence: A Legal dissection. *American Journal of Public Health, 108*(7), 865–867. https://doi.org/10.2105/AJPH.2018.304450

Rothman, K. J., Greenland, S., & Lash, T. L. (2008). *Modern epidemiology* (Vol. 3). Wolters Kluwer Health/Lippincott Williams & Wilkins Philadelphia.

Ruich, P. (2017). *The use of cause-and-effect language in JAMA Network journals.* AMA Style Insider. https://amastyleinsider.com/2017/09/19/use-cause-effect-language-jama-network-journals/

Schell, T. L., Peterson, S., Vegetabile, B. G., Scherling, A., Smart, R., & Morral, A. R. (2020). *State-Level Estimates of Household Firearm Ownership.* RAND Corporation. https://www.rand.org/pubs/tools/TL354.html

Webster, D. W., McCourt, A. D., Crifasi, C. K., Booty, M. D., & Stuart, E. A. (2020). Evidence concerning the regulation of firearms design, sale, and carrying on fatal mass shootings in the United States. *Criminology & Public Policy, 19*(1), 171–212.

Wiebe, D. J. (2003). Homicide and suicide risks associated with firearms in the home: A national case-control study. *Annals of Emergency Medicine, 41*(6), 771–782.

21

Do Gun Control Laws Prevent Mass Shootings in the United States?

A Review of the Evidence

EMMA E. FRIDEL

Introduction

Defined as the killing of four or more individuals (excluding the potential death of the offender) with a firearm within twenty-four hours, mass shootings occur between twenty and thirty times a year on average and account for less than 1 percent of all homicides in the United States (Fridel, 2021a; Krouse & Richardson, 2015). Although public massacres are the most notorious type of mass shootings, this crime includes all types of incidents, such as those that take place in private spaces (e.g., family killings), involve gang activity or drug trafficking, or occur in schools and workplaces. Despite their rarity, mass shootings have engendered moral panics, fomented social movements like March for Our Lives, and galvanized calls for policy change on both sides of the political aisle. The majority of American adults experience stress related to mass shootings, and approximately one-third go so far as to avoid certain places and events due to their fear of victimization (American Psychological Association, 2019).

As a result of this outpouring of public concern, mass shootings have become the most prominent ideological battleground for the gun control debate in the United States, with each additional tragedy prompting calls for both increased restrictions and expansions of Second Amendment rights. Indeed, Luca et al. (2019) found that each mass shooting increases the number of firearm bills introduced in any given state's legislature by 15 percent. Despite frequent claims that these policy changes would have saved lives or prevented an incident from occurring entirely, few studies have explored the complicated relationship between firearms legislation and the frequency and severity of mass shootings in the United States.

Seeking to clarify the mass confusion over mass shootings, the present chapter reviews the evidence for gun control laws popularly thought to address this unique form of violence, including bans on assault weapons and large-capacity magazines, concealed carry permitting, extreme risk protection orders or "red flag" laws, and possession prohibitions for perpetrators of domestic violence. Each section provides a brief summary of the law and the theoretical mechanism by which it impacts mass violence before turning to the anecdotal and empirical evidence.

Assault Weapons and Large-Capacity Magazine Bans

Assault weapons are semiautomatic firearms that accept detachable magazines and have military-style features, such as pistol grips, flash hiders, folding rifle stocks, bayonet mounts, grenade launchers, barrel shrouds, and/or silencers (Koper, 2004). Assault weapons are often equipped with large-capacity magazines (LCMs), or ammunition-feeding devices with more than ten rounds. Although LCMs are often used in assault weapons, they also can be used in many common semiautomatic pistols and rifles without military-style features. From 1994 to 2004, the United States federal government prohibited the possession, manufacture, or transfer of assault weapons and LCMs. Following the expiration of the federal ban, seven states and the District of Columbia have enacted bans on both assault weapons and LCMs, two states have increased regulations on assault weapons alone, and two states have banned LCMs only.

Assault weapons paired with LCMs are more lethal than other types of firearms and enable many rounds to be fired in quick succession, reducing the number of times an individual needs to reload. Opponents of these weapons argue that they increase the number of casualties in a mass shooting and reduce opportunities for victims to escape or intervene (Klarevas et al., 2019). In contrast, pro-gun advocates contend that assault weapons and LCMs are no deadlier than other firearms, as some military-style features are largely cosmetic and individuals can easily utilize multiple guns and/or magazines in lieu of LCMs (Kleck, 2016).

The extant literature on the efficacy of assault weapons bans remains murky yet suggests that these laws have minimal impact on the frequency and severity of mass shootings. Although several studies have found that the federal and/or state assault weapons bans significantly reduced mass shooting incidents and/or casualties (Gius, 2015; DiMaggio et al., 2019; Klarevas, 2016; Blau et al., 2016), Koper (2020) argues that the effect may be an artifact of the specific subsamples used (e.g., public mass shootings, higher minimum victim thresholds), unreliable data sources (e.g., Mother Jones), and a general decline in mass shootings overall during the ban period rather than mass shootings with assault weapons in particular. Consistent with this view, more recent work utilizing data from the FBI's Supplementary Homicide Reports and/or media reports finds no evidence of an effect (Fox & DeLateur, 2014; Siegel et al., 2020; Webster et al., 2020; Fridel, 2021a). This is not too surprising, however, as the federal assault weapons ban was criticized for prohibiting a limited number of specific models (which manufacturers slightly modified to avoid the ban) and permitting the use of grandfathered weapons produced prior to the ban's passage (Koper, 2004). These loopholes guaranteed that the benefits of the ban would take years to fully develop, and these effects were still developing at the time of its expiration (Koper, 2020).

In contrast to the research on assault weapons, growing evidence tentatively supports the use of LCM bans to prevent and mitigate mass shootings. LCMs are disproportionately used in mass shootings relative to gun crime more generally: approximately 20 percent of all incidents involve LCMs, a figure that increases to 50–66 percent for public mass shootings in particular (Koper, 2020). Prior work similarly indicates that cases involving LCMs have higher numbers of victims killed and wounded, on average, in comparison to incidents without LCMs, even when multiple guns and/or magazines are used (Koper et al., 2018; Klarevas, 2016). While this descriptive evidence is compelling, empirical studies examining the effect of state LCM laws over time are more inconclusive. Focusing specifically on high-fatality mass shootings, Klarevas et al. (2019) found that states with LCM bans experience significantly fewer attacks and fatalities, both for cases with and without LCM usage. In contrast, studies utilizing the more traditional victim threshold of four or more killed have alternatively found that LCM bans decrease the incidence rate of mass shootings, but have no impact on the number of victims (Webster et al., 2020) or conversely have no impact on the likelihood of an event occurring, yet significantly decrease casualties when one does (Siegel et al., 2020); still others find little support for LCM bans at all (Fridel, 2021a). Given the different samples utilized across studies, these results suggest that LCM bans may differentially impact mass shootings by type, with stronger effects for incidents that occur in public and involve many victims (Koper, 2020).

Taken together, the extant literature suggests that LCM bans may prove a more effective intervention for mass shootings than restrictions on assault weapons. Nevertheless, studies examining the effects of both policies on gun violence in general remain mixed (see Koper, 2004), suggesting more research is needed in this area.

Concealed Carry

The United States currently has three types of right-to-carry or concealed carry laws, including permitless carry, "shall-issue," and "may-issue" policies. Permitless carry is the most permissive type of legislation, allowing firearms owners to carry concealed weapons without additional documentation. In contrast, both shall- and may-issue states require individuals to apply for an additional concealed carry permit, but they differ in the degree of discretion granted to the issuing law enforcement agency. In the more permissive shall-issue states, law enforcement has minimal discretion and must grant concealed carry permits to all applicants who meet certain basic requirements outlined by the state. In contrast, the more restrictive may-issue states grant additional latitude to law enforcement officers, who may require applicants to provide a heightened showing or establish good cause and can deny a permit application even if all prerequisites are fulfilled. Although historically, most states maintained restrictive no-issue or may-issue policies, the United States has experienced a dramatic shift toward more permissive concealed carry legislation over the past thirty years. As of 2020, fifteen states were permitless carry, twenty-six were shall-issue, and only nine were may-issue (Siegel, 2021).

Proponents of expanded Second Amendment rights suggest that increased gun carrying by the public deters would-be offenders from committing mass violence in the first place by increasing the costs of the crime (i.e., being mortally wounded by a victim) and reduces casualties through the intervention of armed bystanders even if an attack occurs (Lott, 2000; Lott & Landes, 2000). For example, Suzanna Gratia Hupp famously advocated for fewer restrictions on concealed carry, claiming that she could have stopped the 1991 massacre at Luby's cafeteria in Killeen, Texas, if she had been legally permitted to bring her firearm inside the restaurant (Hupp, 2009). In contrast, gun control supporters argue that more permissive concealed carry laws are an unlikely deterrent, as many offenders are suicidal, are mentally ill, and/or seek to engage in a firefight (Fridel, 2021a). Given that responding law enforcement officers cannot immediately differentiate the offender and the so-called good guy with a gun, armed citizens may be more likely to be wounded themselves or kill innocent bystanders than stop the shooter (Donohue et al., 2019).

Although most state legislatures and the majority of Americans support more permissive concealed carry legislation (Newport, 2015), empirical research has not consistently found an association between these laws and the frequency and severity of mass shootings. Indeed, the only study to support a deterrent effect was an extension of Lott and Mustard's (1997) highly publicized—and highly criticized—work on right-to-carry laws and violence in general. In an unpublished manuscript, Lott and Landes (2000) used a series of Poisson regression models to predict the number of public shootings in which two or more victims were killed or wounded in twenty-three states from 1977 to 1997, finding that right-to-carry legislation decreased the overall number of shootings by 67 percent and the number of victims by 78 percent. Replications of this study, however, have found no evidence of a significant relationship between permissive concealed carry legislation and mass shootings, despite utilizing more traditional definitions (four or more victims killed), improved analytical strategies, additional controls for state-level confounders, and more reliable and recent data (Duwe et al., 2002; Webster et al., 2020; Siegel et al., 2020; Fridel, 2021a). Anecdotal evidence also casts doubt on the "good guy with a gun" hypothesis, as only one active shooter incident in the United States from 2000 to 2013 was resolved by an armed bystander (who was notably an active-duty marine); in contrast, twenty-one incidents were stopped by unarmed citizens without such training during the same time period (Blair & Schweit, 2014).

In sum, there is little empirical evidence to support more permissive concealed carry laws as an effective policy intervention for mass shootings. The transition from more restrictive to more permissive legislation in the United States is deeply concerning, however, as recent research indicates that these laws are associated with higher firearms homicides rates overall, if not mass shootings in particular (Crifasi et al., 2018; Donohue et al., 2019; Doucette et al., 2019; Siegel et al., 2017; Fridel, 2021a).

Extreme Risk Protection Orders (ERPOs)

Colloquially known as "red flag" laws, extreme risk protection orders (ERPOs) or gun violence restraining orders (GVROs) allow law enforcement officers and family members to petition a state court to temporarily remove firearms from an individual deemed to be dangerous to themselves or to others. Proponents argue that such laws may be effective in preventing mass violence, as many perpetrators leak their intentions to family members and friends prior to the attack (Silver et al., 2018). Unlike most other forms of firearms legislation, ERPO provisions were developed in direct response to mass shootings with evidence of leakage, including the 1998 lottery massacre in Connecticut, the 2014 Isla Vista killings in California, and the 2018 Marjory Stoneman Douglas High School shooting in Florida. Indeed, the most recent of these incidents sparked a flurry of legislation, as the number of states adopting some form of ERPOs increased from five in 2017 to nineteen and the District of Columbia as of 2020 (Giffords Law Center, 2021). Provisions of red flag laws dramatically vary from state to state regarding who is allowed to petition, whether the order is temporary or ex parte, the duration of the order, and the standard of evidence required to obtain an order.

Although ERPOs were largely inspired by mass shootings, research in this area remains limited to case study evidence due to the recency of most red flag laws and the impossibility of proving a counterfactual (that an incident would have occurred in the absence of the law). In their preliminary analysis of ERPOs in California from 2016 to 2018, Wintemute et al. (2019) identified twenty-one cases in which an ERPO was issued in response to a credible mass shooting threat. Firearms were recovered in ten cases, and pending purchases were blocked in another three; the ERPOs also led to eleven arrests for possession of illegal weapons, criminal threats, and assault with a deadly weapon. Outside of California, two other cases of ERPOs used to prevent potential mass violence were documented in 2018; these included an eighteen-year-old man who glorified the Marjory Stoneman Douglas shooting and threatened to commit a similar massacre at his school in Vermont and a twenty-year-old man who posted anti-Semitic content on social media and threatened to kill thirty people at a synagogue and a school in Washington State. Although it is impossible to establish a causal relationship, no suicides or homicides were committed following the issuance of any of these orders.

While this anecdotal evidence is promising, it remains unclear whether ERPOs are effective in preventing mass shootings. Nevertheless, prior work suggests that red flag laws do reduce another, more common form of lethal violence: suicide. Research on ERPOs in Connecticut and Indiana has found that approximately one suicide is averted for every ten gun seizures (Swanson et al., 2017; Swanson et al., 2019). Similarly, Kivisto and Phalen (2018) estimate that firearm suicides were reduced by 7.5 percent in Indiana and 13.7 percent in Connecticut following enforcement of firearm seizure laws, although the latter's reduction was offset by an increase in suicide utilizing other weapons. Therefore, even if ERPOs are ineffective as a mass shooting prevention measure, enacting such policies will likely still be beneficial for reducing lethal violence more broadly.

Prohibitions for Perpetrators of Domestic Violence

In the United States, the Federal Gun Control Act of 1968 prohibits the purchase and possession of firearms for individuals who are subject to a domestic violence restraining order (DVRO) or have been convicted of a misdemeanor crime of domestic violence (MCDV) (see 18 U.S.C. § 922). Several states have enhanced domestic violence prohibitions designed to close three major loopholes in federal law: (1) violence between unmarried persons who do not cohabitate or have a child in common is excluded (i.e., the "boyfriend loophole"); (2) persons subject to ex parte (temporary or emergency) restraining orders are not prohibited from purchasing firearms; and (3) there are no enforcement provisions to ensure that prohibited possessors relinquish their guns. As of 2020, only twenty states included dating partners for firearms prohibitions, ten extended restrictions to ex parte DVROs, and four required law enforcement officers to remove firearms from DVRO subjects (Siegel, 2021).

Preventing domestic abusers from obtaining firearms is arguably the most important of high-risk possession prohibitions for preventing mass shootings, as offenders in 17 percent of all mass killings and 28 percent of familicides have documented histories of domestic violence (Fridel, 2021b), estimates that are likely to be conservative due to underreporting. Nevertheless, only one study has explored the effect of domestic violence firearms prohibitions on mass shootings. In their case study analysis of incidents from 2014 to 2017, Zeoli and Paruk (2020) determined that federal domestic violence prohibitions were largely ineffective in restricting access to firearms for mass shooters with a history of domestic violence (31 percent; N = 28). In eight cases, prosecutors either failed to charge or convict offenders of an MCDV that would have precluded them from possessing firearms, likely due to prosecutorial preferences for felony over misdemeanor charges. Four offenders were convicted of an MCDV, yet were not prohibited from firearms ownership by either state or federal law due to the so-called boyfriend loophole. Three incidents were also linked to issues with DVROs—one offender's wife and future victim was denied a protective order following a hearing, while two other perpetrators were considered for ex parte orders in states without firearms restrictions for these types of emergency orders. Finally, implementation issues related to the failure to submit prohibitions to National Instant Criminal Background Check System (NICS) accidentally allowed the perpetrator of the 2017 Sutherland Springs shooting to purchase a gun. In contrast to this anecdotal evidence, Webster et al. (2020) found no effect of state laws that mandate firearm surrender or include dating partners and ex parte orders on mass shootings.

While findings are mixed, some evidence suggests that closing federal loopholes in firearms prohibitions for perpetrators of domestic violence (and properly implementing and enforcing these laws) may prevent some potential mass shooters from legally acquiring guns. Even if such prohibitions are ineffective in this regard, prior research indicates that state laws that require relinquishment and extend restrictions to dating partners and/or ex parte DVROs are associated with reductions in intimate partner homicide more generally (Diez et al., 2017; Giffords Law Center, 2021).

Discussion and Conclusion

While both sides of the aisle clamor for changes in gun control policy in the wake of a mass shooting, the empirical evidence for most of these recommendations remains weak. The extant literature evaluating the impact of specific firearms laws on mass shootings in the United States is still in its infancy and has only recently moved beyond case study analysis. This chapter explored the evidence on four types of legislation speculated to prevent and/or mitigate mass shootings, finding preliminary support for large-capacity magazine bans, extreme risk protection orders, and increased possession restrictions for perpetrators of domestic violence. In contrast, assault weapons bans and more permissive concealed carry laws appear to have a minimal impact on mass shootings, and in the case of the latter, they may contribute to increased rates of firearms homicide more generally.

While many view gun control legislation as a potential panacea to mass violence, the empirical evidence for these policy recommendations is tentative at best, due to a number of challenges in this area of research. Mass shootings are inherently rare events, which limits the sample size and statistical power of quantitative analyses; indeed, work on mass killings in decades past was restricted exclusively to anecdotal evidence for this reason. Several of the more recent studies described above, for example, examined samples of fewer than one hundred incidents, which limits the generalizability of their results (Klarevas et al., 2019; Zeoli and Paruk, 2020).

A related issue is the recency and prevalence of certain laws of interest. One of the most rigorous ways to explore the effect of firearms laws on mass shootings is via a quasi-experimental design that takes advantage of natural variation in state policies over time. These cross-sectional panel models inherently require sufficient variation in gun control laws both across states (between-unit variation) and over time (within-unit variation). Given the rarity of mass shootings, such approaches also require a lengthy panel of twenty to thirty years to combat low statistical power. Accordingly, there is simply not enough data to adequately evaluate laws that have not been passed in many states and/or have been adopted relatively recently, including ERPOs and expanded possession prohibitions for domestic violence.

Complicating the matter further, there is no consensus on how to define a mass shooting, as researchers disagree on the minimum number of victims (generally ranging from three to six), whether injuries should be included in addition to fatalities, and whether incidents should be restricted to those occurring in public spaces. Accordingly, it is difficult to compare findings across studies, as they may employ the same term to describe entirely different phenomena. For example, while large-capacity magazine bans may be effective for mass shootings that occur in public (Siegel et al., 2020) and target many victims (Klarevas et al., 2019), it is unlikely that they are equally beneficial for familicides in private homes (Fridel, 2021a). In other words, firearms legislation likely has differential effects across distinct types of mass shootings.

Although inconsistent findings with many caveats are frustrating to policy makers and the public alike, these limitations make it nearly impossible for researchers to provide concrete recommendations on how to prevent the next mass shooting. As the extant literature continues to advance, however, it is critical that potential gun control laws are evaluated for their effects, both on mass shootings as well as more common forms of gun violence that impact thousands of Americans each year; this is especially crucial considering that laws may have unique—and opposite—effects on different forms of lethal violence (see Fridel, 2021a). Accordingly, legislators should prioritize laws that reduce firearms suicide and homicide in general, rather than designing policy to prevent the rare mass shooting, however tragic such incidents may be. In this vein, passing ERPO laws and increased possession restrictions for perpetrators of domestic violence likely represent fruitful approaches, as these laws *do* reduce firearms suicide and/or homicide and *may* also prevent mass shootings.

REFERENCES

American Psychological Association. (2019). One-third of US adults say fear of mass shootings prevents them from going to certain places or events. https://www.apa.org/news/press/releases/2019/08/fear-mass-shooting

Blair, J. P., & Schweit, K. W. (2014). *A study of active shooter incidents, 2000–2013*. Federal Bureau of Investigation, U.S. Department of Justice.

Blau, B. M., Gorry, D. H., & Wade, C. (2016). Guns, laws and public shootings in the United States. *Applied Economics, 48*(49), 4732–4746.

Crifasi, C., Merrill-Francis, M., McCourt, A., Vernick, J., Wintemute, G., & Wesbter, D. (2018). Association between firearm laws and homicide in urban counties. *Journal of Urban Health, 95*(3), 383–390.

Diez, C., Kurland, R. P., Rothman, E. F., Bair-Merritt, M., Fleegler, E., Xuan, Z., Galea, S., Ross, C. S., Kalesan, B., Goss, K. A., & Siegel, M. (2017). State intimate partner violence-related firearm laws and intimate partner homicide rates in the United States, 1991 to 2015. *Annals of Internal Medicine, 167*(8), 536–543.

DiMaggio, C., Avraham, J., Berry, C., Bukur, M., Feldman, J., Klein, M., Shah, N., Tandon, M., & Frangos, S. (2019). Changes in US mass shooting deaths associated with the 1994–2004 federal assault weapons ban: Analysis of open-source data. *Journal of Trauma and Acute Care Surgery, 86*(1), 11–19.

Donohue, J. J., Aneja, A., & Weber, K. D. (2019). Right-to-carry laws and violent crime: A comprehensive assessment using panel data and a state-level synthetic control analysis. *Journal of Empirical Legal Studies, 16*(2), 198–247.

Doucette, M. L., Crifasi, C. K., & Frattaroli, S. (2019). Right-to-carry laws and firearm workplace homicides: A longitudinal analysis (1992–2017). *American Journal of Public Health, 109*(12), 1747–1753.

Duwe, G., Kovandzic, T., & Moody, C. E. (2002). The impact of right-to-carry concealed firearm laws on mass public shootings. *Homicide Studies, 6*(4), 271–296.

Fox, J. A., & DeLateur, M. J. (2014). Weapons of mass (murder) destruction. *New England Journal on Criminal and Civil Confinement, 40*(2), 313–344.

Fridel, E. E. (2021a). Comparing the impact of household gun ownership and concealed carry legislation on the frequency of mass shootings and firearms homicide. *Justice Quarterly, 38*(5), 892–915.

Fridel, E. E. (2021b). A multivariate comparison of family, felony, and public mass murders in the United States. *Journal of Interpersonal Violence, 36*(3–4), 1092–1118.

Giffords Law Center to Prevent Gun Violence. (2021). *Gun Laws.* https://giffords.org/law center/gun-laws/

Gius, M. (2015). The impact of state and federal assault weapons bans on public mass shootings. *Applied Economics Letters, 22*(4), 281–284.

Hupp, S. G. (2009). *From Luby's to the legislature: One woman's fight against gun control.* Privateer Publications.

Kivisto, A. J., & Phalen, P. L. (2018). Effects of risk-based firearm seizure laws in Connecticut and Indiana on suicide rates, 1981–2015. *Psychiatric Services, 69*(8), 855–862.

Klarevas, L. (2016). *Rampage nation: Securing America from mass shootings.* Prometheus Books.

Klarevas, L., Conner, A., & Hemenway, D. (2019). The effect of large-capacity magazine bans on high-fatality mass shootings, 1990–2017. *American Journal of Public Health*, e1–e8.

Kleck, G. (2016). Large-capacity magazines and the casualty counts in mass shootings: The plausibility of linkages. *Justice Research and Policy, 17*(1), 28–47.

Koper, C. S. (2004). *An updated assessment of the Federal Assault Weapons Ban: Impacts on gun markets and gun violence, 1994–2003.* Report to the National Institute of Justice.

Koper, C. S. (2020). Assessing the potential to reduce deaths and injuries from mass shootings through restrictions on assault weapons and other high-capacity semiautomatic firearms. *Criminology and Public Policy, 19,* 147–170.

Koper, C. S., Johnson, W. D., Nichols, J. L., Ayers, A., & Mullins, N. (2018). Criminal use of assault weapons and high-capacity semiautomatic firearms: An updated examination of local and national sources. *Journal of Urban Health, 95*(3), 313–321.

Krouse, W. J., & Richardson, D. J. (2015). *Mass murder with firearms: Incidents and victims, 1999–2013.* Washington, DC: Congressional Research Service.

Lott, J. R. (2000). *More guns, less crime: Understanding crime and gun control laws.* Chicago: University of Chicago Press.

Lott, J. R., & Landes, W. M. (2000). *Multiple victim public shootings* [Unpublished paper].

Lott, J. R., & Mustard, D. B. (1997). Crime, deterrence, and right-to-carry concealed handguns. *Journal of Legal Studies, 26,* 1–68.

Luca, M., Malhotra, D., & Poliquin, C. (2019). The impact of mass shootings on gun policy. Working Paper 16-126. Harvard Business School. https://www.hbs.edu/faculty /Publication%20Files/16-126_ce055015-fc1c-4a8c-9a8a-8a9361d808bb.pdf

Newport, F. (2015). *Majority say more concealed weapons would make U.S. safer.* Gallup. https://news.gallup.com/poll/186263/majority-say-concealed-weapons-safer.aspx

Siegel, M. 2021. State firearm law database: State firearm laws, 1976–2020 [Computer file]. Compiled by Boston University School of Public Health, Department of Community Health Sciences.

Siegel, M., Goder-Reiser, M., Duwe, G., Roque, M., Fox, J. A., & Fridel, E. E. (2020). The relation between state gun laws and the incidence and severity of mass public shootings in the United States, 1976–2018. *Law and Human Behavior, 44*(5), 347–360.

Siegel, M., Xuan, Z., Ross, C. S., Galea, S., Kalesan, B., Fleegler, E., & Goss, K. A. (2017). Easiness of legal access to concealed firearm permits and homicide rates in the United States. *American Journal of Public Health, 107*(12), 1923–1929.

Silver, J., Horgan, J., & Gill, P. (2018). Foreshadowing targeted violence: Assessing leakage of intent by public mass murderers. *Aggression and Violent Behavior, 38*, 94–100.

Swanson, J. W., Easter, M. M., Alanis-Hirsch, K., Belden, C. M., Norko, M. A., Robertson, A. G., Frisman, L. K., Lin, H.-J., Swartz, M. S., & Parker, G. F. (2019). Criminal justice and suicide outcomes with Indiana's risk-based gun seizure law. *Journal of the American Academy of Psychiatry and the Law, 47*(2), 188–197.

Swanson, J. W., Norko, M. A., Lin, H.-J., Alanis-Hirsch, K., Frisman, L. K., Baranoski, M. V., Easter, M. M., Robertson, A. G., Swartz, M. S., & Bonnie, R. J. (2017). Implementation and effectiveness of Connecticut's risk-based gun removal law: Does it prevent suicides? *Law and Contemporary Problems, 80*, 179–208.

Webster, D. W., McCourt, A. D., Crifasi, C. K., Booty, M. D., & Stuart, E. A. (2020). Evidence concerning the regulation of firearms design, sale, and carrying on fatal mass shootings in the United States. *Criminology and Public Policy, 19*, 171–212.

Wintemute, G. J., Pear, V. A., Schleimer, J. P., Pallin, R., Sohl, S., Kravitz-Wirtz, N., & Tomisch, E. A. (2019). Extreme risk protection orders indended to prevent mass shootings. *Annals of Internal Medicine, 171*, 655–658.

Zeoli, A. M., & Paruk, J. K. (2020). Potential to prevent mass shootings through domestic violence firearms restrictions. *Criminology and Public Policy, 19*, 129–145.

22

Gun Purchasing Patterns in the United States

Trends Surrounding Mass Shootings

LACEY N. WALLACE

Introduction

Writing in the 1970s, historian Richard Hofstadter described the United States as a gun culture, stating that the United States remained the "only industrial nation in which the possession of rifles, shotguns, and handguns is lawfully prevalent among large numbers of its population" (Hofstadter, 1970). His assessment of widespread gun ownership was accurate. In a 1972 Gallup poll, 43 percent of U.S. adults reported a gun in their home (Gallup, 2015). As of 2020, that figure had hardly budged, with 43 percent of adults reporting household gun ownership in response to the same survey question (Gallup, 2015). Almost a third of Americans personally owned a firearm in 2019 (Gramlich & Schaeffer, 2019). Although some states require gun owners to register certain types of firearms with state authorities, there is no nationwide list or registry of all gun owners (Giffords Law Center, 2021). That means we can only estimate the number of guns in the United States. Ingraham (2015) estimated the number of civilian-owned guns in the United States in 2015 at more than 350 million, and Karp (2018) placed the 2017 count at 393 million. These figures do not reflect the jump in gun sales that occurred in 2020 (Mannix et al., 2020). Even so, either figure indicates that there are as many guns as there are people in the United States.

While gun ownership remains more common among whites (36 percent own a gun) and males (39 percent own a gun), gun owners have become more diverse, particularly since 2015 (Parker et al., 2017). As of 2017, nearly a quarter of Black Americans reported gun ownership, and 22 percent of women reported the same. During the spike in gun sales in 2020, the National Shooting Sports Foundation (National Shooting Sports Foundation, 2021b) reported sharp increases in sales to Black men and women. No longer is gun ownership as restricted to the "old, white, male" stereotype as it once was. Indeed, Lacombe et al. (2019) found that gun ownership and gun owner identity (subjective affinity with gun owners as a group) were distinct concepts. The authors found that women actually had a stronger sense of gun identity than men. Most U.S. gun owners say they could not imagine life without their guns; most also say that their right to own guns is essential to their sense of freedom (Parker et al., 2017).

The links between gun culture and gun violence are murky and subject to frequent debate. For many individuals, the notion of a gun culture is exclusively positive. In 2016 alone, 11.5 million U.S. residents ages sixteen and older participated in hunting, roughly 5 percent of the U.S. population; about 1.2 million of these individuals were youth ages six through fifteen (U.S. Fish and Wildlife Service, 2017). After decades of decline, the number of hunters in the United States increased in 2020 in the midst of the COVID-19 pandemic (Brown, 2020). For other individuals, gun exposure carries a more negative association. In a 2017 survey, 44 percent of U.S. adults said they personally knew someone who had been shot, either accidentally or intentionally (Parker et al., 2017). Gun violence in the United States is all too common. According to the Centers for Disease Control and Prevention (2021), there were 39,707 firearm-related deaths in the United States in 2019. About three in five were suicides, and more than fourteen thousand were homicides. For perspective, there were 37,595 deaths due to motor vehicle accidents in 2019 (Centers for Disease Control and Prevention, 2021).

This chapter focuses on an extreme, though rare, form of homicide: mass shootings. The pages to follow discuss gun purchasing trends that surround mass shootings and the social and psychological mechanisms that may explain these trends. These include factors such as fear, inaccurate assessments of risk, the divisive nature of gun control rhetoric, and societal changes that coincide with recent mass shootings. This chapter also describes the cyclical nature of mass shootings and gun purchasing whereby mass shootings are associated with increased gun sales, which are then associated with increased prevalence in mass shootings.

Mass Shooting–Gun Purchasing Cycle

Mass Shootings and Increased Gun Sales

Several studies have documented increased gun sales following highly publicized mass shootings. One study focused on the state of California used data from 1996 to 2015 to document changes in state gun sales (Callcut et al., 2019). The authors identified eighty-two mass shootings nationwide during this time period, defined as four or more deaths excluding the shooter. Prior to 2011, the authors found no evidence of a sustained spike in gun sales following mass shootings. From 2012 onward, however, the authors observed an increase in gun sales for several months following each mass shooting event. Sales remained elevated post-2011. The authors attributed these trends to the Sandy Hook Elementary School shooting of 2012 as well as an apparent increase in shootings in the post-2012 era (Callcut et al., 2019). Studdert et al. found similar results in California when focusing on two specific mass shooting events (2017). Of course, some may argue that these results are not representative. California is known for restrictive gun policies, and California's political, social, or economic context may not reflect other areas in the United States.

However, other work has replicated these patterns in other states and nationwide. Iwama and McDevitt (2021) studied Massachusetts gun transactions from 2006 to 2016. The authors found a temporary spike in gun sales following both the Sandy Hook shooting in 2012 and the San Bernardino shooting in 2015. In a nationwide study, Wallace (2015) documented temporary increases in federal background checks (a requirement for firearm sales from a licensed dealer) following six mass shootings. Brock and Routon (2020) found that the increases lasted for about two months. Another nationwide study found that handgun purchases tended to increase after highly publicized shootings (Liu & Wiebe, 2019). High-fatality shootings, in contrast, were associated with a decrease in handgun purchases. The authors argued that the difference in these two trends may relate to media focus on perpetrators (increase in sales) versus victims (decrease in sales). Stroebe et al. (2017b), who studied gun purchasing intentions after a mass shooting in Florida, argued that those who feel compelled to buy a gun after a mass shooting are a minority and that most Americans are not impacted in this way.

It can be difficult to isolate a jump in gun purchases from the ongoing increase in gun purchases over the past decade. Although an imperfect measure, federal law requires individuals purchasing from a federally licensed dealer (FFL) or those applying for certain other permits to undergo a federal background check. These are processed through the National Instant Criminal Background Check System, also called NICS. As shown in Figure 22.1, the number of background checks completed each year has increased ever since 1999, the first full year the NICS system was available.

Yet, the existing evidence suggests that mass shootings may not only impact gun sales but potentially concealed carry as well. Depew and Swensen (2019) found that the number of concealed carry permit applications increased after homicides, at least in those areas near where the homicide occurred. The effects were more pronounced for whites, males, and those who self-iden-

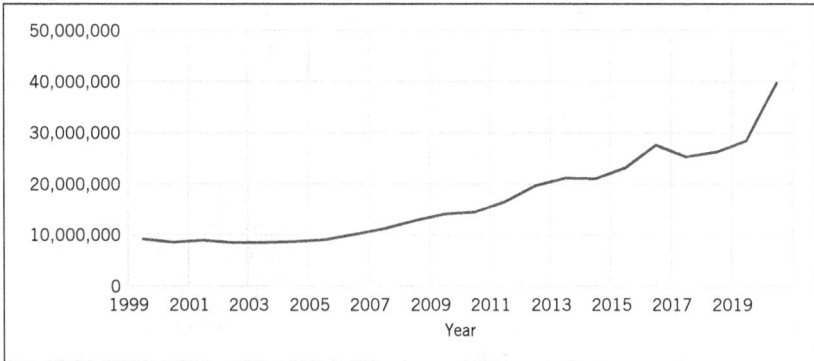

Figure 22.1 Total Federal Background Checks by Year. *(Data Source: Federal Bureau of Investigation, NICS Data)*

tified as Republican. Further, applications were more likely among those who shared demographic characteristics with the victim. Carter and Binder (2018) found that firearm violence had a small positive impact on concealed carry applications. Turchan et al. (2017) noted an increase in handgun carry permits in Tennessee after some high-profile mass shootings. Other research similarly found that individuals were more likely to carry loaded firearms in the days immediately after a mass shooting (Cordova, 2018).

Fear and Perceived Risk

To date, there have been several proffered explanations for why gun sales might spike (or not) following a mass shooting. One is that individuals purchase firearms as a self-defense tool either in fear of a mass shooting occurring or because they see the risk as nonnegligible. Self-defense is, after all, the top-reported motivation for gun ownership in the United States (Parker, 2017). Fear of mass shootings is common. A 2019 nationwide survey found that 79 percent of U.S. adults reported feeling stress about the possibility of a mass shooting occurring (American Psychological Association, 2019). Nearly a third of adults said that fear of a mass shooting prevents them from visiting certain types of public places or events. Further research found that people who were already fearful were also more likely to think school shootings happened with more frequency than they actually do (Schildkraut et al., 2015). This overestimation was also found among school administrators (Madfis, 2016). Fear can motivate some individuals to purchase a gun for self-defense (Hauser & Kleck, 2013; Yuan & McNeeley, 2016). However, it remains unclear whether it is fear of mass shootings specifically, and not other types of violent crime, that motivates this reaction.

In 2020, for example, the National Shooting Sports Foundation (2021b) reported a 58 percent increase in gun sales to Black men and women compared with 2019. The NSSF also estimated that 40 percent of gun purchases in 2020 went to first-time buyers. Some of these purchases may have occurred in response to widespread protests following the death of George Floyd (ABC News, 2021) rather than in response to any mass shooting during that time period. Anestis and Bryan (2021), similarly, found that gun sales early in the COVID-19 pandemic were more related to general uncertainties, COVID-19-related fears, and general anxieties than to any specific threat or perceptions of risk in the community. Other work noted increases in public worries about violence during the pandemic for all violence types *except* mass shootings (Kravitz-Wirtz et al., 2021).

The role of the media in contributing to fear and public understandings of mass shootings cannot be understated. Mass shootings typically receive widespread media coverage. Yet, this coverage may be inaccurate and fear inducing. Schildkraut (2016), for example, found that media coverage of mass shootings tended to place extensive emphasis on the shooters (rather than other people or factors), used extreme examples for comparison, and reported statistics like victim counts without placing these in the context of firearm violence more generally. In doing so, Schildkraut (2016) argued that the media contributed to the public's inaccurate perceptions of mass shootings. Thompson et al. (2019) determined that exposure to media coverage of a mass shooting contributes to high distress, which leads to increased media consumption. Increased consumption, in turn, can lead to further distress.

Media misrepresentation of mass shootings can lead to an inaccurate perception of risk. Existing research found that most Americans perceived the risk of a mass shooting as much greater than it really is (Schildkraut & Elsass, 2016). Mass shootings are far less common than other forms of firearm violence (Centers for Disease Control and Prevention, 2021). Like fear, perceived risk can motivate gun purchasing. Kleck et al. (2011), for example, found that both perceived risk and past victimization were positively associated with gun purchasing intentions. Stroebe et al. (2017a) found that both specific perceived risk as well as the general perception that the world is a dangerous place predicted gun ownership. Those with strong political beliefs have capitalized on these fears. Lott (2019b), for example, argued that existing gun control policies created "gun-free zones" that were vulnerable to attacks by mass shooters. Although the validity of the research is questionable, this notion of vulnerability could motivate a gun purchase for some individuals.

It is also possible that some people overestimate their ability to defend themselves or others with a firearm. The Federal Bureau of Investigation (2016) found that 69.8 percent of mass shootings between 2000 and 2013 (of those cases in which the duration of the event was known) ended in five minutes or less. More than a third ended in two minutes or less. It is rare for an active shooter to be stopped by an armed civilian. Of the twenty-eight events identified by the FBI in 2019, the shooter was killed by a civilian with a firearm in only one instance (Federal Bureau of Investigation, 2020). In three other cases, it was unarmed civilians who ended the altercation by confronting and subduing the shooter. Most authors have found that increases in concealed carry, increases in gun ownership, and/or making the requirements for a permit less restrictive do not seem to prevent mass shootings from occurring (Fridel, 2020; Hamill et al., 2019; Reeping et al., 2019). However, there are several prominent researchers, politicians, and organizations like the National Rifle Association that argue that arming civilians is the best way to prevent and respond to mass shootings (Lott, 2019a; Rupertus, 2016). These are powerful and influential voices.

Concerns about Gun Control Legislation

Another contributing factor to gun purchasing spikes following mass shootings may be fear or uncertainty regarding new gun control measures. In the wake of mass shootings, it is not uncommon for legislators and others to call for increased gun control, though the measures themselves may or may not become law. Luca et al. (2019) observed a 15 percent increase in state-level-proposed firearm legislation after mass shootings. Some individuals may purchase guns just after a shooting to be able to do so before such laws take effect. Porfiri et al. (2020), who examined both self-protection and fear of restrictive gun policies as competing explanations for gun purchases, found that fear of restrictive gun polices was actually a stronger predictor of gun purchasing than the desire for self-protection. Wallace (2015), likewise, found evidence of increased gun purchasing in response to proposed firearm restrictions by the Obama administration. Porfiri et al. (2019) identified media coverage as a key mechanism in this process. Media coverage can increase awareness of proposed legislation and raise public concern about more restrictive gun control measures, thereby increasing gun sales. Interestingly, however, past research determined that whether or not more restrictive policies pass in state legislatures depends on the party in power. Luca et al. (2019) found that laws that loosened gun restrictions actually increased after mass shootings in states with Republican-controlled legislatures.

To date, there remains significant disagreement in the United States on how best both to respond to mass shootings and manage gun ownership. Gun owners are less likely than nonowners to feel that guns themselves are a key contributing factor to mass shootings (Joslyn & Haider-Markel, 2017). Gun owners are more likely to blame parenting, the shooter, and popular culture instead. There are also divisions along party lines. In a 2021 poll, 73 percent of people identifying as Democrats said there would be fewer mass shootings if it were harder for people to legally obtain guns (Pew Research Center, 2021). Only 20 percent of Republicans felt the same way. There were also wide partisan divides in beliefs about whether more people should be able to carry a concealed firearm without a permit, whether concealed carry should be permitted in a greater number of locations, and whether K–12 teachers should be armed (Pew Research Center, 2021). These divisions may contribute to defensiveness or uncertainty about the legal future, especially in the politically intense periods following mass shootings.

Furthermore, several studies have documented gun ownership stigma that may exacerbate feelings of being left out, judged, or persecuted for owning a firearm. Blithe and Lanterman (2017), for example, documented common stigma management practices at gun shows and other events. Wallace (2017) found that concern over how other people might react was a key factor in a person's decision over whether to disclose gun ownership or not. Research has found an increase in the number of self-identified Republicans who refuse to answer questions about gun ownership (Urbatsch, 2019). Buttrick (2020) argued that gun ownership can serve as a coping mechanism, not only for people to manage fear or anxiety about safety, but also to manage perceived threats to their sense of belonging. In other words, the intense and combative nature of the gun control debate might actually contribute to gun purchasing as people seek comfort in what they can control.

Increased Gun Availability and Mass Shooting Prevalence

An increase in gun purchases, regardless of the reason, reflects an increase in citizen demand for firearms in the United States. The National Shooting Sports Foundation estimated that 8.4 million U.S. residents purchased a firearm for the first time in 2020 (2021b). This level of demand supports and encourages supply: increased manufacturing, sales, and growth in the firearms industry. According to the National Shooting Sports Foundation 2021 report, the firearms industry experienced a 106 percent increase in jobs between 2008 and 2020 and accounted for more than $63 billion in U.S. economic activity in 2020 alone (2021a). The growth of the firearm industry has made it easier to purchase firearms over time. Today, consumers can browse firearms online, post and sell used firearms through websites, as well as visit traditional FFL brick-and-mortar locations.

This growth has consequences. Increased firearm availability is associated with increased risk of both homicide and suicide (Knopov et al., 2019; Stansfield & Semenza, 2019). Countries with higher gun ownership rates have more mass shooters than other nations, even after accounting for factors like mental health (Lankford & Silva, 2021). Within the United States, researchers found that mass shootings were more likely to occur in states with higher levels of gun ownership (Fridel, 2020; Reeping et al., 2019). However, the underlying mechanism that explains this correlation is not that firearm sales are made to violent individuals. In most instances, that is not the case. Rather, by making firearms more easily accessible to everyone, we inadvertently make them more easily accessible to those who do wish to harm others.

Most gun owners and purchasers are law-abiding and nonviolent (Lott & Wang, 2020). An FBI investigation of active shooters determined that it was more common for an active shooter to purchase or obtain a firearm explicitly for the attack (40 percent of active shooters) than it was for an active shooter to already be in possession of firearms (35 percent of active shooters) (Silver et al., 2018). Other work noted a similar pattern for mass shooters (Lankford & Silva, 2021). According to Everytown Research (2018), however, only about a third of mass shooters from 2009 to 2017 were legally prohibited from purchasing a firearm at the time of the shooting. This means it remains relatively easy for a would-be shooter to purchase or acquire a firearm. The increase in gun purchasing and the growth of the firearms industry that ensues contribute to mass shootings by creating an environment where it is easier for the rare individual who wishes to commit a mass shooting to purchase and acquire the firearms they need to do so. When this person commits a mass shooting, gun purchases increase as a result, and the cycle begins anew.

What We Still Do Not Know

Much remains poorly understood about gun purchasing before and after mass shootings. One topic, for instance, that merits further study is the purchase of gun accessories, including magazines, bump stocks, and other features that became the subject of political debate following high-profile mass shootings. In 2017, a mass shooter in Las Vegas killed sixty people and wounded more than four hundred (LaCroix, 2018). This level of destruction was possible, in part, due to the shooter's use of a bump stock. This device attaches to semiautomatic weapons and allows them to fire more rapidly. Even as states called for a ban on bump stocks in the aftermath of the shooting, anecdotal reports of sales increases began to surface (Kaste, 2019). To date, however, studies of gun accessory purchases are largely absent from the literature. Part of the reason for this is that they are more difficult to track and document compared with gun purchases.

A second challenge for researchers is that most research focusing on gun purchasing does not track the same individuals over time. Some studies focus on overall trends in gun purchases over time (Callcut et al., 2019). The data used by these studies may be able to indicate the percentage of sales to first-time buyers but usually little else about those buyers, their motivations, or their characteristics. Other studies have used cross-sectional data to document gun purchasing or gun purchasing intentions after a mass shooting (Stroebe et al., 2017b). With these studies, a key concern is that we do not know individuals' perceptions or intentions prior to the shooting event. While we can ask respondents about how their intentions or actions have changed, this is retrospective and subject to recall and recency bias. As a result of these difficulties, it is still quite difficult to draw conclusions about how mass shootings affect gun purchasing or attitudes toward guns.

Conclusion

Mass shootings have many impacts beyond those detailed in this chapter. Mass shootings have been found to reduce both community well-being and emotional health (Soni & Tekin, 2020). The firearms industry in the United States is large; stock prices and industry-related jobs are negatively affected by mass shootings (Gopal & Greenwood, 2017). The emotional trauma caused by a mass shooting not only affects individuals in the moment but also affects their long-term perceptions, pessimism, and financial decisions (Balasubramaniam, 2021).

The impact of mass shootings on gun purchasing is concerning partly for its potential to contribute to a cyclical effect. Several studies found that mass shootings were more likely to occur in states with higher levels of gun ownership (Fridel, 2020; Reeping et al., 2019). Most gun owners and concealed carry permit holders are nonviolent and law-abiding (Lott & Wang, 2020). For those who cannot legally purchase a gun, however, it is relatively easy to obtain a gun from another source: a family member, an acquaintance, or through a private purchase without a background check. As a result, the role of firearm availability cannot be ignored. Additionally, firearm availability raises risk of suicide (Knopov et al., 2019) and domestic homicide (Stansfield & Semenza, 2019). This means that mass shootings may contribute to other forms of firearm violence through their influence on gun purchasing. Further study is needed to examine these pathways of violence and to identify the best means of preventing their occurrence.

REFERENCES

ABC News. (2021). *George Floyd*. ABC News. https://abcnews.go.com/alerts/george-floyd

American Psychological Association. (2019, August 15). One-third of US adults say fear of mass shootings prevents them from going to certain places or events. https://www.apa.org/news/press/releases/2019/08/fear-mass-shooting

Anestis, M. D., & Bryan, C. J. (2021). Threat perceptions and the intention to acquire firearms. *Journal of Psychiatric Research, 133*, 113–118. https://doi.org/10.1016/j.jpsychires.2020.12.033

Balasubramaniam, V. (2021). *Lifespan expectations and financial decisions: Evidence from mass shootings and natural disaster experiences* (SSRN Scholarly Paper ID 3289627). Social Science Research Network. https://doi.org/10.2139/ssrn.3289627

Blithe, S. J., & Lanterman, J. (2017). Camouflaged collectives: Managing stigma and identity at gun events. *Studies in Social Justice, 11*(1), 113–135.

Boine, C., Siegel, M., Ross, C., Fleegler, E. W., & Alcorn, T. (2020). What is gun culture? Cultural variations and trends across the United States. *Humanities and Social Sciences Communications, 7*(1), 1–12. https://doi.org/10.1057/s41599-020-0520-6

Brock, J., & Routon, P. W. (2020). The effect of mass shootings on the demand for guns. *Southern Economic Journal, 87*(1), 50–69. https://doi.org/10.1002/soej.12454

Brown, A. (2020, December 14). *The pandemic created new hunters: States need to keep them.* Pew Research Center. https://pew.org/34lpuA7

Buttrick, N. (2020). Protective gun ownership as a coping mechanism. *Perspectives on Psychological Science, 15*(4), 835–855. https://doi.org/10.1177/1745691619898847

Callcut, R. A., Robles, A. M., Kornblith, L. Z., Plevin, R. E., & Mell, M. W. (2019). Effect of mass shootings on gun sales—A 20-year perspective. *Journal of Trauma and Acute Care Surgery, 87*(3), 531–540. https://doi.org/10.1097/TA.0000000000002399

Carter, J. G., & Binder, M. (2018). Firearm violence and effects on concealed gun carrying: Large debate and small effects. *Journal of Interpersonal Violence, 33*(19), 3025–3052. https://doi.org/10.1177/0886260516633608

Centers for Disease Control and Prevention. (2021). *Injury: WISQARS Data.* Injury Prevention and Control. http://webappa.cdc.gov/sasweb/ncipc/dataRestriction_inj.html

Cordova, R. D. (2018). *Public mass shootings impact on the public's firearm carrying habits: Evidence of a moral panic* [Arizona State University]. https://core.ac.uk/download/pdf/158457022.pdf

Depew, B., & Swensen, I. D. (2019). The decision to carry: The effect of crime on concealed-carry applications. *Journal of Human Resources, 54*(4), 1121–1153. https://doi.org/10.3368/jhr.54.4.1016.8287R2

Everytown Research. (2018). *Mass shootings in America, 2009 to 2017.* https://everytown research.org/reports/mass-shootings-analysis/

Federal Bureau of Investigation. (2016). *Mass casualty shootings fact sheet.* National Center for the Victims of Crime. https://ovc.ojp.gov/sites/g/files/xyckuh226/files/media/document/2016ncvrw_6_masscasualty-508.pdf

Federal Bureau of Investigation. (2020). *Active shooter incidents in the United States in 2019.* Federal Bureau of Investigation. https://www.fbi.gov/file-repository/active-shooter-incidents-in-the-us-2019-042820.pdf/view

Fridel, E. E. (2020). Comparing the impact of household gun ownership and concealed carry legislation on the frequency of mass shootings and firearms homicide. *Justice Quarterly, 0*(0), 1–24. https://doi.org/10.1080/07418825.2020.1789693

Gallup. (2015). *Guns.* Gallup.Com. http://www.gallup.com/poll/1645/Guns.aspx

Giffords Law Center. (2021). *Registration.* https://giffords.org/lawcenter/gun-laws/policy -areas/owner-responsibilities/registration/

Gopal, A., & Greenwood, B. N. (2017). Traders, guns, and money: The effects of mass shootings on stock prices of firearm manufacturers in the U.S. *PLOS One, 12*(5), e0177720. https://doi.org/10.1371/journal.pone.0177720

Gramlich, J., & Schaeffer, K. (2019, October 22). *7 facts about guns in the U.S.* Pew Research Center. https://www.pewresearch.org/fact-tank/2019/10/22/facts-about-guns -in-united-states/

Hamill, M. E., Hernandez, M. C., Bailey, K. R., Zielinski, M. D., Matos, M. A., & Schiller, H. J. (2019). State level firearm concealed-carry legislation and rates of homicide and other violent crime. *Journal of the American College of Surgeons, 228*(1), 1–8. https://doi.org/10.1016/j.jamcollsurg.2018.08.694

Hauser, W., & Kleck, G. (2013). Guns and fear: A one-way street? *Crime & Delinquency, 59*(2), 271–291. https://doi.org/10.1177/0011128712462307

Hofstadter, R. (1970). America as a gun culture. *American Heritage, 21*(6). https://www.americanheritage.com/america-gun-culture

Ingraham, C. (2015). There are now more guns than people in the United States. *The Washington Post.* https://www.washingtonpost.com/news/wonk/wp/2015/10/05/guns-in-the-united-states-one-for-every-man-woman-and-child-and-then-some/?utm_term=.d14fde410266

Iwama, J., & McDevitt, J. (2021). Rising gun sales in the wake of mass shootings and gun legislation. *Journal of Primary Prevention, 42*(1), 27–42. https://doi.org/10.1007/s10935-021-00622-7

Joslyn, M. R., & Haider-Markel, D. P. (2017). Gun ownership and self-serving attributions for mass shooting tragedies. *Social Science Quarterly, 98*(2), 429–442. https://doi.org/10.1111/ssqu.12420

Karp, A. (2018). *Estimating global civilian-held firearms numbers.* Small Arms Survey. http://www.smallarmssurvey.org/fileadmin/docs/T-Briefing-Papers/SAS-BP-Civilian-Firearms-Numbers.pdf

Kaste, M. (2019, February 4). *Bump stocks will soon be illegal, but that's not stopping sales.* NPR.Org. https://www.npr.org/2019/02/04/691287471/bump-stocks-will-soon-be-illegal-but-thats-not-slowing-sales

Kleck, G., Kovandzic, T., Saber, M., & Hauser, W. (2011). The effect of perceived risk and victimization on plans to purchase a gun for self-protection. *Journal of Criminal Justice, 39*(4), 312–319. https://doi.org/10.1016/j.jcrimjus.2011.03.002

Knopov, A., Sherman, R. J., Raifman, J. R., Larson, E., & Siegel, M. B. (2019). Household gun ownership and youth suicide rates at the state level, 2005–2015. *American Journal of Preventive Medicine, 56*(3), 335–342. https://doi.org/10.1016/j.amepre.2018.10.027

Kravitz-Wirtz, N., Aubel, A., Schleimer, J., Pallin, R., & Wintemute, G. (2021). Public concern about violence, firearms, and the COVID-19 pandemic in California. *JAMA Network Open, 4*(1), e2033484–e2033484. https://doi.org/10.1001/jamanetworkopen.2020.33484

Lacombe, M. J., Howat, A. J., & Rothschild, J. E. (2019). Gun ownership as a social identity: Estimating behavioral and attitudinal relationships. *Social Science Quarterly.* https://doi.org/10.1111/ssqu.12710

LaCroix, J. (2018). *The politics of bump stocks, 1 year after Las Vegas shooting.* NPR.Org. https://www.npr.org/2018/09/26/650454299/the-politics-of-bump-stocks-one-year-after-las-vegas-shooting

Lankford, A., & Silva, J. R. (2021). The timing of opportunities to prevent mass shootings: A study of mental health contacts, work and school problems, and firearms acquisition. *International Review of Psychiatry, 0*(0), 1–15. https://doi.org/10.1080/09540261.2021.1932440

Liu, G., & Wiebe, D. J. (2019). A time-series analysis of firearm purchasing after mass shooting events in the United States. *JAMA Network Open, 2*(4), e191736–e191736. https://doi.org/10.1001/jamanetworkopen.2019.1736

Lott, J. R. (2019a). *Schools that allow teachers to carry guns are extremely safe: Data on the rate of shootings and accidents in schools that allow teachers to carry* (SSRN Scholarly Paper ID 3377801). Social Science Research Network. https://doi.org/10.2139/ssrn.3377801

Lott, J. R. (2019b, June 24). *Mass public shootings keep occurring in gun-free zones*. Archive. Is. http://archive.is/L1Qhq

Lott, J. R., & Wang, R. (2020). *Concealed carry permit holders across the United States: 2020* (SSRN Scholarly Paper ID 3703977). Social Science Research Network. https://doi.org/10.2139/ssrn.3703977

Luca, M., Malhotra, D. K., & Poliquin, C. (2019). *The impact of mass shootings on gun policy* (SSRN Scholarly Paper ID 2776657). Social Science Research Network. https://papers.ssrn.com/abstract=3357531

Madfis, E. (2016). "It's better to overreact": School officials' fear and perceived risk of rampage attacks and the criminalization of American public schools. *Critical Criminology, 24*(1), 39–55. http://dx.doi.org/10.1007/s10612-015-9297-0

Mannix, R., Lee, L., & Fleegler, E. (2020). Coronavirus Disease 2019 (COVID-19) and firearms in the United States: Will an epidemic of suicide follow? *Annals of Internal Medicine, 173*(3), 228–229. https://doi.org/10.7326/M20-1678

National Shooting Sports Foundation. (2021a). *Firearm and ammunition industry economic impact report*. https://www.nssf.org/wp-content/uploads/2021/03/2021-Firearm-Ammunition-Industry-Economic-Impact.pdf

National Shooting Sports Foundation. (2021b, January 7). *Taking stock of record-setting 2020 firearm year*. https://www.nssf.org/articles/taking-stock-of-record-setting-2020-firearm-year/

Parker, K. (2017, July 5). *Among gun owners, NRA members have a unique set of views and experiences*. Pew Research Center. http://www.pewresearch.org/fact-tank/2017/07/05/among-gun-owners-nra-members-have-a-unique-set-of-views-and-experiences/

Parker, K., Horowitz, J. M., Igielnik, R., Oliphant, B., & Brown, A. (2017, June 22). *America's complex relationship with guns*. Pew Research Center's Social & Demographic Trends Project. http://www.pewsocialtrends.org/2017/06/22/americas-complex-relationship-with-guns/

Pew Research Center. (2021, April 20). *Amid a series of mass shootings in the U.S., gun policy remains deeply divisive*. Pew Research Center, U.S. Politics & Policy. https://www.pewresearch.org/politics/2021/04/20/amid-a-series-of-mass-shootings-in-the-u-s-gun-policy-remains-deeply-divisive/

Porfiri, M., Barak-Ventura, R., & Marín, M. R. (2020). Self-protection versus fear of stricter firearm regulations: Examining the drivers of firearm acquisitions in the aftermath of a mass shooting. *Patterns*, 100082. https://doi.org/10.1016/j.patter.2020.100082

Porfiri, M., Sattanapalle, R. R., Nakayama, S., Macinko, J., & Sipahi, R. (2019). Media coverage and firearm acquisition in the aftermath of a mass shooting. *Nature Human Behaviour, 3*(9), 913–921. https://doi.org/10.1038/s41562-019-0636-0

Reeping, P. M., Cerdá, M., Kalesan, B., Wiebe, D. J., Galea, S., & Branas, C. C. (2019). State gun laws, gun ownership, and mass shootings in the US: Cross sectional time series. *BMJ, 364*, l542. https://doi.org/10.1136/bmj.l542

Rupertus, E. (2016, July 20). *A good guy with a gun*. NRA. https://www.nrablog.com/articles/2016/7/a-good-guy-with-a-gun/

Schildkraut, J. (2016). Mass murder and the mass media: Understanding the construction of the social problem of mass shootings in the US. *Journal of Qualitative Criminal Justice & Criminology, 4*(1). https://doi.org/10.21428/88de04a1.0e3b7530

Schildkraut, J., Elsass, H. J., & Stafford, M. C. (2015). Could it happen here? Moral panic, school shootings, and fear of crime among college students. *Crime, Law and Social Change, 63*(1), 91–110. https://doi.org/10.1007/s10611-015-9552-z

Schildkraut, J., & Elsass, H. J. (2016). *Mass shootings: Media, myths, and realities.* ABC-CLIO.

Silver, J., Simons, A., & Craun, S. (2018). *A study of the pre-attack behaviors of active shooters in the United States between 2000 and 2013.* Federal Bureau of Investigation.

Soni, A., & Tekin, E. (2020). *How do mass shootings affect community wellbeing?* (No. w28122). National Bureau of Economic Research. https://doi.org/10.3386/w28122

Stansfield, R., & Semenza, D. (2019). Licensed firearm dealer availability and intimate partner homicide: A multilevel analysis in sixteen states. *Preventive Medicine, 126,* 105739. https://doi.org/10.1016/j.ypmed.2019.05.027

Stroebe, W., Leander, N. P., & Kruglanski, A. W. (2017a). Is it a dangerous world out there? The motivational bases of American gun ownership. *Personality and Social Psychology Bulletin, 43*(8), 1071–1085. https://doi.org/10.1177/0146167217703952

Stroebe, W., Leander, N. P., & Kruglanski, A. W. (2017b). The impact of the Orlando mass shooting on fear of victimization and gun-purchasing intentions: Not what one might expect. *PLOS ONE, 12*(8), e0182408. https://doi.org/10.1371/journal.pone.0182408

Studdert, D. M., Zhang, Y., Rodden, J. A., Hyndman, R. J., & Wintemute, G. J. (2017). Handgun acquisitions in California after two mass shootings. *Annals of Internal Medicine, 166*(10), 698. https://doi.org/10.7326/M16-1574

Thompson, R. R., Jones, N. M., Holman, E. A., & Silver, R. C. (2019). Media exposure to mass violence events can fuel a cycle of distress. *Science Advances, 5*(4), eaav3502. https://doi.org/10.1126/sciadv.aav3502

Turchan, B., Zeoli, A. M., & Kwiatkowski, C. (2017). Reacting to the improbable: Handgun carrying permit application rates in the wake of high-profile mass shootings. *Homicide Studies, 21*(4), 267–286. https://doi.org/10.1177/1088767917699657

Urbatsch, R. (2019). Gun-shy: Refusal to answer questions about firearm ownership. *The Social Science Journal, 56*(2), 189–195. https://doi.org/10.1016/j.soscij.2018.04.003

U.S. Fish and Wildlife Service. (2017). *2016 National survey of fishing, hunting, and wildlife-associated recreation: National overview.* U.S. Fish and Wildlife Service. https://wsfrprograms.fws.gov/Subpages/NationalSurvey/nat_survey2016.pdf

Wallace, L. N. (2015). Responding to violence with guns: Mass shootings and gun acquisition. *The Social Science Journal, 52*(2), 156–167. https://doi.org/10.1016/j.soscij.2015.03.002

Wallace, L. N. (2017). Concealed ownership: Americans' perceived comfort sharing gun ownership status with others. *Sociological Spectrum, 37*(5), 267–281.

Yuan, Y., & McNeeley, S. (2016). Reactions to crime: A multilevel analysis of fear of crime and defensive and participatory behavior. *Journal of Crime and Justice, 39*(4), 455–472. https://doi.org/10.1080/0735648X.2015.1054297

23

Mass Shootings and Mental Health in the United States

Key Dynamics and Controversies

JILLIAN PETERSON AND JAMES DENSLEY

Mass public shootings, defined here as four or more people killed in a public space (Huff-Corzine & Corzine, 2020), are often blamed on untreated mental illness by politicians and the media (Duxbury et al., 2018; Craighill & Clement, 2015). Mental illness refers to a wide range of mental health disorders that affect an individual's mood, thinking, and behavior, including depression and anxiety, and Metzl et al. (2021, p. 81) argue construction of the mass shooting problem "relies on an elastic and pejorative definition." They add that while symptoms of certain mental illnesses, such as schizophrenia, raise the risk for serious violence for a minority of individuals, any mass shooter's "diagnosable psychopathology" must be situated "within larger social structures and cultural scripts" (Metzl et al., 2021, p. 81).

For example, the United States has more permissive gun laws and higher rates of gun ownership than almost any other country, meaning it is easier for people with a diagnosed mental illness to legally or illegally access the types of weapons used in mass public shootings (Lankford, 2016b; Siegel et al., 2020). The United States also has higher rates of mental illness and lower rates of treatment than comparable nations. Owing to a lack of accessible community mental health treatment in the United States, individuals with serious mental illness can become entangled in the criminal justice system, which is currently the country's primary mental health treatment provider (Roth, 2018). This may inadvertently create barriers to mass shooting prevention and intervention.

This chapter examines the landscape of mental illness and mental health treatment in the United States—the key dynamics and controversies—and how this feeds the broader discussion about America's unique experience of mass shootings (Lankford, 2016a, 2016b; Peterson & Densely, 2021). We begin but putting mental illness in context.

Mental Illness in the United States

The United States has higher rates of mental illness compared with the rest of the world, according to data from the Global Burden of Disease study (Ritchie & Roser, 2018). The data show 17.3 percent of the United States population meets the criteria for a mental illness compared with 13.0 percent of the worldwide population. Rates of depression (world, 3.4 percent; United States, 4.8 percent) and anxiety (world, 3.8 percent; United States, 6.6 percent) are especially elevated. National Survey on Drug Use and Health estimates are even higher, reporting that 20.6 percent of all U.S. adults meet the criteria for a mental health disorder at any given point in time (Substance Abuse and Mental Health Service Administration, 2019).

Harvard Medical School (2003) examined data from Canada, Chile, Germany, the Netherlands, and the United States. Compared with these other countries, the United States not only had higher prevalence rates of serious mental illness but also a lower treatment rate. In the United States alone, treatment was more associated with the ability to pay rather than the need for care. And in every country, the population least likely to receive treatment for serious mental illness was poorly educated young men.

Current treatment options are often difficult to access because of a shortage of qualified health-care providers in the United States, especially outside of urban centers. Treatment can also be prohibitively expensive because many Americans are uninsured or underinsured. The United States remains the only large rich country without universal health care or a robust social safety net. During the global recession of 2008 and 2009, about 3.9 million American adults lost their health insurance owing to the U.S. practice of tying health care to employment, and an estimated one in ten American adults— approx. 23 million people—owe medical debt (Dorn, 2020). As a result of high medical costs and limited treatment options, many Americans self-medicate mental health problems with drugs and alcohol, which only exacerbates symptoms.

Mental health treatment for children and adolescents at the age when many mental health disorders first onset also is lacking. The American School Counselor Association recommends a ratio of 250 students per counselor, but over 90 percent of students attend schools with higher ratios (the national average is 444:1). A ratio of five hundred students per psychologist is also recommended, but to reach that goal, public schools across America would need to hire more than fifty thousand new psychologists—the national average today is 1,500:1 (Whitaker et al., 2020).

Criminalization of Mental Illness

For some individuals, a lack of affordable, accessible mental health treatment can result in criminal justice involvement. The phrase *criminalization of mentally disordered behavior* was first coined by Abramson (1972). According to the criminalization hypothesis, people with mental illness become entangled in the legal system because the mental health resources that they need are not available in their community (Roth, 2018). Deinstitutionalization, which refers to the process of depopulating the state asylums and hospitals that historically housed and treated people with mental illness, is held largely responsible for criminalization (Roth, 2021).

Deinstitutionalization resulted from several intersecting factors (Abramson, 1972), including the following: the deterioration of state mental health institutions; the advent of psychotropic medications in the 1950s to treat mental illnesses like schizophrenia and bipolar disorder; the creation of Medicaid in 1965, which accelerated the shift from inpatient to outpatient care; mental health legislation, namely the 1963 Community Mental Health Act, designed to bring treatment out of psychiatric hospitals and into the community; and increased civil rights for people with mental illness (e.g., Addington v. Texas 1979, Lessard v. Schmidt 1975, O'Connor v. Donaldson 1975). These radical changes in the mental health landscape saw the use of long-term inpatient psychiatric care decline significantly, with the mean length of stay in a psychiatric hospital falling from 421 days in 1969 to 189 days in 1978 (Kiesler, 1982). In 1955, there were 559,000 persons institutionalized in state mental hospitals out of a total national population of 165 million (339 beds per 100,000 population). By 2016, the number of people institutionalized was 37,679 for a total population of approximately 324,000,000 (11.7 beds per 100,000 population) (Lamb & Weinberger, 2020).

Federal support for mental health programs declined consistently over this period. Instead of national funding for mental health, responsibility was passed onto state governments, where budgets failed to cover the costs of community mental health care and community-based alternatives to defunded state psychiatric hospitals were never stood up (Roth, 2021). When individuals with mental illness could no longer access needed psychiatric care, they moved from the medical system into the criminal justice system (Torrey, 1995; Lamb & Weinberger, 2020), the one "institution that cannot say no" (Teplin,

1984, p. 795). At the same time, the criminal justice system itself changed to facilitate a tough-on-crime response to rising violence and civil unrest (Decker et al., 2022). The so-called war on drugs, broken windows policing, more punitive sentencing, and so on (Alexander, 2010), dialed up the number of incarcerated people from two hundred thousand in 1970 to more than 1.6 million today (Dvoskin et al., 2020).

The vast majority of incarcerated people with mental illness today belong to a subset of the population (e.g., poor, ethnic minority) that likely would never have been served by state psychiatric hospitals in the past (Roth, 2021). Further, only a minority of individuals with serious mental illness become justice-involved directly *because* of their untreated mental health symptoms. For example, Peterson et al. (2014) used a continuum to assess the role of mental health symptoms in 429 crimes committed by justice-involved individuals with a diagnosed serious mental illness. Overall, 65 percent of crimes were completely unrelated to any mental health symptoms, 7.5 percent of crimes were committed in direct response to mental health symptoms, and 28 percent fell somewhere in between. For many individuals, mental illness leads to crime through more complex pathways, most often mediated by substance use or poverty, including homelessness (Peterson et al., 2014; Dvoskin et al., 2020). Whether individuals with serious mental illness become justice-involved due to untreated symptoms, substance use, or poverty, jails and prisons have become the largest mental health treatment providers in the country (Gosselin, 2019).

Law enforcement is the de facto first responder to most mental health crises (Lurigio, 2012). One study found that calls related to mental health disorders outnumbered calls for larceny, traffic accidents, and domestic disputes combined (Biasotti, 2011). But the police typically only have two options at their disposal on a mental health crisis call: arrest or hospitalize (Peterson et al., 2020). Arrest in these situations contributes to the criminalization of mental illness. Hospitalization is often an inadequate response as well. While police officers have the authority to take someone into custody for medical treatment if they need a mental health evaluation and are in danger of harming themselves or others if not immediately detained (Gosselin, 2019), this is only ever a temporary fix because the goal of psychiatric hospitalization is short-term stabilization, not long-term care. The dehumanizing and stigmatizing term *frequent flier* often is used to describe individuals with serious mental illness who have repetitive and frequent contact with the police due to their mental illness, jumping between the psychiatric emergency room and jail (Akins et al., 2016). This, in turn, becomes a barrier to reporting and treatment, which may prevent some individuals on the pathway to serious violence from getting the attention and intervention they need.

The Relationship between Mental Illness and Violence

Though it is widely known that mental illness is overrepresented in the criminal justice system, the relationship between mental illness and violence is more difficult to untangle. First, there are hundreds of mental illnesses ranging from eating disorders to developmental disorders to psychotic disorders, and approximately half of the population in the United States will meet the criteria for one at some point in their lifetime (Schaefer et al., 2017). It is difficult to assess the role of symptoms of certain serious mental illnesses in motivating violence because some symptoms are traits that motivate violence for individuals both with *and* without serious mental illness (Peterson et al., 2014; Skeem & Mulvey, 2020). For example, irritability and hopelessness are symptoms of depression that may contribute to violence for people with and without a diagnosed mental disorder. Likewise, impulsivity is a symptom of bipolar disorder, but it is a trait that influences violence among people both with and without a diagnosed mental illness (Krueger et al., 2007).

Furthermore, serious mental illness and violence have overlapping risk factors, such as childhood physical and sexual abuse (Machisa et al., 2016). Symptoms of serious mental illnesses like psychosis wax and wane over time depending on stress (Douglas & Skeem, 2005), and mental health symptoms and violence alike can be triggered by stressors such as unemployment, strained family relationships, and community factors (Armstead et al., 2021; Alegria et al., 2018). For individuals who are at a higher risk for violence, symptoms of serious mental illness may hold less influence than other risk factors, such as previous antisocial behavior, poverty, or substance use. There is evidence that symptoms of serious mental illness play a larger role in influencing violence among people who are otherwise at a lower risk of violent offending (for a review, see Skeem & Mulvey, 2020).

The link between mental illness and violence is commonly made in media accounts of high-profile violent crimes. An examination of four hundred randomly selected news articles about mental illness found the most frequently mentioned topic was violence (McGinty et al., 2016). This is worrisome when population studies show the majority of people with a serious mental illness are not violent (Glied & Frank, 2014), and less than 5 percent of violent crimes in the United States are committed by people with serious mental illness (Appelbaum, 2006; Fazel & Grann, 2006). Research using the MacArthur Violence Risk Assessment Study (Monahan et al., 2001) found a 2 percent prevalence rate of violence committed with a firearm in a large sample of individuals with serious mental illness released from a psychiatric facility (Steadman et al., 2015).

American Mass Shootings

In addition to having higher rates of mental illness in America compared with the rest of the world, the United States also has more mass shootings (Lankford, 2016b, 2019). Surprisingly, there is no universally accepted definition of a mass shooting (see Huff-Corzine & Corzine, 2020). The concept itself is relatively new and is a subset of "mass killing," which since the 1980s has been used by researchers and the U.S. Federal Bureau of Investigation (FBI) to mean four or more people killed—not including the perpetrator—by the same offender(s) in a twenty-four-hour period (Krouse & Richardson, 2015, p. 4). A mass shooting is simply a mass killing perpetrated with a firearm. To differentiate between mass shootings that occur in domestic settings versus relatively public places, like schools, workplaces, and places of worship, and to separate offenders who only target family members or intimate friends from those who indiscriminately select their victims, researchers have developed the concept of "mass public shooting" (Duwe, 2018).

Evidence suggests that mass public shootings are getting more frequent and deadlier (Densley & Peterson, 2019). Lankford and Silver (2020) argue that the rise of celebrity culture in the age of mass media and social media has led to more mass public shooters who are motivated to kill large numbers of victims for fame or attention, as well as to more shooters who have been directly influenced by past mass shooters. Part of the appeal of past mass shooters, Peterson and Densley (2021, p. 100) argue, is that they provide "social proof," or a model of behavior, for people struggling with the uncertainty of social and psychological strain, including mental illness.

Mental Illness among Mass Shooters

A small number of studies to date have systematically analyzed the role of serious mental illness in mass violence (Dutton et al., 2013; Meloy et al., 2001; Stone, 2015). Rocque and Duwe (2018, p. 31) found that 59 percent of 185 perpetrators in their analysis of mass killings over the last century had either been diagnosed with a serious mental illness or had "demonstrated serious signs of a mental illness prior to the shooting." Taylor (2018) examined 152 mass murders, finding that 30 percent of the perpetrators had either a confirmed or suspected serious mental illness. A more recent study of 1,315 mass murderers since 1900 found psychotic symptoms among 11 percent of perpetrators (Brucato et al., 2021).

Data from the Violence Project Mass Shooter Database, which codes perpetrators who killed four or more people since 1966 using publicly available records (Peterson & Densley, 2019), show 19.8 percent had a history of previous hospitalization for psychiatric reasons, 29.1 percent had a history of counseling, and 23.3 percent had a known history of taking psychiatric medication (comparable to rates among the U.S. general population; Moore & Mattison, 2017). In terms of diagnosis, 15.7 percent showed evidence of a mood disorder diagnosis (compared with 9.7 percent of the U.S. population in a given year), 6.4 percent showed evidence of an autism spectrum disorder diagnosis (compared with 1.8 percent of the general population), and 26.7 percent showed evidence of a psychotic disorder diagnosis (compared with 1 percent of the general population). According to the TVP Database, 31 percent of perpetrators had no known psychiatric disorder according to publicly available data. If hospitalization, counseling, psychiatric medication, and previous diagnosis are combined, 58.7 percent of perpetrators had a mental health history, which is somewhat higher than general population levels (Kessler et al., 2005). Lankford and Cowan (2020) reanalyzed the mental health coding in the Violence Project Database, finding that even the more "mentally healthy" perpetrators could be recoded as having some signs of mental illness, highlighting the difficulty in both defining and coding mental illness using publicly available records (see also Metzl et al., 2021). If not mentally ill, therefore, no one who commits a mass shooting is mentally healthy.

Psychosis among Mass Shooters

Of all the symptoms of mental illness, it is perhaps easiest to conceptualize how delusions (i.e., a fixed false belief system), hallucinations (i.e., perceiving something that is not there), and cognitive symptoms (i.e., confused, disturbed, or disrupted patterns of thought) directly motivate violence (Peterson et al., 2014; Douglas et al., 2009; McNiel et al., 2000). These are all symptoms of psychosis, which is a feature of several mental health disorders such as schizophrenia spectrum disorders, mood disorders, dementia, and substance-induced or traumatic brain injuries. Americans increasingly see people with psychosis as dangerous not only to themselves but to others (Pescosolido et al., 2019).

The vast majority of people who experience psychosis are not violent, but a meta-analysis of 204 studies of psychosis as a risk factor for violence found that "compared with individuals with no mental disorders, people with psychosis seem to be at a substantially elevated risk for violence" (Douglas et al., 2009, p. 702). Persecutory delusions, where someone believes they are being targeted, and command hallucinations, where someone hears a voice telling them to hurt someone, can increase the risk of violence for a minority of people (DeAngelis, 2021). Skeem et al. (2016) used data from the MacArthur Violence Risk Assessment Study to examine 305 incidents of violence among high-risk individuals with a previous inpatient hospital stay, finding that symptoms of psychosis immediately preceded the violent incident in 12 percent of cases.

A recent study of mass shooters using the Mother Jones database found that in twenty-eight of thirty-five cases where the perpetrator survived the shooting, twenty had a psychotic disorder (schizophrenia or delusional disorder), and in a random sample of twenty cases where the perpetrator died, eight had a diagnosis of schizophrenia (Glick et al., 2021).

However, a perpetrator having a psychotic diagnosis does not necessarily mean that hallucinations and delusions directly motivated their shooting. Of course, it is impossible to read anyone's mind or know exactly when and how impaired thoughts might have affected someone's behavior. But based on available evidence, Peterson et al. (2021a) found that in the majority (69.8 percent) of mass public shootings, psychotic symptoms played no role whatsoever. In 11 percent of cases, psychosis may have played a *minor* role in the shooting (i.e., the perpetrator experienced delusions or hallucinations while planning and/or committing the crime, which may have influenced their thinking and decision-making, but the perpetrator had another primary motivation or precipitating event), and in 8.7 percent of mass shootings, psychosis played a *moderate* role (i.e., the perpetrator experienced delusions and/or hallucinations while planning and/or committing the crime, was responding to delusions or hallucinations in planning and/or committing this crime, but also had additional motive[s]). Psychotic symptoms played a *major* role in about 10.5 percent of all mass public shootings, meaning the shooter was known to have experienced psychosis both before and during the crime, was responding to delusions or hallucinations in planning and committing this crime, and had no other known motive. For these perpetrators, access to high-quality and long-term mental health treatment may have prevented the shooting from occurring. However, for the other 89.5 percent of cases, the motivation to commit the shooting was more complex, so intervention would likely need to be more nuanced than the treatment of psychotic symptoms alone.

Psychopathy among Mass Shooters

The term *psychotic* is used frequently and interchangeably with *psychopathic* to explain mass violence in the media and popular culture, though they are two distinct concepts. Psychopathy is a personality disorder, albeit not listed in any editions of the American Psychiatric Association's Diagnostic and Statistical Manual of Mental Disorders. The term *psychopath* describes someone charming, grandiose, lying, manipulative, emotionally shallow, callous, easily bored, impulsive, irresponsible, and lacking in goals (Hare, 2003). There is a vast academic literature on the exact nature of psychopathy (for a review, see De Brito et al., 2021), but colloquially, psychopaths are often described as narcissists with little conscience, which is a natural description for many mass shooters (e.g., Langman, 2009).

People get labeled psychopaths often based on the results of a psychological evaluation tool called the Hare Psychopathy Checklist-Revised (PCL-R; Hare, 2003). After years of research, however, expert psychiatrists and psychologists have concluded that the test cannot precisely or accurately predict an individual's risk for committing serious violence. Importantly, violence and criminality are not diagnostic features of psychopathy (Skeem & Cooke, 2010). Cleckley (1941), who originally conceptualized psychopaths in his book *The Mask of Sanity*, describes psychopaths as charming and glib, without empathy or the ability to experience the full range of human emotion. In his framework, Cleckley describes psychopaths as calm individuals, distinctly not anxious, which makes them immune to suicide. However, studies have shown that a majority of mass shooters are not resistant to suicide (see Lankford, 2013), and they show signs of agitation, isolation, and paranoia in the days, weeks, and months leading up to a shooting (Peterson & Densley, 2021). Dutton et al. (2013) argue that the obsessive qualities of the perceptions of mass shooters are more consistent with paranoid thinking than with psychopathy overall. Other studies have shown that the vast majority of mass shooters have not been psychopaths (Lankford & Cowan, 2020).

Suicidality among Mass Shooters

It is important to note that although there is a significant overlap between mental illness and suicide, one can be suicidal without meeting the criteria for a mental illness. The majority of suicides are related to depression, psychosis, or substance use disorders; however, the risk for suicidality is multifaceted and also related to trauma and other stressors (Brådvik, 2018). In the United States, only about 4 percent of perpetrators who commit murder also commit suicide at the same time (Eliason, 2009; Lankford, 2015). However, the numbers are significantly higher among mass shooters (Lankford et al., 2021). Previous studies have shown that approximately 38 percent of mass shooters die by suicide and an additional 10 percent provoke law enforcement to kill them (Kelly, 2010). Peterson and Densley (2021) found that 31.5 percent of mass public shooters were actively suicidal before their attack (defined as previous attempts of suicide, writing or telling others about suicidal thoughts), and an additional 40.5 percent of perpetrators die by suicide during their shooting. A rise in mass shootings in the United States corresponds with a rise in deaths by suicide, drug overdoses, and alcohol-related conditions, often referred to as deaths of despair (Case & Deaton, 2020). In a related analysis of the motivation behind any communication of intent to do harm, or "leakage," among 170 mass public shooters, Peterson et al. (2021b) found shooting threats were statistically most associated with previous counseling and suicidality, especially among younger shooters, thus indicative of a cry for help as opposed to seeking fame or attention.

Policy Implications

Importantly, the role that mental illness plays in the lives of mass shooters varies from perpetrator to perpetrator. Mental illness is one factor on a long pathway to violence, and symptoms are often triggered by stress, unemployment, relationship struggles, violence, and trauma (Peterson & Densley, 2021). A history of crime and violence is more common than a history of mental illness for mass shooters. Most perpetrators had a prior criminal record (64.5 percent) and a history of violence (62.8 percent), including domestic violence (27.9 percent), and 28.5 percent had a military history (Peterson & Densley, 2021). Nonetheless, the prevalence of mental illness and mental health concerns among perpetrators of public mass shootings has implications for policy and practice.

Crisis Response

Much more common than formally diagnosed mental illness, studies have found that 82 percent of perpetrators showed signs of a crisis in the days, weeks, and months leading up to the shooting, though not necessarily a mental health crisis (Peterson & Densley, 2021). Parents, spouses, friends, coworkers, neighbors, pastors, mental health professionals, and even law enforcement often report observing significant behavior change in a majority of mass shooters. Perpetrators showed increased agitation, mood swings, or abusive behavior before the shooting. They isolated themselves, lost touch with reality, became paranoid, and were noticeably depressed or unable to perform daily tasks (Peterson & Densley, 2021). Four out of five shooters showed more than one of these signs, and nearly 60 percent showed three or more different signs of atypical behavior. Therefore, crisis intervention and suicide prevention skills could be critical components of mass shooting prevention and intervention.

Crisis response teams in schools and workplaces, where perpetrators tend to be insiders (i.e., students of the school or employees of the workplace) may also help identify individuals who are at risk for violence against self or others and determine appropriate intervention strategies (Borum et al., 1999). In the wake of several post office shootings in the 1980s and early 1990s, for example, the United States Postal Service implemented a workplace threat assessment program, using district-level threat assessment teams, as part of its broader workplace violence prevention initiative. To avoid disciplinary outcomes that may exacerbate risk factors for violence and increase criminal justice involvement (Crepeau-Hobson & Leech, 2021), these programs could extend beyond the usual notion of threat assessment and instead use a crisis response team model to provide nonpunitive supports for anyone experiencing a mental health crisis (Peterson & Densley, 2021).

Relatedly, police and mental health worker co-responder models, where a specially trained officer and a mental health crisis worker respond together to mental health calls for service (for a review, see Puntis et al. 2018), could help tackle the criminalization of mental illness (Abramson, 1972), which is a barrier to reporting and treatment. For myriad reasons (for a discussion, see Roth, 2018), law enforcement responds first to many if not most mental health crises in the United States (Peterson et al., 2020). Co-responder models draw on the combined expertise of the officer and mental health professional to link people with mental illnesses to appropriate services or provide other effective and efficient responses. Had the Santa Barbara County Sheriff's Office used this model when conducting a welfare check on the 2014 Isla Vista shooter a month before his deadly rampage, for example, perhaps they would have found cause to enter or search his residence and find the arsenal he had amassed for his crime, thus preventing it.

Access to Firearms

Gostin and Record (2011) argue that owing to the ineffectiveness of current restrictions on access to firearms for "dangerous people," the government must instead improve safeguards against the "dangerous weapons" implicated in mass violence. The Gun Control Act of 1968 (18 U.S.C. § 922) generally restricts "prohibited persons" from purchasing firearms, including those involuntarily committed to mental health or substance abuse treatment, people adjudicated as incompetent or dangerous, or those who receive a verdict of not guilty by reason of insanity. However, federal law is the floor not the ceiling when it comes to restricting firearms, and states interpret and implement the law differently, resulting in variable outcomes. Rather than limiting someone's access to firearms for life based on their mental health history, states could adopt systems to identify and disarm gun possessors who are particularly at high risk for violence. The California Armed and Prohibited Persons System, for example, uses state gun sale records to identify prior gun buyers who have since become disqualified possessors (Laqueur & Wintemute, 2020). This is especially important because, as discussed, mass shooters with serious mental illness share many of the same risk factors for violence as mass shooters without mental illness (Skeem & Mulvey, 2020).

Allowing for temporary removal (and reinstatement) of a firearm based on a wider range of factors might also encourage reporting from family and friends and incentivize treatment. Red flag laws, properly known as extreme risk protection orders, allow family members to petition a court to temporarily remove a person's access to firearms if they pose a threat to themselves or others. Evidence suggests such laws may help prevent mass shootings (Laqueur & Wintemute, 2020; Zeoli & Paruk, 2020).

Access to Mental Health Treatment

For people experiencing a serious and persistent mental illness like psychosis for the first time, the biggest barriers to seeking treatment are generally stigma, a lack of knowledge or difficulty recognizing mental illness, and not knowing where to seek help (Scholten et al., 2003). It is possible that access to affordable, community-based mental health treatment and assistance services may help prevent mass shootings in a minority of cases. However, the fact that approximately half of the mass shooters who were motivated by psychosis—a serious and persistent mental illness—in any way had received previous treatment implies that the quality of treatment matters in addition to its quantity. The efficacy of having mental health practitioners assess clients for mass shooting risk is also an area for future research (Meloy, 2018).

On a larger scale, serious investment is needed in the social and political determinants of health and well-being—the social and economic conditions, such as those in housing, employment, food security, and education, that have a major influence on individual and community mental health and safety (Metzl et al., 2021). We need a stronger social safety net in the United States so that the loss of a job does not mean the loss of one's home, identity, and health insurance (and therefore access to mental health care). Universal health care, paid maternity leave, and access to affordable childcare are examples of policies common in other wealthy democracies with lower rates of mental illness that reduce stress and financial strain (Case & Deaton, 2020). In addition, an investment in school-based mental health resources including counselors, social workers, and social-emotional learning curricula could help with the early detection of mental health concerns and identifying healthy coping mechanisms, particularly for young boys.

REFERENCES

Abramson, M. (1972). The criminalization of mentally disordered behavior: Possible side-effect of a new mental health law. *Hospital and Community Psychiatry, 23,* 101–105. https://doi.org/10.1176/ps.23.4.101
Akins, S., Burkhardt, B. C., & Lanfear, C. (2016). Law enforcement response to "frequent fliers": An examination of high-frequency contacts between police and justice-involved person with mental illness. *Criminal Justice Policy Review, 27*(1) 97–114.

Alegria, M. NeMoyer, A., Falgas, I., Wang, Y., & Alvarez, K. (2018). Social determinants of mental health: Where we are and where we need to go. *Current Psychiatry Reports, 20*(11), 95.

Alexander, M. (2010). *The new Jim Crow*. New Press.

Appelbaum, P. (2006). Violence and mental disorders. *American Journal of Psychiatry, 163*(8), 1319–1321.

Armstead, T. L., Wilkins, N., & Nation, M. (2021). Structural and social determinants of inequities in violence risk: A review of indicators. *Journal of Community Psychology, 49*(4), 878–906.

Biasotti, M. C. (2011). The impact of mental illness on law enforcement resources. *Treatment Advocacy Center*. https://www.treatmentadvocacycenter.org/storage/documents/The_Impact_of_Mental_Illness_on_Law_Enforcement_Resources__TAC.pdf

Bijl, R. V., de Graaf, R., Hiripi, E., Kessler, R. C., Kohn, R., Offord, D. R., Bedirhan Ustun, T., Vicente, B., Vollebergh, W. A. M., Walters, E. E., & Wittchen, H-U. (2003). The prevalence of treated and untreated mental disorders in five countries. *Health Affairs, 22*(3), 122–133.

Borum, R., Fein, R., Vossekuil, B., & Berglund, J. (1999). Threat assessment: Defining an approach for evaluating risk of targeted violence. *Behavioral Sciences & the Law, 17*(3), 323–337.

Brådvik L. (2018). Suicide risk and mental disorders. *International Journal of Environmental Research and Public Health, 15*(9), 2028. https://doi.org/10.3390/ijerph15092028

Brucato, G., Appelbaum, P. S., Hensson, H., Shea, E. A., Dishy, G., Kathryn Lee, K., Pia, T., Syed, F., Villalobos, A., Wall, M. M., Lieberman, J. A., & Girgis, R. R. (2021). Psychotic symptoms in mass shootings v. mass murders not involving firearms: findings from the Columbia mass murder database. *Psychological Medicine*, 1–9. https://doi.org/10.1017/S0033291721000076

Case, A., & Deaton, A. (2020). *Deaths of despair and the future of capitalism*. Princeton University Press.

Cleckley, H. (1941). *The mask of sanity*. Mosby.

Craighill, P. M., & Clement, S. (2015, October 15). What Americans blame most for mass shootings (Hint: it's not gun laws). *Washington Post*. https://www.washingtonpost.com/news/the-fix/wp/2015/10/26/gun-control-americans-overwhelmingly-blame-mental-health-failures-for-mass-shootings/

Crepeau-Hobson, F., & Leech, N. (2021). Disciplinary and nondisciplinary outcomes of school-based threat assessments in Colorado schools. *School Psychology Review*. https://doi.org/10.1080/2372966X.2020.1842716

DeAngelis, T. (2021). Mental illness and violence: Debunking myths, addressing realities. *Monitor on Psychology, 52*(3), 31.

De Brito, S. A., Forth, A. E., Baskin-Sommers, A. R., Brazil, I. A., Kimonis, E. R., Pardini, D., Frick, P. J., Blair, R. J. R., & Viding, E. (2021). Psychopathy. *Nature Reviews Disease Primers, 7*, 49.

Decker, S., Pyrooz, D., & Densley, J. (2022). *On gangs*. Temple University Press.

Densley, J., & Peterson, J. (2019, Sept. 1). We analyzed 53 years of mass shooting data. Attacks aren't just increasing, they're getting deadlier. *Los Angeles Times*. Retrieved October 27, 2022 from https://www.latimes.com/opinion/story/2019-09-01/mass-shooting-data-odessa-midland-increase

Dorn, S. (2020). *The COVID-19 pandemic and resulting economic crash have caused the greatest health insurance losses in American history*. Families USA. https://familiesusa

.org/resources/the-covid-19-pandemic-and-resulting-economic-crash-have-caused -the-greatest-health-insurance-losses-in-american-history/

Douglas, K. S., Guy, L. S., & Hart, S. D. (2009). Psychosis as a risk factor for violence to others: A meta-analysis. *Psychological Bulletin, 135*(5), 679–706.

Douglas, K. S., & Skeem, J. L. (2005). Violence risk assessment: Getting specific about being dynamic. *Psychology, Public Policy, and Law, 11*(3), 347–383. https://doi.org/10 .1037/1076-8971.11.3.347

Dutton, D. G., White, K. R., & Fogarty, D. (2013). Paranoid thinking in mass shooters. *Aggression and Violent Behavior, 18*(5), 548–553.

Duwe, G. (2018). Mass shootings: A new name for a familiar problem. In S. H. Decker & K. A. Wright (Eds.), *Criminology and Public Policy: Putting Theory to Work* (2nd ed., pp. 169–188). Temple University Press.

Duxbury, S. W., Frizzell, L. C., & Lindsay, S. L. (2018). Mental illness, the media, and the moral politics of mass violence. *Journal of Research in Crime and Delinquency, 55*(6), 766–797.

Dvoskin, J., Knoll, J., & Silva, M. (2021). A brief history of the criminalization of mental illness. In Warburton K, Stahl S (Eds). *Decriminalizing mental illness* (pp. 14–29). Cambridge University Press.

Eliason, S. (2009). Murder-suicide: A review of the recent literature. *Journal of the American Academy of Psychiatry and the Law, 37*(3), 371–376.

Fazel, S., & Grann, M. (2006). The population impact of severe mental illness on violent crime. *American Journal of Psychiatry, 163*(8), 1397–1403.

Glick, I. D., Cerfolio, N. E., Kamis, D., & Laurence, M. (2021). Domestic mass shooters: The association with unmedicated and untreated psychiatric illness. *Journal of Clinical Pharmacology, 41*(4), 366–369.

Glied, S., & Frank, R. G. (2014). Mental illness and violence: Lessons from the evidence. *American Journal of Public Health, 104*(2), e5–6.

Gosselin, D. K. (2019). *Crime and mental disorders.* West Academic Publishing.

Gostin, L. O., & Record, K. L. (2011). Dangerous people or dangerous weapons: Access to firearms for persons with mental illness. *JAMA, 305*(20), 2108–2109.

Hare, R. D. (2003). *The Hare Psychopathy Checklist-Revised (PCL-R) manual* (2nd ed.). Toronto, Ontario, Canada: Multi-Health Systems.

Harvard Medical School. (2003, May 7). Survey finds U.S. has high rate of mental illness, low rate of treatment compared to other countries. *ScienceDaily.* www.sciencedaily .com/releases/2003/05/030507080958.htm

Huff-Corzine, L., & Corzine, J. (2020). The devil's in the details: Measuring mass violence. *Criminology & Public Policy, 19*(1), 317–333.

Kelly, W.R. (2010). Active shooter: Recommendations and analysis for risk mitigation. New York City Police Department.

Kessler, R. C., Berglund, P., Demler, O., Jin, R., Merikangas, K. R., & Walters, E. E. (2005). Lifetime prevalence and age-of-onset distributions of DSM-IV disorders in the national comorbidity survey replication. *Archives of General Psychiatry, 62*(6), 593.

Kiesler, C. A. (1982). Mental hospitals and alternative care: Noninstitutionalization as potential public policy for mental patients. *American Psychologist, 37*(4), 349–360.

Kivisto, A. J., & Phalen, P. L. (2018). Effects of risk-based firearm seizure laws in Connecticut and Indiana on suicide rates, 1981–2015. *Psychiatric Services, 69*(8), 855–862.

Krouse, W. J., & Richardson, D. J. (2015). *Mass murder with firearms: Incidents and victims, 1999–2013.* Congressional Research Service.

Krueger, R. F., Markon, K. E., Patrick, C. J., Benning, S. D., & Kramer, M. D. (2007). Linking antisocial behavior, substance use, and personality: An integrative quantitative model of the adult externalizing spectrum. *Journal of Abnormal Psychology, 116*(4), 645–666.

Lamb, H. R., & Weinberger, L. E. (2020). Deinstitutionalization and other factors in the criminalization of persons with serious mental illness and how it is being addressed. *CNS Spectrums, 25,* 173–180.

Langman, P. (2009). *Why kids kill.* Palgrave Macmillan.

Lankford, A. (2013). *The myth of martyrdom.* St. Martin's Press.

Lankford, A. (2015). Mass shooters in the USA, 1966–2010: Differences between attackers who live and die. *Justice Quarterly, 32*(2), 360–379. https://doi.org/10.1080/07418825 .2013.806675

Lankford, A. (2016a). Are America's public mass shooters unique? A comparative analysis of offenders in the United States and other countries. *International Journal of Comparative and Applied Criminal Justice, 40,* 171–83.

Lankford, A. (2016b). Public mass shooters and firearms: A cross-national study of 171 Countries. *Violence and Victims, 31,* 187–199.

Lankford, A. (2019). Confirmation that the United States has six times its global share of public mass shooters, courtesy of Lott and Moody's data. *Econ Journal Watch, 16,* 69–83.

Lankford, A., & Cowan, R. G. (2020). Has the role of mental health problems in mass shootings been significantly underestimated? *Journal of Threat Assessment and Management, 7*(3–4), 135–156. https://doi.org/10.1037/tam0000151

Lankford, A., & Silver, J. (2020). Why have public mass shootings become more deadly? assessing how perpetrators' motives and methods have changed over time. *Criminology and Public Policy, 19*(1), 37–60.

Lankford, A., Silver, J., & Cox, J. (2021). An epidemiological analysis of public mass shooters and active shooters: Quantifying key differences between perpetrators and the general population, homicide offenders, and people who die by suicide. *Journal of Threat Assessment and Management, 8*(4), 125–144. https://doi.org/10.1037/tam0000166

Laqueur, H. S., & Wintemute, G. J. (2020). Identifying high-risk firearm owners to prevent mass violence. *Criminology & Public Policy, 19*(1), 109–127.

Lurigio, A (2012). Responding to the needs of people with mental illness in the criminal justice system: an area ripe for research and community partnerships. *Journal of Crime and Justice, 35,* 1–12.

Machisa, M. T., Christofides, N., & Jewkes, R. (2016). Structural pathways between child abuse, poor mental health outcomes, and male-perpetrated intimate partner violence. *PLOS One, 11*(3), e0150986.

Mcginty, E. E., Kennedy-Hendricks, A., Choksy, S., & Barry, C. L. (2016). Trends in news media coverage of mental illness in the United States: 1995–2014. *Health Affairs, 35*(6), 1121–1129.

McNiel, D. E., Eisner, J. P., & Binder, R. L. (2000). The relationship between command hallucinations and violence. *Psychiatric Services, 51*(10), 1288–1292.

Meloy, J. R. (2018). The operational development and empirical testing of the Terrorist Radicalization Assessment Protocol (TRAP-18). *Journal of Personality Assessment, 100*(5), 483–492.

Meloy, J. R., Hempel, A. G., Mohandie, K., Shiva, A. A., & Gray, B. T. (2001). Offender and offense characteristics of a nonrandom sample of adolescent mass murderers. *Journal of the American Academy of Child & Adolescent Psychiatry, 40*(6), 719–728.

Metzl, J., Piemonte, J., & McKay, T. (2021). Mental illness, mass shootings, and the future of psychiatric research into American gun violence. *Harvard Review of Psychiatry, 29*(1), 81–89.

Monahan, J., Steadman, H., Silver, E., Appelbaum, P., Robbins, P., Mulvey, L. H., Roth, Grisso, T., & Banks, S. M.(2001). *Rethinking risk assessment: The MacArthur study of mental disorder and violence.* Oxford University Press.

Moore, T., & Mattison, D. (2017). Adult utilization of psychiatric drugs and differences by sex, age, and race. *JAMA Internal Medicine, 177*(2), 274. https://doi.org/10.1001/jamainternmed.2016.7507

Pescosolido, B. A., Manago, B., & Monahan, J. (2019). Evolving public views on the likelihood of violence from people with mental illness: Stigma and its consequences. *Health Affairs, 38*(10), 1735–1743.

Peterson, J., & Densley, J. (2019). *The Violence Project database of mass shootings in the United States, 1966–2019.* The Violence Project. https://www.theviolenceproject.org

Peterson, J., & Densley, J. (2021). *The violence project: How to stop a mass shooting epidemic.* Abrams Press.

Peterson, J., Densley, J., & Erickson, G. (2020). Evaluation of "the R-Model" crisis intervention de-escalation training for law enforcement. *The Police Journal, 93*(4), 271–289.

Peterson, J., Densley, J., Knapp, K., Higgins, S., & Jensen, A. (2021a). Psychosis and mass shootings: A systematic examination using publicly available data. *Psychology, Public Policy, and Law.* https://doi.org/10.1037/law0000314

Peterson, J., Erickson, G., Knapp, K., & Densley, J. (2021b). Communication of intent to do harm preceding mass public shootings in the United States, 1966–2019. *JAMA Network Open, 4*(11), e2133073.

Peterson, J. K., Skeem, J., Kennealy, P., Bray, B., & Zvonkovic, A. (2014). How often and how consistently do symptoms directly precede criminal behavior among offenders with mental illness? *Law and Human Behavior, 38*(5), 439–449.

Puntis, S., Perfect, D., Kirubarajan, A., Bolton, S., Davies, F., Hayes, A., Harriss, E., & Molodynski, A. (2018). A systematic review of co-responder models of police mental health "street" triage. *BMC Psychiatry, 18*, 256.

Ritchie, H., & Roser, M. (2018). *Mental health.* Our World Data. https://ourworldindata.org/mental-health

Rocque, M., & Duwe, G. (2018). Rampage shootings: An historical, empirical, and theoretical overview. *Current Opinion in Psychology, 19*, 28–33.

Roth, A. (2018). *Insane.* Basic Books.

Roth, A. (2021). The truth about deinstitutionalization. *The Atlantic*, May 25. Retrieved from https://www.theatlantic.com/health/archive/2021/05/truth-about-deinstitutionalization/618986/

Schaefer, J. D., Caspi, A., Belsky, D. W., Harrington, H., Houts, R., Horwood, L. J., Hussong, A., Ramrakha, S., Poulton, R., & Moffitt, T. E. (2017). Enduring mental health: Prevalence and prediction. *Journal of Abnormal Psychology, 126*(2), 212–224.

Scholten, D. J., Malla, A. K., Norman, R. M., Mclean, T. S., Mcintosh, E. M., McDonald, C. L., Eliasziw, M., & Speechley, K. N. (2003). Removing barriers to treatment of first-episode psychotic disorders. *Canadian Journal of Psychiatry, 48*(8), 561–565.

Siegel, M., Goder-Reiser, M., Duwe, G., Rocque, M., Fox, J. A., & Fridel, E. E. (2020). The relation between state gun laws and the incidence and severity of mass public shootings in the United States, 1976–2018. *Law and Human Behavior, 44*(5), 347–360.

Skeem, J., & Cooke, D. (2010). One measure does not a construct make: Toward reinvigorating psychopathy research. Reply to Hare & Neumann (2010). *Psychological Assessment, 22,* 455–457.

Skeem, J., Kennealy, P., Monahan, J., Peterson, J., & Appelbaum, P. (2016). Psychosis uncommonly and inconsistently precedes violence among high-risk individuals. *Clinical Psychological Science, 4*(1), 40–49.

Skeem, J., & Mulvey, E. (2020). What role does serious mental illness play in mass shootings, and how should we address it? *Criminology & Public Policy, 19*(1), 85–108.

Steadman, H. J., Monahan, J., Pinals, D. A., Vesselinov, R., & Robbins, P. C. (2015). Gun violence and victimization of strangers by persons with a mental illness: Data from the MacArthur Violence Risk Assessment Study. *Psychiatric Services, 66*(11), 1238–1241.

Stone, M. H. (2015). Mass murder, mental illness, and men. *Violence and Gender, 2*(1), 51–86.

Substance Abuse and Mental Health Service Administration. (2019). *2019 National Survey of Drug Use and Health (NSDUH) Releases.* https://www.samhsa.gov/data/release/2019-national-survey-drug-use-and-health-nsduh-releases

Taylor, M. A. (2018). A comprehensive study of mass murder precipitants and motivations of offenders. *International Journal of Offender Therapy and Comparative Criminology, 62*(2), 427–449.

Teplin, L. (1984). Criminalizing mental illness: The comparative arrest rate of the mentally ill. *American Psychologist, 39,* 794–803.

Torrey, E. F. (1995). Jails and prisons: America's new mental hospitals. *American Journal of Public Health, 85,* 1611–1613.

Whitaker, A. Torres-Guillén, S., Morton, M., Jordan, H., Coyle, S., Mann, A., & Sun, W-L. (2020). *Cops and no counselors: How the lack of school mental health staff is harming students.* American Civil Liberties Union. https://www.aclu.org/sites/default/files/field_document/030419-acluschooldisciplinereport.pdf

Zeoli, A. M., & Paruk, J. K. (2020). Potential to prevent mass shootings through domestic violence firearm restrictions. *Criminology & Public Policy, 19*(1), 129–145.

Contributors

Melanie Brazzell is a graduate student and Chancellor's Fellow at the University of California Santa Barbara and currently a predoctoral fellow at the SNF Agora Institute at Johns Hopkins University. Their dissertation focuses on transformative justice alternatives to prison and policing for gender-based violence. Their participatory research and community engagement are housed within the What *Really* Makes Us Safe? Project. Most recently, they authored the "Building Structure Shapes" report in collaboration with the Realizing Democracy Project and six social movement organizations.

Tristan Bridges is Associate Professor of Sociology at the University of California, Santa Barbara. He currently coedits the journal *Men and Masculinities* (Sage Publications) and coedited the anthology *Exploring Masculinities: Identity, Inequality, Continuity, and Change* (Oxford University Press, 2016). His research is broadly concerned with shifts in gender and sexual identities and transformations in systems of gender and sexual inequality, with a specific focus on masculinities as an important piece of this larger process. His research has been published in *Gender & Society, Signs, Sociology Compass, Sociological Perspectives, Contexts,* and more.

Ryan Broll is Associate Professor in the Department of Sociology and Anthropology at the University of Guelph. His research focuses on trauma and resilience, with an emphasis on youth well-being after experiences of bullying and other forms of victimization. He also studies the policing of youth and mass murderer fandoms. His recent research has been published in the *Journal of Interpersonal Violence, Deviant Behavior, British Journal of Criminology,* and *Journal of School Violence,* and he is author of *Becoming Strong: Impoverished Women and the Struggle to Overcome Violence* (University of Toronto Press, 2018).

F. Chris Curran is Associate Professor of Educational Leadership and Policy and Director of the Education Policy Research Center at the University of Florida's College of Education. Prior to joining the University of Florida, he was a faculty member in the School of Public Policy at the University of Maryland, Baltimore County (UMBC). He received his Ph.D. in Leadership and Policy Studies with a doctoral minor in quantitative methods from Vanderbilt University's Peabody College in 2015 and holds a master's in Curriculum and Instruction from the University of Mississippi. Dr. Curran's research focuses on issues of equity in education with a particular focus on the ways that school discipline and safety contribute to racial disparities in educational outcomes. His work has been supported by grants from the National Institute of Justice and the National Science Foundation, among others. His research has been published in outlets including *Educational Evaluation and Policy Analysis, Educational Researcher, AERA Open, Social Problems, Law and Society Review,* and *Education Finance and Policy.* He is a regular contributor to *The Conversation,* and his work has been featured in a number of media outlets, including *NPR, Politico, Education Week,* and the *Atlantic.* Prior to his roles in academia, Dr. Curran was a middle school science teacher.

Sarah E. Daly, Ph.D., is a senior consultant for a private IT and business consulting firm and a visiting scholar with the Department of Criminal Justice at SUNY Oswego in the United States. In her research, she focuses primarily on involuntarily celibate men, or incels. Her recent research has been published in *Sex Roles, Qualitative Criminal Justice & Criminology,* and *Forum: Qualitative Social Research.* She is the cofounder and coeditor of the *Journal of Mass Violence Research.* She has also examined the experiences of Asian American faculty in academia in an article in *Critical Criminology* as well as the use of movies, video games, and television as a teaching tool in the edited volume *Theories of Crime through Popular Culture* (Palgrave Macmillan, 2021). Dr. Daly previously taught courses on mass violence, school violence, and issues of race and gender. She earned degrees in criminal justice, applied psychology and school counseling, and Spanish literature from Rutgers University, University of Pennsylvania, and University of Notre Dame, respectively.

Salvatore D'Angelo is a criminal justice graduate student at the University of Delaware. He received his master's degree in criminology from the University of Pennsylvania in spring 2016 and was employed as Visiting Lecturer of Sociology at Susquehanna University from fall 2016 to spring 2018. His research interests include incidents of gun violence, crime prevention through environmental design, and racial disparities in the criminal and civil justice systems. He is a recipient of the James A. Inciardi Fellowship at the University of Delaware from 2018 to 2021.

James Densley is Professor of Criminal Justice and Department Chair of the School of Law Enforcement and Criminal Justice at Metro State University, part of the Minnesota State system. He is also cofounder and copresident (with Jillian Peterson) of the Violence Project, a nonpartisan, nonprofit research center best known for its NIJ-funded database of mass shooters in the United States. Densley has received global media attention for his work on street gangs, criminal networks, violence, and policing. He is author or coauthor of seven books, including, *The Violence Project: How to Stop a Mass Shooting Epidemic* (Abrams Press, 2021), more than fifty peer-reviewed articles in leading scientific journals, and more than ninety book chapters, essays, and other works in outlets such as the *Los Angeles Times, USA Today,* the *Wall Street Journal,* and the *Washington Post.* Densley is a former middle school special education teacher and earned his doctorate in sociology from the University of Oxford.

Tom Diaz is a retired lawyer and former journalist who lives in the metropolitan Washington, DC, area. He has written a number of monographs and articles about crime, terrorism, and firearms, including *Broken Scales: Race and the Crisis of Justice in a Divided America* (Rowman & Littlefield, 2021), *Tragedy in Aurora: The Culture of Mass Shootings in America* (Rowman & Littlefield, 2019), *The Last Gun: How Changes in the Gun Industry Are Killing Americans and What It Will Take to Stop It* (New Press, 2013), *No Boundaries: Transnational Latino Gangs and American Law Enforcement* (University of Michigan Press, 2009), *Lightning Out of Lebanon: Hezbollah Terrorists on American Soil* (with Barbara Newman) (Random House, 2005), and *Making a Killing: The Business of Guns in America* (New Press, 1999). He is a graduate of the University of Florida and of the Georgetown University Law Center. Diaz practiced a variety of civil and criminal law in his legal career. As a journalist, he was assistant managing editor at the *Washington Times* newspaper from 1985 to 1991. Prior to that, he was Supreme Court reporter and later reported on national security affairs. From 1993 to 1997, he was Democratic counsel to then-Congressman Chuck Schumer, chairman of the U.S. House of Representatives Subcommittee on Crime and Criminal Justice. Diaz's subject matter specialties were terrorism and firearms regulation. He was a senior policy analyst at a gun violence reduction organization from 1997 to 2012.

Scott Duxbury is Assistant Professor in the Department of Sociology at the University of North Carolina at Chapel Hill. His research examines mass incarceration, racism, the mass media, public opinion, and criminal network dynamics. It has appeared in outlets such as *American Sociological Review, American Journal of Sociology, Social Forces, Criminology*, and *Sociological Methods & Research*.

Benjamin W. Fisher is Associate Professor of Civil Society and Community Studies in the School of Human Ecology at the University of Wisconsin-Madison. Dr. Fisher's research focuses on school criminalization, with a particular emphasis on issues of equity in school safety, security, and discipline.

Betsy Friauf, a graduate of the University of North Texas, was a longtime journalist. At the *Fort Worth Star-Telegram* from 1980 to 2007, she rose to the position of assistant metropolitan editor. After holding the position of Deputy Chief Communications Officer for the City of Fort Worth, she became a senior communications specialist for the University of North Texas Health Science Center, where she served until 2020. Since 2021, she has served in the same position at Children's Health Hospital—Dallas. With Michael Phillips, she won the 2018 C. K. Chamberlain Award for Best Article of the Year in the *East Texas Historical Journal* and the 2019–2020 Texas Oral History Association Kenneth E. Hendrickson, Jr., *Sound Historian* Best Article Award.

Emma E. Fridel is Assistant Professor in the College of Criminology and Criminal Justice at Florida State University. She primarily studies violence and aggression with a focus on homicide, including homicide-suicide, serial and mass murder, gun violence, and police shootings. Her work has recently been published in *Criminology, Social Forces, Journal of Quantitative Criminology*, and *Justice Quarterly*. She is also coauthor of *Extreme Killing: Understanding Serial and Mass Murder* (Sage, 2019).

Celene Fuller is a sociology doctoral student at the University of Nevada, Las Vegas, who specializes in the sociological subfields of gender and sexuality and social psychology, emphasizing stigmatized sexual and gender identities. Fuller's dissertation research centers on the experiences of sexual and reproductive health stigma surrounding access to abortion and reproductive health care in Nevada.

Daniel Gascón is Assistant Professor in the Sociology Department at the University of Massachusetts, Boston. Professor Gascón's research combines criminology, law and society, and critical race theory. His research employs qualitative methods to study two broad topic areas: police-civilian relations in Black and Latinx communities and the role of stigma in shaping perceptions of deviance and criminal justice outcomes. Professor Gascón's coauthored book, *The Limits of Community Policing: Civilian Power and Police Accountability in Black and Brown Los Angeles* (New York University Press, 2019), looks at community policing—popularized for decades as a racial panacea—which in practice appears not the solution proponents claim it to be. Tracing this policy back to its origins, the book focuses on the Los Angeles Police Department, which first introduced community policing after the high-profile Rodney King riots. It draws on interviews with officers, residents, and stakeholders to show how police tactics in South LA's "Lakeside" precinct amplified—rather than resolved—racial tensions, complicating partnership efforts, crime response and prevention, and accountability. Professor Gascón has also published on police-juvenile relations in scholarly journals such as *Social Problems* and *Race & Justice*. Currently, he is conducting a study of gender and mass violence in the United States and is developing a volume on colonialism and state violence in the Americas.

Patrick J. Gauding is a Ph.D. candidate at the University of Kansas. His research interests in American politics and public policy include criminal justice policy and gun politics.

Brooke Miller Gialopsos is Assistant Professor in the Department of Criminal Justice, Criminology, and Forensics at Seattle University. Her research focuses on the psychological impacts of active assailant protocols, fear of crime and risk perceptions, disparities within jury summons, and barriers to jury service. She has published in *Victims & Offenders, Crime and Delinquency, Journal of Criminal Justice, Journal of School Violence, Journal of Contemporary Criminal Justice*, and *Criminal Justice Review*.

Simon Gottschalk is Professor Emeritus of Sociology at the University of Nevada, Las Vegas. He has published on topics such as terrorism, the mass media, countercultural youth, environmental identity, acceleration, Las Vegas, the transgenerational transmission of trauma, ethnography in virtual spaces, and qualitative research methods, among others. He is coauthor of *The Sense in Self, Society, and Culture* (Routledge, 2012), and his latest book, *The Terminal Self* (Routledge, 2018), explores how our interactions with digital technologies shape our everyday lives and experiences. He is currently researching emotions and interactions on white supremacist websites.

Donald P. Haider-Markel is Professor of Political Science at the University of Kansas. His research and teaching is focused on the representation of group interests in politics and policy, and the dynamics between public opinion, political behavior, and public policy. He has more than twenty years of experience in survey research, interviews, and in policy studies. He has authored or coauthored several books, more than eighty refereed articles, and more than two dozen book chapters in a range of issue areas.

Stephanie Howells is Assistant Professor in the Department of Sociology and Anthropology at the University of Guelph. Her research interests include school shootings, youth violence, qualitative methodology, and the sociology of education. Dr. Howells has published her work in *Higher Education Policy* and *Policing*, and she is author of the textbook *The How To of Qualitative Research* (Sage, 2022).

Cheryl Lero Jonson is Associate Professor in the Department of Criminal Justice at Xavier University. Her research focuses on the effectiveness and psychological impacts of civilian active assailant protocols, the effect of prison sentences on recidivism, and public opinion about gun control. Her work has appeared in *Criminology*, *Criminology & Public Policy*, *Justice Quarterly*, and *Journal of Research in Crime and Delinquency*.

Mark R. Joslyn is Professor of Political Science at the University of Kansas. Professor Joslyn examines attitude formation and change. His research draws from cognitive and motivational theories, recognizing the value of both to understanding the complexities of the political mind. Recently, Professor Joslyn has devoted considerable time to examining the determinants and consequences of people's causal attributions. Specifically, he explores the individual and contextual factors that influence the public's causal reasoning.

Jessie Klein, Ph.D., M.S.W., M.Ed., is Adelphi University Associate Professor of Sociology/Criminal Justice and the founder and director of Creating Compassionate Communities (CCC), a K–12/college empathy and community-building bullying-prevention program. She is author of *Bullying: A Reference Handbook* (ABC-CLIO, 2019) and *The Bully Society: School Shootings and the Crisis of Bullying in America's Schools* (New York University Press, 2012), which was listed in Choice's Outstanding Academic Titles (2013). Her writing appears in scholarly journals, including *Theoretical Criminology*, *School Social Work*, and *Men and Masculinities*; and the popular press, including the *New York Times*, *USA Today*, and *Huffington Post*. She has been interviewed in more than one hundred television, radio, and online media, including CNN, WNPR/NYC, and Slate.com. Previously she served as high school Acting Assistant Principal of Guidance, school social worker, college adviser, social studies teacher, substance abuse prevention counselor, and conflict resolution coordinator. She also worked as a social work professor. You can learn more about Dr. Klein and CCC from her websites: creatingcompassionatecommunities.com; jessieklein.com; and her AU faculty profile, http://www.adelphi.edu/faculty/profiles/profile.php?PID=0326.

Aaron Kupchik is Professor of Sociology and Criminal Justice at the University of Delaware. He studies the policing and punishment of juveniles in schools, courts, and correctional facilities. Dr. Kupchik has published six books, including *The Real School Safety Problem: The Long-Term Consequences of Harsh School Punishment* (University of California Press, 2016), *Homeroom Security: School Discipline in an Age of Fear* (New York University Press, 2010), and *Judging Juveniles: Prosecuting Adolescents in Adult and Juvenile Courts* (New York University Press, 2006). He is the recipient of a number of awards, including the American Society of Criminology's Ruth Shonle Cavan Young Scholar Award and its Michael Hindelang Book Award. He has served as Chair of the American Society of Criminology Division on Corrections and Sentencing and as Executive Counselor for the American Society of Criminology.

Adam Lankford is Professor of Criminology and Criminal Justice at the University of Alabama. He is author of two books and many peer-reviewed journal articles. His research on mass shooters has examined their psychological tendencies, homicidal intentions, mental health problems, suicidal motives, fame-seeking tactics, copycat behavior, and firearms acquisition—along with strategies that could reduce the prevalence of their attacks.

Eric Madfis is Associate Professor in the School of Social Work and Criminal Justice at the University of Washington, Tacoma. His research, which focuses on the causes and prevention of school violence, hate crime, and mass shootings, has been published in academic journals across a range of disciplines and featured in national and international media outlets. His recent book, *How to Stop School Rampage Killing: Lessons from Averted Mass Shootings and Bombings* (Palgrave Macmillan, 2020), utilizes in-depth interviews conducted with school and police officials directly involved in averting potential school rampages to explore the processes by which threats are assessed and rampage plots are thwarted in American public schools.

Alison J. Marganski, Ph.D., is Associate Professor and Director of Criminology at Le Moyne College in Syracuse, New York. Her research focuses on violence, including studying the dynamics of mass murder, intimate partner violence, sexual violence, cyber/technology-facilitated violence, and other offenses through interdisciplinary and intersectional approaches. Her background includes quantitative and qualitative research, and she has experience working with victims/survivors of violence, persons who have perpetrated violence, and justice-related practitioners. She has been published in various academic journals, including but not limited to the *Journal of Interpersonal Violence, Violence Against Women, Family Violence, Violence & Victims, International Journal of Cyber Criminology, Cyberpsychology, Journal of Clinical Psychology, Sociology Compass,* and *International Criminal Justice Review.* She has also written for and been interviewed by various media outlets (e.g., *The Conversation,* Reuters, Mic, *Axios,* Insider, Domesticshelters.org, and Spectrum News). She is a recipient of various grants, fellowships, and awards. Additionally, Marganski regularly collaborates with community partners and has worked with numerous organizations/agencies at local, state, and national levels. Also, she has led workshops, facilitated trainings, conducted evaluations, and engaged in other professional and applied research activities. Marganski received her Ph.D. and M.A. from the School of Criminal Justice at Rutgers University in Newark, New Jersey, and B.S. in Criminology and Justice Studies from the School of Culture and Society at the College of New Jersey in Ewing, New Jersey.

Melissa M. Moon is Professor of Criminal Justice at Northern Kentucky University. Her research focuses on citizen attitudinal surveys, organizational commitment of law enforcement personnel, the bullying–school shooting connection, and psychological impacts of active shooter responses. She has published in *Justice Quarterly, Crime & Delinquency, Journal of School Violence,* and *Victims & Offenders.*

Kristen J. Neville, M.S., is a doctoral student in the College of Criminology and Criminal Justice at Florida State University. Her research interests include gun violence, mass shootings, and intimate partner homicide.

Jaimee Nix is a sociology doctoral student at the University of Nevada, Las Vegas, whose research interests include cultural sociology, environmental place attachment, community studies, and the Burning Man culture.

Daniel Okamura is a sociology doctoral student at the University of Nevada, Las Vegas, studying culture and technology. His recent publications include "Islands in the Stream: How Digital Music Piracy Became a Normal Activity" and "Powering Down: Theoretical Lenses to Examine the Agency of Our Smartphones." He is coeditor of *The Gayborhood: From Sexual Liberation to Cosmopolitan Spectacle* (Lexington Books, 2021).

Patrick F. Parnaby is Associate Professor of Sociology in the Department of Sociology and Anthropology at the University of Guelph. His research interests include risk and expertise, deviant behavior, and the sociology of policing. Dr. Parnaby has published his work in a variety of journals, including *Policing & Society, Pragmatics & Society, Social Media and Society, Canadian Journal of Criminology and Criminal Justice*, and *Deviant Behavior*.

Jillian Peterson is a psychologist and Associate Professor of Criminology and Criminal Justice at Hamline University. She is also cofounder and copresident of the Violence Project, a nonprofit, nonpartisan research center dedicated to reducing violence in society using research and analysis. Dr. Peterson holds an M.A. and a Ph.D. from the University of California, Irvine, and previously worked as an investigator on death penalty cases in New York City. Dr. Peterson is a national speaker, trainer, and media commentator on issues related to mass shootings, mental illness and violence, and violence prevention. Dr. Peterson was principal investigator on a three-year grant from the National Institute of Justice examining the life histories of perpetrators of mass shootings and is coauthor of the new book, *The Violence Project: How to Stop a Mass Shooting Epidemic* (Abrams Press, 2021).

Michael Phillips is a scholar of American racism, right-wing extremism, and apocalyptic religious beliefs. He covered crime as a reporter for the *Fort Worth Star-Telegram* before earning his Ph.D. in history from the University of Texas at Austin in 2002. His first book, *White Metropolis: Race, Ethnicity and Religion in Dallas, 1841–2001* (University of Texas Press, 2006), won the 2007 Texas Historical Commission's prize for Best Book on Texas History. In 2019, he won a Mellon/American Council of Learned Societies Community College research fellowship to examine the history of eugenics in Texas. Phillips and his research partner Betsy Friauf are under contract with the University of Oklahoma Press to write an upcoming book, *The Strange Career of Eugenics in Texas, 1854–1940*.

Paul Reeping is a doctoral candidate in epidemiology at Columbia University Mailman School of Public Health. Previously, he received his M.S. in epidemiology from the Harvard T. H. Chan School of Public Health and worked as a high school science teacher in the South Side of Chicago. It was in Chicago that he saw the impact of gun violence on his students and was motivated to research ways to prevent it by studying the underlying causes. Since then, his research has focused primarily on mass and school shootings, and the topic of his dissertation is the impact of gun-free zones on both interpersonal shootings and active shootings in the United States.

Jason R. Silva is Assistant Professor in the Department of Sociology and Criminal Justice at William Paterson University. His research examines mass shootings, terrorism, and mass media coverage of crime. Silva's recent publications have appeared in *Justice Quarterly, Aggression and Violent Behavior, American Journal of Criminal Justice, Journal of Crime and Justice*, and *Violence Against Women*.

William A. Stadler is Associate Professor in the Society and Social Justice Department at Saint Martin's University. His research involves public opinion about crime and justice; the intersection between technology and justice; and white-collar, corporate, and environmental crime. He has published in *Justice Quarterly, Victims & Offenders, Criminal Justice & Behavior, Criminal Justice Review,* and *Journal of Financial Crime.*

Lindsay Steenberg is Reader/Associate Professor in Film Studies at Oxford Brookes University, where she coordinates their graduate program in Popular Cinema. She has published numerous articles on violence in the media and popular crime genres. She is author of *Forensic Science in Contemporary American Popular Culture: Gender, Crime, and Science* (Routledge, 2013) and *Are You Not Entertained? Mapping the Gladiator in Visual Culture* (Bloomsbury Academic, 2020), for which she was awarded a Research Excellence Fellowship from Oxford Brookes. She is currently working on a project, funded by the Social Sciences and Humanities Research Council of Canada, to map the fight sequence in postmillennial action cinema.

Tara Leigh Tober is Lecturer in the Sociology Department at the University of California, Santa Barbara. Her research concerns culture, memory, and identity.

Jillian J. Turanovic, Ph.D., is Associate Professor and Director of the Crime Victim Research and Policy Institute in the College of Criminology and Criminal Justice at Florida State University. Her research examines various issues surrounding victimization, violence, and incarceration.

Abigail Vegter is Assistant Professor at Berry College. She maintains an active research agenda on religion and politics, primarily investigating the relationship between gun ownership and religion.

Stanislav Vysotsky is Associate Professor of Criminology at the University of the Fraser Valley. Dr. Vysotsky's research began with analysis of supremacist movements with a focus on internal dynamics, subcultural activity, and online discourse. His research agenda later expanded to include analysis of the relationship between threat, space, subculture, and social movement activism of the antifascist movement with an eye toward its interplay with its far-right opposition. This work has been published in journals such as *Interface: A Journal for and about Social Movements, Critical Criminology,* and the book *American Antifa: The Tactics, Culture, and Practice of Militant Antifascism* (Routledge, 2020). He has also published research on far-right and supremacist movements in the *Journal of Political and Military Sociology, Journal of Crime and Justice, Journal of Hate Studies,* as well as several edited volumes. His current research focuses on the emotional labor of research on the far-right as well as analysis of right-wing extremism in Canada.

Lacey N. Wallace is Associate Professor of Criminal Justice at Penn State Altoona. Her research concerns juvenile delinquency as well as the impact of public policy and mass violence on human behavior. Her more recent research has explored gun purchasing, public perceptions of mass shootings and mass shooting risk, and self-protective behaviors.

Index